Thirty Years'
Musical Recollections

HENRY F. CHORLEY

Thirty Years'
Musical Recollections

HENRY F. CHORLEY

*Edited with an Introduction
by Ernest Newman*

NEW YORK
VIENNA HOUSE
1972

This 1972 VIENNA HOUSE edition is reprinted
by arrangement with Alfred A. Knopf, Inc.
International Standard Book Number: 0-8443-0026-8
Library of Congress Catalogue Number: 77-183330
Manufactured in the United States of America

INTRODUCTION

I

It is difficult for the musical critic to achieve any immortality except one of opprobrium. He is remembered solely by his few misses; his many hits are not counted to him. The reason is obvious. If he talks sense, his views become the commonplaces of later musical opinion, and no one thinks of crediting him in particular with them. If he talks nonsense, this is regarded as peculiarly his own, and it is sure to be brought up against him later by some musical biographer or other who wants to intensify the sympathetic atmosphere surrounding his hero by showing how sadly sympathy was lacking to him while he was alive. Thus Hanslick, because the Wagnerians hated him, and Wagner happens to have turned out to be a winning card, has become a by-word to tens of thousands of people who have never read a page of Hanslick for themselves, and are completely ignorant not only of his views on music in general but even of his real attitude towards Wagner. And because Chorley also failed to foresee the overlordship of Wagner he too is "a joke and a sore shame," as Nietzsche says of the ape, in the eyes of modern writers on music who know no more about him at first-hand than they do of Confucius. Chorley, like the rest of us, had his limitations, but he was anything but the fool most people of to-day imagine him to have been. In his own sphere he was a very able man. To say that he did not transcend either his own limitations or those of his epoch is merely to say that he was human. Wagner himself showed equivalent limitations. As regards his judgment of individuals, posterity does not agree with Wagner's judgment of Schumann, Chopin, Brahms and others. As regards general principles, a vast amount of his theorising is dead to-day because it was too purely the expression of the transitory point of view of his own day. I am not attempting to justify Chorley as against Wagner. I am merely pointing out that the greatest of us show our humanity by occasionally erring. Chorley, like other people, came to grief when he tackled a subject that was too big for him; but on a subject of his own size he was a writer of undoubted sense and shrewdness. It is in virtue of these qualities that his *Thirty Years' Musical Recollections* is worth re-issuing to-day, more than sixty years after it was written.

He was a prominent figure not only in the English but in the European musical world of his time; in Germany he was perhaps the only English critic whose opinion counted for anything. In England he exercised a great influence through his long association, extending over thirty years, with the *Athenaeum*. His life was a varied one, and his work contains many a sobering lesson for the musical criticism of this or any future time. For some years before his death he had been engaged on an autobiography. This has never been published, and perhaps the day for a complete issue of it has gone by. But a year or so after his death a full memoir of him by his friend Mr. H. G. Hewlett appeared, in which copious use was made of the autobiography and other private papers.

II

Henry Fothergill Chorley, the third son and fourth child of John and Jane Chorley, was born at Blackley Hurst, near Billinge, Lancashire, on the 17th December, 1808. The family was an old and honourable Quaker one that had come down in the world. John Chorley was an ironworker whose business was none too flourishing; he dropped dead in his counting house on the 15th April, 1816, leaving his widow and children in rather poor circumstances. She was helped, then and later, by her half-brother, John Rutter, a Liverpool medical man. Henry Chorley seems to have inherited from his father a tendency to heart disease. His health was never robust, and a good deal of his melancholy,—perhaps even of the conservatism with which he was so frequently reproached in his later years,—may have been due in part to the excessive demands made by a too strenuous life on a deficient physical vitality.

The irritation that also became more marked during his last few years was the natural outcome of the excessive sensitiveness he showed as a child. As a result partly of the circumstances of the family, partly of his own physical and mental make-up, he was very much alone as a child, not caring greatly for games for which he had not the constitution, and given to the introspective use of his imagination. "If my own recollections go back to a very early date in life," he says, "it is probably because my powers of observation were prematurely sharpened by being either left to myself or living with grown people: As boys from childhood, my two brothers 'cronied' together, leaving the youngest, weakest and ugliest as the odd one; and my sister early became my mother's companion. I have thus, from infancy, been alone as regards family confidence or comradeship; and the subsequent periods of life at which this condition of solitude has been partly counteracted have been few and far between."

The family more than once changed its place of residence during his childhood, though it always remained in Lancashire. His mother, a gentle and imaginative woman, was a moderate pianist, and Chorley seems to have picked up the rudiments of music for himself at an early age. As the years went on, the boy became more and more isolated. He speaks of his life about that time as "years of wakening—years, too, of some suffering; and then, for the first time, I began to feel the yearnings for companionship which beset one of an affectionate nature, a fanciful imagination, and a social humour, placed by circumstances in a solitary position. On her widowhood, my mother possessed herself of my sister as her chosen companion, and my two elder brothers, as I have said, 'cronied' together. I was the smallest, the worst-looking, the most nervous; not a coward, though reported such, because of great physical excitability; totally inexpert with my hands and at all the manly games in which boys delight; therefore mocked at, and left alone, without any excessive persecution, but without any influence to encourage, assist, or befriend me."

Such education as he had at this time was irregular and informal. He learned easily what interested him, and his memory was excellent; later the accuracy of it in musical matters aroused the astonishment of many good musicians. He was self-centred, and the grown man can be seen in the portrait he gives of himself as a child. "From first to last, to me, all schooling was intolerable. I was hopelessly idle—perhaps because, in some things, I was precociously quick, having been started in the world with a memory of no common compass and strength, and with that sort of *divining* nature which is one of the elements of the artist temperament. Had this been understood, and had this been worked towards in forming character and in developing such talents as God gave me, my life might have yielded special results in place of the universal indications which are all it will ever yield. But this was not seen, not apprehended, perhaps could not be; and I had then, as now, a physically feeble temperament, in which irritability and languor were oddly mixed up. . . . Had I been apprenticed to a musician, or to a draftsman, or to an architect, I fancy I might have become distinguished."

About 1819 we find him in Liverpool, where he had the good fortune to be taken up by a leading Liverpool family, the Rathbones, in whose comfortable house he had ample opportunity to develop his culture along the lines that most appealed to him. He had still little or no definite musical schooling, but he had a natural aptitude for the art. "The manner in which I played and picked out tunes on that small, square pianoforte at Green Bank, and began to read music long ere I could name a note, connecting the ideas of sound and symbol, strikes me now—who have since seen much of the beginnings of musicians—as arguing propensity for the art above the average." He was sent to the best Liverpool school of the time—the Royal Institution—where he was as unhappy as boys generally are who are not quite like their schoolfellows. He still seems to have had little formal technical training in music, but he was hearing a certain amount of music at this time in private and in public, and there can be no doubt that at bottom his temperament was genuinely musical, though he had also a touch of the painter and the man of letters in him. He worked tolerably hard at drawing, but only, one gathers, because opportunities for strict musical study were denied him. The vague artistic impulses in the boy had to find some outlet, and they naturally chose the line that the circumstances of the moment made easiest for him. "A musician I should have been," he says: "and since the technical training and the opportunities of self-culture were denied me by circumstance, secondary talents, grouped around the central one, which were more easily indulged and developed, broke out, as it were, to satisfy a want which must find some relief.

Thus I drew (I ought to say, coloured) patiently, for hours upon hours."

When he was writing his autobiography many years later, he was convinced that music had been his real line from the first. "It seems to me now," he says, "in putting together all these revelations, that had my elders understood the signs before them, and apprenticed me to a musical career, I might have done England an artist's service. But I hardly know the middle-class family in the provinces forty years ago (save, perhaps, one so much before its age as that of the Taylors of Norwich), where such a disposition of a boy's life would not then have been considered as a degradation. How the good people of those days resigned themselves to going to theatres and music-meetings I have never been able to understand, even on the most comprehensive theory of inconsistency. I know that my wings were perpetually breaking against the cage, and that unable to get out, as I wished, I had to make other outlets for humour, or taste, or talent which *would not* conform to the life chalked out for me."

He had to begin earning his living immediately on leaving school, and he started as a clerk in a Liverpool business house, that of Cropper, Benson and Co., American merchants. When or why he left this firm we do not know, but later we find him in the office of a firm of Sicilian wine growers, Messrs. Woodhouse. He detested commercial life, and was already dabbling in literature. The Rathbones were unceasingly kind to him, and it was probably in the company and at the charge of his friend and benefactor, Mr. Benson Rathbone, that he paid his first visit to the Italian opera in London, some time in his early twenties. We have a description of him about this time from the pen of Mrs. Procter, the wife of Bryan Procter ("Barry Cornwall"), whose house in London he had visited about 1830: he was "a romantic, enthusiastic youth, plain-featured, with red hair; his manner gentlemanly, but marked by the same nervous timidity that he retained to the last, and a touch of Quaker quaintness, the result of early association—that he soon dropped." Liverpool was in those days a moderately musical provincial town, and from 1827 onwards Chorley heard a good deal of concert music and a certain amount of Italian opera given by companies touring from London. Between 1830 and

1833 he was an active member of a society of musical amateurs in Liverpool; and the only systematic teaching that he ever received in music was given him at this time by Mr. James Z. Herrmann, a German quartet player who had settled in the town, and who afterwards became conductor of the Liverpool Philharmonic Society. Chorley was now not only attending every musical performance he could but was committing his impressions and speculations to paper. "He was evidently," Mr. Hewlett says, "feeling his way to a definite vocation."

His introduction to a larger field of literature than the local journals and annuals of the "Keepsake" class came about in a curious way. In September, 1830, the railway between Liverpool and Manchester was opened, and Chorley was asked by Dilke, the editor of the London *Athenaeum,* to contribute an article on that important event. The ceremony, it may be remembered, had a tragic outcome: Huskisson, a prominent statesman of the time, was killed by the first train that ran. What with one thing and another, the young Chorley found the subject rather too "scientific" for his imaginative pen, and he told Dilke so frankly, at the same time asking if he could not write for the *Athenaeum* occasionally on general literary or musical subjects. Later he "covered" the Dublin musical festival for that paper, and as a result of this and other small contributions he was ultimately invited to join the staff of the *Athenaeum* on probation, at a salary of £50 for six months' services. Chorley jumped at the offer, and left Liverpool for good on the last day of 1833.

III

Those were days of hard thinking and plain living for the conscientious rank-and-file journalist. Chorley did not, on the whole, dislike his drudgery, but drudgery it was for all that; for many years now his life was one of incessant book reviewing and turning out notices of "musical performances, operas, concerts, festivals, and the principal exhibitions of pictures and drawings." Like most journalists, he had a secret conviction that Nature had intended him to be an author. He tried his hand at novels and dramas,—*Sketches from a Small Seaport Town* (1834), *Conti, the Discarded, and other Tales and Fancies in Music* (1833), *Fontibel* (a drama, 1837, not published or performed), *The Lion, a Tale of the Coteries* (published anonymously, 1838), *Old Love and New Fortune* (the Surrey Theatre, 1850), *Pomfret, or Public Opinion and Private Judgment* (1845), *The Lovelock* (a drama, produced in 1854), *Duchess Eleanour* (Haymarket Theatre, 1854), *Roccabella* (a novel published in 1859 under the pseudonym of Paul Bell), *The Prodigy, a Tale of Music* (1866). In addition he translated and edited Savinien Lapointe's fairy tales, under the title of *Fairy Gold for Young and Old* (1857), wrote and translated a number of opera libretti, produced a considerable quantity of verse (his best-known effort being *The Enchantress*, which has been kept alive by J. L. Hatton's excellent musical setting of it), and did a good deal of other literary work. *Old Love and New Fortune* had a moderate run, but none of the other plays and novels made a success. The long line of failures undoubtedly embittered him, in spite of his professed philosophy. For a year (from midsummer 1850 to midsummer 1851) he edited *The Lady's Companion;* and the salary he received for this, he said, brought him financial ease for the first time in his life.

As a critic of books and plays he made no distinction between authors whom he did not know personally and authors with whom he happened to have close personal ties. "It is noteworthy," says Mr. Hewlett, "as evidence of his honesty of purpose, that some of his harshest criticisms are of books written by his personal friends." He was one of the first in England to see the promise of Browning and the quality of Nathaniel Hawthorne. He did much to establish Mrs. Browning's popularity, but vexed her many years later (1860) by a review of her *Poems before Congress* that Mr. Hewlett describes as "severe to the point of asperity." The Brownings' regard for him had led to his being appointed one of the trustees of Mrs. Browning's settlement in 1846. Their relations were disturbed for a little while by his review of *Poems before Congress,* but his honesty was recognised; and Browning testified that Chorley had Mrs. Browning's "very deep and true regard" to the end of his life. The rule of the *Athenaeum* was that the truth should be told without consideration of consequences; and Chorley himself was hurt at what he considered the severe handling of his novel *The Lion* in the columns of his own paper.

Occasionally he could be playful as well as critical, as in his review of Coventry Patmore's *Angel in the House* (20th January, 1855):

"'The Angel in the House—The Betrothal.'

"The gentle reader we apprise, That this new Angel in the House Contains a tale not very wise, About a person and a spouse. The author, gentle as a lamb, Has managèd his rhymes to fit, And haply fancies he has writ Another *In Memoriam*. How his intended gathered flowers, And took her tea and after sung, Is told in style somewhat like ours, For delectation of the young. But, reader, lest you say we quiz The poet's record of his she, Some little pictures you shall see, Not in our language, but in his.

" 'While thus I grieved and kissed her glove,
    My man brought in her note to say
Papa had bid her send his love,
    And hoped I'd dine with them next day;
They had learned and practised Purcell's glee,
    To sing it by to-morrow night:
The postscript was—her sisters and she
    Enclosed some violets blue and white.

*   *   *   *   *   *   *   *   *   *

" 'Restless and sick of long exile,
    From those sweet friends I rode, to see
The church repairs, and after awhile
    Waylaying the Dean, was asked to tea.
They introduced the Cousin Fred
    I'd heard of, Honor's favourite; grave
Dark, handsome, bluff, but gently bred,
    And with an air of the salt wave.'

"Fear not this saline Cousin Fred; He gives no tragic mischief birth; There are no tears for you to shed, Unless they may be tears of mirth. From ball to bed, from field to farm, The tale flows nicely purling on; With much conceit there is no harm In the love-legend here begun. The rest will come another day, If public sympathy allows; And this is all we have to say About the 'Angel in the House.' "

As a musical critic he made, of course, many enemies by his frankness, and received the usual quantity of abusive letters, signed and anonymous. "I kept by me, for some years," he says, "a collection of such flowers of rhetoric, the most exquisite of which was a letter in very blank English, beginning "You WORM!!!"

IV

His multifarious activities can have left him little time for the intensive study of music. He mostly drew his impressions from, and picked up his knowledge in, the concert room or the opera house. He neglected no opportunity to hear new music, and underwent a great deal of discomfort—inseparable from the travelling conditions of that time—to be present at new or notable performances on the continent. The result of an extended tour in 1839 and 1840 was a book published in 1841 under the title of *Music and Manners in France and Germany: a Series of Travelling Sketches of Art and Society* (3 vols.). The book, says Mr. Hewlett, was hastily put together. Chorley reprinted parts of it thirty years later in his *Modern German Music.* The first of these works laid the foundation of his continental reputation. In 1864 he contributed a biographical preface to the second edition of Lady Wallace's translation of Mendelssohn's *Letters from Italy and Switzerland.* He planned a life of his idol Rossini, but abandoned it after a little work upon it. His *Thirty Years' Musical Recollections* was published in 1862. Money had come to him from his deceased brother in his later years, and after 1866 he ceased to write for the *Athenaeum* on any but musical subjects. He retired formally from the paper in 1868, after thirty-five years' service, though he continued to contribute an occasional signed article to it until 1871. His last years seem to have been none too happy. He had been consistently overworked for the greater part of his life; he inherited, as we have seen, an unhealthy heart from his father; and his vitality must often have been unable to meet the heavy demands made upon it. Mr. Hewlett speaks of "the unusual slovenliness of style" in the *Thirty Years' Musical Recollections;* it was probably due to the work having been compiled under conditions of strain. He had a great deal to depress him towards the end. Year after year he had lost by death one or other of his dearest friends; the death of Mendelssohn in 1847 had been a shock from which it took him a long time to recover. In June, 1870, the sudden death of Charles Dickens left him, says Mr. Hewlett, in a "mental prostration painful to witness." He apparently never quite overcame the shyness and sensitiveness that had been characteristic of him as a boy: he was conscious of his physical defects and felt that they barred him from many of the pleasures of the normal man. All his life through he had a pathetic longing for sympathy and understanding. He had two love affairs, both of them unfortunate; his solitary proposal of marriage was rejected. His books and plays were mostly failures. His position in the musical world and his honesty of speech brought him many annoyances and insults, and made him the object of many a malicious intrigue. It is indeed difficult for a musical critic to take any but a cynical view of his fellow-men, since his profession takes up the bulk of his time, and in that profession he is mostly brought into contact with the mean or the absurd side of the class of people whom he knows best. But there is ample evidence that Chorley was held in the highest esteem by some of the most eminent men of the musical and literary worlds of his day. His close friendship with Dickens and with the Brownings has been referred to already. Mendelssohn had a great regard for him. Perhaps a remark of Sydney Smith's is the best summing up of him. Before the old wit's death he called in and destroyed his letters, to prevent possible biographers from making indiscreet use of them. A friend who was delivering up a packet of "intimate and lively communications" asked him if he would mind Chorley reading them first. "No," said Sydney Smith, "he is a gentleman."

Towards the end, the irritability of which he himself seems always to have been conscious, and that was probably the result of imperfect health, overwork, and the consciousness of having failed in so many of the things he most wanted to succeed in, grew upon him to an extent that sometimes made intercourse with him difficult, though his friends were generally ready to make the necessary allowances. The tendency to introspection grew on him, and he became, as Mr. Hewlett says, "obstinate and crotchety." In later life, adds Mr. Hewlett, the "natural bias of his mind to conservatism displayed itself still more prominently, and exposed him, with some show of reason, to the imputation of dogmatism and finality, but it never rendered him insensible to the impression of new ideas." In 1870 he was visibly ageing. He had virtually given up journalistic work, and spent a good deal of his time searching for health at the seaside or in the country. He was engaged on his autobiography, the agreement for which had been

signed.   During the winter of 1871 his health worsened consider-
ably, and in January, 1872, we find him declining a railway journey
because of the possible effect on his heart.   On the 16th February,
a Friday, Sir Michael Costa, Lady Downshire, and a few other
friends were to have dined with him at his house; early on that
morning "he was seized with sudden syncope, and, after lying a
few hours unconscious, expired without apparent suffering."

V

The *Thirty Years' Musical Recollections* was published in two
volumes in 1862.   The book shows Chorley, as far as my knowledge of him goes, at his best.   Whatever may be thought of his
attitude towards Wagner, there can be no question of his compe-
tence as a judge of the old schools of Italian opera and Italian
singing.   It is impossible, of course, to check his verdicts upon
singers whom none of us now living ever heard, and no doubt his
contemporaries often differed as pointedly from him as readers
do from critics to-day.   But even if we admit that his point of
view was possibly only one out of many, we must recognise that
it is always the point of view of a man who knows every in and out
of his profession.   There is hardly a page of these volumes in
which he does not show a remarkably acute sense of the musical
and more especially the vocal values of the operatic world of his
time.   He must have had much the same types to deal with as we
have.   Then, as now, there was the opera performer who could
sing but not act, the performer who could act but not sing, and the
performer who could neither sing nor act.   Then, as now, a vast
amount of bad singing was obsequiously accepted because it came
from Italy.   Then, as now, what he calls "the course and stentorian bawling" of the Italian tenor made certain nights at the
opera a penance for the musical ear.   Then, as now, the art of the
press agent was exercised to eke out the insufficient art of the
singer himself.   Rubini, we are told, "would walk through a given
third of any opera languidly, giving the notes correctly, and little
more," but "when his own moment arrived" he would put forth
all his powers.   The Rubinis we have, and will always have, with
us on the Italian opera stage.   Is it of Herr Wild, again, in 1840,
or of some X or Z in our own sad experience, of whom he writes
thus: "A strenuous tenor veteran was there in Herr Wild,—a

singer who has seen out many dynasties and many composers, but who never could have been accepted as a favourite elsewhere than in Germany"? Then, as now, it was the habit of English singers to go to Italy to get an Italian style and an Italian reputation, only to find that "an Italian success in no wise ensured an English one." And which of us, reading the following without knowing the name or the date, would not instantly swear that it is a description of a certain popular singer of to-day:

"The change for the worse in Mademoiselle Cruvelli began to show itself strongly this season. More at ease with her public than formerly, and by panegyric encouraged to rate herself as equal, if not superior, to the greatest of her predecessors, she began, in fancy, to originate—in reality, to neglect. Every now and then some wild burst of energy in her singing displayed the glorious compass of her voice, but also that its freshness was even then departing, while her acting, though it was animated enough, perpetually missed its mark owing to her extreme self-occupation. She was triumphantly heedless of all her companions on the stage. In her great scenes she was always too soon or too late. She preferred to fly into a fury before the word was spoken that should set fire to the train. She would fall into an attitude just after the moment for the attitude had gone by. Then she performed strange evolutions with her drapery by way of being statuesque, and exhibited things more strange with her costume when it was not antique, by way of being pictorial. So well were these propensities of hers known that later, when, as Queen of the Grand Opera of Paris, she deliberately altered the rhythm of the leading phrase of a grand duet in *Les Huguenots,* the world said, 'Only Mademoiselle Cruvelli's way'; and when, a few months later, the choice of some coming opera was in debate, loungers reported, rather admiringly than otherwise, that 'this time there was to be a part with bare arms in it, for Mademoiselle Cruvelli!'"

But interesting as Chorley's pages are for their many demonstrations that the opera singer type is in the main unchangeable throughout the centuries, they are still more interesting for the light they throw on certain phases of musical mentality that have disappeared, presumably for ever. The old Italian opera presents some almost insoluble problems to the student of musical history. It is, I imagine, the only form of music of which this can be said.

We of to-day have not the slightest difficulty in placing ourselves at the point of view of those who made and those who listened to the music of periods much earlier than that. We hear a song of Dowland's, a madrigal of Byrd's, a Mass of Palestrina's precisely as their contemporaries did. We feel that these were all men like ourselves. Some of their forms may be antiquated, and occasionally the expression itself has not the force for us that we may presume it to have had in its own day—some of the pages, for instance, of Bach's Passions and church cantatas. But even here, though we can no longer enjoy, there is no difficulty in understanding not merely that contemporaries enjoyed this art, but precisely *how* they enjoyed it. But when we come to Italian opera we are confronted with more than one problem that baffles us. These people had certain ways of looking at music that were so different from ours that we cannot enter into them by any effort of the imagination. They were deeply moved by devices that seem to us either tiresome or downright absurd.

Who to-day, for example, can understand the old passion for "ornaments" in vocal music? We must, of course, remember that these were not an invention of the Italian opera singers. From time immemorial the singer who is proud of his powers has "embellished" the composer's melody in his own way to exhibit his vocal agility. The practice can be traced, in European music, as far back as the earliest plain song. In the 16th century a singer would take a part out of a madrigal and decorate it with runs, trills, "divisions," and other ornaments according to his fancy; and Caccini's preface to the *Nuove Musiche* shows that at the beginning of the 17th century the practice of coloratura was firmly fixed upon the Italian solo song. All this, however, presents no difficulty of understanding to the modern musician. The difficulty arises when we find these ornaments regarded not merely as excrescences upon a melody but as vital elements in dramatic expression. We of to-day are inclined to think that these ornaments were only evidences of the bad taste of the singers and the tyranny imposed by them upon audiences, and that while the vulgar among the listeners may have delighted in them, to the genuinely musical ear they must have been intolerable. Chorley's pages will rid us of that complacent misconception. To him, and probably to the majority of the lovers of opera and oratorio of that time,

ornaments were a vital necessity to fine solo music. Chorley regards it as an evil day for musical expression when these ornaments
shall be discarded. Again and again we find a singer com-
mended for his taste in ornament, or blamed for his lack of taste.
Distinctions were made between singers who invented appropriate
embellishments of their own and those who merely took standard-
ised articles out of the common stock. And the crucial fact has
again to be insisted on, that these embellishments were admired
not merely because they served to show off the virtuosity of the
singer but because they gave to the composer's dramatic conception a life it would otherwise have lacked. It is difficult, almost
impossible, for us to place ourselves at the point of view of these
people,—impossible to understand how, for instance, the roulades
and shakes and other vocal fripperies introduced into a mother's
lament over her dead child could give the melody a psychological
force at least as great as that of the melody itself. And, as I
have just said, it was not the mere unmusical who liked this sort
of thing because they were dazzled by the virtuosity of it, but the
solid and serious musicians who were deeply moved by it, and did
not see how musical expression of the finest kind could be maintained in opera without it. Chorley's many remarks on this point
deserve the most careful pondering, for they help to explain, in
part, the horror of some of the older schools at the new spirit
brought into opera by Wagner.

Not less interesting to us of to-day are Chorley's opinions upon
the composers of his time. These opinions are in part those of
his epoch, in part his own; but we need not trouble at this time
of day to attempt to draw a dividing line between the two. These
pages shew Chorley as a patient, knowledgeable, and thoughtful student of the operatic music of his period. They help us to
place ourselves at the point of view of the men for whom this
music was the newest thing. They help us to understand how
Rossini and Meyerbeer attained their enormous vogue, and to
realise the curious differences in musical mentality between that
age and this. Of the future of the opera, Chorley and his contemporaries clearly had no inkling. Wagner had not yet shown
himself in the fulness of his power. We must never forget that
a great deal of the earlier opposition to Wagner came as much
from ignorance as from knowledge of him. No new opera of his

was produced between *Lohengrin* in 1850 and *Tristan* in 1865. We look back indulgently upon *Tannhäuser* and *Lohengrin* through eyes that have seen the glory of *Tristan*, the *Meistersinger,* and the *Ring.* The men of 1850–1860 saw what to us are early works as the *latest* works of a contemporary composer, and judged them with the severity that is always meted out by criticism to contemporary music. The Wagnerian long-windedness, to which we have become accustomed and almost reconciled, must have been at first a sore trial. But the opposition to Wagner was based not so much on his early music as on his prose writings, that were hard enough to understand in their native German, and of which only garbled versions appeared in other languages. The impression that most people gained from these prose works was that of a young composer of fair talent and insufferable arrogance, who disparaged all previous and contemporary opera composers and contended that he alone had the secret of the genuine musical drama. A good deal of gratuitous objurgation of the critics of the period might have been spared us had historians only taken the trouble to look at the dates and the facts.

Chorley's later opinions on Wagner do not come within the scope of this introductory survey. In the concluding pages of the present volume we see Chorley a little doubtful as to the new developments of the day, but certain that music will somehow or other right itself. "Righting itself," for him, meant putting the latest German upstarts, such as Wagner, in their place, and getting back to the sane principles of opera according to Mozart, Gluck, Rossini and Meyerbeer. What the critics of that day left out of their calculations was the genius of Wagner. It was that that altered the whole face of music; had Wagner died after *Lohengrin* it is extremely probable that opera throughout the second half of the 19th century would not have been appreciably different from what it had been in the first half. We cannot in fairness make it a reproach against Chorley that in the eighteen-fifties he did not foresee the future consequences to music of an explosive personal force the existence of which could not even be suspected at that time; we might as well blame the medieval builders of town walls for not having foreseen the invention of the howitzer. Chorley and his fellows did their critical work honestly and painstakingly according to their lights; and the result is that the critical studies of contemporary composers in such a book as this are of the greatest value to the critic and the musical student of to-day. Chorley shows us Rossini and Meyerbeer and the minor operatic composers of that period as they appeared to audiences to whom this music was the newest thing, palpitating with actuality. We see Verdi's star slowly rising, with as yet hardly a hint that it will some day eclipse its older rivals. Present-day criticism may learn some lessons in prudence from Chorley's attitude towards the young Verdi, as also from his enthusiasm for Gounod. The man of the next generation but two after us will be similarly amused and astonished at our under-praise of this composer of to-day and our over-praise of that.

. . . .

In preparing this new edition of *Thirty Years' Musical Recollections* I have had to cut out two chapters, one on Rachel, one on Ristori, in order to bring the book within practicable limits. I should not have ventured to do this had the subjects been musicians; but since something had to be sacrificed on account of space, the non-musical parts of the *Recollections* were obviously marked out for the knife. For the rest, I have mostly excised only a few sentences or paragraphs here and there relating to personalities of the time—chiefly singers—who are now so completely forgotten that a recital of their shortcomings could have no interest for the reader of to-day.

In his later years, Chorley adopted a system of punctuation of his own that more often than not made his pages difficult to read, obscured his meaning, and brought on him the charge of "slovenliness of style" of which Mr. Hewlett speaks. He seems to have sprinkled his commas, semi-colons, colons, and dashes from a pepper-pot, and the majority of them fell in the wrong places. I have re-punctuated the whole book, making, at a moderate estimate, at least ten thousand alterations. Chorley's text, of course, has not been touched; the changes in punctuation have merely made it more readable and more intelligible.

ERNEST NEWMAN

INTRODUCTION

There is one only way in which a book like the following can be written, with any chance of its possessing some value. This is by aid of faithfulness to recollection, and sincerity in offering opinion. In so much as either romance or suppression enter into the record, its worth is impaired.

Personality there must be—and such bias as is decided by individuality. If a judgment beyond appeal can be formed by human creature on any question, it is surely not on a question of art. In that imaginative world and its enjoyments, human sympathies will have their share, let reason be ever so conscientious. Then there is association; that which we have heard during those good moments (of which life contains many for all who will have them), that which we have been obliged to hear when the heart has been sad and the attention unwilling, can in neither case be altogether truthfully presented. I have tried my utmost to be a fair witness. If there be more of myself in these pages than under other circumstances would be graceful or self-respecting, such egotism has been allowed for the express purpose of enabling those who may read to agree or to differ with me in proportion as they approve my predilections, or dissent from my prejudices.

It is impossible to execute a task like mine without speaking of artists still living, as well as of those who have vanished from every scene. With regard to the former, this can only be done by considering them as they have presented themselves or been presented in public—setting on one side such allusion, or anecdote, or experience belonging to rumour or intercourse, as are derived from private knowledge. There can be no offence, however, in writing of actors and actresses that which is to be seen, and may be remembered by every eyewitness, or reader of the news of the hour.

Thus, too, it has seemed best to be silent on all such tales of the green-room as relate to the dealings of manager with artist—to the character of the one, or the grievances of the other. My chronicle is written from *before the curtain,* and with no wish to rake up old quarrels or to pronounce on vexed questions. The result is the thing to be dealt with. The wisdom or the folly of this or the other line of policy may be judged by the evidence offered as to results, and such opinion of the trustworthiness of the witness as he may be able to inspire.

It has been difficult to arrange the matter of this book without going over the same ground more than one, or else making the whole collection tiresome because of its fragmentary nature. Thus it will be seen that in attempting some characteristics of the composers and singers who have ruled the stage a certain liberty of grouping has been taken: while the leading features of every year as it passed have been dwelt upon. I have endeavoured to distribute the portraits and speculations which form substantial essays, so as to vary a story at best liable to the charge of frivality and monotony.

The lists here offered of the special features which have marked the opera-campaigns of the past thirty years may be found useful for purposes of reference.

Lastly, this book of mine is strictly what it professes to be—a book of Recollections. I have merely resorted to former memoranda for the yearly lists of operas and singers,[1] and in *no one case* have consulted them with a view of refreshing my memory, or of fabricating an opinion of that which had passed from my mind. It has been gratifying to me on comparing these pages, after they were written, with the notes thrown off at the time, to have found no discrepancy betwixt past and present judgments worth adverting to. Had I done so, I should have conceived it a duty to have pointed it out.

H. F. C.

* In the case of only two of the principal singers named—Madame Meric-Lalande and Signor David—have I spoken from hearsay.

CONTENTS

CONTENTS

THE YEAR 1830

OPERAS. *Il Pirata,** Bellini; *Il Matrimonio, Gli Orazi,* Cimarosa; *Elisa e Claudio, La Donna Caritea,** Mercadante; *Don Giovanni,* Mozart; *Semiramide, Otello, La Cenerentola, Il Barbiere, La Gazza Ladra, Matilda di Shabran, Il Turco, L'Inganno Felice,* Rossini. PRINCIPAL SINGERS. Mdes. Méric-Lalande,* Blasis, Malibran; MM. Ambrogi, Curioni, Donzelli, Santini, Lablache.* BALLETS. *Flore et Zephyre, Guillaume Tell, Masaniello, La Somnambule.* PRINCIPAL DANCERS. MDES. Brocard. Taglioni,* M. Perrot.

* The asterisk indicates first performance or first appearance.

THE YEAR 1830

HAT a change has passed over the foreign musical drama in England since the foregoing was the programme of London's Italian Opera season! The orchestra in 1830 was, compared with what it is now, meagre and ill-disciplined; the chorus was an ear-torment rather than an ear-pleasure; the scenery and appointments were shabby to penury; but *Guillaume Tell* (desecrated, as *Masaniello* had been, into ballet form) was new. It was the year when Signor Rossini's formidable Italian rival (as the public has since learned to think) first was heard in England. It was the year of the first appearances here of Lablache and of Mademoiselle Taglioni. Each of the three events noted marks an epoch.

Though the predominance of the composer of *Il Barbiere* had as yet given way in no respect, there were other modern Italian composers whose works were worth trying. Signor Mercadante was little known; but the clever and level music of his early operas, in spite of their containing effective airs and concerted pieces, is too utterly devoid of freshness or individuality for them to have stood a chance of taking a permanent root here, so long as Signor Rossini was in the ascendancy. With the temporary mitigation of that master's popularity they were sure to perish for ever, since their life amounted to his forms, reproduced second-hand. It is not so with *Il Pirata*. Weak as that opera is (only containing a couple of tenor airs which are sung now), an individuality exists in Bellini's music. Whenever individuality is not mere eccentricity there is always interest in it—there is always a chance of that interest becoming a charm. But till Rubini adopted "Tu vedrai," the charm was not recognized in this country, and the young Sicilian composer was treated with unanimous contempt.

From Madame Méric-Lalande, a French lady [1] by birth, and a

---

[1] Born at Dunkirk, 1798.

3

pupil of Garcia—who had for six years been reported to be one of the best singers in Italy—much had been expected. Our opera-goers had heard of serenades beneath her windows, of medals struck in her honour. She had been compared with the best of the best. But she arrived in England too late; and her place, moreover, had been filled by women of greater genius. She was a good musician, and sang with taste; but her voice—a soprano —ere she came had contracted a habit of trembling, in those days a novelty (would it had always remained so!) to which English ears were then averse. She gave little satisfaction.

The season could hardly have been carried through without the presence of Mdlle. Blasis—one of those invaluable artists of the second class who are always prepared, always acceptable, complete in what they do, if never exciting their audiences to high pleasure. Her voice was good and her manner intelligent; her appearance, however, was not prepossessing. She had seen much and had studied well; and the main weight of the soprano singing of the season 1830 may be said to have rested on her shoulders. It seems hard that the popularity of artists so modest, so sedulous, so useful as she was, should bear such small proportion to their real value. The subordinate ladies who filled up the company were very poor, the absence of an efficient contralto being less felt than might otherwise have been the case, owing to the versatility of Malibran, who was able to sing either Semiramide or Arsace,[1] as the case required, or as the humour took her.

Ere I attempt some character of her, and of the great artist who made his first appearance in England that season, in detail, a word of recollection is due to Donzelli,[2] who had for some years been singing in England. He had one of the most mellifluous robust low tenor voices ever heard—a voice which had never by practice been made sufficiently flexible to execute Signor Rossini's operas as they are written, but who even in this respect was accomplished and finished, if compared with the violent persons who have succeeded him in Italy, each one louder and less available than his predecessor. The volume of Donzelli's rich and sonorous voice was real, not forced. When he gave out its high notes there was no misgiving as to the peril of his blood-vessels;

---

[1] The soprano and contralto respectively in Rossini's *Semiramide*.—E. N.
[2] Born at Bologna about 1790.

and hence his reign on the Italian stage was thrice as long as that of any of the worse-endowed, worse-trained folk who have since adopted the career of forcible tenors, partly from a wish to split the ears of the groundlings, partly from that innate laziness which, together with the increased facilities in gathering gains during modern time, has so largely corrupted art.

Donzelli had an open countenance and a manly bearing on the stage, but no great dramatic power. In emulation of Garcia, whose fiery southern genius justified him in any usurpation that he chose to make, the less able tenor laid hands on *Don Juan;*[1] unable, however, to vindicate himself as the Spaniard had done. To the hazardous nature of such experiments, and the mischief they produce, I shall have too many opportunities of returning as the opera years go on.

Times are, happily, changed since such a masterpiece among operas as *Guillaume Tell* could only be smuggled into England stripped of nearly all save its overture and dance music, in the form of a ballet, as *Masaniello* had been before it. Yet even as thus presented, and with Mademoiselle Taglioni, in the prime of her grace, to dance the Tyrolienne, our connoisseurs were deaf to its beauty. In the year 1830 a work written with French text, for the Opera at Paris, was, by that very circumstance, condemned in this country. Nor was Taglioni, in spite of that exquisite new style of dancing, in her first season appreciated as she deserved to be.

[1] Chorley always refers to Mozart's *Don Giovanni* in this form.—E. N.

MARIA MALIBRAN

HIS year 1830 may be recorded as Malibran's second regular season at our Italian Opera, after her return from America. It was also her last one, since the few appearances which she made there in 1833 were merely what may be called extra performances, in which she repeated a few favourite parts. Here, then, some recollections and characteristics of one who set the world on fire may be fitly offered.

The task is not an easy one. While I remember Malibran, her appearance, her voice, and certain of her performances, more vividly than I can now recall many good things of yesterday, I feel that there was something feverish, meteoric, ever changing into a new surprise, both in her nature and her art, which dazzled while it delighted, leaving the witness with small readiness available for balance and comparison of impressions. Appreciation and memory do not imply the power of presenting and representing. We know past ecstacies, dreams, terrors, by heart: yet may fail, by any exercise of ingenuity, to convey an idea of them to others.

From the first hour when Maria Garcia [1] appeared on the stage —first in *Il Barbiere,* and subsequently in *Il Crociato*—it was evident that a new artist, as original as extraordinary, was come— one by nature fairly endowed not merely with physical powers but also with that inventive, energetic, rapid genius before which obstacles become as nothing, and by aid of which the sharpest contradictions can be reconciled.

She may not have been beautiful; but she was better than beautiful, insomuch as a speaking Spanish human countenance by Murillo is ten times more fascinating than many a faultless angel-face such as Guido could paint. There was health of tint, with but a slight touch of the yellow rose, in her complexion; great mobility of expression in her features; an honest, direct brightness of eye; a

---

[1] Born in Paris, 1808; made her first appearance in London, 1825; married in America, 1826; rea_,peared in London, 1829; died 1836.

refinement in the form of her head, and in the set of it on her shoulders, more obvious in 1830 than it could be in 1860, when the desire of female beauty seems to be to obliterate that which so thoroughly expresses grace, high-breeding, and character—the turn of the head. But Malibran had her own tastes and fashions in dress. She knew what suited her features. At a time when public singers indulged in crowning themselves with hearses of feathers and gigantic hats (the size of which to-day seem so absurd in some caricature by Chalon) I remember to have seen her braided hair circled by a fine Venetian chain, with one small gold coin, serving for clasp, above her forehead, and attracting every eye by the thorough fitness of the ornament to its wearer. Perhaps the chain and the coin indicated the character of a woman—if not in her life, in her art at least—thoroughly, fearlessly original.

Her voice was not naturally a voice of first-rate quality. It was a mezzo-soprano, extended upwards and downwards by that hardy and tremendous exercise the introduction of which has been ascribed to the appearance of her father, in singing and tuition. To support this no common strength and tenacity of frame are necessary; and perhaps the discipline can never be fully wrought out without some sacrifice of power and certainty. As it was, the girl was early put into possession of an instrument two octaves and a half, if not more, in compass, weakest in the tones betwixt F and F—a weakness audaciously and incomparably disguised by the forms of execution, modification, and ornament which she selected. Her topmost and deepest notes were perpetually used in connected contrast, whatever the song might be—whether it was the bravura from *Inez di Castro,* or Haydn's "With verdure clad." On the stage her flights and sallies told with electric effect. There was much of her restless and impassioned southern nature in them—as much of a musical invention and skill which required no master to prompt or to regulate her cadences; but there was something, too, of an instinctive eagerness on her part to evade display in the portion of her voice to which display would have been the least becoming. In some degree, that which began by being an individuality with her has become a sort of necessity to all who have been subjected to a similar training.

If this be so, a question is inevitably suggested—whether in art it is better to force or to cultivate nature, to ignore defects, or to

admit them and turn them to account.   No founders of a school
of singers can expect that two people, during a century, shall enter
it, so indomitable, so fervid, so full of resource, as the Garcia
sisters; but for its scholars to emulate them might prove a fatal
ambition—and it has done so.

Though creative as an executant, Malibran was not a creative
dramatic artist.   Though the fertility and audacity of her musical
invention had no limits, though she had the power and the science
of a composer, she did not establish one new opera or character
on the stage—hardly, even, one first-class song in a concert-room.
Though she was received with royal honours in Milan, Naples,[1]
Venice, where she excited her audiences to frenzies of enthusiasm,
and where the soldiers presented arms as she passed, on the Italian
stage in London she was unable to possess herself of the succession to Madame Pasta, or to satisfy our public as thoroughly as a
far younger and less accomplished artist, Madame Grisi, did
shortly after her disappearance.   She is best remembered, perhaps, in Italian opera, as Desdemona—especially in the incomparable third act of *Otello;* and no theatrical portrait of modern
time could be named surpassing that by M. Dubufe, of herself in
the chamber scene.   On the whole, she was found unequal, bizarre,
and fatiguing by many of our opera loungers (a public as apt to
be scared as allured by original genius).   Her real stage triumphs
in this country were when she sang in English as Amina, as
Leonora in *Fidelio*—Isolina, in Mr. Balfe's *Maid of Artois,* being
her third character.   In her English performances her exuberance,
not to say extravagance of style, served the purpose of concealing
the mediocrity, and worse, of her playfellows.   To myself it always brought as much of wonder as of delight.   Her vehemence
in *La Somnambula* too nearly trenched on frenzy to be true; in
Fidelio it destroyed that idea of faltering and fear which gives so
much tenderness to the earlier scenes of the tale of woman's devo-

---

[1] It was at Naples that she gave way to one of her oddest caprices. "She played,"
says Madame Merlin, in her Memoirs, "in a new opera, *Amelia,* composed by Rossi.
In this opera Malibran undertook to dance the mazurka.   She never excelled in dancing, though she was excessively fond of it.   Her native grace seemed to forsake her
whenever she attempted to dance; still she seized every possible opportunity of dancing
on the stage.   In this instance, Madame Malibran's Mazurka certainly contributed to
the failure of *Amelia.*—I have elsewhere been assured that she could never dance
in time—a peculiarity which, however singular it seems, has distinguished more than
one perfectly organized musician.

tion. She delivered Beethoven's music wondrously, considering its unsuitability for her voice, making changes and adaptations where they were inevitable with such musician-like science that not the protest of a solitary purist could be raised against them, but the effect produced in the opera by a singer incomparably inferior to her, Madame Schroeder-Devrient, was far deeper and more moving. The Spaniard threw more horror into the scene in the vault than her predecessor; but the German is before me when, in the introduction to the Chorus of Prisoners, as they creep out of their cells, she questioned one ghastly face after another with the heart-piercing wistfulness of hope long deferred. Nothing comparable has since been seen on the musical stage till the other day, when the younger sister of Malibran struck the same chords by her admirable pantomime as Orpheus in Gluck's opera, when he is shown as searching for his Eurydice in the "yellow meads of asphodel."

As a woman, Malibran was ambitious, fond of gain, munificent in giving (and this when no chorus was at hand to applaud the gift) noble, careless, insatiable in her search for excitement and effect. These facts have been so often told by her personal friends and her old comrades that their story need not be returned on.

There is no need to relate minutely the tale of her wretched American first marriage; neither how, by breaking away from it, she flung herself into suspense and perplexity from which one like herself could only find refuge in excitement, and to which may be ascribed many of the caprices and inequalities which, for some years of her life, were supposed by her audiences to be only so many whimsies of a violent and reckless woman. Calmer days might have been in store for her after her second marriage with M. de Beriot, but for her premature decease, hurried on by her wilfulness in concealing the consequences of an accident while she was riding (a favourite pastime of hers). Nothing could possibly be more painful than her agonizing death in the midst of the Manchester Festival of 1836, only a few hours after one of those unexpected outbursts of inspiration in which she was unparalleled. Nothing could be more sad to English eyes than its sequel. Of a woman so bright, so kindly, so ill-starred, and thence (it may be) so unequal, as she, it is impossible to think without a strange and

affectionate regret.   Of the artist it must be recorded that, boundless as were Malibran's resources, keen as was her intelligence,
dazzling as was her genius, she never produced a single type in
opera for other women to adopt.   She passed over the stage like
a meteor, as an apparition of wonder, rather than as one who, on
her departure, left her mantle behind her for others to take up
and wear.

LOUIS LABLACHE

USICAL history contains no account of a bass singer so gifted by nature, so accomplished by art, so popular without measure or drawback, as Louis Lablache. For the most part, the lowest voice of the quartet has habitually been considered as useful rather than interesting, at least in serious Italian opera. It is true that Mozart and other Germans have given it a prominence, this arising from the large supply of bass voices in their country, as compared with tenors.[1] It is as true that, in Italian comic operas, the buffo has always been a prime favourite; though his occupation is more dependent on lively action and rapid delivery of the words than on qualities strictly musical. But the fact, so far as Lablache is concerned, remains as I have stated it. Never, at all events in our memory, has the spell of indifference been so completely broken as by this wonderful artist—taking him for all in all the most remarkable man whom I have ever seen in opera.

The long-treasured notion of French voices being inexpressive and unpleasing in quality (as if our neighbours' country had not produced a Fodor, a Cinti, a Duprez), receives a heavy shock from the fact that Lablache was of French origin, though born in Naples,[2] and trained in the Conservatorio della Pietà di Turchini there. There, too, as M. Scudo's agreeable recollections of Italian singers assure us, he enjoyed the great advantage of the society and counsels of Madame Mericoffre (a rich banker's wife), known in Italy before her marriage as La Coltellini; utterly unknown in England (such was singers' fame then), although

---

[1] Nothing is more curious, or at first sight more capricious, than the distribution of voices. Soprani grow in every country; but the full, as compared with the light, soprano, is rare in France, whereas the latter is seldom to be found in Germany. Neither France nor Germany possesses the contralto voice in which Italy and England are so rich. The south has always been, *par excellence,* the birthplace of tenors, though England is now more productive than formerly. The deep bass, from Handel's time till our own, has always been a German specialty.

[2] A.D. 1791.

described as one of the finest artists belonging to the golden age of Italian singing. But whatever position and training may have done for Lablache, nature, bounteous in his organisation, had done more. An organ more richly toned or suave than his voice was never given to mortal. Its real compass was about two octaves— from E to E. In the upper portion of the register four or five of his tones had a power which could make itself heard above any orchestral thunders or in the midst of any chorus, however gigantic either might be. This remarkable force was not, as in the case of many singers, displayed on all occasions; but it was made to tell in right places, such as in the parts of the deaf and angry Don Geronimo (*Il Matrimonio*) or of Oroveso, the Druid Priest, in *Norma* (from which Bellini repeated its effect in *I Puritani*), with prodigious and resistless lustre, put forth, as it was, without stint or the slightest apparent difficulty.

Then Lablache was gifted with a personal beauty to a rare degree. A grander head was never more grandly set on human shoulders; and in his case time, and the extraordinary and unwieldy corpulence which came with time, seemed only to improve the Jupiter features and to enhance their expression of majesty, or sweetness, or sorrow, or humour, as the scene demanded.

His mother-wit, too, his feeling for propriety in all that concerned his art, combined with genius in the nicest proportion, were as remarkable as his beauty. One never felt on the stage how huge he was. His shoe was as big as a child's boat. One could have clad the child in one of his gloves; and the child could almost have walked (though no Blondin) on his belt. But every article of his dress was so excellently fitted to its wearer, was worn so unconsciously, and was so thoroughly in agreement with all that it accompanied, that there was neither time nor temptation for comparison. I have seen a feat somewhat analogous performed in a totally opposite manner. On the stage, no one (save a Dantan) ever found out that M. Duprez was of small stature.— Nor was this all. One was never reminded by Lablache, when he would be tragic in touch, or turn, or tone, of the comic actor who gave way to the wildest Neapolitan *lazzi* when the artist chose to be comical. I think of his Podestà in *La Gazza Ladra*, of his deaf Don Magnifico in *Il Matrimonio*, of his Doge in *Marino Faliero*, of his Puritan Captain in *I Puritani*, as of so many dif-

ferent creatures, set apart one from the other, in no respect recalling the personality of him who still gave life and soul to all of
them.   Towards the close of his career (as I shall have to record),
at a time of life when anyone save himself would have grown
dull and mechanical, he broke out into the personification of two
beings as different as Shakespeare's Caliban from Scribe's Calmuck
in M. Meyerbeer's Russian opera [1]—with a vivacity, a profound
stage knowledge, and a versatility which were as rare as they were
strongly marked.

But Lablache had qualities as sterling as others which were fascinating.   Whether from organization, or from ambition, or from
industry matters little, this handsome young French-Neapolitan
had got an amount of general and genial and solid musical culture,
ere he appeared in England, which, for a singer, has been something
with too little precedent.   No music was strange to him; no one
has so sung, to compare with himself, Leporello's "Madamina" in
Mozart's *Don Juan;* or the tough air devised for Mephistopheles,
from Spohr's *Faust,* known by its Italian words as "Va sbramando."
The only time that I had an opportunity of drawing near the great
Palestrina music (for ever talked about, never heard) was at one
of our Ancient Concerts.   At this Lablache's perfect acquaintance
with the great Roman style, his marvellous voice and, little less
marvellous, his power of sustaining and animating his comrades
without bearing them down, afforded a distinct idea of how such
music might be sung, and how (when well sung) it might move,
impress, and exalt those who heard it as a portion of a rite.

Thus much by way of general character of one of the greatest
musicians and artists ever seen or heard on the stage or in the orchestra.   The life, the vigour, the variety thrown by him into new
characters till he died, the consummate musical skill with which he
completed every task that he undertook, for the score of years
which followed his appearance, will be told in the sketch of the
events of the seasons as they passed.

[1] *Etoile du Nord.*—E. N.

THE YEAR 1831

OPERAS. *Il Pirata, La Somnambula.** Bellini. *Il Matrimonio.* Cima-rosa. *Anna Bolena.** Donizetti. *Medea.* Meyer. *L'Ultimo Giorno di Pompei.** Pacini. *Il Barbiere, Ricciardo e Zoraide, La Cenerentola, Semira-mide, Otello.* Rossini. PRINCIPAL SINGERS. Mdes. Sigl-Vespermann.* Fanny Ayton. Wood.* Méric-Lalande. Rubini.* Pasta. Beck.* MM. David.* Curioni. Rubini.* De Begnis. Santini. E. Seguin.* Lablache. BALLETS. *Kenilworth.** *Flore et Zephyre. La Bayadère.** PRINCIPAL DANCERS. Mdes. Montessu. Brocard. Taglioni. M. Perrot.

THE YEAR 1831

THE list of the performers and singers who were presented in the year 1831 of itself bespeaks a time of transition, which is rarely a time of prosperity. The power of Signor Rossini's spell was, for the moment, beginning to weaken as rapidly as if four out of the five of his operas performed had not that lasting vigour and beauty which belongs only to works of genius such as his. *Ricciardo e Zoraide,* compared with them, is weak, and yet contains one trio, "Cruda sorte," the best movement of which helped to set a pattern to many a contemporary,[1] and to almost every subsequent Italian composer, Bellini alone excepted.

For awhile, however, the new composers were received timidly. *Anna Bolena,* brought hither under the protection of Madame Pasta's royal robes, was permitted rather than admitted, though in this historical English opera might be discerned something of Donizetti's own; and though three of the characters—those of the Queen (Pasta), Percy (Rubini), and Henry the Eighth (Lablache), were played and sung to perfection. Donizetti, however, was not an utter stranger here. A duet of his, introduced into a pasticcio opera by Bochsa, called *I Messicani,* had, a season or two earlier, excited attention. But he was credited with small individuality by those who then ruled public opinion. So it is curious to recollect how Bellini's second opera, introduced here (also by Madame Pasta), *La Somnambula,* was treated on its introduction with contempt; the want of science on the part of its composer

---

[1] The figure of this is one of Signor Rossini's favourite figures, used to its greatest effect in the quartet, "Ciel il mio labbro," *Bianca e Faliero,* and the incomparable finale to the third act, added to his *Mosè,* for Paris. Perhaps some indication of it is to be found in the operas of Paër, from whom Signor Rossini improved much—compare his overture to *Tancredi* with Paër's to *Sargino.* But those who have borrowed from Signor Rossini—as Signor Mercadante, in the well-known duet, "Ah non lasciarmi" from *Andronico* (Malibran's *last* duet); as Signor Verdi in the screaming stretto which ends the first act of *Il Trovatore*—have not followed his, and Handel's, example, in enriching with some new beauty that which they have appropriated.

17

dwelt on, and that which is true in expression, and which has kept the opera alive, utterly overlooked.   It may have been that possibly truth in expression was not then much cared for by those who frequented our Italian opera.   The time of Donizetti and Bellini, though at hand, was still to come.

A third Italian composer, already of some home note, living and writing in 1860, fared, and has always fared, worse in England than the two composers just mentioned.   Signor Pacini was not unknown here; for a comic opera by him *La Schiava in Bagdad,* had been performed some years earlier, the rondo finale of which —a varied air with violin obbligato—survives to this day as a show song.   This contempt is the more singular because Signor Pacini has shown in such tunes distinct originality.   Three or four of his airs of parade are admirable, and his own—let me instance "Il soave e bel contento" (*Niobe*), and "Lungi dal caro ben" (I forget from what opera), in the last movement of which there is an early example of those syncopations which have been since so largely used and abused by the Riccis, Lillos, Coppolas of modern Italy, and most of all by Signor Verdi.   Yet in spite of this claim as a melodist, not one opera by Signor Pacini (there are eighty, or thereabouts, by this time, a *Medea* among the number) has kept the stage for a month in London or in Paris.

Among the female singers of the year 1831 the only Italian was Madame Pasta.   There were two new tenors, however; one of whom must be spoken of from testimony, the other dwelt on from recollection.   The first was David—the son of the elder David, an artist of great renown some seventy years ago, who had formed Nozzari (another tenor, described by all having Neapolitan recollections as remarkable for brilliancy and grandeur), and his son also.   The latter rose to a great reputation in Italy.   I have listened to travellers who heard David the younger at home, when in his prime; and who have spoken of him with rapture as a sort of Italian Garcia, as a man not endowed with a grateful voice, but whose musical science and natural spirits combined were limitless in their effect, who could sometimes shock, but oftener carry away, his audiences into transports.   He was one of Signor Rossini's Neapolitan troop in the days when the incomparable *Otello* was written; but he crossed the Alps too late, after he had passed the age of forty years, to assault a public habitually averse to every foreign thing that *seems* extravagant (we tolerate any extravagance that conceals itself in our own nationality)—prepared, probably, for ovations, possibly somewhat contemptuous of a rude northern audience. His voice was found to be worn and nasal; his animation was considered as mere caricature; his facility was rated as so much frippery. "When he came to this country," says Lord Mount Edgecumbe in his *Musical Reminiscences,* "he was *passé;* and his voice had become so unsteady that he was obliged to disguise its defects by superfluity of ornaments and passages." The amateur quoted, it may be remarked, was one of the old school, who never heartily recognized Signor Rossini as an Italian conversant with the true opera style. In any event, Signor David had no success either in London or in Paris. In one of his favourite operas, *L'Ultimo Giorno,* by Signor Pacini, he was unlucky as having to sing with Mrs. Wood (Miss Paton) who, whatever might be her merits, did not number among them any knowledge of the modern Italian style.

Of the other southern tenor who appeared in the same year as Signor David, and who never, thenceforward, lost his hold on England, there is more to be said presently.

In the chronicles of the ballet, another example of the taste of the time is to be found in the presentation of M. Auber's *Le Dieu et la Bayadère* (a ballet opera, it is true) with all the opera left out. The luxurious oriental grace of Mdlle. Taglioni, the dancing girl who lured a divinity (as Goethe's ballad assumes) was as remarkable as her Swiss dancing in Signor Rossini's Tyrolienne had been fresh, sprightly—anything but morally vulgar. One of the best of Chalon's opera portraits—unique as a collection, in their taste and appreciation of the world portrayed—remains to bring her fascinations more clearly before the eyes than words, were they as winged as her own feet, could do.

The other new ballet of 1831, *Kenilworth,* is noticeable as having introduced, for the first time, the name of one to whom music in England owes a greater debt than has yet been owned—I mean Signor Costa. This was his first step on a domain in which he has since walked steadily forward, as only (in England) an upright and a competent man can do, supposing the walk prolonged through a life.   His music to *Kenilworth* may be marked as the beginning of the solitary European musical reputation which has ever been made by an unknown foreigner in England, and in England alone.

GIAMBATTISTA RUBINI

F Rubini,[1] "king of tenors," as he was called on the continent, and whose name became "a household word" in England among all opera-frequenters, I shall offer a separate study. As a singer, and nothing beyond a singer, he is the only man of his class who deserves to be named in these pages as an artist of genius. No one, in my experience, so merely and exclusively a singer as he was, so entirely enchanted our public so long as a shred of voice was left to him; no one is more affectionately remembered. His memory is, if possible, more prized than he himself was, fascinating though his sole admitted successor among Italian tenors has been.

Rubini's career in this country was marked by yearly progress in public affection more signally than any of his brother or sister artists. There were peculiarities to which we had to habituate ourselves. He was in no respect calculated to please the eye; for the openness of his countenance could not redeem the meanness of features impaired by smallpox. His figure was awkward; he dressed as any one else pleased, without a thought of his own as to taste, character, or picturesque effect (in this how different from his successor!). He rarely tried to act, the moment of the curse in the contract scene of *Lucia* being the only attempt of the kind that I can call to mind. The voice and the expression were, with him, to "do it all."

Before, however, Rubini came to England his voice had contracted that sort of thrilling or trembling habit, then new here, which of late has been abused *ad nauseam*. It was no longer in its prime—hardly capable, perhaps, of being produced mezzo forte or piano; for which reason he had adopted a style of extreme contrast betwixt soft and loud, which many ears were unable, for a long period, to relish. After a time these vehemences (in themselves

[1] Born at Bergamo, 1795.

21

vicious) were forgotten for the sake of the transcendent qualities by which they were accompanied, though in the last years of his reign they were exaggerated into the alternation of a scarcely audible whisper and a shout; and it was said, not untruly, that it would be hardly possible to form any idea of a new tenor part were it presented for the first time by Rubini, so largely did memory and knowledge of his intentions aid his public.   Further, he was to be easily surpassed by every one in his declamation.   Here and there (as in the garden scene in *Otello* with Iago) he roused himself to give point and passion to his recitative.   But such an awakening was exceptional, since for the most part he went through this part of his task with correct accent but without any remarkable intelligence—in this respect an utter contrast to M. Duprez.   One remembers Rubini not by this or by the other character, but by his songs.   Yet more, his taste in ornament was often questionable. His facility was apt to tempt him into enormous roulade cadenzas which had little variety.   In Paolino's great song, "Pria che spunti" (*Il Matrimonio*), he revelled in embroideries of the phrase in retarded time which occurs just before the close, which, however ingenious and wonderful as vocal displays, I always felt to be superabundant.

The most enthusiastic admirers of Rubini cannot dispute the truth of these characteristics; the fact being that the idol of the public made them all forgotten and forgiven by his excessive vocal finish, and by a geniality of expression that was resistless.   There was never an artist who seemed so thoroughly and intensely to enjoy his own singing—a persuasion which cannot fail to communicate itself to his audiences.   Again, there was never an artist more sure of his own effects than Rubini.   He would walk through a good third of any given opera languidly, giving the notes correctly, and little more; in a duet, blending his voice intimately with that of his partner (in this he was unsurpassed) ; but when his own moment arrived there was no longer coldness or hesitation, but a passion, a fervour, a putting forth to the utmost of every resource of consummate vocal art and emotion, which converted the most incredulous, and satisfied those till then disposed to treat him as one whose reputation had been overrated.   As a singer of one song, who has equalled Rubini?—whether the song was "Vivi tu" in *Anna Bolena,* or his air "Tutto e sciolto" in the second act of *La Som-*

nambula, or his bravura in the second act of Donizetti's *Marino Faliero,* or his "A te o cara" in *I Puritani,* or his "Il mio tesoro" in *Don Giovanni,* or his scene from Signor Costa's *Malek Adhel* (containing that resplendent song, "Tiranno cadrai," which no creature to come, in our time, may be ever able to attempt). These songs did not create a success for him so much as an ecstasy of delight in those who heard them. The mixture of musical finish with excitement which they displayed has never been equalled within such limits, or on such conditions, as the career of Rubini afforded. He ruled the stage by the mere art of singing more completely than any one, woman or man, has been able to do in my time. He had as many devoted admirers of the fair sex (of both sexes) as if he had been an Adonis—people ready to swear that his voice did not vibrate, to pour out their homage in sonnets, to maintain that he was an original and vigorous actor, that his declamation admitted of no improvement, he being all the while merely an honest, homely man, with few graces of manner, and none of that natural quickness which stands many of his countrymen in the stead of culture: a little vain—and who can wonder?—but not offensively so.

In one wise respect Rubini did not resemble the majority of tenors—in foolishly flinging away the treasure which he had amassed by his songs. He is understood to have left behind him one of the largest fortunes ever gained on the opera stage. The traditions of his method died with him. He may be said to be the last of the remarkable company of Italian tenors for whom Signor Rossini wrote, and compared with whom the best of those we hear to-day, nine out of ten, with finer natural voices than his, are incomplete, unsatisfactory, and whose reign in favour is brief, as it deserves to be.

SIGNOR ROSSINI'S OPERAS

CHARACTERISTICS

ERE, as belonging to a year of transition—to the temporary wane of Signor Rossini's popularity, and to his final retirement from composition for the stage—some remarks on the greatest musical genius of southern Europe are not unseasonable.

The world is only beginning to appreciate this genius at its real value. Yet that Signor Rossini, on his first appearance, intoxicated the general public as no other composer, earlier or later, has done, is equally true. The vivacity of his style, the freshness of his melodies, the richness (for an Italian) of his combinations, the room and verge afforded to the singers, make up a whole in comparison with which the brightest splendours of Cimarosa and Paisiello and Paër (to whom Signor Rossini is indebted for many of his forms) are but so many faded and pale emanations from luminaries of a second order.

There is no such luxury of beauty in any former Italian writer. I have never been able to understand why this should be contemned as necessarily false and meretricious—why the poet may not be allowed the benefit of his own period and his own manner, why a lover of architecture is to be compelled to swear by the Dom at Bamberg, or by the cathedral at Monreale, that he must abhor and denounce Michael Angelo's church on the Baths of Diocletian at Rome, why the person who enjoys *Il Barbiere* is to be denounced as frivolously faithless to Mozart's *Figaro* and as incapable of comprehending *Fidelio,* because the last act of *Otello* and the second of *Guillaume Tell* transport him into as great an enjoyment (after its kind) as do the duet in the cemetery betwixt Don Juan and Leporello, and the "Prisoner's Chorus." How much good genial pleasure has not the world lost in music owing to this pitting of styles one against the other!

To some such unfair construction as that typified in the above paragraph was Rossini subjected by "the judges" of opinion, so-called, who ruled during the noontide of his popularity. That was held to be a mere passing madness, which could not last. The old amateurs who delighted in the delicate music of Paisiello and the clear merriment of Cimarosa pronounced the works of the young Pesarese master overcharged, out of taste, and were not to be charmed by the fascinations of his melody, which no composer has poured forth in such delicious abundance, or by his exquisite and new concerted effects, as in *Il Turco, Cenerentola, Otello, La Gazza,*—in every opera from his pen. They declared, and declared truly, that he had borrowed from other composers largely—from Haydn in his "Zitti, Zitti" (*Barbiere*), from Paër, from Generali; but what of that? They might just as fairly have railed against Shakespeare because he quoted Plutarch and Holinshed verbatim; or against Handel, who scrupled not to appropriate any material that suited his purpose for the moment; having forgotten what a gorgeous treasure of originality remains to each of the three when every debt has been owned to the uttermost! We are *now* aware of the glow, the colour, the emotion thrown into Italian opera by Signor Rossini, as compared with his predecessors; but the purists, thirty-five years ago, saw none of these things—none of the enrichment and enlargement brought into his art by the master, without any such innovations as imply destruction. They resigned themselves, with a sort of fastidious self-pity, to the enthusiasm of the hour,—as wise men will to a passing frenzy,—preferred to talk of the composers and singers whom they had thoroughly delighted in when they were young, in the days when Art was Art indeed—quiet and select, however beautiful,—not a delirious orgy, which could only intoxicate those feeble-brained and hot-blooded folk who courted intoxication. In a humour such as this were the operas of Signor Rossini treated by such English amateurs of music as Lord Mount-Edgecumbe and his contemporaries.

They had also to run the gauntlet of criticism totally different in argument and spirit. At the time of their sudden outburst the world of Europe was beginning also to waken to the solid and lasting claims of the great writers of the German school. Mozart was comparatively unhackneyed; Beethoven was just beginning to pierce the sympathies of the imaginative and enterprising (in spite of the imperfect execution of his works). Weber had got hold of a fresher stage than that of Italy by the fascination of a wild and popular nationality.   There is more to master in the music of all these three men than in that of Signor Rossini.   Germany was newer than Italy.   Orchestral art was then in the first freshness of its youth; and hence the sagacious, the scientific, and the sour set their faces against the facile author of *Il Barbiere* as the spoiled idol of fashion, as a mere flimsy tune-spinner whose seductions (supposing any one willing to be honestly seduced) must prove transient, palling, unreal.   When the composer was in England, singing at Marlborough House for H.R.H. the Prince Leopold, or under the wing of the Duke of Wellington (a man as genuine in his musical amateurship as in everything he set himself to study or to do), it was a fashion with the narrow (let me say, the pedantic) members of the English profession—then proud to be able to comprehend German music—to show their pride by depreciating the newest and greatest of the Italians.   There were such things as good and cultivated Englishmen who, on principle, when Signor Rossini entered one music shop, repaired to another.   So that this unprecedented Italian popularity of his was not without its countercheck, not only in London but in every metropolis on this side of the Alps.   Even when he consented to attach himself to the Opera of Paris for a time, he himself (subtlest among the subtle, most experienced among the experienced) found it well to change his manner—to be more careful, to attend more closely to finish—as his operas, *Le Siège de Corinthe, Le Comte Ory, Moise,* and last, and greatest of all, *Guillaume Tell,* attest.

Another cause may be ascribed for the pause of Signor Rossini's popularity besides the newly-acquired importance of what may be called the scientific school of stage composition.   It is wonderful that one so far in advance of his age as Signor Rossini should have consented to waste his genius on subjects so utterly unworthy of it as are the majority of his opera-books.   Considered as a series, their want of dramatic interest is perplexing and remarkable—so much so as to have suggested to sagacious persons the idea that the composer of *Tancredi* and *Otello* could not treat dramatic passion and situation, and was nothing when he was not sensually musical. No folly more baseless ever presented itself to fantastic spinner of theories.   It would be difficult to name any more forcible example of musical expression than the third act of *Otello,* than the apparition scene in *Semiramide,* than the second act of *Guillaume Tell;* or (to change the humour) than *Il Barbiere,* from its first to its last note.   Then, for colour, what can exceed in freshness certain scenes of *La Donna del Lago?*—in intensity, the Plague of Darkness in *Mosè?*

Evidences of power without limit present themselves in the music of this great genius.   That such power has been, in his case, not unaccompanied by a self-disregard closely trenching on cynicism, it is unhappily impossible to question; and this may have been crossed by a vein of self-assertion amounting to arrogance.   Too inattentive to the march of time, the musician may have fancied that he could retain, after fascinating, his theatrical audience by the spell of music alone.

That this was a mistaken idea (supposing idea it was), the event proved.   Dramas weaker in music than Signor Rossini's kept the stage, for the sake of the scope afforded to the actors.   Medea, Romeo, the shame-crazed father in *Agnese,* the peasant Nina of Paisiello's opera, even during the time of his early triumph, still attracted such great singers as were conscious that powers of personation were strong within them.   This may explain what Signor Rossini is reported to have said concerning Madame Pasta—"She always sang false."   Her greatest victories were not in his music. Her dignified and knightly demeanour, it is true, her superb declamation, animated his *Tancredi.*   Her queenly grandeur of bearing relieved the lengthiness of the songs and duets in his *Semiramide.*   In *Otella,* finding the part of Desdemona, throughout two-thirds of the opera, somewhat pale, she was driven by her instincts towards what is terrible and impassioned in art—"to attempt" (her own modest phrase) the stormy and vindictive character of the Moor married "to the gentle lady"; and unsatisfactory as all such assumptions must be, her personation printed deep on the minds of those who saw it an impression of something fierce, masterful, oriental, the like of which had hardly, till she came, been expressed in music.   But one recollects Madame Pasta by her Medea, her Romeo, her Norma, her Anna Bolena.   When she could be dramatic, the defects of intonation to which she was liable either disappeared, or were forgotten in the consummate union of vocal art with human emotion.

Thus an assertion which at first sight may seem a paradox, if examined will prove to be tenable as a truth.   The time on which Signor Rossini fell was unfortunate to the steady duration of his popularity—the more so since, owing to his indifference to what was passing in the world round him, he did not sufficiently provide for the exigencies of the hour.   The phrase of "no man's enemy but his own" applies in fullest force, to the direction given by this man of superb musical genius to his career.

Yet after everything has been admitted and regretted, as a body of imperishable music the operas of Signor Rossini will endure so long as the art of music lasts.   Now when the heat of immediate partisanship has died out, musicians of every country can admit his wondrous grace, his fertility of invention,[1] his admirable treatment of the voice, his simple and effective taste in arrangement of the orchestra.   He has already lived down some of his rivals and successors.   He can never be made a model; neither can any man of spontaneous inspiration who owes so little to rule as he.   The day may never come in which commentators will wrangle about his outer forms and inner meanings; but that every year as it flows on will deepen and ripen his fame, I no more doubt than that wood grows and water runs.

The strange, obstinate retirement from creation of such an artist as Signor Rossini, in the prime of his powers, with *Guillaume Tell* just made, and myriads of fancies still unexpressed, has always reminded me of nothing so much as of the old story, true in the main, which, however, has been added to and coloured and lectured on till small truth, it may be, is left in it—the story, I mean, of the man who left his wife in pique, without bidding her farewell, and who dwelt, for a long term of years, undiscovered, in a house on the opposite side of the street, long after her agony of wish to discover him had died out in blank hopelessness.   After holding out for a certain time, pride forbade him to go home.

Who has ever weighed the strength of perversity, the self-punishment of the implacable, or the comfort of their conviction

---

[1] Let one example of this be mentioned:—the beginnings of his Overtures—to *Il Barbiere*, to *L'Italiana*, to *La Cenerentola*, to *La Gazza*, to *Otello*, to *Semiramide*, to *Le Siége de Corinthe*, to *Guillaume Tell*—all how different one from the other, all how arresting to the listener by the very first phrase! In this first requisite for a dramatic prelude, the Italian (though professedly no instrumental composer) ranks on a par with Beethoven and Weber. The three are followed, at a long interval, by M. Auber.

that if the outer world suffers by it, so much the better! Thus it may be that the perpetual reference to, and solicitude concerning, Signor Rossini during the past thirty years, the anxiety to be allowed to hope that his last words were not said, the return to his best operas (in spite of their feeble stories), after one and another writer has been praised, become wearisome, and been laid by, may have amounted to so many incitements to persistence in the course of musical perversity, by which we have lost so much. No stranger story is, at all events, recorded in the annals of art, with respect to a genius who filled his own world with its glory, and then chose to vanish "not unseen."

THE YEAR 1832

OPERAS. (In Italian.) *La Straniera,** Bellini; *L'Esule di Roma,** *Olivo e Pasquale,** Donizetti; *Elisa e Claudio* Mercadante; *Agnese,* Paër; *Gli Arabi,** Pacini; *Otello, Il Barbiere, Pietro l'Eremita, Elisabetta La Donna del Lago,* Rossini; *La Vestale,** Spontini; *Giulietta e Romeo,** Vaccai. (In German.) *Macbeth,** Chelard; *Fidelio,* Beethoven; *Don Juan,* Mozart; *Der Freischütz,* Weber. (In French.) *Robert le Diable,** Meyerbeer. PRINCIPAL SINGERS. Mdes. de Méric,* Cinti-Damoreau,* Giuditta Grisi,* Rosa Mariani,* Schroeder-Devrient,* Schneider;* MM. Winter,* Curioni, Donzelli, Haitzinger,* Nourrit,* Tamburini, Giubilei, Lablache, Pellegrini,* Galli. BALLETS. *La Somnambula, L'Anneau Magique.** PRINCIPAL DANCERS. Mdes. Le Compte, Heberlé,* Brugnoli;* M. Samengo.*

THE YEAR 1832

T HIS was a strange year; in more than one respect important to the future of foreign opera in England, however ruinous to the manager who adventured an amount of experiment so large as is shown in its table of contents. Not one in the list of Italian operas, old or modern, contented the public. *L'Esule di Roma* made a certain mark in favour of Donizetti because of a terzetto, which was found new; but the other novelties from the south fell dead in the hour of their appearance. Spontini's grand French opera, *La Vestale,* has never been suffered to exist in England, never having been here prepared with care enough to harmonize the barrenness of certain portions of the composer's setting of M. Jouy's drama with the musical grandeur of his strong scenes.

No Italian prima donna of first class appeared. Giuditta Grisi [1] failed to enchant her public; a singer, however meritorious, with a harsh, limited voice, though with real dramatic intentions.

The leading woman of the Italian season, at its commencement, was a French lady, Madame de Méric; and later the delicious artist born, Mademoiselle Cinthie Montalant, who sang in Italian opera as Mademoiselle Cinti, afterwards as Madame Cinti-Damoreau.

To the value and cleverness and skill of Madame de Méric, as one able to carry out any part, whether it was one in Italian, or French, or German opera, sufficient tribute has not been paid. As to her countrywoman—among and above all the singers of her class, as an artist commanding boundless volubility without deep sentiment, charming by the delicious suavity of her voice and by an easy variety of embellishment, which never, for an instant, seemed to be mannered or studied for, do I recollect Madame Cinti-Damoreau. This admirable vocalist seems to have only wanted a steady direction of her fascinations to have controlled such world as waits on singing. But she quarrelled with the Grand Opera of Paris (after having been Signor Rossini's chosen heroine

[1] Not to be confused with *the* Grisi (Giulia.)—E. N.

there) ; came and went in England and America for a while; after at the Comic Opera of Paris, having given to M. Auber the heroines of his *Ambassadrice* and of that French *Barbiere,* the *Domino Noir.* She subsequently slipped out of sight and beyond ken, as no one so deliciously endowed and accomplished as she was should have done so early.

This was the year of Signor Tamburini's first appearance in England—if not an artist of genius, as a brilliant bass singer and actor combining more attractive qualities than any other (save Lablache) who could be named. He was a singularly handsome man; his voice was rich, sweet, extensive and equal—ranging from F to F two perfect octaves—and in every part of it entirely under control. His execution has never been exceeded, establishing him as one of the best singers of Signor Rossini's music. No one since himself has so thoroughly combined grandeur, accent, florid embellishment, and solidity; nor has approached him in such music as the aria "Sorgete!" from *Maometto,* in the part of Assur, in *Semiramide,* of Fernando, in *La Gazza Ladra.* How admirable he was as one of a company we knew for many a year. His acting, whether tragic or comic, was sensible and spirited, if it did not show those flashes of passion or irresistible drollery which have since atoned for so much vocal imperfection in Signor Ronconi. Something of high breeding was wanting to him when such a part as Don Giovanni had to be played; his pronunciation, too, of Italian became mannered and impure during his later years; but as a brilliant artist of the great school of Italian opera singers who appeared during a great period, Signor Tamburini will not soon be forgotten. One importation after another has come across the Alps to interfere with or replace him, but always without success.

This was the year when (happy event for England!) the Italian orchestra was placed under the direction of Signor Costa.

The German performances claim separate notice; but in addition to these the theatre,—by way of a novelty, and when just about to close under circumstances of disappointment and ruin—introduced nothing less strange to England, less elaborate, and less costly, than *Robert le Diable,* which, as the first of M. Meyerbeer's extraordinary French revelations, was at that time turning Paris crazy. In England some ill fortune, as will be seen, has always attended this opera, which has never been accepted as a favourite by our public. It is impossible to account for inconsistencies like these, frequent as they are in the world of music. In 1832, however, *Robert,* with its piquant melodies, its daring stage effects, and magnificent instrumentation, had no chance of establishing itself in London, since it was only completely performed once, and then after insufficient rehearsal. The singers quarrelled with the management, and had to be replaced by inferior ones. The work was curtailed, and on it, given in this mutilated form, descended the curtain of the season 1832—a season of disasters, in which, nevertheless, there was something like a foretaste and prophecy of the performances which have since raised the Italian Opera at Covent Garden to a place of supremacy among the musical theatres of Europe.

GERMAN OPERA IN ENGLAND

HE most noticeable feature of the year 1832 was the introduction to England of German opera in its original form; and the effect of the experiment which, in some respects, has proved alike important and lasting.

There are few subjects in art concerning which so many popular fallacies are current as German musical drama. The range of its claims is much narrower than has been dreamed of, confusions having been largely fallen into owing to the parentage of certain composers. This does not warrant classification of their music. Lulli, who settled the forms of opera for France, in the French taste, was Italian. Hasse, the Saxon, and Mysliweczek, the Bohemian, wrote Italian operas. The five operas of Gluck which keep the stage are assuredly French in every characteristic (*Orpheus* the least so). Mozart only fairly arrived on the national ground when he wrote his *Zauberflöte* for a faëry theatre at Vienna (and this had imported its distinctive character from the *Extravaganzas* and *Commedie delle arte* of the south). The real serious German operas that can be named are the one by Beethoven, those left by Weber and Spohr, some by Dr. Marschner and Herr Lachner; and from these we must step at once to the much-canvassed productions of Herr Wagner. Many, even in the above narrow list, can be said only to exist, not to live, on the stage of their own country, because that has been fed from France. There is no need here to dwell on the works of a lighter style, as without character or reality or beauty, seeing that none of them has had the existence of half an hour of passing fashion in this island. Dittersdorf, Conradin Kreutzer, and (latest) Lortzing, are so many names next to unknown in England.

Though some small attempt had been made to present German operas some years earlier in London, consequent on the popularity of the version of *Der Freischütz*, mutilated in English, it was not till Mr. Monck Mason held our Italian Opera house in his hand, for the single season of 1832, that our untravelled folk were enabled to form an idea of the power or the peculiar characteristics of pure German opera. *Fidelio,* as given by artists "to the manner born," amounted to a revelation. It was the solitary success of a management which was as disastrous as it was enterprising, and as such worthy of honourable commemoration.

A study of *Fidelio* has yet to be made, from more points of view than one. The book, of French origin, by M. Bouilly—the same dramatist who wrote *Les Deux Journées* for Cherubini— would be laughed to scorn if nowadays presented to a composer or a manager. "No part for the tenor in the first act," would be the remark, fatal to its acceptance—as if one work was to be precisely like another, according to the same Chinese model of exactness! How stupid is such a fancy, all concerned in art have often and again had occasion to see of late.

Belonging to the family of stories the strength and simplicity of which defy cavil and time is this story of *Fidelio,* twice set— once by Gaveaux, once by Paër—before Beethoven took it in hand; after (so anecdote says) his bearish reception of the Italian score, on the same being shown to him by its composer—if the tale be true—"I like your story," said he, "and will set it to music." The anecdote may concern the score of Gaveaux, not of Paër. Beethoven certainly re-set a twice-told story, full of passion and reality.

On considering the music to which Beethoven set M. Bouilly's story, such fault as may be found with the opera of *Fidelio,* as the music stands, is not to be charged against the unartificial disposition of the scenes so much as on the rugged nature of the master, on his limited and uncomplying views in respect to vocal art, and on his want of sympathy for the capacity and charm of the voice, which he never showed when writing for instruments. There are no melodies in *Fidelio* comparable to those which exist in Beethoven's symphonies, quartets, pianoforte sonatas. These are so symmetrical as often to amount to the vulgar things called "tunes," which the transcendental Germans of to-day, of whom Beethoven has served for prophet, do so contemptuously spurn when they are met on the stage.[1] The part of the heroine is one of extreme vocal

---

[1] Yet that Beethoven could be as richly captivating in this branch of his art as any musician who ever lived he showed in his stage music, as in his Choral Sym-

difficulty wherever she is called on to appear alone, so much so as to preclude the possibility of much individual pathos being thrown into it.   Even in the adagio of Leonora's great air, the best singer must be hampered by the florid obbligato accompaniment of horns, which but once in twenty times can be played correctly, so uncertain and hard to manage is the instrument.   The singer must in this song reduce her individuality to that of an organ stop.   Again, there are pages in *Fidelio* which are weak and commonplace.   The march is but colourless; the concerted finale end in the first act, during which the prisoners are returned to their cells, is, for Beethoven, uninteresting; and the grand closing scene of the opera begins and ends with phrases which, were they found elsewhere, might be treated with disparaging epithets.

Throughout the opera—need it be said?—the orchestral portion of *Fidelio* is sonorous, varied, original, and following the situations with a pertinence as wonderful as it is unobtrusive.   But (two or three pieces set apart) the orchestra, the story, and the acting, are the first and main attractions of *Fidelio;* and the voice, which should be the protagonist in opera, as declaiming musically, as leading the work from commencement to close, principal and predominant, and most effective when its position is the best considered, comes after them as secondary and assistant, a permitted accessory, not an indispensable fascination.

Be these things as they may, the sensation produced by *Fidelio* in 1832 is not to be forgotten.   The Italians, that year not very strong in muster, were fairly beaten out of the field by the Germans.   The intense musical vigour of Beethoven's opera was felt to be a startling variety, wrought out as it was in its principal part by a vocalist of a class entirely new to England.

This was Madame Schroeder-Devrient,[1] whose best character was Leonora.   Within the conditions of her own school she was a remarkable artist.   She was a pale woman.   Her face—a thoroughly German one—though plain, was pleasing, from the intensity of expression which her large features and deep tender eyes conveyed.   She had profuse fair hair, the value of which she thor-'

phony and his Choral Fantasia. The Greek and the Turkish marches in his *Ruins of Athens,* the "Hungarian Chorus" in his *King Stephen* (the last exquisite piece of music too little known), attest this sufficiently.

[1] Born at Hamburg, in 1805.

oughly understood, delighting, in moments of great emotion, to fling it loose with the wild vehemence of a Mœnad. Her figure was superb, though full, and she rejoiced in its display. Her voice was a strong soprano—not comparable in quality to other German voices of its class (those, for instance, of Madame Stöckl-Heinefetter, Madame Bürde-Nye, Mademoiselle Tietjens)—but with an inherent expressiveness of tone which made it more attractive on the stage than many a more faultless organ. Such training as had been given to it belonged to that false school which admits of such a barbarism as the defence and admiration of "nature-singing." Why not as well speak of natural playing on the violin or other instrument which is to be brought under control? A more absurd phrase was never coined by ignorance conceiving itself sagacity. Why as well not have nature-civilization?—nature-painting?—nature-cleanliness? But on the rock of this difficulty the German singers and German composers for voices have split. A man whose fingers cannot control the strings would hardly have a second hearing, did he attempt instrumental music. But a woman, supposing she can correctly flounder through the notes of a given composition, has been allowed, too contemptuously, to take rank as a singer. Such a woman was not Sontag—neither, of later days, Mdlle. Lind. The two had learned to sing; Madame Schroeder-Devrient *not*. Her tones were delivered without any care, save to give them due force. Her execution was bad and heavy. There was an air of strain and spasm throughout her performances, of that struggle for victory which never conquers.

But then as an actress, the devouring suspense of the disquieted wife, throughout the first half of the tale, enabled the German Leonora to exhibit all her passion of by-play, in judicious interpretation of the situation. Her eyes, quickened by the yearnings of her heart, were everywhere; her quivering lip, even when her countenance was the most guarded, told how intensely she was listening. It was impossible to hear the "Prisoners' Chorus" as given by the Germans in London during that year, and to see the eager woman as she unclosed cell after cell, and ushered its ghastly tenants into the fresh air, questioning face after face, all in vain,—without tears. Nor less earnestly wrought up was her scene in the vault, ending with her rapturous embrace of the rescued captive, for whom she had waited so long and dared so much. By no one has

Madame Schroeder-Devrient been equalled in this opera. In no other opera was she seen to such advantage; her fatal and sinister acting as the Lady in Chelard's *Macbeth* was hampered, in some measure, by the music; for this demanded an executive facility which she did not possess. Subsequently she made the mistake of appearing in Italian opera; a season or two later attempted to sing in English, without having mastered the language, and lost her hold on our public. As years went on, she exaggerated every peculiarity as a singer and as an actress. The last time I heard her in her own theatre at Dresden, her restlessness on the stage had reached a monopolising point of torment to every spectator, so resolutely did she seem determined that no one else should be seen or attended to when she was in presence.

The tenor who played with her, Herr Haitzinger, a man of great German reputation, was a meritorious musician, with an ungainly presence and a disagreeable throaty voice—an actor whose strenuousness in representing the hunger of the imprisoned captive in the dungeon trenched closely on burlesque. How he patted his stomach I well recollect. This, by the way, is a characteristic of the German theatre. The actors partake of stage meals with a gusto—not to say greediness—and a noisy obtrusive enjoyment, which hardly meets the taste of England or France.

But the principal feature of the German performance of *Fidelio* which marked an epoch in London was the spirit and reality of the stage chorus—things till then totally unknown here. The rueful, shabby people who used to shout their easy Italian tunes out of tune, in meagre, motionless semi-circle—so many scarecrows, instead of singers—were in these German operas replaced by a company of earnest folk with stout voices (and those of the women fresh), who showed that they took pride in their work by rendering the music, and all its lights and shades, with instant steadiness, and that they understood the scene, by the assistance their appropriate action afforded to every situation in which they took part. Their forcible and intelligent performances did not fall on deaf ears. The English people (since Handel's time, at least) have always cultivated a taste and relish for chorus singing. Their example was not lost. Year by year this most important feature in musical drama, which has been studied as such more and more closely by modern composers—German or not German—has excited increasing attention in this country, and to such good purpose that we are now, as to excellence, in advance of the great theatres of Paris, Berlin, Vienna, or Milan. The spark, however, was laid to the tinder by the results obtained by M. Chelard, the conductor of these German operas, from his chorus singers in *Fidelio*.

THE YEAR 1833

OPERAS. *Il Pirata, Norma,** *I Montecchi,** Bellini; *Anna Bolena,* Donizetti; *Medea,* Mayer; *Le Nozze di Figaro, Don Giovanni,* Mozart; *Agnese,* Paër; *La Cenerentola, Matilda di Shabran, Il Barbiere, La Gazza Ladra, Semiramide, Tancredi,* Rossini. (In German.) *Fidelio,* Beethoven; *Der Freischütz,* Weber; *Zampa,** Hérold. PRINCIPAL SINGERS. Mdes. Boccobadati,* De Méric, Schiasetti,* Nina Sontag,* Cinti-Damoreau, Pasta, Pirscher;* MM. Donzelli, Rubini, Tamburini, De Begnis, Giubilei, Galli. BALLETS. *Faust,** *Flore et Zephyre, Nathalie, Inez de Castro,** *La Sylphide,** *La Bayadère.* PRINCIPAL DANCERS. Mdes. Leroux, Montessu, Teresa and Fanny Elssler,* Taglioni; M. Perrot.

THE YEAR 1833

HOUGH the list of operas performed in 1833 be long, the performances fell short of giving entire satisfaction. Of the novelties by Bellini introduced, only one was relished—for the critics of the hour flouted *Norma* as a poor work. Nor till a year or two later did that opera take its place among the stock favourites of England. None of the new singers became popular. The German company was made up of mediocrities, the men not being worth naming: the sensation of 1832 was accordingly not repeated. The glory of Madame Pasta already showed signs of waning: she steadily began her evening's task half a tone too flat. Her acting was more powerful and striking than ever, if that could be. This, however, was her last season of being the presiding divinity of the opera. She only sang here on an engagement, once again, after an interval of some years; with regard to which appearance I shall speak in detail. This, too, was the season of Malibran's few last Italian performances in England. She had astounded rather than edified our fastidious dilettanti by singing in English at Drury Lane; [1] and thenceforth a sort of pique grew up between our despotic aristocracy and the wayward Spanish prima donna, and *Semiramide* was sung for the last time by herself, Madame Pasta, and Signor Tamburini, then in his prime—to an empty theatre.

Such life and excitement as were to be found in the Opera House in 1833, belonged to a world more attractive to many of its frequenters than the world of music—that of ballet. The year which showed us *La Sylphide,* with Madame Taglioni in the prime and perfection of her grace, which introduced an artist so incomparable, in another style, as Madame Fanny Elssler, was in its way a memorable one.

La Sylphide marks a ballet epoch, as a work that introduced an

[1] In an English version of *La Somnambula,* in an operetta by M. Chelard, called *The Students of Jena,* and, absolutely, as Count Belino in *The Devil's Bridge.*

element of delicate fantasy and fairyism into the most artificial of all dramatic exhibitions—one which, to some degree, poetized it. After *La Sylphide* were to come *La Fille du Danube,* and *Giselle,* (containing some of Adam's best music), *L'Ombre,* and a score of ballets in which the changes were rung on Naiad and on Nereid life—on the ill-assorted love of some creature of the elements for some earthy mortal. The purity and ethereal grace of Mdlle. Taglioni's style doubtless suggested the opening of this vein, as it also founded a school of imitators. Then her mimic powers, however elegant, were limited. Her face had few changes. Her character dances, as in *Guillaume Tell, La Bayadère,* were new and graceful; but their seduction, piquancy, and national chagrin were to be outdone. When she touched our cold English ground, however, The Sylph excited as much enthusiasm as the most idolized songstress can now do. Yet those were days in which the pretensions of the most favourite of favourites were trifling as compared with those of their inferiors now. While diamond bracelets were flung to her on the stage by magnificent patrons of the art, while the European world of playgoers was ringing with the fascinations of the young Swedish artist, she was contented (alternately with one of those creations which filled the theatre) to take such accessory parts as that of the Swiss peasant in Signor Rossini's opera, or the ghostly Abbess in M. Meyerbeer's *Robert.*

It was long and late before the star of Mdlle. Taglioni waned, before her lightness failed her, before it was whispered that there might be some little sameness in her effects. Even then its wane was accelerated by the growing success in the dancing world of a rival in a style and of a humour totally different—Mademoiselle Fanny Elssler. This last-named woman of genius had to "bide her time" both in Paris and London. Our public, at least, has not room in its heart for two sensations at once. Those who were captivated by the tenderness and the elegance—even when her flights were the boldest—of Mdlle. Taglioni, maintained that there was too little of the *semi-reducta Venus* in the presentations of the young, fresh, and bold dancer from Vienna. As to personal attractions, there could be no comparison between the two women. Mdlle. Elssler's dignified and triumphant beauty of face and form would have made her remarked whatever dress she wore, in whatever world she appeared. There was more, however, of the Circe than of the Diana in her smile, a quiet if not imperious consciousness of power and accomplishment, a *bravura* of style in her intercourse with the public, which was too keen for some eyes to bear. A mistress of the grand and artificial art of dancing, she possessed many more resources than Mdlle. Taglioni. She had studied Heberle closely; she had gone through every species of exercise which can give firmness and suppleness and the completest concord among all parts of the body, whether the same was in rapid motion, or flung into those unnaturally graceful and conventional postures which in dancing astonish rather than allure the uninitiated. The exquisite management of her bust and arms (one of the hardest things to acquire for the dancing) set her apart from everyone whom I have seen before or since. Nothing in execution was too daring for her, nothing too pointed. If Madame Taglioni flew, she flashed. The one floated on to the stage like a nymph; the other showered every sparkling fascination round her like a sorceress, with that abundance which finds enjoyment in its own exercise. Her versatility, too, was complete. She had every style, every national humour, under her feet: she could be Spanish for Spaniards, or Russian for the northerns, or Neapolitan for those who love the delirious Tarantella, with as much variety as certainty.

The above qualities, however, though great, may be numbered among those technical ones which every thoroughly-trained dancer is expected to exhibit as a matter of course. But beyond these Mdlle. Elssler as an actress commanded powers of high and subtle rarity—powers unsuspected during the period when her rival was queen of the stage, when invention was set to work principally to fit *her* with proper occupation. It was not till *The Gipsy* was produced that Mdlle. Fanny Elssler's full genius was known. This ballet, given on a reduced scale in London (and here best known as the theme of Mr. Balfe's *Bohemian Girl*), as seen in Paris, was a performance never to be forgotten. Much of the lovely music of Weber's *Preciosa* was used in it: the Bolero which opens his overture was allotted to a scene where the gipsy girl compels her sulky mates to dance. When she appeared on the stage of Paris the folk lay couched in fifties, huddled together in their wild and picturesque clothes, as only the French stage managers know how to group forms and colours. How she moved hither and thither, quick and bright as a torch, lighting up one sullen heap of tinder after another, gradually animating the scene with motion, till at last the excited rout of vagabonds trooped after her with the wild vivacity of a chorus of bacchanals, made a picture of many pictures, the brightness and spirit of which stand almost alone in the gallery of similar ones.   There have been Gitanas, Esmeraldas, Mignons by the score, but no Gipsy to approach Mdlle. Fanny Elssler.

In the next act of the same ballet came the scene of the minuet danced by the heroine to gain time, and to distract attention from her lover in concealment hard by, whose life was perilled.   Lord Byron, when speaking of his own dramas, has subtly dwelt on the power of suppressed passion.   Few things have been seen more fearful than the cold and measured grace of Mdlle. Fanny Elssler in this juncture, than the manner in which every step was watched, every gesture allowed its right time, so that neither flurry nor faltering might be detected, than the set smile, the vigilant ear, the quivering lip controlling itself.   It is in moments like these that genius rises above talent.   It was by representations such as these that Mdlle. Fanny Elssler gradually established a fame among the few as well as the many, which could have been built up by no pirouettes nor entrechats, but in right of which she is enrolled among the great dramatic artists of the century.

In the year 1833 an attempt was made, in *Inez di Castro,* to introduce one of those exhibitions of which the Italians are so fond, a "ballet of action," in which the impassioned story, told in dumb show, is the main matter, not the serious or sprightly dancing to garnish certain scenes.   Signor Cortesi's ballet had no success, was not understood here; indeed, it may be questioned whether, even had it been supported by La Pallarini herself (that wonderful tragic mime commemorated by so many southern travellers during the early part of this century), any such entertainment would have borne transportation into this northern clime of ours.

A monograph on ballet music is much wanted, for the interest and importance of the subject have been too universally overlooked by writers on our art.   Such influence as the dance with its rhythms has exercised on lyrical poetry and music has never been sufficiently considered, though there is hardly a fancy in musical composition which may not be traced back to it.   A mere list of the works of sterling and peculiar value written for the express use of dancing, and to accompany action, would be a contribution to the history of art as suggestive as it is valuable. We should find in the catalogue Gluck, as pioneer to Mozart, by his *Don Juan*,—Beethoven, the rigid and rugged, as regarded anything that might be called seductive, not merely conceding to a dance theatre his *Prometheus*, but, as I have said, in such accessory music to drama, as his Kotzebue's *Ruins of Athens*, and to *King Stephen* giving out some of his freshest inspirations. The Hungarian chorus (with ballet?) in the latter is not beaten in its easy appeal to the ear and delicious elegance of melody by the Tyrolienne in *Guillaume Tell*. Then there is Weber's *Preciosa* music— shadowed out in his earlier *Sylvana*—dance music of extraordinary beauty yet as inexorable in form as the veriest French galoppe. If we leave the renowned men of what is called classical art, and descend to such mere ballet makers as the Count de Gallenberg, whose *Anneau Magique* is noted on a foregoing page; as Herr Schneitzöffer, who wrote the music to the delicious *Sylphide;* it may be found that there is much to delight in, something to learn. The prelude to the second act of this faëry ballet, during which the curtain rises on a wood scene, is full of delicious poetry, mystery, and melody and attractive sound. Again, those who have mixed ballet with opera, according to the French taste, such as Rameau (in the well-known chorus from *Les Indes Galantes*), Gluck, whose dance music, whether choral or without voices, is wondrously alluring, Signor Rossini, MM. Auber and Meyerbeer, have, in this portion of their stage music, shown as much of the sacred fire of inspiration, if not of the "midnight oil" of science, as in the portions devoted by them to the setting out of words by sounds. We have lived into a period when everything that pleases is scouted by the severe and unimaginative, who conceive themselves transcendentalists. Possibly, then, such a protest as the above, giving creditable examples in favour of melody, symmetry, and beauty (if even the same be not "improved" by the devices and designs of counterpoint), may not be misplaced.

THE YEAR 1834

OPERAS. (In Italian.) *La Sonnambula,* Bellini; *Anna Bolena,* Donizetti; *Don Giovanni,* Mozart; *La Gazza Ladra, Semiramide, Il Barbiere, Otello, l'Assedio di Corinto, La Donna del Lago,* Rossini. (In German.) *La Dame Blanche,** Boieldieu; *Das unterbrochene Opferfest,** Winter. PRINCIPAL SINGERS. Mdes. Féron-Glossop,* Kynterland,* Salvi,* Caradori-Allan, Giulia Grisi,* E. Seguin,* Degli Antoni.* MM. Curioni, Rubini, Ivanoff,* Schmetzer,* Tamburini, Zuchelli, Giubilei. BALLETS. *La Sylphide, La Bayadère, Le Sire Huon,** Armide,** Masaniello.* PRINCIPAL DANCERS. Mdes. Taglioni. Duvernay.* Teresa and Fanny Elssler. M. Perrot.

THE YEAR 1834

HE prosperity of this year, so far as opera was concerned, was referable to the appearance of Mdlle. Grisi, and to the immediate place of supremacy—then less easy to conquer than now—which she assumed on a stage from which a Pasta and a Malibran had only just vanished. The small number of operas produced tells of itself a tale of the complete success of the new singer's fascinations. There was only one novelty—the Italian version of *Le Siège de Corinthe,* by Signor Rossini, arranged for the Opera of Paris from his *Maometto,* with some important additions.

The world has been too willing to let this work go, perhaps because the cause of Greek liberty, to which it was meant to appeal, soon ceased to warm any one; the dull arrangement of the story, too, precluding its finding a place among such dramas "for all time" as are *Masaniello* and *Les Huguenots.* Yet *Le Siège de Corinthe* contains music too noble to be forgotten—first among these the Overture. A Rossinian prelude though this be—and as such to be derided by classical souls, who are enamoured of many a piece of unidea'd German dullness—there is a grandeur in the introduction, there is a burning and brilliant force in the allegro, only in character and vivacity outdone by the prelude to *Guillaume Tell.* The quickstep forming the second subject of the allegro is more dependent for its character on rhythm than most of its master's themes; but the spirit with which it is wrought up is rare, even for Signor Rossini. Then where is there a bass aria of parade which can compare with the entry of Maometto?—especially if it be given with such temperance and florid grandeur combined as Signor Tamburini could throw into it. Since himself, no one has been able to sing this air properly, owing to the modern idea of accomplishment, which now denounces a shake as beneath the dignity of a hero, and a roulade to be nothing less meretricious than a dancer's pirouette. The opera also contains a grand and spirited duet betwixt bass and soprano, which was admirably sung by the two principal artists, a Turkish chorus, which may be cited with those of Mozart's *Seraglio,* and the banner solo and chorus, added (I think) for Paris—the poorest of which movements would, in this day of dearth, sound like marvels of fresh fancy. The opera, however, had not, nor has anywhere had, a long life. The world had not in those days ceased to measure Signor Rossini by himself.

During this year, 1834, Bellini, or rather his *La Somnambula,* began to creep on in public favour. This change may, in part, have been owing to the performances of that opera in English by Malibran; but doubtless, too, the simple interest of the story, and the artless expressiveness of the music, were found to have in them something permanent, entitling the young Sicilian to rescue it from the wholesale contempt which had been heaped on him. At the close of the season the part of Amina was taken, not successfully, by Mdlle. Grisi—earlier it had been presented by Madame Cara-dori, one of those first-class singers of the second class with whom it would be hard to find a fault, save want of fire. Elegance of person, purity of voice, a method beyond reproach, thorough musical skill, familiarity with many languages, were all combined in herself. Yet she only really pleased on the stage, when she sang in such second parts as Giulietta to Romeo. Her Zerlina was correct but cold; and it seemed, ere long, to be somehow agreed, by the tacit consent of every one, that her place was not the stage but the orchestra. There, in every part of Europe, she subsequently found honourable and profitable occupation for many a year.

As a young singer from whom much was hoped—not afterwards to be fulfilled—Signor Ivanoff must be commemorated: with the sweetest voice, as a gentle tenor, that ever sang in Italian or in Muscovite throat. Nothing could be more delicious as to tone, more neat as to execution: nothing, assuredly, ever so closely approached an automaton not wound up, as did he, on the stage, by his insignificance of aspect and his nullity of demeanour. In England he was never seen to attempt to act. Subsequently, he essayed to do so in Italy, I have heard: but by that time the voice had begun to perish. In 1834 it was so exquisite as, for a period, to make its owner's utter spiritlessness forgotten. No such good

Rodrigo in *Otello* has been heard here since I have known the opera.

The German company was beneath mediocrity. What has been said about the narrow limits of their repertory was signally proved in 1834. Though Winter's opera was, during some thirty years, a universal favourite in Germany, north and south, it seemed to us, in this country, merely a diluted piece of weary writing in the style of Mozart, in no wise comparable to the composer's *Ratto di Proserpina,* written professedly for the Italian stage, in which there is some pleasing and tuneable music.

The other opera new to our foreign stage was a version of *La Dame Blanche,* of Boieldieu—in which work, again, Germany has always taken infinite delight, England not much. The French composer tried hard to Scotticize himself by using a northern melody in his overture, "The Bush aboon Traquair," and to lay out his composition on such an ample scale as befits a story of sentimental romance with a touch of the supernatural in it; but never succeeded in ridding himself of French slightness, and in assuming Italian sweetness or German solidity. I have always found the music faded as well as feeble, especially when laboured through (not played with) by the average race of German singers. This was the humour of our public generally as regarded *La Dame Blanche.*

OPERA-GOERS IN 1834

FROM the year 1834 till the present one I am able to speak of foreign opera in England with more minute recollection: having since that period not, so far as I am aware, missed one new work or one first appearance which has taken place in London, nor one of the changes which have passed over that world within a quarter of a century.

How is everything changed! The seasons were then much more protracted than they have since become: and began as early as February with inferior singers, who disappeared at Easter, when their betters took their places. In this respect the alteration has been for good which has abolished the idea of bad performances as sufferable: not so, perhaps, the increased number of opera nights in the week. This may be in part a necessary consequence of the numbers of strangers who come and go through London, and snatch their entertainments as they pass. The non-subscribers are now of as much consequence to the treasury as the habitual frequenters of the theatre; but the strain on the musicians is sadly increased, and with it the difficulty of finding time for such nice preparation of the works performed as, happily, has become a necessity. By this, too, a certain air of private society, where known persons are sure to be found in known places, which used to distinguish the Opera, has all but departed from it.

Let me number a few of the familiar figures and faces which, from 1834 to 1838, were pointed out to "the friend from the country" as so many belongings of the Italian Opera. There was no escaping from the entrance of Lindley and Dragonetti into the orchestra: a pair of favourite figures, whose sociable companionship for some thirty years was as remarkable as their appearance was contrasted—no two faces imaginable being more unlike than the round, good-humoured, comely visage of the Yorkshireman from that of the gaunt Venetian, as brown and as tough as one of his own strings. On what the affectionate regard maintained between them was fed it is hard to say; for both were next to unintelligible in their speech—the Englishman from an impediment in utterance, the Italian from the disarranged mixture of many languages in which he expressed his sentiments and narrated his adventures. They talked to each other on the violoncello and double bass, bending their heads with quiet confidential smiles, which were truly humorous to see. Nothing has been since heard to compare with the intimacy of their mutual musical sympathy, nor is a pair of figures so truly characteristic now to be seen in any orchestra. Those two are among the sights of London that have vanished for ever.

There were then conspicuous figures in the boxes, in their places as regularly as the opera nights came round. Among these were a couple of Royal Dukes, one of whom was resolute to be heard as well as seen, and whose criticisms on things as they passed in society or on the stage sometimes broke most comically into the midst of pause or cadence—without intention on his part, since a better natured and more considerate man never breathed. Then, on Saturday nights, *The* Duke [1] was rarely absent: and the sight of his eagle profile advancing from behind the red curtains of his box was sure to be accompanied by a motion of eager heads and eager whispers in the pit.

Opposite the Royal box was to be seen another celebrity, much observed, as much misunderstood: one concerning whom rumour ran more mercilessly riot than concerning most notorious and beautiful women recollected. There was nothing which people would not say and believe of Lady Blessington. Her queenly and sweet beauty (animated, withal, whenever she spoke, and set off by her peculiar dress) was of itself sufficient to attract remark— and disfavour. Her wit, too, which her books in no respect represent, was still less pardonable. It enchanted the men; it repaid the women for their slighting curiosity. Her own friends knew her by something better than either her beauty or wit—by a generosity and kindliness of heart, by a constancy in gratitude, rare indeed in one so spoiled by fortune and misfortune as she had been. I have never known any one so earnest in defence of the absent and unpopular as herself, never one placed in a position so peculiar, so utterly devoid of caprice or time-serving. Her so-

[1] Of Wellington.—E. N.

ciety included distinguished men of all ranks and all classes,—
statesmen, ambassadors, foreign grandees, an exiled prince since
become an Emperor, actors, musicians, painters, poets, historians,
men of science, of renown, and the man of letters as yet without
a name, to whom she opened her circle.   For all she had the same
attentive natural courtesy.   There was no chief guest, no ebb and
flow in the warmth of her welcome, whether she was alone and
glad of a single listener, or surrounded by the most brilliant talkers
and the deepest thinkers of the time.   Had those whom she be-
friended with a zeal that knew no limit or prudence, repaid her
untiring affection and munificence with only common gratitude,
with only a small share of consideration in their claims on her
influence, her time, her money, her life would have been far happier and longer.   As it was, there is no remembering her without
regret and pain: as a woman to whom hard measure was dealt,
and who had to atone for all that seemed gay in her life and
brilliant in her social position by hours of suffering and disappointment and hope deferred, little dreamed of during many a year,
at least by those who looked up from the pit of the Opera, and
saw her there in all the state and bravery of her diamonds, or in
the simple gauze cap, fitting close to her beautiful head, the sight
of which made the outer world insist that she was going to turn
Quaker.

There, too, was Count d'Orsay to be seen, who had for many
years been a member of her husband's family.   It is needless to
describe "the King of the French" (as the hunting farmers in the
Vale of Aylesbury used to call him), as one endowed with rare
personal beauty, with talents by the thousand never ripened, with
luxurious and original fancies enough to turn the heads of a good
third of the gay noble youths of London; needless to put on record
that he had a readiness and richness of wit, uniting the best qualities of English humour and French *esprit,* and a buoyancy of spirit
which no embarrassment could put down, or reduce into the common laws of prudence.   That he was extravagant to recklessness,
and beyond any fortune he possessed, is no secret.   That he was
the unprincipled adventurer which many fancied him when he was
living, and in which character some have described him since his
death, is most false.   He had been set wrong in his very childhood,
by the doting vanity of those who had pampered and indulged a boy

so vivacious, so fascinating, so rarely endowed, to an excess little short of insanity. He was bred to think of enjoyment as not merely the business of everyone's life, but to order his own as if he had an extra right to it. And in this he was cheered on by every creature who approached him. His gaiety, his fancy, his affectionate nature, his instant wit, were irresistible. The rich and the great, the dull who wanted ideas, the bright who delighted in repartee for repartee, all agreed (it was next to impossible to help it) to minister to him. He was encouraged, he was assisted to realize every whim as it rose, at no matter what cost, to organize all manner of pleasures, and to invent new forms for them, by way of varying the monotonous costliness of fashionable routine. There was no one at his ear to tell him what the certain end of all this must be; or if there was, the voice was drowned, and the warning was deprived of its authority by some outburst of high spirits in which it was drowned. It seemed impossible to him to be melancholy or to take thought. Then he had the sanguine temper of a projector in perfection. He was always going to increase his fortune tenfold, long after the fortune was only a heap of debts—always on the point of finding some sure extrication from the labyrinth, the intricacy of which, I truly believe, he never knew. In short, he was a man of genius, fatally, irremediably spoiled on the very threshold of boyhood; but, so far as such a man could be, a man of honour, and further than many a man of unimpeachable probity has been, a man of kind thoughts, generous impulses, and deep affections. It was impossible for any one who approached him nearly to forbear becoming attached to him. It would be impossible to count up one tithe of the unprompted and delicate acts of beneficence and kindness, demanding memory and time, and performed in secrecy, by which a life, which the outer world deemed to be merely one of reckless licence and folly, was varied. I speak of what I know, having for many long years seen as much of this dazzling meteoric career as any bystander could see whose objects and purposes in life ran in a different path, and were pursued in a different fashion. I can speak of hundreds of good offices, small and great, done to those who had nothing to give in return, of shrewd counsel offered in difficult cases, of a ready practical sense that could pierce to the heart of a dilemma. There are many living beside myself who have cause to regard the memory of this ill-starred victim to indulgence with such gratitude as belongs to a real friend, who helped them with his best will, and who harmed them never.

As for wit!—I have heard more in that opera box in one hour than I have heard during months of latter times. Then, moreover, there was no want of wit "in the town" with which to compare it; I do not mean the mechanical pleasantry of such diners out, men like Theodore Hook and James Smith, who were never contented except when telling some anecdote, or exhibiting some snip-snap of words, but the real, genial, spontaneous, or intellectual frolics of Sydney Smith and Thomas Hood—not to be ordered like the soup and the ice—which broke out unexpectedly in the abundant gaiety of the moment. Those were so many true brighteners of society, men who enjoyed and made others enjoy, who, when they had thrown the ball, waited till it should be thrown back to them, in place of monopolizing the eyes and ears and laughter of audiences by any deliberate and exclusive exhibition. Such wit, of his own original quality, Count d'Orsay commanded, with as much courteous good-nature as instant readiness. I have never heard so brilliant and impulsive a talker more entirely devoid of bitterness.

This could not be said of another Opera-frequenter in those days, whose polished bald head, pale face with its closed eyes, and drooping figure, were always in the stalls, as though their owner was dutifully exhibiting there some act of worship by his presence, in which mind and sympathy took small part. I speak of Mr. Rogers,[1] whose connoisseurship of music was represented by himself to be something super-refined—whereas it was merely slender, and based on a few traditions and pleasures of memory. He had elegant tastes, no doubt—a certain balance in his imaginative faculties, derived from much experience of life and travel on easy terms: he was consulted as an authority on poetry, painting, architecture and music; but it is difficult to remember a saying of his, on any of these subjects, save by some covert sarcasm or open depreciation. His tongue was as mercilessly cruel as his hand was generous. The private munificence and courtesy with which he ministered to many a poor artist who could never trumpet abroad the relief, were not more abundant than the antipathy with which

[1] The poet, Samuel Rogers.—E. N.

he persecuted all whom he declined to admit into the select sanctuary of his grace.   If Signor Rossini was the question, he raised his eyebrows (where eyebrows were not) and spoke of Paisiello. When Mdlle. Grisi came out, and on her coming naturally excited cordial hopes, which have not been unfulfilled, he would wander far afield, and murmur something about Mdlle. Grisi's aunt, "La Grassini," or about Banti.   How such an elaborate advocate of the "good old times" could so diligently bend himself to keeping pace with despised modern pleasures as Rogers did, was, as an inconsistency, remarkable, if it did not imply some resolution of acting a part till the last.   I have never seen a man so devoted to public amusements who, on principle, appeared to enjoy them so little as he.   He used to sleep at the Opera, and at the Exeter Hall Oratorios, which he religiously frequented.   But the evening service gone through furnished remarks for his breakfast table.

The above recollections are so strongly associated with my impressions of the Haymarket Theatre that they are perhaps not out of place here, though, if considered as a "curtain tune," they may be found something of the longest.

THE YEAR 1835

OPERAS *La Somnambula, I Puritani,** Bellini; *Anna Bolena, Marino Faliero,** Donizetti; *La Prova d'un Opera Seria,* Gnecco; *Tancredi, La Gazza Ladra, Semiramide, Otello, Il Barbiere, L'Assedio di Corinto,* Rossini. PRINCIPAL SINGERS. Mdes. Finklohr,* E. Sequin, Grisi, Brambilla. MM. Rubini, Ivanoff, Taglioni, Lablache, F. Lablache. BALLETS. *Nina, Paul et Virginie,** *Zephir Berger,** *La Chasse des Nymphes,** *Mazila,** *La Somnambule.* PRINCIPAL DANCERS. Mde. Tagloni. M. Perrot.

THE YEAR 1835

N the year 1835 the return of Lablache to Paris and London completed that quartet of accomplished singers and artists, which for many following years was to present performances unprecedented in their evenness and finished concord. The admirable union thus made up was improved to its utmost by the Parisian managers—always more courageous in catering for novelty than our London ones have been. It was by them that Donizetti's *Marino Faliero* and Bellini's *I Puritani* were commissioned from their composers, Signor Rossini having retired into the obstinate silence which no temptation could induce him to break.

The production of these two new operas, then, in London, was the event of the season. On such occasions there is always a success and a failure. The public will not endure two favourites. In spite of the grandeur of Lablache as the Doge of Venice, in spite of the beauty of the duet of the two basses in the first act of *Marino,* in spite of the second act containing a beautiful moonlight scene with a barcarolle, sung to perfection by Ivanoff, and one of Rubini's most incomparable and superb vocal displays, *Marino Faliero* languished, in part from the want of interest in the female character—a fault fatal to an opera's popularity. On the other hand, from first to last note, *I Puritani* was found enchanting. The picture of Grisi leaning against Lablache to listen in the second scene, the honeyed elegance of Rubini's song of entrance, the bridal polacca in the first act, in the second, the mad scene and the duet between the two basses (a feebler repetition of effects already produced in *Norma*), entranced "the town." In the third act, Rubini, who had not appeared since an early stage of the story, carried every one to the seventh heaven by a display of his powers of expression, potent enough to make the severest for a while forget the platitude of the materials with which they had to deal.

London was *steeped* in the music of *I Puritani;* organs ground it, adventurous amateurs dared it, the singers themselves sang it to such satiety as to lose all consciousness of what they were engaged in, and, when once launched, to go on mechanically.   I must have heard Mdlle. Grisi's Polacca that year alone, if once, one hundred times, to speak without exaggeration.   In short, Bellini had "the luck."   Donizetti's turn of triumph was to come later, and, to my judgment, in a work very inferior to his *Marino Faliero*.   This, then, is the year for attempting some character of the composer who displaced for a while Signor Rossini, seeing that it was the year of his last opera.

There was no novelty among the singers worth naming, since Mdlle. Brambilla had appeared some years earlier, together with Mdme. Pasta.   In those days she had been a handsome girl, with magnificent dark eyes, a rich, though limited, contralto voice, and no very great vocal skill.   When she came back she was a mature woman, with her beauty overblown, her voice impaired to the last point of feebleness and fatigue.   There were hardly two tones one alike to the other left in her register.   In some passages they were nothing more than hoarse whispers, almost devoid of musical sound or association.   But in the interim betwixt the young bloom and the premature fading of physical gifts Mdlle. Brambilla had learned how to sing; and whether from her own taste or from obedience to the *maestro* who prepared her exhibitions, her choice and variety of ornament carried her through the season to the satisfaction of her public.

BELLINI'S OPERAS

CHARACTERISTICS

THOUGH Vincenzo Bellini—born at Catania, in 1802—was ostensibly educated at Naples, under Tritto and Zingarelli, and commenced his career by composing little pieces for instruments, fifteen overtures and symphonies (say biographers), three masses, and other church music,—his less boyish works make it clear that the acquirements with which he began to write must have been of the slenderest possible quality and quantity, a little exceeding those of any amateur[1] who can combine a few chords, originate simple tunes, and show some feeling for the grouping of voices and instruments. Nor is there in music an example more signally showing than Bellini's on what a narrow base such decided individuality as distinguishes inventor from copyist can rest. More trite and faded themes and phrases than many of his (among them some the best-loved by the singers) can hardly be imagined. Few, however, are without some rescuing touch which gives life and colour to the combinations of notes habitually sickly; for there is nothing more fatiguing and mawkish, even in Spohr's incessant chromatics, than Bellini's abuse of appogiatura. In the well-known duet, "Mira o Norma," from his best tragic opera, this amounts to a yawn: which is distasteful. Yet, as counterbalance, Bellini wrote so as to draw out and display the expressive power of the singer, enabling him by its aid to illustrate the situation, feebly though that be sketched in his music. It would be difficult to imagine anything essentially weaker than the melody of the favourite song from *Il Pirata,* by which Rubini brought the new

---

[1] This was curiously proved during many seasons subsequent to 1834, at every performance of *Norma* in London. The overture then played was not Bellini's prelude, but the composition of an English amateur, Mr. C. Raper—so thoroughly tinctured with the Italian spirit that its parentage passed unquestioned and unsuspected.

composer into notice; [1] but who felt its feebleness when Rubini
filled every tone of it with the spirit of the scene? The same
criticism, in a less degree, applies to the favourite tenor air in *La
Somnambula*—another of the great tenor's triumphs. A third example in the last scene of *I Puritani* is noticeable because its theme
is identically that of Simon Mayr's "Donne l'Amore," fitted with
English verse by Haynes Bayly as, "O! 'tis the melody." Mayr's
original tune was written to slight words; Bellini's repetition or
plagiarism fitted it to the life-and-death suspense of a lover
doomed to execution, on being forced from the idol of his heart,
whom misadventure has driven mad, and whom he quits to mount
the scaffold, leaving her in a swoon which (for her sake) he would
fain hope is the sleep of death. Yet Rubini contrived, by the in-
flexions of his voice, to make this unmarked cantabile lacerate with
its distress the heart, through the ear.

These are peculiarities worth dwelling on, because on the principle involved in them depends the existence of opera music. To
insure this, the singer must be permitted play and display. It is
idle to say that the composer's thought, irrespective of means to
impress it, should dominate,—idle to appeal to drama, and to ask
whether a Shakespeare or a Siddons is the stronger in *Macbeth;*
and for this reason. The admitted conventionalities of drama are
doubled by the conditions of opera. The tale must be carried on,
not in verse, but in rhythmical music, solitary or combined—must
be wrought out on the stage, not merely with footlights before it,
but with an orchestra betwixt these and the audience. But that
the singer of an opera tale ought to predominate in the opera
(very well if the tale and its words be good, still the better if the
music be good, not the more ill if the instrumental portion be good,
none the worse if the scenery be probable, and the theatrical accessories are wrought to any degree of refinement), is a fact no
more to be disputed than the platitude that a ball is not a walking
party, or that a chamber quartet of stringed instruments is not a
sonnet by Wordsworth.

That the great German instrumental composers have (since

---

[1] The list of Bellini's known operas is as under:—*Adelina e Salvina* (1824);
Bianaca e Gernando (1826); *Il Pirata* (1827), given with great success at Milan; *La
Straniera* (1828), one of Mdme. Méric-Lalande's triumphs in the same opera-capital;
I Capuleti (Romeo and Juliet); *La Somnambula* and *Norma* (written for Mdme.
Pasta); *Beatrice di Tenda;* lastly, *I Puritani,* composed for Paris in 1834.

Mozart's period) despised the art of singing, and, on some confused theory of "idea," have tried to subjugate the singer and to destroy the singer's powers of individual expression, in no respect whatever decides the value of Italian opera, or of German instrumental science and fantasy. It would be as hard for the best woodman to determine which was the lovelier among trees—the chestnut, when flowering in spring, with its pyramidal spires of bloom, or the slow-growing, evergreen, harsh-cornered cedar, pushing its iron elbows right and left all the year round with the same pertinacity.

Only by reference to some sympathies such as those here shadowed out can the merit of Bellini, and the reason for his popularity, be judged aright. It is true that the final rondo in *La Somnambula,* that certain passages in *Norma* (for instance, Oroveso's battle-chant in the opening scene, and Norma's outbreak of rage in the trio to the first act), prove that he *could* be distinct and forcible; and, by his force, bind his singers, as well as be obliged to them, in his gentleness. The same character is applicable to his mad scene in the second act of *I Puritani.* In this, the largo, "Qui la voce," is more wayward, woeful, and afflicting, by intense misery, than any similar mad-song in recollection—the painful recitatives in Purcell's *Delirous Lady* not forgotten.

Then, that Bellini could be originally gay, the polacca in *I Puritani* remains to prove. He might, if life had been spared to him, have arrived at a greater versatility than his early efforts promised. But it may be insisted that in point of science, from first to last, Bellini was little more than an amateur, promising an artist. His power of construction was a mere nothing. His modulations might be pronounced awkward and hampered, had not we lived to see crudities cruder than his set forth, in the case of young German writers, as discoveries belonging to an era of emancipation. His treatment of the orchestra was violently noisy, or else uselessly feeble. The warbling flute of the prelude to "Casta Diva," Norma's favourite song, could not well be poorer, nor further apart from any idea of such support to the vocal prayer of the Druid Priestess to her goddess, as the hearer naturally expects in our days, when an orchestra has ripened, and when orchestral writing should bear up—not supersede—the situation, the voice, and the singer.

But Bellini was picturesque; and this few modern Italians are. They have some feeling for passion; they have less for humours; they have none for the aspects of nature—for the solemnities of night, for the wakings at the dawn.   In spite of the inexperience with which the instrumental score is filled up, the opening scene of *Norma,* in the dim druidical wood, bears the true character of antique sylvan mystery.   There is day-break, again—a fresh tone of *reveillée*—in the prelude to *I Puritani*.   If Bellini's genius was not versatile in its means of expression, if it had not gathered all the appliances by which science fertilizes nature, it beyond doubt included appreciation of truth, no less than instinct for beauty. And for this, I fancy, he will be long set apart from the superficial and ephemeral manufacturers who have done so much to bring the name of Italian opera into discredit.   His death, in 1836, may have prevented his developing resources of the existence of which, when he started in his race for fame, he did not entertain the remotest idea.[1]

[1] The above character of Bellini has received an interesting illustration in the letter from himself to his publisher at Milan, respecting his last opera, *I Puritani,* and future works, which has been just published (September, 1861).   The composer writes of himself and of his prospects with a modesty of claim, on the part of a man who had already the ear of Europe, strange indeed, but as welcome as it is rare, in these our grasping times, when the singer who makes popular a song expects to receive a larger sum than was paid for an opera score in days when composers *were*.   More remarkable still, to those who are familiar with the haste of southern genius, is Bellini's tone in regard to his power of writing.   He did not care to be paid exorbitantly; he did not care to produce hastily.   But he sought that which was real; that to which he could do the best justice; and he sought to enrich his alphabet of expression—eagerly in proportion as he was successful; and by his success he may have tested his want of much sound and real knowledge.   In brief, he had within him the material of which a real artist is made.

THE YEAR 1836

OPERAS. *La Straniera, Beatrice di Tenda,** *Norma, I Puritani,* Bellini; *Anna Bolena,* Donizetti; *La Prova d'un Opera Seria,* Gnecco; *I Briganti,** Mercadante; *Don Giovanni,* Mozart; *La Gazza Ladra, Il Barbiere, Otello, L'Assedio di Corinto,* Rossini. PRINCIPAL SINGERS. Mdes. Grisi, Colleoni-Corti,* Assandri.* MM. Rubini, Winter, Cartagenova,* Tamburini, Lablache, F. Lablache, Galli. BALLETS. *Le Rossignol,** *Beniowsky.** PRINCIPAL DANCERS. Mdes. Saint-Romain,* Carlotta Grisi.* M. Perrot.

THE YEAR 1836

THERE was no novelty this year of much importance, either among the works performed or those who performed them. *Beatrice di Tenda* is one of Bellini's feeble operas, which will never sustain itself in this country. *Norma* set itself in its place, once for all. Madame Pasta's Adalgisa (for such had been Mademoiselle Grisi) had not drawn so near that wondrous actress without having imbibed some of her deep and true dramatic spirit. She was then, too, in all the splendour of her beauty of voice and person, and mounted the throne of her predecessor with so firm a step, that the world of the moment might be well beguiled into doubting which of the two was the greater queen.

Mademoiselle Assandri, by whom she was seconded, was promising, graceful, and fresh, as a "second woman," in no common degree. The duets of the two (and in *Norma* the duets are as important as in *Semiramide*) were delicious in the charm which they exercised not merely over ear but over eye also. Mademoiselle Assandri, however, was merely a passing artist. Her engaging promise was borne out by no after fulfilment. She disappeared early from the stage, without reason given. Still, as Adalgisa, there was something about her tender, in tone of voice, in look, and in feeling, such as no study can produce—which suited the character admirably. She sang carefully and with expression, and vanished too soon.

I Briganti, by Signor Mercadante, commissioned for Paris—as an opera by Bellini, and as another by Donizetti, before it had been commissioned—failed to please here; in this following the fate of all its clever composer's operas on our side of the Alps. The music was well made. Rubini had a beautiful cantabile in the second act: but the transformed version of Schiller's *Robbers* proved merely a *"Transformed Deformed."* Great as Lablache was, he could not present the famine-starved old man in the tower. Popular as Mademoiselle Grisi was, she could not force on public ac-

ceptance the calculated solfeggi which, in her part, were laid out
to do duty for airs and graces.   In short, there was a mediocre
respectability in the music not to be endured: and accordingly the
opera died, without any one lamenting its death.   That its composer has written single songs which last, such as the contralto airs
from *Nitocri* and *Il Giuramento,* such as the tenor melody from
I due Illustri Rivali, in which Signor Mario has been so fascinating, does not prevent his being found, when met in the larger field
of entire dramas, tiresome, characterless—not to be blamed, not
to be admired; an industrious man of talent, in short, but no
genius.

Beniowsky, a dashing and elaborate Russian ballet, was thoroughly successful.   The music, by Bochsa, was brilliant, if not
new; the scenic glories of it were, in those days, something extraordinary.   There was a national dance, "Krakoviak," by Mademoiselle Saint-Romain, which was popular and piquant.   In the
ballet, too, appeared Mademoiselle Carlotta Grisi, who was then
gracious and promising, with a young face, a complexion like that
of the briar-rose, a shy, sparkling pair of eyes, and a certain modest
grace, accompanied with fearless and firm execution.

But the golden age of ballet was beginning to wane—or (to put
it otherwise) no new-comers could as yet succeed to the thrones of
Mademoiselle Taglioni and Mademoiselle Fanny Elssler.   Many,
since they danced, have been applauded, and have gathered laurels
and bouquets.   No one has originated anything since their day;
no one, therefore, as they did, has marked a period.

MADAME GRISI

QUARTER of a century is a fair length of reign for any queen—a brilliant one for an opera queen of these modern times, when "wear and tear" are so infinitely greater than they used to be. The supremacy of Madame Grisi has been secured and prolonged by a combination of qualities rare at any period. In our day there has been no woman so beautiful, so liberally endowed with voice and with dramatic impulse, as herself—Catalani excepted. In many respects Madame Grisi has been more satisfactory than her gorgeous predecessor—more valuable to her public, because less exacting. By choice or by chance, Catalani preferred to be associated with and to be surrounded by pigmies, to wander Europe hither and thither without a fixed theatrical settlement, a habit totally destructive of the fortunes of the authors who would invent and can nowhere find material to be relied on for execution. Madame Grisi has always formed one of the most equally-distinguished opera companies ever collected. She had, during fifteen years, two homes—one in London, one in Paris—where she was certainly to be found at certain seasons; and by such constancy in arranging her career, kept alive (in England especially) the loyalty of her subjects to a degree which is rare, but which was as largely well-merited. This manner of arranging her life precluded usurpation. It seems already a long time since favourite singers on the other side of the Alps, who have long perished and passed away, spoke of the favourite prima donna of London and of Paris as one of "the Old Guard," with ill-concealed envy. Madame Grisi was in 1860 a favourite still; with only the remnant of her powers more attractive and commanding than her successors who one after another have ventured hither with ambitious projects, and have departed abusing English obstinacy, because they were unable to wrest the sceptre out of her hands.

That this is matter of history there is no gainsaying. With the many, no opera queen has prolonged her reign so successfully as

she. The few have admitted it without reluctance, though they
may have never held her to be the absolute divinity of opera. I
find no part of my task harder than the endeavour fairly to estimate the qualities of this remarkable artist, and to ascertain the
height of the pedestal (so to say) on which she should be exalted
in the gallery of first-class Italian singers of the nineteenth century.

The remarkable beauty—which time informed with expression,
and ripened into the semblance of majesty—of the girl who ran
on the stage to sing Signor Rossini's "Di piacer," on a raw March
evening in 1834, at once secured her a cordial welcome. That
which her figure and her gestures then wanted in grace was already
supplied by symmetry of feature, by a rich southern smoothness
of complexion, by an "air of the head" which enchanted without
any petty over-consciousness of their owner. Never has so beautiful a woman as Madame Grisi been so little coquettish on the
stage. I remember no solitary instance of smile or sign which
could betray to the closest observer that she was attempting any of
those artifices which are so unpleasing to all who love art and who
do not regard the theatre as a slave-market.

Though, naturally enough, in some respects inexperienced on
her first appearance in England, Giulia Grisi was not incomplete.
And what a soprano voice was hers!—rich, sweet, equal throughout its compass of two octaves (from C to C) without a break, or a
note which had to be managed. The voice subdued the audience
on her first appearance ere "Di piacer" was done. In 1834 she
commanded an exactness of execution not always kept up by her
during the after years of her reign. Her shake was clear and
rapid; her scales were certain; every interval was taken without
hesitation by her. Nor has any woman ever more thoroughly
commanded every gradation of force than she—in those early
days especially; not using the contrast of loud and soft too violently, but capable of any required violence, of any advisable delicacy. In the singing of certain slow movements pianissimo—such
as the girl's prayer on the road to execution in La Gazza, or as
the cantabile in the last scene of Anna Bolena (which we know as
"Home, sweet home")—the clear, penetrating beauty of her reduced tones (different in quality from the whispering semi-
ventriloquism which was one of Mademoiselle Lind's most favour-

ite effects) was so unique as to reconcile the ear to a certain shallowness of expression in her rendering of the words and the situation.

At that time the beauty of sound was more remarkable (in such passages as I have just spoken of) than the depth of feeling. When the passion of the actress was roused—as in *La Gazza,* during the scenes with her deserter father, with the villainous magistrate, or in the prison with her lover, or on her trial, before sentence was passed—her glorious notes, produced without difficulty or stint, rang through the house like a clarion, and were truer in their vehemence to the emotion of the scene than were those wonderfully subdued sounds in the penetrating tenuity of which there might be more or less artifice. From the first, the vigour always went more closely home to the heart than the tenderness in her singing and her acting and her vocal delivery—though the beauty of face and voice, the mouth that never distorted itself, the sounds that never wavered, might well mislead the generality of her auditors, and were to be resisted by none.

As an artist calculated to engage and retain the average public without trick or affectation, and to satisfy, by her balance of charming attributes—by the assurance, moreover, that she was giving the best she knew how to give—she satisfied even those who had received much greater pleasure, and had been impressed with much deeper emotion, in the performances of others. I have never tired of Madame Grisi during five-and-twenty years: but I have never been, in her case, under one of those spells of intense enjoyment and sensation which make an epoch in life, and which leave a print on memory never to be cancelled by any later attraction— never to be forgotten so long as life and power to receive shall endure.

Madame Grisi has been remarkable for her cleverness in adopting the effects and ideas of others more thoughtful and originally inventive than herself. With two exceptions, her most popular personations have followed those of other actresses. Her Norma, doubtless her grandest performance, was modelled on that of Madame Pasta—perhaps, in some points, was an improvement on the model, because there was more of animal passion in it; and this (as in the scene of imperious and abrupt rage which closes the first act) could be driven to extremity without its becoming repulsive, owing to the absence of the slightest coarseness in her personal beauty. There was in it the wild ferocity of the tigress, but a certain frantic charm therewith which carried away the hearer [1]—nay, which possibly belongs to the true reading of the character of the druid priestess, unfaithful to her vows. I think this must be so, from recollecting how signally the attempt of a younger Norma to colour the part differently, failed; I allude to Mademoiselle Lind. That singer's Julia, in Spontini's *Vestale,* was a real, pathetic, admirable piece of acting—by much her best tragic character. But however successful she was when trying to express the intense delicacy of emotion which characterizes the noble Roman Virgin, in her rendering of the impassioned pagan priestess her failure was something as entire, as aimless, as it is possible for so remarkable an artist to make. The actress and the play had no agreement; yet in Germany, where critics distort their vision to fathom depths which are merely so many mystified shallows, I have heard this "maidenly" reading of Norma by Mademoiselle Lind lauded as among the master-strokes of never-sufficiently-to-be-wondered-at thoughtfulness. So that Madame Grisi's reality kept the stage, and swept Mademoiselle Lind's novelty from it as with a whirlwind of fire.

On a level with her Norma was Madame Grisi's Lucrezia Borgia, even more original as a conception, ripened and coloured into a superb and glowing picture as years went on. In this opera, however, she had the advantage of being supported as no Norma can be. The charm and grace of Gennaro, so exquisitely adapted to that most pictorial of tenors, Signor Mario, by contrast gave enormous vigour to her sinister and voluptuous beauty; and sharpened the agonies of the secret, in the hideous conflict with her fourth husband, undertaken for the defence of the son she dare not own. More repulsive and abominable some of the situations

---

[1] It is impossible to advert to a quarter of a century of *Norma* in England without putting on record that the only artist able to dispute the part with Madame Grisi was an English singer—the last of a great dramatic family. But Miss Adelaide Kemble, if in passages more subtle than her Italian contemporary (perhaps as a matter of temperament and intellect, perhaps as the condition of a voice only to be subjugated by merciless labouring) virtually wrought out the character in the same one way. There is no stopping, no reserve, possible in certain moments of emotion. A storm made "sad and civil" (as Olivia hath it) amounts to little more than a futile attempt at bad weather.

could not be—belonging to the nightmare days of French drama—but their power can hardly be exceeded.

Yet Madame Grisi has been surpassed, I have been told, by the original Lucrezia; a woman far less splendidly gifted by nature—Madame Ungher—whose serpentine and deep malevolence, subtly veiled at the moment when its most diabolical works were on foot, has been described as fearful. Madame Grisi had less astuteness, more violence. The moment of villainous rage and revenge, when Lucrezia is recognized and unmasked in Venice by the young nobles, was magnificent in expression and attitude—a true prophecy of the supper of retribution to which she treated her persecutors at Ferrara. Her appearance, too, in the scene with the jealous Duke, her husband, and the young soldier, was gorgeous, especially when she first represented the part. She then wore a black dress richly embroidered with gold, with a crimson scarf round her waist, which set off her bared arms to their utmost advantage. The passionate haste, too, with which she administered the counter-poison was made doubly forcible by the despairing strength she could throw into the notes of the agitated movement—one of Donizetti's best. In the last act, her reception of her guests at the death-banquet might have been more impressive. Something was wanted of the quiet triumph of satisfied vengeance with which Rachel subdued her hearers into horror in certain scenes of her Roxana. The half-repressed concentration of scorn and duplicity —of crime that broods, and, when the hour comes, satisfies itself deliberately by witnessing the agony of its victims—was not within her reach. With her, all, it seemed, must be impulse and rapid movement.

Madame Grisi's attitudes were always more or less harsh, angular, and undignified; and when she was in her prime, and had no reason to manage or spare her resources, there was a fierceness in certain of her outbursts which impaired her effects. In short, her acting did not show reflection so much as the rich, uncultivated, imperious nature of a most beautiful and adroit southern woman.

Of her, too, however, as of Lablache, I shall have to speak again and again, as the passing years are noticed—the above being merely an outline. While I am writing, in May, 1861, the vision of all her glory, so long protracted, is rapidly passing from the stage. The hour of her parting with her subjects has come. It is hardly in the course of possibility than any such phenomenon as a career like hers in this country will be witnessed by the chronicler —if such should be—who, thirty years hence, would carry on the tale of foreign opera in England.

THE YEAR 1837

OPERAS. *Il Matrimonio*, Cimarosa; *Malek Adhel*,* Costa; *Norma, I Puritani*, Bellini; *Anna Bolena, L'Elisir d'Amore*,* *Belisario*,* Donizetti; *Ildegonda*,* Marliani; *Medea*, Mayer; *Don Giovanni*, Mozart; *La Donna del Lago, La Cenerentola, Semiramide, Pietro l'Eremita*, Rossini; *Romeo e Giulietta*, Zingarelli. PRINCIPAL SINGERS. Mdes. Blasis, Giannoni,* Albertazzi,* Assandri, Grisi, Pasta. MM. Catone,* Deval,* Bellini,* Curioni, Inchiadi,* Ivanoff, Rubini, Tamburini, Lablache, F. Lablache, BALLETS. *Fra Diavolo*,* *Le Corsaire*.* PRINCIPAL DANCERS. Mdes. Duvernay, Herminie Elssler,* Montessu.

THE YEAR 1837

DURING the winter of 1836–7 an attempt had been made at the Lyceum Theatre to establish a Comic Opera. To this we owed the introduction in this country of Donizetti's *L'Elisir,* an effort to make England like Signor Ricci's *Scaramuccia* and Signor Coppola's *Nina Pazza,* also the revival, after twenty years, of Mozart's *Le Nozze.* The speculation, though resumed in the early winter of 1837–8, was understood not to have been successful. The new Italian compositions were not relished.

Nor was this disregard unjust. The prettiness of Signor Ricci's comic music could not conceal its writer's want of style and science. The story he set is puerile, in the worn-out Italian taste, and so far as I know, his name has already died away in Italy, except in those third-rate theatres to listen to music in which gives a shock to every sense; where the singers are bad, the buffoonery is violent, and the audiences (to be lenient) want washing. The only one time when I was ever seduced into sleep at a theatre was over an opera of Ricci's at Florence: and not because the opera was poor, but because the vocalists were execrable, and the atmosphere of garlic and from crowding humanity amounted to a smell strong enough, as the Irishman said, "to hang one's hat on."

Signor Coppola's *Nina* stood a still poorer chance with us. Though, for a while, it displaced the better "Ninas" of Paisiello and Dalayrac, and was even translated for the Opéra Comique of Paris—there to bring out Madame Eugenie Garcia—even the simple prettiness of the story, and the scope afforded the actress, could not save music so utterly stale.

These smaller Lyceum operas, however, gave the greater theatre what for the first time during many seasons it had not enjoyed —a passable company before Easter.

The season of 1837 was musically interesting, though it put the splendid genius of Signor Rossini still further into retreat by the bringing out of many who aspired to succeed him. Donizetti's

Belisario was a failure.   His *L'Elisir* has never won a profitable
stage success in England—a work infinitely poorer than *Le Philtre*,
by M. Auber, the book of which (French again!) Donizetti laid
hold of.   The music has been in concert rooms hackneyed to a
death after which it is hard to fancy any possible resurrection.

Signor Costa's *Malek Adhel* is to be viewed in a light altogether
different; not as a chance work flung out by a fluent writer, but as
the deliberate essay of a musician—strong and quick in one capacity—to change his ground of action.   Whether a great conductor can ever be a great composer is a doubtful matter.   No
modern example of the kind exists, save, perhaps, in the case of
Mendelssohn; and he was lively, rather than certain, as a conductor.   When at the head of his own Leipsic band, no one could
be more successful than he: elsewhere he was fretted by want of
understanding and sympathy among his forces, and fretted them
accordingly.   In England he obtained no great result as a conductor, save in his own compositions.   In those, the effect of his
presence and presidence was magnetic.

From the first evening when Signor Costa took up the baton, a
young man from a country then despised by every musical pedant,
a youth who came to England without flourish, announcement, or
protection, as a singer without much voice, to do what was never
done in England before, it was to be felt that in him were combined the materials of a great conductor—nerve to enforce discipline, readiness to the second, and that certain influence which only
a vigorous man could exercise over the disconnected folk who
made up an orchestra in those days.   Times are changed since
then.   Good taste, good feeling, good manners, are now the rule
(rather than the exception) in the world of subordinate music; but
they were not so thirty years since.   The stranger had to work,
and to work his way up, with the coarsest of materials.

Such occupation is hardly to be braved and conquered by the
strongest of mortals without some loss of fancy.   Then, there is
little or no possibility of writing well for the stage (unless the man
be called Beethoven) without writing fluently and frequently.   Signor Costa's *Malek Adhel,* however, is a thoroughly conscientious
work, containing an amount of melody with which he has never
been duly credited.   In the first act there are a delicious tenor
song for Rubini, and an elegant romance for the contralto, which

pleased in spite of the lifelessness of Madame Albertazzi; in the second, a terzetto to the one forcible situation of the opera; in the third, a grand scena for Madame Grisi, which she sang consummately—and *what* a song for Rubini! No one to come (as I have already said) will be able to touch "Tiranno cadrai." The air, though strained in its passion—demanding an E flat on the treble scale—was wondrously calculated for the singer; *too* wondrously, since it renders the revival of the opera (of which it is the culminating point) difficult almost to impossibility.

Of Marliani's *Ildegonda* I recollect nothing beyond the conclave of the grandest-looking people who could have been assembled at any price (had they never tried to sing) sitting on the stage in old Italian dresses, when the curtain drew up. Marliani died young, ere he justified his pretensions to compose; having tried his hand twice in Paris—once among the Italians with this *Ildegonda,* once, with *La Xacarilla,* among the French. But he is worth a word because of a certain air, "Stanca di più combattere," which Madame Grisi used to introduce on her entrance in *Otello*—which she never sang well, but which, nevertheless, was a great Italian air of parade.

MADAME PASTA

S an artist who could turn natural deficiencies into rare beauties, who could make us forgive others which cannot be thus transformed by the presence and power of genius, truth, and thought in one, who has printed deeper impressions on the memories of those that heard her than any other female singer, Madame Pasta must be placed first in the first rank of all who have appeared in England during the last thirty years. Her great triumphs, however, belong to a period somewhat earlier.

My earliest recollection of the Italian Opera in London is of Signor Rossini's *Zelmira* [1]—of all his serious operas the most gorgeously florid; in which will be found more than one foretaste of *Semiramide,* and, I venture to think, pieces equal in force and originality to its more popular successor. In England the opera could not establish itself. The story is alike dreary and monstrous, containing, I think, merely one strong situation—an arrested murder, or something of the kind. The men who appeared in *Zelmira*—with the exception of Signor Porto, with a hard, deep, bass voice—were utterly inefficient; but I remember, as if it was a thing of yesterday, the entirely new sensation created in me by the entrance of the heroine, and by the first sounds which issued from her lips. I remember her exquisite delivery of the opening phrases of "Perchè mi guardi" (a duettino which she sang with Mademoiselle Brambilla, then a girl with a dark, speaking face, and a rich, untrained, contralto voice); the thrill of terror caused

---

[1] There is small chance of this opera being ever revived, not merely because of its absurd and wearisome story but because it demands tenor singers the race of which is extinct—commanding a brilliancy which it has been, of late, the fashion to denounce, as so much musical frippery. But the introduction to the first act, the air for the deep bass voice, "Ah gia trascorse," the terzetto (best known among its musical pieces), the pompous duet for soprano and tenor, with chorus, the finale to the first act, very carefully written for Vienna, the delicious scena, "Ciel pietoso," for contralto (not to be tedious), seven-eighths of the opera, are in Signor Rossini's highest Italian style; and most vexatious is it that, in a time when novelty is becoming as precious as the last leaf of the Sybil's last book, the peculiarities alluded to prevent the possibility of presenting *Zelmira* in its present form.

by her gesture and declamation at the one tragic moment of her part; her singing of a cavatina by Bonfichi, "Ah che forse," which she introduced in place of the finale originally written as a close to the opera; and her magnificent, queenly smile, as she received the applause of a theatre crowded with a brilliant audience. For those were the days when full dress was demanded for the Opera —before Fop's Alley had ceased to be. Attendance there, especially for men, was more costly and troublesome than it is now; but in many points, whereas the stage has since gained, the audience has lost in magnificence. This is, perhaps, as it should be. But among that gorgeous assembly, I remember well the central figure in the blue robe and the classical diadem adorned with cameos; who stood forth like a sovereign in the midst of her subjects, with a grace and a majesty which put many a born Royalty and Ambassadress to shame. I saw her afterwards in *Otello*, and in a poor opera by Meyer, *La Rosa rossa e la rosa bianca.* This was in 1828. The impression of those three nights was indelible, as "a thing of beauty," of might, belonging to the highest world of high art, which nothing could overpass. Ere I could return on it, I had heard with delight Sontag, Malibran, Grisi, successively; but none had displaced Madame Pasta, nor in the least interfered with her supremacy, as possessing qualities and fascinations superior to theirs. As I thought in 1828, and in 1837—when she returned for a few performances, with her vocal powers painfully impaired—I think now, when writing these Recollections in 1861.

The way was long and laborious by which Madame Pasta arrived at her throne. The ninety-nine requisites of a singer (according to the well-known Italian adage) had been denied to her. Her voice was originally limited, husky, and weak, without charm, without flexibility, a mediocre mezzo-soprano. Though her countenance *spoke,* the features were cast in that coarse mould which is common in Italy. Her arms were fine, but her figure was short and clumsy. She walked heavily, almost unequally. No candidate for musical sovereignty ever presented herself with what must have seemed a more slender and imperfect list of credentials; and by these, accordingly, she was rated at the outset of her career.

She was born at Como, biographical dictionaries tell us, in the year 1798; and when about eighteen, after having received some

training at Milan, was to be found among the insignificant myrmidons whom Catalani chose to assemble round her on the stage.
It has been said that Giuditta Pasta was more than overlooked—
openly flouted—in this very Opera House of ours, in the year 1817,
and by a wardrobe woman.   The affront may have done with her
what neglect and insolence have done with other people of genius—
Byron among the rest.

At all events, whether roused by it or not, she subjected herself
to a course of severe and incessant vocal study, to subdue and to
utilize her voice.   To equalize it was impossible.   There was a
portion of the scale which differed from the rest in quality and remained to the last "under a veil," to use the Italian term.   There
were notes always more or less out of tune, especially at the commencement of her performances.   Out of these uncouth materials
she had to compose her instrument, and then to give it flexibility.
Her studies to acquire execution must have been tremendous; but
the volubility and brilliancy, when acquired, gained a character
of their own from the resisting peculiarities of the organ.   There
were a breadth, an expressiveness in her roulades, an evenness and
solidity in her shake, which imparted to every passage a significance totally beyond the reach of lighter and more spontaneous
singers.

Madame Pasta was understood to be a poor musician, a slow
reader; but she had one of the most essential musical qualities in
perfection—a sense for the measurement and proportion of time.
This is more rare than it should be, and its absence strangely often
passes unperceived even by artists and amateurs who are sensitively
cultivated in other respects.   It is not such mere correctness as is
ensured by the metronome, not such artful licence in giving and
taking as is apt to become artifice and affectation, but that instruc-
tive feeling for propriety which no lessons can teach—that due
recognition of accent and phrase—it is that absence of flurry and
exaggeration, such as make the discourse and behaviour of certain
persons memorable in themselves, be the matter and occasion what
they may—that intelligent composure without coldness, which at
once impresses and reassures those who see and hear it.   As examples of what is meant may be named Hummel, among pianoforte
players, M. de Bériot and Herr David among violinists.   I may

allude, among singers, to the noble artist in question, to M. Duprez, and to Madame Persiani.

But the greatest grace of all, depth and reality of expression, was possessed by this remarkable artist as few (I suspect) before her—as none whom I have since admired—have possessed it. The best of her audience were held in thrall, without being able to analyse what made up the spell, what produced the effect, so soon as she opened her lips.

Her recitative, from the moment when she entered, was riveting by its truth.   People accustomed to object to the conventionalities of opera—just as loudly as if all drama was not conventional too—forgave the singing and the strange language for the sake of the direct and dignified appeal made by her declamation.   Madame Pasta never changed her readings, her effects, her ornaments.[1] What was to her true, when once arrived at, remained with her true for ever.   To arrive at what stood with her for truth, she laboured, made experiments, rejected, with an elaborate care, the result of which, in one meaner or more meagre, must have been monotony.   But the impression made on me was that of my being always subdued and surprised for the first time.   Though I knew what was coming, when the passion broke out, or when the phrase was sung, it seemed as if they were something new, electrical, immediate.   The effect is as present to me at the moment of writing as the impression made by the first sight of the sea, by the first snow-mountain, by the first hearings of the organ, by any of those first emotions which never utterly pass away.   These things are totally distinct from the fanaticism of a *laudator temporis acti*. With honest people, I dare to believe and hope, death only takes away the power of honest admiration.

The spell of Madame Pasta was to the last, with some of us,

---

[1] Of this a curious proof was given during the course of the two last disastrous appearances of Madame Pasta in England, made by her some years later. Nobody (the admirers of Rubini must forgive me) ever sang the great air from Pacini's *Niobe,* "Il soave e bel contento," as Madame Pasta did—though everyone has tried to sing it. Her execution of it, at a provincial concert long ago, marks a period in my musical experiences. When she essayed to repeat it, at a concert for the Italian cause given some twenty years later—past middle age, out of practice, and with her voice in a state of wretched dilapidation (for which my epithet is not too strong)—not a change, not a *cadenza* of the old times was left out. She called for them all, though "they would not come."

unbroken.   When she returned to England in 1837, and occupied a box in the centre of the dress circle of the King's Theatre,—the pit, as with one accord, turned towards her with such an immediate gaze of interest and welcome as befits a royal personage.   I was afraid to see and to hear her again, aware of the illusions which eager persons are apt to cherish in regard to objects of early admiration.   During this last visit referred to her voice was steadily out of tune, with some exceptional moments.   Painful as this was to the ear, she was none the less the

                              "Queen
          And wonder of the enchanted world of sound,"

in right of all those attributes which age cannot wither, neither custom stale.   The grandeur of her style had undergone no decay, her wonderful musical perception was unimpaired; so were her incomparable taste, courage, and yet moderation, in ornament.   She no longer looked the Romeo of Zingarelli's opera.   Her first appearance distressed those who recollected her; but I *hear,* at this moment of writing, her large and stately delivery of a duet from *Aureliano in Palmyra* (I think) which was introduced by way of strengthening a score sweet but feeble, and the passion and finish thrown into the airs, "Sommo ciel" and "Ombra adorata."   These no one since Madame Pasta has been able to touch successfully: in the last, particularly, her rich and original ornaments gave a sort of superb Italian charm to the tomb-scene, in no respect contradicting that burst of despair from the heart with which, raising tenderly a long lock of hair from the brow of the deceased, she used to exclaim, "Ah, mia Giulietta."   I *see,* too, her magical and fearful Medea—a part musically and dramatically composed by herself out of the faded book and correct music of Simone Mayr's opera.   On the outward presentment of this, time told, of course, less cruelly than in the case of her Romeo.   The air of quiet, concentrated vengeance seeming to fill every fibre of her frame,—as if though deadly poison was flowing through her veins—with which she stood alone, wrapped in her scarlet mantle, as the bridal procession of Jason and Creusa swept by, is never to be forgotten.   It must have been hard for those on the stage with her to pass that draped statue, with folded arms, that countenance lit up with aw-

ful fire, but as still as death, and as inexorable as doom.[1] Where,
again, has ever been seen any exhibition of art grander than her
Medea's struggle with herself ere she consents to murder her children?—than her hiding the dagger, with its fell purpose, upon her
bosom, under the strings of her distracted hair?—than her steps to
and fro, as of one drunken with frenzy, torn with the agonies of
natural pity, yet still resolved on her awful triumph? These
memories are so many possessions to those who have seen them,
so long as reason shall last; and their reality is all the more assured to me because I have not yet fallen into the old man's habit
of denying or doubting new sensations.

"There's always Morning somewhere in the world."

God be thanked! there is always also genius. I never thought
of the Medea of Madame Pasta with greater enthusiasm of regard
than after enjoying, with sensations not less strong, the Medea,
in spoken drama, of Madame Ristori. Nothing could be more different than the two performances, than the two plays (admitting
an opera to be a play), than the two women, than the two concep-
tions of the character of the magical enchantress. But the past
delight helped the present one, and the present justified the sincerity
of the past. There is no final and canonical treatment of any dramatic subject. There might, there *should* be yet, a new *Medea* as
an opera. Nothing can be grander, more antique, more Greek,
than Cherubini's setting of the "grand fiendish part" (to quote the
words of Mrs. Siddons on Lady Macbeth). But, as music, it becomes simply impossible to be executed, so frightful is the strain on
the energies of her who is to present the heroine. Compared with
this character, Beethoven's Leonora, Weber's Euryanthe, are only

---

[1] This is not a mere hyperbole, thrust in for the sake of effect. I remember to
have seen a stage crowd absolutely appalled by an actress—Madame Viardot—in
the last act of *La Juive,* at the Royal Italian Opera. She was supported on the
stage, hardly conscious (as the luckless Rachel) of time, place, or the frightful fate
so near. The odious drone of the death-music roused her. She raised her languid
eyes, and saw the tremendous cauldron in the distance. The scene demands that,
shrinking to her father, the Jewess should say, "Mon père! j'ai peur!" (the excla-
mation loses much terror in the Italian translation). Eleazar, the Jew, was on the
opposite side of the stage. His daughter disengaged herself from the executioners
and tottered towards him, fascinated as by a basilisk by that hideous machine of
torture; with her back to the audience. There have been few such impressions of
mortal terror received in any theatre, as that conveyed to the audience by the
countenances of every one on the stage, whom the gestures of the actress, seconded,
no doubt, by the expression of her features, obviously terrified.

so much child's play.   There is a later *Medea* by Signor Pacini
—a pretty version of the tremendous story.   The real presentment
of it in music may be yet to come, supposing the taste for ancient
fable not to die out, and so, too, there *may* be a new enchantress,
differing in every respect from the two superb Italian women of
genius who have wrought out the first idea, each incomparably.

There remains a strange scene to be spoken of—the last appearance of this magnificent musical artist, when she allowed herself,
many years later, to be seduced into giving one performance at
Her Majesty's Theatre, and to sing in a concert for the Italian
cause at the Royal Italian Opera.   Nothing more inadvised could
have been dreamed of.   Madame Pasta had long ago thrown off
the stage and all its belongings, and any other public than those who
have made their boatmen linger on the lake of Como, hard beneath the garden walls of her villa, with the hope of catching a
glimpse of one who in her prime had enthralled so many.   Her
voice, which at its best had required ceaseless watching and practice, had been long ago given up by her.   Its state of utter ruin on
the night in question passes description.   She had been neglected by
those who, at least, should have presented her person to the best
advantage admitted by time.   Her queenly robes (she was to sing
some scenes from *Anna Bolena*) in nowise suited or disguised her
figure.   Her hairdresser had done some tremendous thing or other
with her head—or rather, had left everything undone.   A more
painful and disastrous spectacle could hardly be looked on.   There
were artists present who had then, for the first time, to derive
some impression of a renowned artist—perhaps, with the natural
feeling that her reputation had been exaggerated.   Among these
was Rachel, whose bitter ridicule of the entire sad show made itself heard throughout the whole theatre, and drew attention to the
place where she sat—one might even say, sarcastically enjoying the
scene.   Among the audience, however, was another gifted woman,
who might far more legitimately have been shocked at the utter
wreck of every musical means of expression in the singer, who might
have been more naturally forgiven, if some humour of self-
glorification had made her severely just—not worse—to an old
prima donna; I mean Madame Viardot.   Then, and not till then,
she was hearing Madame Pasta.   But truth will always answer to
the appeal of truth.   Dismal as was the spectacle, broken, hoarse,

and destroyed as was the voice, the great style of the singer spoke to the great singer. The first scene was Ann Boleyn's duet with Jane Seymour. The old spirit was heard and seen in Madame Pasta's "Sorgi!" and the gesture with which she signed to her penitent rival to rise. Later she attempted the final mad scene of the opera —that most complicated and brilliant among the mad scenes on the modern musical stage, with its two cantabile movements, its snatches of recitative, and its bravura of despair, which may be appealed to as an example of vocal display, till then unparagoned, when turned to the account of frenzy, not frivolity—perhaps as such commissioned by the superb creative artist. By that time, tired, unprepared, in ruin as she was, she had rallied a little. When, on Ann Boleyn's hearing the coronation music for her rival, the heroine searches for her own crown on her brow, Madame Pasta wildly turned in the direction of the festive sounds, the old irresistible charm broke out; nay, even in the final song, with its roulades, and its scales of shakes ascending by a semitone, the consummate vocalist and tragedian, able to combine form with meaning—the moment of the situation with such personal and musical display as form an integral part of operatic art—was indicated: at least to the apprehension of a younger artist. "You are right!" was Madame Viardot's quick and heartfelt response (her eyes full of tears) to a friend beside her; "You are right! It is like the *Cenacolo* of da Vinci at Milan—a wreck of a picture, but the picture is the greatest picture in the world!"

THE YEAR 1838

OPERAS. *Falstaff,** Balfe; *La Somnambula,* Bellini; *Lucia,** *Parisina,** Donizetti; *Don Giovanni, Le Nozze di Figaro,* Mozart; *Otello, Matilda di Shabran,* Rossini. PRINCIPAL SINGERS. Mdes. Persiani,* Grisi, Albertazzi, Ekerlin,* Caremoli.* MM. Tati,* Borrani,* Rubini, Tamburini, Morelli,* Lablache, F. Lablache. PRINCIPAL DANCERS. Mdes. Taglioni, Teresa and Fanny Elssler.

THE YEAR 1838

ROM the list of performances this year it will be seen how entirely Signor Rossini's star had waned. A new singer had been added to the company, by whose agency a new composer was set in the place which he has since maintained. The singer was Madame Persiani, the composer was Donizetti.

His *Parisina,* though it was superbly acted by Madame Grisi and Signor Tamburini, did not please; his *Lucia* did.

The third new opera was Mr. Balfe's *Falstaff,* one of the many chances which this man of indisputable genius has been fortunate enough to obtain—I must add, willing to fling away. There has been hardly a great singer in Europe since the year 1834 for whom he has not been called on to write; hardly a great and successful theatre in which his works have not been heard. He has the gift— now rare, in late days—of melody, and a certain facile humour for the stage, which can hardly be over-prized. His tunes are in our streets: but his best works cannot be said to last.

The reason for this may be found partly in a certain unsettlement of style, not to be confounded with eclecticism; for in spite of its being neither purely French, Italian, nor German, the opera music of Cherubini, Spontini, or Meyerbeer lasts in esteem. Each of the three distinguished men may be designated as "composite"; yet each differs from each in his marked individuality. With something of his own, there is something not so much of every country as of every composer in Mr. Balfe's music. Here we meet an Italian rhythm, there a French interval, anon a German harmony, sometimes a strain of artless Irish melody. The listener most ready at identification would be puzzled to pronounce on the parentage of one of his English operas from the music itself—still more from those written by him to foreign text. This characteristic is too general among our composers who have written for the stage during the past five-and-twenty years. Perhaps it has been always so, as Arne's *Artaxerxes* (the one serious English opera which kept the stage) reminds us.

Not further to venture on ground very delicate to be trodden, other reasons for the ephemeral duration of Mr. Balfe's operas may be cited—his disregard of character, accent, and situation, for the sake of catching effects, and his peculiar taste in instrumentation. The latter, though sometimes effective, sometimes piquant, is too often thin; the stringed instruments are so carelessly grouped as to lose that nourishing sonority which is to the body of sound a central support, analogous to that which the spine affords to the human frame.

The above may be so generally remarked as peculiarities in this fertile and successful composer's writings, that comment on them is no more indelicate than on the spasmodic climax of Signor Verdi, or on M. Meyerbeer's particular habit of self-interruption. Owing to them it may be that of *Falstaff* only the animated trio of the two wives (Madame Grisi and Mademoiselle Caremoli) and Anne Page (Madame Albertazzi) lives to tell the tale of Shakespeare's *Merry Wives,* set in Italian for England by an Irishman, and with such a French-Neapolitan artist for its protagonist as would have made Shakespeare's heart leap for joy to look on.

The crowd at the revival of *Le Nozze di Figaro* is a thing to recollect. So crammed was the theatre, and the audience overflowed on the stage in such a resolute swarm, that the curtain could not be raised for half an hour by reason of their intrusion. The contest to keep and to clear the space approached a riot, within a narrow step. The Figaro was Lablache; the Almaviva was Signor Tamburini. Madame Grisi was too indifferent as Susanna—she never took to the opera kindly. Madame Persiani sang the music of the Countess like a true artist; and though her voice was not one which blended willingly with any other soprano, the letter duet was excellently given by the two ladies.

MADAME PERSIANI

THIS most accomplished singer was always a greater favourite with the artists and the connoisseurs than with the public, for reasons easy to explain.

Never was there woman less vulgar, in physiognomy or in manner, than she; but never was there one whose appearance on the stage was less distinguished. She was not precisely insignificant to see, so much as pale, plain, and anxious. She gave the impression of one who had left sorrow or sickness at home; and who therefore (unlike those wonderful deluders, the French actresses, who, because they will not be ugly, rarely *look* so) had resigned every question of personal attraction as a hopeless one. She was singularly tasteless in her dress. Her one good point was her hair, which was splendidly profuse, and of an agreeable colour.

Then, such even sensual charm as her voice may, in its early days, have possessed, had been left on the other side of the Alps ere she appeared in Paris and London. It was an acute soprano, mounting to E flat altissimo—acrid and piercing rather than sweet, penetrating rather than full, and always liable to rise in pitch; a voice in the sound of which, considered as sound, no one could by any possibility find pleasure; one, too, which, owing to the peculiar qualities described, never blended with other voices willingly. These defects combined would, with ninety-nine out of a hundred women, have amounted to a chasm betwixt their owner and public favour, to be bridged over by no magic. What made matters worse was, that their owner had to cope with an artist then so resplendent as Madame Grisi; and, worst of all, that passionate action was beyond her reach.

Madame Persiani, however, had one excellent quality, the might and completeness of which made the want of many others forgiven by the public—forgotten by all real judges and artists—and which enabled her to keep the stage, as an invaluable and admirable member of a first-rate opera company, till Nature failed her.

She was such a mistress of the art of singing as few women in our, or in any time, have been.   Her father, Tacchinardi, the tenor, though among the most unsightly to look on of men, null as an actor, and of whose voice there is little on record, knew every secret of his art, having, on the one hand, a fair knowledge of instrumental effects, and, on the other, having modelled himself after "the famous tenor, Babbini."   Most, if not at all, that he knew, Tacchinardi imparted to his daughter.   Her voice was developed to its utmost capacities.   Every fibre of her frame seemed to have a part in her singing.   There was nothing left out, nothing kept back.   She was never careless, never unfinished; always sedulous —sometimes to the edge of strain (I speak of her as a singer)— and occasionally, in the employment of her vast and varied resources, rising to an animation which, if not sympathetic as warmth kindling warmth, amounted to that display of conscious power which is resistless.   The perfection with which she wrought up certain songs—such as the *Somnambula* finale, or the mad scene in *Lucia*—if considered in respect to style, and to what style can do, has not in my experience been exceeded, has been very rarely approached.

She had the finest possible sense of accent—a gift, as I may have somewhere else said, sparingly given; one hardly to be acquired by those who possess it not by nature.   From her, every phrase had its fullest measure.   Every group of notes was divided, and expressed by her with as much precision as the best of violinists (who *has* the gift of accent) brings into his bowing.   And this was done with that secure musical ease which made her anxious, mournful face, and her acute, acid voice, forgotten.   It mattered not whether the movement was as rapid as the stretto in the known duet of Donizetti's *Linda,* with its staccato theme—as one of the florid passages of eight quavers in common time, twice or four times divided, such as abound in the Rossinian operas—or whether it was some largo, large and expressive, such as the well-known "Che mi frena" from the second act of *Lucia*—Madame Persiani's *attack* (thus to present the French word *aplomb*) was not more unfailing than the delicate sensibility with which she gave every note its fullest value, never herself becoming breathless, rarely heavy.   This was the second of her rare musical qualities and attractions.

The third (perhaps the *first* with the least thinking part of the public) was her taste and extraordinary facility in ornament. Whether she invented or commissioned her changes and cadenzas is not to be ascertained easily; but she rarely produced one which was wrong in style, and in many of her songs exhibited a variety, more or less brilliant, in proportion as she was better or worse in voice. Strange to add, her shake (a grace which it is the humour of the day to contemn) was the least brilliant of her executive passages. In every other form of acomplishment she was incomparable among Italians: always trying to throw some expression into her embroideries and flourishes—thereby, however, less voluble, less easy, than certain great executive artists of other countries such as Sontag, or Madame Cinti-Damoreau, or a later French singer or two who could be named.

The only time (to illustrate) that I recollect Madame Persiani short of the mark, was once when she chose to introduce the great show song of Angela from M. Auber's *Domino Noir* into the lesson-scene of *Il Barbiere*. There she was heavy. On the other hand, nothing could be more poignant, clear, audacious, ready to the moment, than her execution of the variations to Paisiello's "Nel cor": a form of vocal music originated in obedience to Catalani's bad taste. Certain of her freaks and fancies in this (in particular, a variation on enormously distant intervals), recur to me as best among the best of exhibitions of the kind.

"The kind" is now disdained. Such absurd use of the voice by way of instrument, as these solfeggi imply, can hardly be too severely disdained, whether the place be the stage or some arena where such warbling is wanted as the birds give without teaching —and not beauty and sentiment enriched by ornament. But because of these abuses, to disdain altogether the science of vocal ornament as superfluous, absurd, meretricious, is equivalent to preferring the brute diamond, spoiled from the Hindoo, to the same jewel when all its lustre has been brought out, and when, after having been set by art, it strikes its fire to far and dark places from the crown of some Christian Prince. The new-fangled pedantry which declares that a composer writing for singers shall avoid everything showing that they know how to sing, if carried out to its extreme would simply make an end of music—bring us back to the tom-tom and the tortoise-shell lute, and abrogate all that science and culture have done. A wigwam may be sincere in point of architecture (and there be those now who could discourse eloquently on the wigwam as the best of buildings).   A Gregorian chant may be awkward in its intervals, and thereby wholesome and nourishing, because hard to swallow.   It may be unfortunate for the world that we cannot return to the sincerity of wigwams, or to the crude symmetry of the Gregorian chants; but we cannot do this, at least, without a protest against the barbarisms in which we are invited to find aliment, rest, and enjoyment.   In art, no one perfection extinguishes another.   So far from this, apart from all eclecticism (because eclecticism is an affair of mind rather than of material), one perfection embellishes another, giving room for individual display, and keeping the while, high and intact, the supremacy of poetical thought and invention over forms of utterance.

"So many hard and pompous words about a few flourishes?" The whole life and perpetuation of the art of singing, and of composition for the voice, are involved in the question, into considering which my recollections of Madame Persiani's admirable accomplishments have accidentally broken the way.   Every conceivable passage was by her finished to perfection—the shake, as I have said, excepted, which might be thought indistinct and thin.   In the attack of intervals distant one from the other, in the climbing up a series of groups of notes, ascending to the highest notes of the scale, she was unrivalled.   Her variety, too, was great.   When she was encored, she rarely repeated her cabaletta without some change or enhancement to its brilliancy.   When she was uncertain as to the state of her powers (a matter of frequent occurrence), she could retrench, and substitute graces so acceptable as to conceal from her audience that her voice was more weary or less strong than she could wish it to be.

How convincingly these rare and remarkable merits were felt when, after a few years of absence from our stage, Madame Persiani reappeared in London—how, in comparison with her, her younger successors sounded like so many immature scholars of the second class—may appear in the course of these remembrances.

On her gala nights, to the last, the spirit—the splendour, it may be said—of her expressive execution, was irresistible.   I remember especially one evening when she sang the part of Amenaide at the Royal Italian Opera, in *Tancredi*, with Mademoiselle Alboni, as a perfect revel of vocal skill, daring, triumphant, perfect, riveting

by its display of art.   It was with reference to some such performance that Mendelssohn—true German as he was, but just to Italy,
as few German musicians are nowadays—said, to the amazement
of the pedantic few among his audience, "Well, I do like Madame
Persiani dearly.   She is such a thorough artist and she sings so
earnestly, and there is such a pleasant, *bitter* tone in her voice!"

DONIZETTI'S OPERAS

CHARACTERISTICS

HIS was the year when Donizetti was recognized in England, thanks to the sensation made by Rubini and Madame Persiani in *Lucia*. Italian opera music has declined so sadly since he wrote (the vogue of Signor Verdi admitted), that it is something like taking leave of the subject to attempt a character of this facile, fertile man. There was much in him to value—something peculiar to apprehend, alien to certain habits of mind and sympathy. I find myself thinking of his music as I do of Domenichino's pictures of "St. Agnes" and the "Rosario" in the Bologna gallery, of the "Diana" in the Borghese Palace at Rome, as pictures equable and skilful in the treatment of their subjects, neither devoid of beauty of form nor of colour, but which make neither the pulse quiver nor the eye wet; and then such a sweeping impression is arrested by a work like the "St. Jerome" in the Vatican, from which a spirit comes forth so strong and so exalted that the beholder, howsoever trained to examine, and compare, and collect, finds himself raised above all recollections of manner, by the sudden ascent of talent into the higher world of genius. Essentially a second-rate composer, Donizetti struck out some first-rate things in a happy hour—such as the last act of *La Favorita*.

He is remarkable as an instance of freshness of fancy, brought on by incessant manufacture. Such a change is almost exclusively confined to Italian genius in its workings. It learns and grows while creating. If it be moved by no deep purpose, it avails itself of self-correction; it strengthens its force on unconscious experience. Whereas German after German has gone deeper and deeper into fog-land when aspiring to produce what music cannot give, Italian after Italian has not merely perfected his own peculiar style, but has enlarged his science and arrived at novelty at a period of his career when it might have been fancied that nothing but truism remained to be given out.

The "craft" belonging to incessant production has been too much despised. The scholar can retire for a quarter of a century to elaborate works for scholars to come, and has his just and high reward, accordingly. Those (on the other hand) who wish to speak less learnedly to the public can hardly present themselves to the public too often. They may never make themselves scholars by retreat or reserve; but they may nerve their powers of expression by exercise, if it be accompanied by self-scrutiny. Cavillers have too pedantically assumed that, by restriction and concentration, creative genius could with all men be *forced* into becoming something far more precious than it may have originally been. In music, at least, this is a huge and untenable fallacy. Dangerous though it seem to afford encouragement to idleness, to presumption, to invention by chance, to a spirit of money-making cupidity, the perpetuation of falsehood is yet more dangerous: and there are few falsehoods more complete than the reproach conveyed in the above assertions. With few exceptions, all the great musical composers have been fertile when once educated, and capable of writing with as much rapidity as ease. Bach, Handel (whose *Israel* was completed in three weeks), Haydn (more of whose compositions are lost than live), Mozart—all men remarkable as *discoverers,* and renowned as classic authors, held the pens of ready writers. Signor Rossini's *Il Barbiere,* again, which has now kept the stage for upwards of half a century, was the work of thirteen days, the *insouciant* composer being spurred to his utmost by a disparaging letter from Paisiello, who had already set Beaumarchais' comedy. Those on whom the gift of fertility has been bestowed run some danger of becoming "nothing if not fertile,"—timid, restrained, affected. Their minds are impulsive rather than thoughtful; their fancies are strengthened by the very process and passion of pouring them forth.

In the case of Donizetti it is obvious that his invention was, year by year, becoming enlarged by incessant use and practice. There are no melodies in any of his earlier works so delicious as those of the quartet and serenade in *Don Pasquale.* His instrumentation, too, always correct, became richer and more fanciful with each successive effort. It has elsewhere been remarked that, considering Donizetti was called to write for particular singers, an unusual number of the operas thus fashioned to order have become stock pieces: thereby proved to be essentially superior to the generality of works of their class.

He was born at Bergamo in 1797; he was trained by Simone Mayr at Bologna; he was drawn for a soldier in 1816, and extricated himself by the small gains from his first opera, *Enrico di Borgogna,* produced at Venice.   Then came some score of operas, all forgotten, except, perhaps, *Il Borgomastro di Saardam,* for the sake of a poor but tuneable duet.   His twenty-first was *L'Esule di Roma,* of which some mention has been made; his thirty-second was *Anna Bolena.*   Thirty-three more were to come ere the brain of the busy man perished, under the influences of an unbridled life of indulged appetite.   Gradually—Signor Rossini remaining silent, Bellini dead, and Signor Verdi as yet partially owned—Donizetti became the man to whom Europe looked for Italian opera.

Lucia would generally be named as Donizetti's best opera.   I am not able to share in the admiration it has excited.   Never, assuredly, was a story so full of suggestion for music as Scott's *Bride of Lammermoor* tamed into such insipid nothingness, even by an Italian librettist, as this.   The supernatural tone of the legend entirely taken away; the dance on the bridal night, with its ghastly interruption, replaced by a sickly scene of madness, such as occur by scores in every southern serious opera; the funeral, with its one superfluous mourner and unbidden guest, abolished to make room for the long final scene so cherished by tenors; the character of Lady Ashton, affording such admirable material for contrast, obliterated; here are so many injuries to one of the most moving tragic tales existing in any literature.   It would be a good deed to arrange Scott's novel anew—and anew to set it.

For only in one scene—that of the contract, which closes the second act—is Donizetti equal to the occasion.   In the first act may be noticed a slight trait, meant to be Scotch, in the opening chorus; and the slow movement for two voices in the duet by the Mermaiden's Well.   The song of entrance for the heroine, like others of Donizetti's show songs, is faded, in spite of the opportunities for the vocalist which it contains.   In the second act, the letter duet, so high in favour with baritones who love to rage, is a piece of sounding platitude.   In the concerted finale to the second act, its crescendo of passion (how admirably animated when Signor Tamburini supported and spurred it!) repeats the working-out of a form already indicated in the first finale of *Anna Bolena*. The "malediction" solo of Edgardo is in the true style of operatic declamation. He who speaks ill of the third act, closed by its long-drawn death-scene (the darling scene of tenor singers), may prepare himself to be stoned for heresy. Yet throughout that scene (with the exception of the dialogue between Ravenswood and the chorus), there is to be found little beyond singer's effects, a sadly small amount of vigour or freshness in the musical treatment of the situation—nothing to be compared with analogous passages in *Lucrezia Borgia,* or even in that less popular work (a very fine specimen of the master, nevertheless), *Marino Faliero.*

Donizetti's best serious music (as I have said) is to be found in *La Favorita*. In this opera—written originally to another book, for Paris, and altered and extended when transferred to the Grand Opera—there is musical and dramatic beauty enough to make a story painful to the verge of vileness, forgiven. The chorus with dance which heralds the appearance of the King's mistress, protectress of the youth whom she has allured to break his monastic vows, is delicious. The anathema scene in the second act is forcible; the romance for the baritone is one of the best romances written for the voice. There is a voluptuous tone in the heroine's grand air, in the third act, which raises it above the commonplace level of similar scenas, and there is no song more becoming to a singer who has the needful voice and warmth of conception. The fourth act, it has been said, was showered out on paper during an incredibly brief period and at the last moment. There is no church chant on the stage more solemn and affecting than the hymn in the monastery (a good example of the deep pathos which is consistent with the use of the major key). So passionate is the romance for the tenor that it is hardly possible to sing it without effect. As given by such singers as M. Duprez and Signor Mario, it is to be ranked among the most thrilling songs of the Italian stage; yet it is built on one of the simplest scale passages. The duet which closes the opera rises still higher in emotion in the ecstacy of despair, succeeded by almost delirious exaltation. The stretto is hardly possible to spoil, so resistless is the sweep of the rhythm, provided it be only sung in time. The only singer of any merit from whose lips it has failed to move our audiences has been Signor Giuglini, whose delight in his clear and finished tones often seduces him into a languor devoid of proportion and measure, which, in music like that of the movement alluded to, becomes fatiguing and fatal. On the whole, this fourth act is Donizetti's noblest serious music. The ideas pertain to the situations and are always striking; the voices are judiciously employed and displayed; the orchestral portion is treated with care. In *La Favorita* he proved himself worthy of admission to the stage which a Rossini and a Meyerbeer had studied with solicitude.

Among his comic operas, *L'Elisir* is the general favourite; but here again I fancy the popular judgment may be hardly fair. In *L'Elisir* the Italian composer had to measure himself against the brilliant Frenchman, M. Auber, who, in the prime of his vivacity, treated the selfsame subject as *Le Philtre*. The gaiety of *L'Elisir* is flat and characterless as compared with that of *La Figlia del Reggimento*—a work which, having been tepidly received with the French text to which it was written, has gained universal acceptance out of Paris, and, under translation, has established itself as among the brightest and the last of comic Italian operas. There is a careless gaiety amounting to merriment, there is a frankness, always military, never vulgar, in this music. One might fancy it to have been thrown off during some sunny period of high spirits, when the well-spring of melody was in a sparkling humour. It is slight, it is familiar, it is catching, it is everything that pedants find easy to condemn.

I happened once in London to hear it laid hold of by a party of such connoisseurs, including more than one composer who would have found it hard to write eight bars having the faintest echo of hilarity in them. Some were decrying it, too, for the poor reason of anticipating the presumed censure of the one genius of the company. This was Mendelssohn. He let them rail their fill for a while, saying nothing. Then he began to move restlessly on his chair:

"Well, I don't know," said he, at last; "I am afraid I like it. I think it very pretty—it is so merry." Then, bursting into one of those fits of hearty gaiety which lit up his beautiful countenance in a manner never to be forgotten, "Do you know," said he, "I should like to have written it myself!"

The dismay and wonderment of the classicists, who had made sure of his support, were truly droll.

The last of Donizetti's operas—the last comic opera worth having which Italy, once so gay, has yielded—*Don Pasquale,* was written in a few weeks, when that bodily exhaustion had begun which was so soon to take the form of mental imbecility, followed by death.   Under such circumstances, that the sixty-fifth opera of one who had for a quarter of a century been supplying the stage should have any freshness at all, is marvellous—more marvellous that the music should prove its composer's very freshest.   The entrance of the coquettish Norina; the duet betwixt herself and her brother which closes the first act; in the second act, the entire finale, during which the widow springs a mine of provocations against the foolish old uncle of the man she intends to marry, including one of Donizetti's most individual concerted pieces, the quartet; in the third, the exquisite serenade behind the scenes—bear no traces of a weary brain, of a hand in which the numbness of palsy was already working.   It is true the master was incited to do his best for a quartet no less admirable than Madame Grisi, Signor Mario, and Tamburini, and Lablache.   How they seemed to revel in the light music to this airy comedy, after having borne one another company through many direful stories, set to violent sounds!   For the present it may be feared that we have taken leave of mirth in Italian music, and must look for it in the Comic Opera of Paris; and even in the home of Grétry, Boieldieu, Auber, and Adam the fountain of laughter seems to be slowly dwindling and drying up. We are becoming graver without becoming more learned; we are showing our ambition at the expense of our command over melody. Compare, for instance, the old trio, "Lei faccio," from *Il Matrimonio,* with any other modern trio for three female voices—say that from Mr. Balfe's *Falstaff,* or that from M. Halévy's *Fée aux Roses* (in which there is some finesse, as in all that M. Halévy writes), and the poverty of the time, in fancy and in power of treating the voice effectively, and the absence of real gaiety become dolefully evident.   Nay, as decay inevitably engenders decay, the very art of instrumental combination and effect for which so much has been sacrificed is in course of deterioration, owing to careless treatment, under the pretext of dash and originality.

To return from this digression, a peculiarity or two remain to be pointed out. The amount of characteristic music produced by Donizetti is very small. There is not one march, or good waltz, or minuet in any of his works. There is nothing to pair off with the march in *Norma,* or with the Polacca in *I Puritani.* Some of his overtures are written with care—as, for instance, that to *Maria di Rohan,* produced to propitiate Vienna, and the one to *Linda;* but there is none which arrests the ear. He had a way of his own in grouping voices. He employed the device, so abused by Signor Verdi, of unisonal effect, with transparency and skill, and is, accordingly, oftentimes more forcible, though less noisy, than his successor. His works demand and repay real singers, showing the latter to advantage without straining them. He wrote comparatively little for that most expressive of voices, the contralto—though that he could write charmingly for it the parts of Pierrotto, in *Linda,* and of Gondi, in *Maria di Rohan,* remain to prove. Compared with the music of these, the more popular Brindisi, in *Lucrezia,* is chargeable with vulgarity. Although not enterprising in his instrumentation, he was neither meagre nor incorrect. In short, it may be said that, though there be no startling beauties in the operas of Donizetti, none of those seizing melodies which, like "Di tanti," or "Largo al factotum," or "Assisa al piè d'un salice," ring through the world, neither such intensity of sentiment as reconciles us to the very limited alphabet in which Bellini wrote, they contain so much of what is agreeable, so many happy combinations and excellent opportunities for vocal display, such frequent harmony between the sounds and the situations to be portrayed, as to justify musical annalists in giving the fertile master a high place in the records of his time.

THE YEAR 1839

OPERAS. *La Somnambula, I Puritani, Norma,* Bellini; *Belisario,* Anna Bolena,* Lucrezia Borgia, L'Elisir d'Amore,** Donizetti; *Otello, La Cenerentola, Guillaume Tell,** Rossini. PRINCIPAL SINGERS. Mdes. Monnani,* Alban Croft,* Grisi, Persiani, Ernesta Grisi,* Pauline Garcia.* MM. Tati, F. Lablache, Rubini, Lablache, Tamburini, Mario.* BALLETS. *Robert Le Diable,* Un Nuit de Bal,* La Gitana,* La Gipsy.** PRINCIPAL DANCERS. Mdes. Taglioni, Fanny Elssler.

THE YEAR 1839

Y this year's list of operas it will be seen that the ascendancy of Donizetti's music was on the increase. It was the first year in England of his *Lucrezia Borgia,* since so associated with the names of Madame Grisi and Signor Mario. The only other opera, unknown, though not precisely new, which was presented, was Signor Rossini's *Guillaume Tell. Lucrezia* took hold of London from the first moment, though it is not Donizetti's best work. Signor Rossini's masterpiece has never done so, till this year of writing (1861).

Such fact in no respect determines the value of the music accepted or rejected—merely figuring as one item in a long list of similar cases. Dear as is Mozart's *Zauberflöte* to all musicians and lovers of melody, on the stage that opera has been only tolerated. The reason, in both cases, is the same—the stupidity of the story. It would appear, as I have remarked, as if the greatest of Italians had taken a despotic pride in choosing a subject without reference to dramatic treatment, and without a leading female interest, always of the first importance to opera, be the part long or brief.

The music, however, will grow so long as music lives and lasts. Year by year will be more and more seen the rare and characteristic beauty royally showered over the work from its earliest to its latest note. In the long opening act—with no incident whatsoever till the finale is reached, and that incident (the flight of a culprit) one belonging to mechanist rather than to actor—the freshness and charm and Swiss character of the music sustain the opera, though such heroine as it possesses has not till then appeared. Not to speak of the overture (in which the storm and the opening of the quickstep are open to cavil—the close of the latter movement redeeming the puerility of the theme by its amazing animation), the opening chorus and quartet, the concerted close of the first scene, with the well-known "Ranz des Vaches" so wonderfully interwoven, the duet for the two principal men, the bridal chorus,

113

the ballet music, lastly, the finale, including its prayer, and its vehement, anxious stretto, cling to the ear and the heart with such power that nothing beyond music is thought of or desired.

After this comes a second act unparagoned in opera-writing; composed of five pieces worth dwelling on for a moment—though it is needless, in a work so familiar, to detail one by one the situations which they represent.   The first gives the tone of the scene and the hour—a hunting-chorus, opening with a flourish of horns, and the shout of the gathered mountain rangers.   A simpler melody could not be found, nor yet one more clear of the vulgarity which a triple rhythm, and the restricted powers of the instruments employed, are somewhat apt to stamp upon all music *à la chasse*. But it is evening, and a pause allows the measured chime of a distant bell to be heard, with a sunset hymn of herdsmen accompanying in mellow harmony the decline of day, and the approach of a time of repose.   The burden of the hunters' song is resumed, with a diminished vivacity; there is a *farewell* in the reiterated notes and the dying fall of the wind instruments, and in the detached tones given to the voices as the singers withdraw, leaving the margin of the lake to the stars and the dew, silent and lonely— the very field for expectation.   And expectation (unless fantasy has misled me into the folly of Sterne's simile maker) is expressed strongly in the second change—in Matilda's recitative and romance which follow, from the first symphony to the close of the air, which is built on a phrase so expressive that it is next to impossible that a singer should utter it coldly.   The calm of the hour, the gentle stir of leaves, the murmur of night airs across the bosom of the lake, are not more strongly expressed in the accompaniment than the tenderness and anxiety of human affection in the vocal part.   But expectation is not to be fruitless.   The third change opens out its fulfilment: the passionate dialogue, the delicious repose of mutual confession, the rapture of assured love.   It would seem hard, at its close, to sustain the excitement to which the hearer has been wrought.   This, however, Rossini has sustained —nay, surpassed—in the fourth musical piece of the act, where the lover is aroused from his dream by his indignant friends, and where the struggle betwixt passion and patriotism is stirred by their detailing to him that his own father has become a victim to

Gessler's tyrannous cruelty; till the desire to avenge his country at length absorbs every softer feeling.   I know not whether it has ever occurred to any one beside myself that in the leading idea, both of the commencement and of the close of this trio, a distant but not indistinct reminiscence of "La Marseillaise" is traceable. Be this as it may, courage never uttered its unselfish defiance with a more enkindling animation than in the final Tyrtean hymn.   The finale to the second act—the last of the five gradations mentioned —has yet to be spoken of.   It was well done of Rossini, after the trio, to allow an interval of comparative repose, the occasion being furnished by the covert approach and gradual entrance of the men of the three Cantons.   What invention is here! what variety! How characteristic and distinct is the music of each tribe; yet how naturally and solidly are the three different airs bound together by a few emphatic and significant phrases, till they burst out in the inspiriting triple chorus, *"Guillaume, tu le vois!"* and afterwards reply to the hero's address in antiphony, which, wrought up to a climax, leads to the solemn dedication of their swords and lives to the cause of freedom!   Here the situation is far more the work of the musician than of the poet, so intensely picturesque and appropriate is the chain of movements by which the effect is wrought up.   At first we have snatches of melody like the sighing of the night wind over the shadowy lake and among the columnar pines; then airs which themselves suggest motion and number and diversity of costume; then an outburst of fiery impatience; then the stern catechism and the eager reply; and lastly a whole people devoting itself to a noble purpose, in the presence of their ancestral mountains.[1]

The wondrous beauty of this act, though sustained by singers no less admirable than Madame Persiani [2] and Signor Rubini, Tamburini, and Lablache, could not, twenty years ago, save the opera in England.   Sedulously prepared as it was, the public had not become used to grand musical drama, and preferred any musical melodrama of Donizetti because of the scope for acting afforded by the story.

[1] I have transferred this passage from a former work out of print—*Music and Manners in France and North Germany.*
[2] A cadence made by this lady, at the close of "Sombres forêts," lives to be remembered as one of the happiest, most fearless, most characteristic, and best executed pieces of ornament which I have ever heard, even from Madame Persiani.

Two singers who have since, in widely different orbits, set the world on fire, were brought forward this year.

The new Garcia (sister to Malibran), the new tenor, demand separate future studies. Suffice it here to say that the first appeared in her girlhood, for the first time on any stage, as Desdemona, with an amount of musical accomplishment and of original genius the combination of which was unique. Signor Mario had been trained at the Grand Opera of Paris before he sang here in public. There the charm of his voice and appearance and the elegance of his manner had already, though imperfectly, asserted themselves. I had seen and heard him there in a now-forgotten opera by M. Halévy, *Le Drapier;* but I have not to this day forgotten the skill there shown by him in his dress, the beauty of his tones (then belonging to the half-cultivated voice of an amateur), nor his expressive saying of a romance, of which the burden was "un seul instant." When he appeared here, in *Lucia,* the vocal command which he afterwards gained was unthought of; his acting did not then get beyond that of a southern man with a strong feeling for the stage. But physical beauty and geniality such as have been bestowed on few, a certain artistic taste, a certain "distinction," not exclusively belonging to gentle birth, but sometimes associated with it, made it clear, from Signor Mario's first hour of stage life, that a course of no common order of fascination was begun. Pity that events should be of such frequent occurrence as the singer not beginning to sing well till the bloom is off his voice, as the actor not being able to act till time has thinned his flowing hair, and channelled the round cheek, and set a knob in the Grecian throat! Such has not been altogether Signor Mario's case. Nevertheless his best triumphs have come not so much in the noon as in the afternoon of his charming genius. When will artists begin seriously to study before they present themselves to be judged? when learn, that youth has a beauty of its own, which can be got back by neither prayers nor tears when it has once vanished? when forbear to trade on such youth, as a quality which shall stand in stead of culture? Pauline Garcia was a ripe musician, with many natural defects bespeaking indulgence, ere she began to sing; but Signor Mario was a Hyperion born, who had only to be seen and heard and the enchantment was complete.

The other new appearances were beneath mediocrity.   In the ballet, Mdlle. Fanny Elssler increased her fame by dancing in the *Gipsy,* though the presentment of that capital work seemed pale and starved to those who had seen it at the Grand Opera of Paris.

THE YEAR 1840

OPERAS. *Il Matrimonio Segreto*, Cimarosa; *La Somnambula, Beatrice di Tenda, Il Pirata, I Puritani*, Bellini; *Torquato Tasso*,* *Lucia di Lammermoor, L'Elisir d'Amore*, Donizetti; *Il Giuramento*,* Mercadante; *Don Giovanni*, Mozart; *Inez di Castro*,* Persiani; *Otello, La Gazza Ladra, Il Barbiere, La Donna del Lago*, Rossini. PRINCIPAL SINGERS. Mdes. de Varny,* Persiani, Tosi,* Ernesta Grisi, Grisi. MM. Ricciardi,* Coletti,* Lablache, Rubini, Tamburini, Mario. (In German Opera, at the St. James's Theatre.) Herr Staudigl. BALLETS. *La Tarantule*,* *Le Lac des Fées*,* *La Gitana, L'Ombre*.* PRINCIPAL DANCERS. Mdes. Fanny Elssler, Cerito,* Taglioni. M. Bretin.*

THE YEAR 1840

N 1840 the Opera management, which for half-a-dozen years had gone on from strength to strength, began to change its plans and to show symptoms of uneasiness, decomposition, and pretext. Since the day when Signor Costa took up the baton its orchestra had steadily improved under his discipline, intelligence, and resolution to be contented with nothing short of the best. Then the excellent company of singers, who moved from Paris to London, with the rare advantage of perfect mutual understanding one with the other, had shown in their performances an equality and finish unattainable under any other circumstances than those of habitual intercourse. It is true that new compositions did not come forward as in the time when Signor Rossini was pouring out his treasures no less fluently than, in his world, Walter Scott had done. But our public was well satisfied; and for once in its life knew that it was content, and asked for no immediate change.

The spell of ruin, in the shape of litigation, complicated enough to bewilder the most cunning Chancery (or Chicanery) barrister, had hung for years on years over the Haymarket Opera House. Season after season had the world been wearied by reports of this or the other trial in which the property figured as yet one more of those cases displayed by our admirable modern novelist in his *Bleak House*. It would seem to be an indispensable ingredient in operatic speculation that it should be entered on without money, without foresight, without special knowledge, by way of sheet anchor. To meet the exigencies of law and debt, prices of admission were raised; the season (formerly dependent on subscription) was shortened; and, what was least supportable, an attempt was made to replace the good artists by others less good. The result will be seen.

One of the liveliest evenings of the season of 1840 was that of the Tamburini riot, on the night when Mademoiselle Cerito was to make her first pirouette here. The intention of ousting this excellent artist, then in his prime, to replace him by Signor Coletti—another excellent singer, though second in order of merit and accomplishment—was resented with such fiery indignation as has not been often witnessed. The public would not receive the new dancer; it would demand reason for the substitution for the singer —*would* have its own favourite back again, and became violent beyond reason and propriety. It carried its point, however, for the year: after having treated those who are amused by uproar to a performance of such disorder and discord as must have gratified them to their hearts' content.

The Italian new compositions, one and all, failed.

During this year there was, in a smaller theatre (the St. James's), a German opera company, which brought to light some stage works till then little known here—such as Weber's *Euryanthe,* Spohr's *Faust* and *Jessonda,* Dr. Marschner's *Templer und Jüdin*—and which revived Gluck's second *Iphigenia.* The intrinsic worth of all these operas, as compositions, made itself felt somehow; but the mediocrity of all (except one) of those who presented the music did not slay the creations of the great German masters, old and young, so much as put them to sleep. Yet the best soprano voice of this half-century was to be heard among these German singers in Madame Stöckl-Heinefetter (one of the four Heinefetter sisters); and a strenuous tenor veteran was there in Herr Wild—a singer who had seen out many dynasties and many composers, but who never could have been accepted as a favourite elsewhere than in Germany.

It is heresy, I know, to dwell on the disenchantment which persons who are sensible to the charms of singing have to undergo in the course of their acquaintance with German opera. It will be thought worse to say that to hear many of the masterpieces of its limited repertory mated with German language and presented by German artists, be they ever so strenuous, is a trial only to be got through by abstracting the work itself from the vehicle of its interpretation. Yet to me the average German execution of German opera—setting aside the choral portions—is as little welcome as it would be to see one of Shakespeare's plays industriously laboured through by provincial Romeos and Juliets. Partly the indifference to vocal grace and beauty, which has become so universal as to be all but generic, may arise from the superior attention given since Haydn's days to purely instrumental music; but in part it would seem as if a sense was wanting to the people, so strangely ungracious is the rule of vocal stage performance in the country of such great instrumental composers. It was least unsatisfactory at Vienna, perhaps because that capital has held on to its commerce with southern art longer than Berlin or Dresden or Munich. The few most acceptable singers of later time—Madame Jenny Lutzer, Madame Van Hasselt-Barth, and Herr Staudigl—belonged to the Kärnther Thor Theatre. I can recall not one German tenor whom I have heard on the stage with much pleasure save Herr Tichatschek, at Dresden; nowhere a contralto—a voice apparently withheld from Germany, as also from France. Of some among the above named, as they passed, I may have to speak with reference to their appearances in Italian opera, or opera in Italian. For the present it must suffice to point out their peculiar qualities (for better for worse), as one among other reasons why German opera has never cordially thriven in London since the year of its first real revelation here.

Having named a few exceptions I must dwell for a moment on the name of Staudigl, who was first heard in London in 1840. He is probably the best example of a German basso that ever existed. So long ago as Handel's time, managers repaired to Germany when they were in want of this particular voice. A certain Waltz, who had been the great master's cook,[1] figured on the London stage in Handel's operas. There has been, from the time of Waltz downwards to that of Herr Formes, a line of Germans richly endowed with deep and ponderous organs, such as is to be found in no other country. The only very deep-toned Italian basso that I recollect was Signor Porto (if he was an Italian); the only French voice of the kind that of M. Levasseur; but the French sing in every register, and, not having been genially endowed by Nature, manage to press every possibility and impossibility which study and stage tact can secure for them into the service of music and declamation.

Staudigl was a great singer—a great artist also: a man born with a real vocation for the stage and for music. Placed, when young, in that paradise for lazy youths with small means, the Benedictine

---

[1] Possibly the cook to whom Handel alluded in the *mot* which has been worked so hard to Gluck's disparagement, and in which the composer of *The Messiah* is described as having said that the composer of *Orpheus* knew no more of counterpoint than his cook.

Monastery of Mölk, on the Danube, there was no quiet for him, no possibility of his remaining there. Yet the quasi-monks of Mölk have liberty enough within its lazy limits. They can go down the Danube to the Vienna theatres; they can lay by their monastic dress when they travel. When they are at home they are lodged royally. Nevertheless it is hard to keep their number up, even in Austria; and Staudigl broke out from thence on the strength of a noble bass voice, compassing two octaves—from F to F—equal, rich, sonorous, in no common degree; fairly trained and subject to the prompting of a genial, careless nature, which wanted outlet for its abundance. When he came to London, from the first he towered above all his fellow German singers in German opera. There could be no question with anybody that this was a voice which belonged to a musician of no common order, and also to a man, warm, kindly, impulsive; who threw his life and his temperament into every note that he gave out. He was not well educated, I have been told—I never knew, nor spoke with, him—but he had that which the French call "distinction"—that innate, cheerful, courteous self-assertion which belongs to no rank, to no training, to no ancestry, and which engages at once and for all those who are willing to enjoy, let them be ever so closely obliged to compare.

Among the new Italian singers Signor Coletti must be named first, as an expressive, manly artist, with a fine baritone voice less flexible and versatile than Signor Tamburini,—an artist of whom the public, after a few seasons, tired somewhat unjustly. He has now, for years, sung only at Rome and Naples. Madame Tosi was a mediocre singer who had studied good models—one of the class which can hardly be expected to exist for the future, so few and far between are the examples left in Italy worthy of imitation. Those Italians now sing the best who have had the least to do with their own stage. The reinforcements of Italian opera have of late come from every other source than the south.—1840, then, cannot be chronicled as among the years of the Golden Age of musical drama in London.

It was the year, however, of the last comic ballet which excited any enthusiasm here. This was the *Tarantule*—incomparably acted and danced by Mademoiselle Fanny Elssler. She put forth in it all her mimic power, all that audacious and exuberant execution which made the critic say that if Taglioni was "the Poetry," she was "the Wit," of motion. The story could not be matched for absurdity, being the tale of a girl who pretends to be tarantula-*mad* in order that she may dance a stupid old suitor forced on her into declining her hand; but absurd as it is, as canvas for Mademoiselle Elssler's embroideries it could hardly be surpassed in comedy. The manner in which she wrought its whimsical scenes up to a climax; the grace, the daring, the incessant brilliancy, the feverish buoyancy, and the sly humour with which she managed to let the public into her secret that her madness was only feigned, raised this ridiculous farce to the level of a work of art. No one, probably, will attempt to revive it, since the silver age of ballet was already beginning to set in even before Mademoiselle Fanny Elssler's departure. Not long after this creation—the last of her comic ones—was exhibited, this fascinating artist was bitten by that tarantula desire to roam, on the temptation of fabulous gains, which has done so much to bring about the downfall of our theatres, and virtually gave up Paris and London to undertake the voyage to America, concerning which so much was written at the time. Our relatives on the other side of the water were then almost as deliriously transported by the seductions of the dancer as they proved themselves to be, a few years later, by the munificent charities and lovely singing of Mademoiselle Jenny Lind. In Mademoiselle Fanny Elssler's case there was no pretence, even, of extraordinary virtue. That she was graceful and fascinating in her manners everyone can bear witness who met her in private. The most prudish woman—or man—might have passed days in her society without being recalled to any recollection of the scanty stage dress, and the attitudes, fitter for sculpture than for social life— in short, by any look, gesture, or allusion belonging to the dancer's craft, on her part. She spoke and behaved in private with the ease, quietness, and taste of a gentlewoman; but this could only be known to a few, whereas her pirouettes and battements, and the whole artillery of her sorceries, were, without stint, public property. And on the hint of the sorcery, the States, Puritan and Catholic—rigid Boston and hot New Orleans—were up in arms. She was caressed and courted as lions can be caressed and courted only on the other side of the Atlantic. Divines offered her their pews in meeting houses. Students from every country under the sun serenaded her; her lap was filled with gold with a prodigality recalling those reckless times when noblemen flung purses, with diamonds among the coin, to the Sallé or Guimard of the hour when she took her benefit at the Paris Opera.   It was a grotesque rehearsal, in short, of the more stately and orthodox pageant of enthusiastic belief and rapture which, a few years later, was to be enacted—with Mr. Barnum for High Priest—in honour of the real claims (howsoever by artful circumstance exaggerated) of the greatest singer whom Sweden has ever sent forth to captivate the world.

THE YEAR 1841

OPERAS. *Beatrice di Tenda, Norma, La Straniera,* Bellini; *Gli Orazi, Il Matrimonio,* Cimarosa; *Lucia, Fausta,* Roberto Devereux,* Marino Faliero, Lucrezia Borgia,* Donizetti; *Don Giovanni,* Mozart; *Il Tancredi, Semiramide, La Cenerantola, Il Barbiere, Il Turco,* Rossini. PRINCIPAL SINGERS. Mdes. Viardot-Garcia, Nunn, Persiani, Granchi, Löwe,* Grisi. MM. Mario, Flavio,* De Bassini, Tamburini, Rubini, Lablache. BALLETS. *Le Diable Amoureux,* La Sylphide, La Gitana, La Magie Amoureuse.* PRINCIPAL DANCERS. Mdes. Guy Stephan,* Cerito, Taglioni. M. Albert.* FRENCH TRAGEDY. Mademoiselle Rachel Felix.

EITHER of Donizetti's new operas had any success. Not a bar of *Fausta* lives; and only a song and a duet from *Roberto Devereux* are remembered. Queen Elizabeth has never been fortunate as an opera heroine: neither (by the way) has been Mary Stuart.

It was a matter of no common interest to be allowed to hear Cimarosa's *Gli Orazi,* though the tragedy was only executed "after a fashion." But the hearing of the opera, when due allowance was afforded for all drawbacks, revealed the vast change which had passed over musical drama since that operatic setting of Corneille's play had been written. The music—the final duet excepted—seemed, on its revival, pleasing, but feeble beyond the power of acting to animate; telling of a time when the pleasure of the ear was cared for on the opera stage, without any close reference to dramatic truth or dignity. The old heroes and heroines stepped the boards rather than presented characters. Lord Mount-Edgecumbe recollects how the Gabrielli (in her day more talked of than Mademoiselle Lind) "tucked up her hoop," as Dido, ere she sidled into the flames of Carthage. Even Malibran's sister, full of young dramatic fervour, could do nothing for the heroine, as draped by Cimarosa, analogous to that which Rachel did when she electrified all Paris in the revival of the formal *Les Horaces* of Corneille. *Gli Orazi* is a weak opera, let it be taken how it will.

Yet that Cimarosa was not, of necessity, dramatically weak, is to be seen in that scene from his oratorio, *Il Sacrifizio d'Abramo,* "Deh parlate," which will always tempt Italian singers of the highest class. The dispensation under which he wrote was one (as every musical stage dispensation has been—save, possibly, in France) in which a single interest was allowed to predominate—technical, sensual, musical pleasure, over deep emotion, the singing-master's art over the temptation to the tragedian to express any or every deep emotion. The pendulum has now oscillated to its furthest extreme.

A criticism somewhat analogous could be passed on the once-famed *Tancredi* of Cimarosa's successor, which was also revived this year, and with singers no less able than Madame Persiani and Madame Viardot. The latter, it is true, had to fight up against recollections of Madame Pasta as Tancredi; but the music, in spite of Signor Rossini's vivacity and fluency of melody (how superior both to Cimarosa's!), in spite of the vocal magnificence and charm of the duets, came over the ear as something behind our time, because it had never been wholly consistent with its purpose. *Il Tancredi* is already old, without being ancient. Gluck's operas are ancient, without being old.

Signor Rossini's *Il Turco* was likewise tried again—an opera containing some of its writer's most exquisite and spontaneous comic music, in which, again, Cimarosa is utterly beaten on his own ground. On this work that archimage of comedy, Lablache, lavished his best drollery and most superb singing. But the world had got past *Il Turco,* owing to the puerile stupidity of the story; and it is too probable that the opera is buried "for ever and a day," owing to the thoughtless disregard of the man of genius who flung it out.

There were no new artists this year who could gain, or ought to have gained, favour in London at our Italian Opera. With regard to one of the ladies English curiosity had been excited, and not without reason. On my first visit to Germany in 1839 every *table d'hôte* was ringing (and loudly tables *do* ring with talk there!) with enthusiasm for a charming singer then to be heard at Berlin, a Sontag come back again—yes! and better than Sontag! When their enthusiasm is aroused our "cousins German" do not spare asseveration. I was to hear Madamoiselle Löwe at Berlin, or else I had heard nothing! I *did* hear her. With my London and Paris remembrances fresh in my mind, and hearing her only in translated French and Italian operas, I was colder in acquiescence than my hospitable hosts liked. I saw in her a tall, handsome woman, somewhat of the type of Mademoiselle Fanny Elssler and of a more modern prima donna, Mademoiselle Cruvelli; who looked intelligent, was dressed with taste, and acted with an animated attempt at the French style of stage eloquence; obviously a lady to be set apart from the list of average German songstresses. But I could not like Mademoiselle Löwe's voice—a weak, wiry, high soprano, without charm; and I could not close my ears to the fact that she belonged to the class of vocalists who think they are florid and who do their best accordingly, but who are not really so —how different from the Sontags, Cintis, Persianis, with whom, for the instant, their admirers class them! Trying at the most audacious feats of execution as she did, Mademoiselle Löwe achieved no success. Everything, however well-aimed, fell short of its mark; and insomuch as the ornate and florid style of singing is to be defended, on every principle of art the plated ware in place of the real precious metal, the mechanical web-work in place of the delicate *hand*-lace, cannot content those who would rather have plain and massive simplicity than false ornament. Great was the Berlin sarcasm which a stranger, compelled to speak (silence being mistaken for accusation), had to bear if he offered comparisons such as these. "No! If the Löwe were to come to London, I should see! Everybody knew" (this in 1839) "that Grisi's voice was gone. Everybody knew that there was no singer in Europe like the Löwe!"

Such enthusiasm naturally made its object believe in herself somewhat immoderately. It came into Mademoiselle Löwe's mind to leave Berlin (even as Sontag had done) for brilliant Paris, and for stupid but well-paying England. She was absolutely (I have been told) after quitting her own subjects for new conquests, appealed to at the frontier by an offer of recall sent after her, entreating her to return, at an enormous increase of salary. She was deaf—would go on; and, confident in what her subjects had encouraged her to believe, would measure herself against "those Italians!" In Paris she was unable to find an engagement; but in London a less costly Grisi was, possibly, at that juncture an object of importance to a management in which second-rate artists were, on principle, preferred; and so to London Mademoiselle Löwe came; and so it was whispered east, and asserted west, before she came, that this real idol of the Berlin public (as Sontag had been before her) was better than Grisi—even as the Germans had said.

The lady herself I conceive to have been thoroughly self-deceived. When she tried to mount her throne here, in *La Stra-*

niera (an unlucky opera) of Bellini, every one characteristic and quality of those I have mentioned came to full light and fair appreciation.   She was not allowed to consider herself a failure; but the truth could not be long escaped from.

And here I must tell that, for a past season or two, the foreign system had been introduced of fabricated applause, in the determination to force on the public what and whomsoever the opera manager adopted.   Men and women, as notoriously hired for such mystification as the howlers at an Irish funeral, began to be seen in known places every night, obtruding their stationary raptures (which were paid for) at the serviceable times and places.   The extent to which this nuisance grew was one among other causes of the decay of the old Italian opera, and its increasing dis-esteem in the judgment of all real connoisseurs.   The English are in some things supine, too slow to believe in the existence and practice of trickery; but an impression once made on them is made for ever.   The poor artists, deluded and degraded by such false shows, run a risk of faring badly when the hour of disenchantment arrives.

For a night or two Mademoiselle Löwe may have dreamed that the succession to Madame Grisi was to be hers.   Ere a week or two had gone she must have felt that she was to be either a substitute or a "second woman" in London.   In the latter capacity she might have become very valuable.

She was the best Donna Elvira in *Don Giovanni* that I have ever seen, assuming the dignified, half-devotee post of that ill-used and rather troublesome woman to perfection.   She sang the music conscientiously, and the *harpsichord* quality of her voice told well, rather than ill, for the opera—the *quill*-tone in it (musicians will understand my word) giving a sort of fantastic excuse for the Don's vicious vagaries in favour of something sweeter.   Later in the year, as La Dogaressa, in *Marino Faliero* (revived with a vain hope of settling that fine opera on the stage), her demeanour as the Venetian patrician lady was unimpeachable, and her dress superb and pictorial.   Could these accessories save a weak and ungracious female part in an opera, they would have done so in her case.   Later, Mademoiselle Löwe was accepted in Italy, during the season of opera dearth even then setting in.   A little later still she left the stage (it was said) for a great marriage.   She was a graceful, accomplished woman, with much tact; never a great artist, but one of the least disagreeable German singers who have adventured on the Italian opera stage in this country.

Of the other new vocalists in the year 1841 there is no need to speak. This was the last season, for many years, of Madame Viardot's performances. When she returned it was to a world entirely transformed, and with her own peculiar genius in its own peculiar place. Yet even so early in her career her singing in *La Cenerentola* could not be exceeded for invention and brilliancy of style. When she appeared with Rubini she had to subdue her voice so as to match his musical whisper; but for the final rondo she had already invented that reading and those admirably ingenious changes (changes not so much allowed as demanded by Signor Rossini's music) most of which have since been quietly appropriated by less imaginative singers—to name but one, Madame Alboni. During this season Signor Mario stepped into the place of first tenor, never since vacated by him. Musically, however, the year, as concerned Italian opera, was not rich.

There was a German company at another theatre, of which the only endurable member was Staudigl. A stinted and slovenly version of M. Meyerbeer's *Robert* failed to bring that romantic and difficult work into fashion. To this day London has been obdurate in disregard of it. Something worse happened in respect to another opera, which, were it duly presented, has every quality recommending it to English admiration.

This is Mozart's *Die Entführung*, one of the most delicious comic operas in being—Mozart's *only* comic opera, for his *Figaro* is sentimental, in the teeth of Beaumarchais' situations; and his *Cosi fan tutte* is as grand in style as *Don Juan*, wheresoever the stupidity of the story could be thrown off by the composer. The local colour and clear distinction of character in *Die Entführung* were never subsequently outdone by the composer. It has fun for the thoughtless, construction for those who will not accept an opera "without counterpoint," a flow of melody belonging to the opening days of its owner's well-spring, in no later work enriched, and amplest opportunity for vocal display given to the highest of soprani, to the lowest of bassi, to the most luscious of tenors, to the shrewdest of soubrettes. Here, except by Staudigl, it was simply disguised and murdered by Mozart's countrymen, and therefore undervalued and overlooked. Its recent disinterment in

Paris, at the Théâtre Lyrique, with the changes and retrenchments in the opera book rendered indispensable by the taste of our times, may lead to its being replaced in the theatre by such lively persons as can sing no less than act—if it should prove that the humour for comic opera has not died out past revival.

THE YEAR 1842

OPERAS. *Norma, Beatrice di Tenda, I Puritani,* Bellini; *Malek Adhel,* Costa; *Gemma di Vergy,** Lucia, Torquato Tasso, Lucrezia Borgia, Anna Bolena,* Donizetti; *Le Cantatrice Villane,** Fioravanti; *Elena da Feltre,** Mercadante; *Don Giovanni, Cosi fan tutte,* Mozart; *Il Barbiere,* Rossini. PRINCIPAL SINGERS. Mdes. Molteni,* Persiani, Frezzolini,* Ronconi.* MM. Guasco,* Ronconi,* Poggi,* Rubini, Lablache, F. Lablache, Stella.* BALLETS. Giselle,* Alma. PRINCIPAL DANCERS. Mdes. Carlotta Grisi,* Cerito. M. Perrot.

THE YEAR 1842

HIS was a bad and disappointing season, marked with little novelty worth commemorating. Donizetti's *Gemma di Vergy* and Signor Mercadante's *Elena da Feltre* were new to our Italian stage. Neither produced the slightest sensation. The latter had been more fortunate in an English dress, owing to the remarkable acting and singing of Miss Adelaide Kemble.

And here, seeing that a young English lady, in spite of the disadvantages of a translated version, and of comrades unused to Italian music, could gain a success for an unknown opera in London, which an Italian prima donna, in all the plenitude of promise and power—I mean Madame Frezzolini—was unable to do, a word or two are not misplaced, in a chronicle of great singers, regarding another great interpreter.

Such was Miss Adelaide Kemble: a musical artist in right of resolution rather than liberal nature. Her voice, originally limited, had been moulded, rendered flexible, and extended in compass, by study and incessant practice, till it became capable of every inflexion, of every possible brilliancy. More honest singing than its owner's I have never heard; add to this, command of four languages and four styles of music, and poetical aspiration borne out by intellectual culture, by habitual commerce with all that is most refined and most thoughtful, and the result could only be what it was—the greatest English singer (though not the best of this century), a poetical and thoughtful artist, whose name will never be lost so long as the art of dramatic singing is spoken of. That Miss Kemble's singing had always the heaviness of style belonging to one who has had to wrestle with rebellious natural means, belonging, also, to one too full of intelligence to allow the smallest point or particle to pass without its being wrought out, is true. She was too fond of drawing out those high notes to gain which had cost her so dear; of delivering every syllable in every word spoken, with equal emphasis, so that a certain fatigue of impression could not but be the result.   But these mannerisms (which might have worn off) had nothing to do with the genius, skill, and knowledge of their possessor; since these (with her instinctive and inherited powers of acting) enabled her here to carry Signor Mercadante's opera triumphantly through in its English version; [1] while on our Italian stage it died out, without disapproval, there to be heard of no more.

How pretty was Fioravanti's comic opera!   But the showy terzett, "Io dirò" is the only musical piece by which even the name of *Le Cantatrice Villane* will be recollected.   We have grown graver, morally (if not musically)—Italians and English both—since the days when farces of this quality sufficed for the contentment of the public.

A proof more emphatic still was to be seen, in the want of success for Mozart's *Cosi fan tutte,* when that opera—silly in story, rich in beauty and skill—was revived.   As regards mere attraction for the ear, Mozart never outdid the first act; so full is it of grace, harmony, constructive power, and that melody which was like an instinct with that wondrously endowed artist.   The concerted music is marvellous in its beauty and ingenuity.   In the second act there are some superb songs; there is a magnificent close to the opera.   Yet what do they avail?   The tiresome folly of the fable is even more fatal here than in the case of *Die Zauberflöte.*   The utterly stupid trick put on two girls by their two lovers, abetted by a nimble Abigail, cannot pass at this time of day; and thus, because of utter indifference on the composer's part, a mine of treasure is, as it were, drowned for ever and for ever. There is no hope for *Cosi fan tutte* on the stage as the work stands.

It was very well given, though, on this occasion,—and Rubini's singing of "Un' aura amorosa" is not to be forgotten, as one of the most caressing, highly-finished, and exquisite specimens of Rubini's singing.

[1] Nor must it be forgotten that Miss Kemble's Norma could be compared with that of Madame Pasta,—could be preferred (apart from comparisons of voice and person) to that of Madame Grisi.   In comedy, too, how charming were her Suzanna and her Carolina!—good enough for any opera house in Europe, no matter how high the standard, how famous the playfellows of the prima donna.   On the English stage she created and sustained a reputation as a first-class artist, the early termination of whose career left a void which there is small chance of our seeing filled.

Among the musical events of the year 1843, the production of Signor Rossini's *Stabat* must not be forgotten. There was the usual amount of cavil, of course, concerning it, by the would-be wise persons who will only recognize one style of music, and who forget that, ever since the days when opera separated itself from miracle play, and the orchestra was allowed its place in the church, that which is rich and florid has always been permitted to enter there. Signor Rossini's *Stabat,* as considered in reference to its epoch, is no more trivial and secular than was Pergolesi's— about which such shallow musical critics as Mr. Rogers used to shake their heads and sigh, simply because it was old, and because no one could quote it against the new music, themselves, probably, the least able of the party—no more trivial and secular than Jomelli's Requiem, less so than Haydn's and Mozart's Masses. The fugue at the end is bad; but not worse (as I am dealing with comparisons) than Spohr's fugues. The introduction, how admirable, serious, and mournful!—the close of "Cujus animam," the entire "Pro Peccatis," the duet for female voices (with its prelude, incomparable in the contrast of instruments), the opening and close of the unaccompanied chorus, "Eià mater," the episodes in the quartet, the entire contralto song (how admirable as an example of broken rhythm!), the gorgeous "Inflammatus," the "Paradisi gloria," are all so many passages—inspirations, I will say—to recall which makes the blood run quicker in one's veins, let the cavillers complain as they please. The work stands, and should and will stand, if not a model to composers, a delight to singers; a work which bears as little trace of manner or period as do the best passages in *Moise,* or the incomparable second act of *Guillaume Tell.*

This year there was, again, at another theatre, a German company, headed by the best brilliant German singer I have ever heard (Sontag and Mdlle. Lind not coming into the category). This was Mdlle. Jenny Lutzer. It would not be easy to accomplish more, or to execute what was undertaken more perfectly, than she did. Her voice, too, had a clear, ringing tone, which lent itself well to the style chosen by her. There was a want, however, of charm, a sort of hardness of manner, in her performance and execution, which stood between her and the highest honours. The company of which she formed one, together with Madame Stöckl-

Heinefetter and Herr Staudigl, attempted M. Meyerbeer's *Les Huguenots,* in German. But the day of that magnificent opera had not yet come for England; and indeed, when given with German text it loses effect to a degree which is hardly explicable. Then the utmost care and luxury must be expended on its production, or the work becomes heavy and tiring, and its effect chill. This, a company of strangers, who were only here for a few weeks, and in a theatre of insufficient resources, could not afford; and *Les Huguenots,* accordingly, was overlooked and judged; and people who had not seen the opera in Paris found it in no respect remarkable, nor worthy of its reputation. How often has the same story to be hold!

There remains but one more event of this poor year to be mentioned—the arrival of Mademoiselle Carlotta Grisi. This dancer is the only one, since Mdlles. Taglioni and Fanny Elssler, who exhibited something like individuality as compared with imitation, or repetition of known effects. She had not the dancer's face, with its set smile put on to disguise breathless distress and fatigue; but she looked shy, and young, and delicate, and fresh. There was something of the briar rose in her beauty. How she came to dance, always puzzled me; then, too, she had a sweet little singing voice which, for want of outlet and enrichment, perished, next to unknown. *Giselle* was written for her, on an invention of Heine's, by Adolphe Adam. This lively, facile French musician, too much undervalued—happiest in his ballet music—was never happier, even in his *Fille du Danube,* than in *Giselle.* Some of the melodies in it are excellent; the dance tunes are full of life; the instrumentation, if somewhat coarse, is sparkling and provocative (a first requisite in dance-music). In short, *Giselle* was a charming ballet, even before Mdlle. Fanny Elssler came, who turned the romantic and gently melancholy story into a piece of tragic pathos, as powerful as was ever exhibited by mime.

The music to *Alma* was by Signor Costa—his last and his best ballet music.

THE YEAR 1843

OPERAS. *La Somnambula, Norma, I Puritani,* Bellini; *Adelia, Belisario, Linda di Chamouni, Don Pasquale,* Donizetti; *Don Giovanni,* Mozart; *Semiramide, Il Barbiere, La Gazza Ladra, Guillaume Tell,* Rossini. PRINCIPAL SINGERS. Mdes. Persiani, Molteni, Grisi, Brambilla; MM. Conti,* Fornasari, Mario, Lablache, F. Lablache. BALLETS. *La Tarantule, Giselle, Ondine, Alma, Le Delire d'un Peintre.* PRINCIPAL DANCERS. Mdes. Fanny Elssler, Dumilatre,* Cerito; MM. St. Léon, Perrot.

THE YEAR 1843

S regarded music, the Italian season of 1843 was dry and unsatisfactory. The opera houses had come to an absolute dependence on Donizetti for novelties, the star of Signor Verdi not yet having risen on this side of the Alps. His name had reached England by the agency of an Englishwoman—Mrs. Alfred Shaw —who had made her first appearance on the stage, in Italy, in his *Oberto* (I think his first opera), and whose letters home spoke of the maestro as a composer of promise; but for the hour there was no one to be heard excepting Donizetti. He was then near the end of his creations, since, shortly after *Don Pasquale* was produced, his mind gave way (as has been told), and his life of incessant brain and fancy and bodily indulgence came to its painful solution in imbecility, and, not long afterwards, in death.

That *Linda* is a work which has not had its fair share of success among Donizetti's works I feel so often as the long list of them comes before me. It was written with a careful solidity not tried for in many of the operas slightly flung off by him. The story, founded on a sentimental French drama, *La Grâce de Dieu* (which Madame Albert used to act in London so pathetically), is balanced betwixt what is lachrymose and what is disagreeable, and fails to provide that direct appeal to the sympathies which another sentimental opera story, kindred to it in quality (that of *La Somnambula*), furnishes.

But among the music to this opera there is some of Donizetti's best. The Savoyard tune, belonging to the Savoyard peasant boy with his hurdy-gurdy, is more characteristic than was the habit with the composer. The duet of soprano and tenor in the first act has become a stock piece; the finale, showing the departure of the simple hill people for the town, has in it something real and touching. The second act is weaker, because the opera book maker overwhelmed his heroine with four duets; the first, betwixt the deluded peasant girl and her faithful boy friend who finds her out;

143

the second, with the insolent rake who persecutes her with his coarse solicitations; the third, with the courtly lover who deluded her, in quiet disguise; the fourth, with her father, in which she offers him alms, and he—little having guessed to whom he was applying—in his homely virtue denounces the child who has marked the hill châlet with shame. All this is ill-considered, because too tightly straining the artist who has to present herself in these four doubtful situations; and after these, to conclude this luckless act, comes one of those scenes of incipient madness by which it would almost seem as if Donizetti had been prophetically fascinated, so frequently do they recur in his operas. The drama, I repeat, is one ill laid out for music; since the third act—in which the crazed maiden's sense returns, and her lover does her justice, and her tempter is confounded, and her parents are thankfully ecstatic—is (for opera) a situation as old as the hills—of Chamouni.

Of *Don Pasquale* I have already spoken as the last, and not the least blithe, of comic Italian operas. The perfection with which its comedy was rendered by Madame Grisi, Signor Mario, and Lablache will not, it may be feared, be presently seen again. They revelled in the easy music, and Lablache seemed especially to court favour by presenting the farce of fatness trying to make itself seductive. It used to be said in Paris that the bouquet which the dear, silly hero of the farce-opera wore in the coat which stuck to him with as terrible a closeness as the outside garment of a sausage does to the contents within, was offered, night after night, by anonymous admirers. But throughout the entire farce of Lablache's performances nothing was more admirable than his entire avoidance of grossness or coarse imitation. There was, with him, that security which only belongs to persons of rare and admirable tact; and, with that security, the highest power of expressing comedy, tragedy, or grotesque,—because it belongs to one who will risk nothing hazardous, but who is not afraid of daring anything extraordinary. When I hear of this person's style, and that person's high note, and when I think of Lablache, I am tempted to feel as if I had parted company with real comic genius on the musical stage for ever!

To return to Donizetti's share in this work of his dying brain,— the serenade, with its burthen of voices and guitars, written for

Signor Mario, tells no tale of a dying brain, but rather is the song of one young in love, in life, in gaiety. Now it is hardly to be heard without a certain sadness, when the impending close of its composer's busy and wasted life is recollected. The opera, it is said, was the work of three weeks. It is certainly one of Donizetti's gayest.

The company this year was not satisfactory. The process of imperceptible substitution of what was second for what was first-rate had steadily set in as a principle of management. The great singers of the troop left sang under discouragement. Inferior ones were thrust forward, with too obvious a hardihood.

For some time there had been employed a system of cajoling the press till then tried on a very small scale; and, howsoever complimentary to those of "the fourth estate," anything but flattering to the taste and judgment of our amateurs. The "puff preliminary," by aid of which whiting's eyes were to be made to pass for pearls, had begun, with regard to our Italian Opera, to assume forms of an invention and a courage hitherto unknown in England. By way (it may be presumed) of reducing the expenses of an establishment the name of which was synonymous with Chancery suits, mortgages, and their consequences, a steady intention of substituting cheaper and less perfect artists for the excellent ones who had satisfied the public, not merely by their individual genius, but by their mutual understanding in combination, began to manifest itself. It was to be draped and masked, however, by every possible device. Curiosity and mystery were to be set to work by the artful aid of the paragraph-monger. It being gently intimated that the *corps* of our Italian Opera (as it stood) was growing indolent and senile, and that its members were overweening in their pretensions, we next began to read of *this* peerless voice, secured at a fabulous price, of *the other* Southern beauty, with eyes like the moon and a "cypress waist," of some magnificent Don Juan—the real, original Don Juan, and the finest bass in the world —who had been known as the "Terror of Husbands" in Mexico. No one henceforth, were he a star of second or third magnitude, was allowed to arrive in London without a symphony in the style of Caleb Balderstone—about Mysie's red herrings.

This year the management resolved to make a success for Signor Fornasari, as substitute for Signor Tamburini. The new baritone was a tall, dashing man; he possessed a very handsome face, a sufficient voice, though its quality was not pleasant—and pretension enough and to spare. He was one who sang with bad method and confidence, and who, though not obtrusively vulgar, must have impressed everyone with the conviction that he could merely have been successful among inferior artists, and in second-rate capitals. His first appearance in *Belisario* imposed on many persons. I confess to have been among the many imposed on. There was something fresh, intense, and original, in the ways of Signor Fornasari, whether as singer or actor, which seemed to bespeak a pleasant and honest nature. May none of us ever grow too old to welcome a young talent, nor too critical when a new appeal is made to our sympathies! Signor Fornasari's triumph in *Belisario* was complete. It was the first of very many similar triumphs. There were plaudits, glowing criticisms, a full theatre, and myrmidons running to and fro to prime the half-instructed or those timid in pronouncing judgment with an assurance that this new singer was the greatest marvel whom opera had yet seen in baritone form. The world likes to believe (up to a certain point); but well-a-day for those who have memories, and who cannot shut their ears to the past, let the present be ever so forcibly thrust into them! That sensibility and excitement which gave to Signor Fornasari's first appearance a false air of genius, dwindled, flattened, and faded, night after night, part after part. The tremulous quality of his voice (that vice of young Italy, bad schooling, and false notions of effect) became more monotonous and tiresome than the coldest placidity could have been. His execution (there was none required in *Belisario,* but much in Signor Rossini's operas) proved rough, and belonging to a school of pretext, not of reality. I think (great as was the seeming success of the hour) that Signor Fornasari's name might be totally forgotten in England, were it not that the chronicler has to tell all that has passed within his experience. But the success was a step on the stair downward so far as the art of dramatic singing is concerned.

The orchestra of the Opera, on the other hand, had been worked up, by this time, into great beauty and European renown; and the chorus had, by the same able conductor, been made respectable, if not (as now) attractive.

THE YEAR 1844

OPERAS. *I Puritani, Norma,* Bellini, *Il Matrimonio,* Cimarosa; *Don Carlos,** Costa; *Adelia, Don Pasquale, Lucia, Lucrezia, Anna Bolena,* Donizetti; *Zampa,* Hérold; *Don Giovanni,* Mozart; *Corrado d'Altamura,** Ricci; *La Cenerentola, Semiramide, Otello, La Gazza,* Rossini. PRINCIPAL SINGERS. Mdes. Persiani, Favanti,* Grisi, Rosetti;* MM. Corelli,* Fornasari, Felice,* F. Lablache, Paltoni,* Lablache, Mario, Moriani. BALLETS. *Esmeralda,** *La Vivandière,** *Zélie,** *La Paysanne.** PRINCIPAL DANCERS. Mdes. Carlotta Grisi, Cerito, Fanny Elssler; MM. Perrot, St. Léon.

THE YEAR 1844

IT is impossible to forget the odd events of this season, by which the ruin of Italian opera, in the Haymarket, was pushed a substantial step forward. There was great apparent bustle, small real result.

Three new operas were produced. The worthiest of these was Signor Costa's *Don Carlos,* which opera had nevertheless not the good fortune to please the public. Everyone knows the honours paid to a prophet in his own country; but there may have been other reasons why a work so conscientiously written in the Italian style was denied a place on the stage. Elsewhere the general possibility of any great conductor being a great composer has been considered. An inventor must have the strength of a Hercules and the self-abstraction of a Simon Stylites who, having dealt with the inventions of others incessantly, can give to his own fantasies and creations any remarkable individuality and freshness. Then the story of *Don Carlos* is a singularly gloomy and painful one for an opera book. The contriver of words and situations for music has no power of redeeming the oppressive sorrow of its incidents, as a Schiller could do for the spoken drama by the elevated nobility of his De Posa. Divested of subtleties of character, the play becomes a strained melodrama without any redeeming novelty of situation. Yet *Don Carlos* is full of good music; the orchestra throughout it is handled with a thorough knowledge of effect and colour; Signor Costa, in this part of his writings, having proved himself a countryman of Cherubini, whose skilful, natural, yet striking use of instruments cannot be too earnestly recommended as model. One trio, for three male voices, is so solid and fine that it ought not to have been so soon forgotten.

The attempt to place Hérold's *Zampa* on the stage here, in a translated form, had been already tried by a German company; but in England we have never taken very kindly to French serious opera. No acceptance here has been procured for Spontini's *Vestale; Robert le Diable* is received with indifference till this day.

Till 1844, it may have been remarked that many of the musical dramas most cherished in Paris have been, in London, stripped of much of their most important features and served up in the form of ballet.   The Italians since the days of Rameau have, as a nation, set their faces against French opera; and our dilettanti have no less foolishly confined themselves to the pleasure derived from two schools of music, in place of enjoying three.   Only very lately has the Chinese Wall of such prejudice been forced down in a place or two.   To myself, since the hour when my musical understanding began to wake such narrowness has seemed inconceivable.   But I have never been able to rate *Zampa* as highly as it has been rated in France or in Germany, nor to join in the enthusiasm which the name of Hérold, or in the regret which his death in full manhood, have excited.   There is something harsh in his brilliancy, something far-fetched in his sentiment; his tunes are often sickly and puerile, or fail to satisfy the ear by some far-fetched interval or rhythm which, however national, sound somewhat out of place. For here and there it is evident that Hérold, during his occupation as accompanist at the Italian Opera in Paris, had caught some of those peculiarities of Signor Rossini's manner which that subtle master modified when he wrote for Paris, with wondrous grace in *Le Comte Ory,* with surprising power of transformation in *Guillaume Tell.*   This want of nature and settlement, which could be hardly illustrated here, is increased by the fact of the hero's part in *Zampa* having been written for one of those mixed voices, common enough in France,[1] exceptional everywhere else.   Indeed, it might be fairly said that M. Chollet, the original Zampa, was an excellent actor and an adroit musician, but one who had no real voice, his organ being a composition of baritone, tenor, falsetto, in no part of it tuneable or graciously delivered.   Thus the music of Zampa's part has, under alterations, been committed to both bass and to tenor singers in Italy and Germany—of course losing some of its peculiar effects in either case.   Here it was entrusted to a

---

[1] It is impossible to make acquaintance with French opera and not become cognizant of the fact. Allowing for every possible difference of the diapason caused by modern desire for effect, it must be seen that the male parts in many of Gluck's operas (to give a most striking instance) were written for French voices—baritones with high notes—which have no representatives elsewhere, save, perhaps, in such a case as Herr Pischek's. Martin, at the Opéra Comique, was a type-singer of this kind, and Chollet was his representative, as is now M. Montaubry (1861) the representative of Chollet.

French gentleman who had no voice at all, no stage experience, was totally untried in Italian; the same who sang in London under five different names, as Signor Felice, Signor Planco, Monsieur Félix, Monsieur Planque, and M. Delmar.   The luckless calculation on which this aspirant had been fished out of the depths of France, and been brought hither for his own mortification and for the discredit of a first-class theatre, must be left to be settled by those who write the story of affairs behind the curtain.   But the year 1844 was a year when experiments of the kind, as will be presently seen, took the wildest form of offence to public common sense.   A more rueful failure than this deceived Frenchman's I have never seen.   The promises made for him in print beforehand availed him nothing. He was modest enough, however, to lose presence of mind, and to be aware of the disgraceful absurdity of his attempt ere he had been ten minutes on the stage: failed in every point—of music, of singing, of entrance.   I think I now see Madame Persiani (who had always a somewhat anxious and ill-used look), in utter despair at some vagary transacted by him, seat herself resolutely down, with an appearance of giving up the entire matter as hopeless, and of contemptuous compassion for herself, which were almost farcical, and which provoked laughter at her helpless situation, in the midst of hisses for Zampa's incompetence.   This was her last season at the Haymarket Opera House.

Subsequently Signor Fornasari was prevailed on to attempt the unlucky opera, but in vain.   Under better circumstances the work was tried again in another Italian theatre here, a few seasons ago, but with the same result.   It may be doubted whether the day for Zampa will ever come in England; in spite of the success which always attended its dashing overture (here played marvellously) and in spite of the breadth of the final duet, where Hérold rises, for the only time, into the broad, sweeping passion of serious opera.

Not more successful was the essay to introduce Signor Frederico Ricci as a composer, by his *Corrado d'Altamura,* though at that time he was enjoying a certain vogue in Italy—a vogue completely extinguished by Signor Verdi's successes.   Yet that there is an inkling of the new effects in Signor Ricci's music seems to me, so far as I can recollect this opera, which was once (or twice only, at the utmost) played.   There is the same rude noise in the instrumentation, under pretext of passion, the same violence in breaking the phrases of the show music for the prima donna, by jerks and sharp cries, of pushing the animation onwards by the use of unisons and syncopations, of driving every effect to a spasmodic crescendo, as have since become the law; the same devices which have worn their authority out by their extravagance and falsity. One bravura, given with amazing vigour by Madame Grisi—who could then bring any desired amount of force to bear, and seemed to like grappling with a novelty—excited the audience. There is also a pleasing terzetto towards the close of the opera, which might have been recognized had the music been decently rendered, or had our public been in its usual mood of somewhat torpid indulgence. But this was the last character attempted by the English lady who sang as Mademoiselle Favanti; and her story—a repetition of Signor Felice's, with variations—had, in its progress of her singing one part after another worse and worse, so torn to pieces the patience of the audience that she was ignominiously treated; and the distaste of the public to pretensions so utterly baseless as those advanced for her—and fought for till the last with a desperation which became offensive—may have unconsciously helped to the rejection of Signor Ricci as a composer. Since then none of his works have been tried here. Of the lady it is necessary to speak separately.

A singer with claims far superior to those of Mademoiselle Favanti—Signor Napoleone Moriani—brought to England, is the last novelty of the year 1844 to be spoken of. He came with a real Italian reputation; but he came too late in his own career, and too early for a public that had not forgotten what the great Italian tenors had been at. Then, too, Signor Mario was already on that vantage-ground as first favourite, which he has since never left for an hour. Signor Moriani must have had one of the most superb and richly-strong tenor voices ever heard, with tones full of expression as well as of force. But either the reign of false taste had set in, encouraging him to drawl and to bawl, or his voice had never been trained. Ere it came here, his command over it was gone. Yet I was deceived for a while, by its remarkable beauty, into fancying the newcomer an artist from whom much might be obtained. He had a striking, though heavily-moulded face, resembling that of the great man whose name he bore; he was earnest in action. This again was some variety in a man aspiring to the succession of Rubini, whose indifference and powerlessness in scenes of passion had begun to be felt in proportion as his voice came near being inaudible.   This earnestness deceived me.   I saw Signor Moriani twice in *Lucia* ere I began to be aware that the extreme prolongation of his last scene was wearisome—for other reasons than because the scene itself has always wearied me. Later it occurred to me that he had made its sickliness doubly heavy, instead of redeeming it by delicacy.   When one compared him in it with that of M. Duprez (also a weighty tenor and an impassioned actor, and whose voice was already on its wane), the difference betwixt what is false and true in style—whether it be ponderous or florid, impressive or subtle—made itself felt, once and for ever.

Night by night, part by part, did the new tenor lose some of his first favour.   A public once disposed to be wearied can never be enkindled afterwards.   Better even (it has been said) to shock the world than to make it yawn.   The most strenuous resolutions behind the curtain, represented in the criticisms of the hour, could not sustain Signor Moriani.   Yet how many worse tenors from Italy, with good voices, who have since arrived, have I not lived to hear —and to see!

While the talk is of tenors, Signor Mario's attempt at the most difficult part in the Italian repertory—Otello—must not be overlooked.   Why and how it was a flight beyond his reach, even when his voice was in full bloom, and when he had every grace of manly beauty to recommend the personification, may be perhaps gathered in pages to come.

ENGLISH SINGERS AT THE ITALIAN OPERA

INCE the days of Mrs. Billington, who could hold her own against a Southern no less fascinating than Madame Grassini, it may be asserted that no female artist belonging to this country has been able to maintain anything approaching to a first position at the Italian Opera House in London. Yet many have appeared there,—more than will be remembered by the generality of hearers and readers, even during the period to which these notes refer.

A step for a year or two over their boundary, so far as 1827, may be permitted in order to commemorate one of the cleverest of the company, who might have done good service to the stage had not her natural powers, at first barely sufficient, prematurely given way. This was Miss Fanny Ayton, who was more in the form and order of an Italian singer for comic opera than any of my countrywomen whom I have since heard or seen attempt it. Her voice had been trained by good masters; it was a weak voice—not unlike that of Mdlle. Piccolomini, but more supple and flexible; and it had a certain sprightly life in it. She had considerable execution, a certain piquancy and taste of her own, and—what English artists generally lack so largely—accent. Her appearance was pleasing; if it was not distinguished, not vulgar. Were such a singer as she was to appear now, I can imagine her succeeding in a certain range of parts. But the young girl had the misfortune to arrive here at a time when the great foreign artists were the rule rather than the exception, and when "the Town"—totally differently composed from "the Town" of to-day—was in no respect disposed to be merciful to any newcomer who came without an immense foreign reputation. The new Rosina and Fiorilla excited some attention and a little wonderment by her clever ease on the stage and her fluent Italian; but this was merely for the moment. Her voice had small charm; and she had hardly sung here for three months ere its intonation gave way at once and for ever, the tone becoming at the last too painful to be endured. She struggled on for a second season, in what then passed for paraphrased foreign opera on the English stage; she went down with Italian companies (in those days rarities) into our provincial towns; she fought up courageously against disappointment and the failure of means for a year or two; and then passed out of public sight.

About the same time it was that Madame Vestris made her last appearance on our Italian stage. There, if she had possessed musical patience and energy, she might have queened it; because she possessed (half Italian by birth) one of the most luscious of low voices—found, since Lear's time, excellent in women—great personal beauty, an almost faultless figure, which she knew how to adorn with consummate art, and no common stage address. But a less arduous theatrical career pleased her better; and so she too could not, one might perhaps say because she *would* not, remain on the Italian stage.

The next British lady who attempted the feat was Miss Paton. Those who recollect that lady's style, and the means of popularity which she preferred to cultivate, need no words to explain why there was not the slightest chance of her grouping with any foreign playfellows.

Indeed, whatever be his, or her, endowments, it must be always an ill chance for a home artist to sing in a foreign language on the stage in England. We are curiously bad linguists ourselves (*were*, I perhaps should say), but, before the curtain, we cannot endure bad language in those who amuse us. We are too apt to spend on others the critical labour which, were it applied at home, would be greatly to the ease and advantage of polyglot society. The very few among us that are *not* bad linguists are given to be unmercifully severe in the pride of their own acquirements and facility. Behind the curtain, on the other hand, there are pitfalls and sunken rocks still more difficult to cope with—small and great perfidies, ungenerous rivalries, certain to be found in a calling so largely engaging personal vanity, and impossible to evade in a world where people must work with comrades whom they dread or despise, with whom they are perpetually thrown into contact, having abundant idling time for scandals to breed in. All such evils come out in a form more or less pronounced wherever there is a theatre; but

nowhere with so vehement a power to thwart, injure, and discon-
cert, as in the case which I am considering.

In the early time of our Royal Academy of Music, a young English lady or two might be occasionally brought thence, as filling the
second and third parts at the Opera House; but the next of our
countrywomen who need be named as making some position there
was Madame Albertazzi. She had many things in her favour—an
agreeable presence and a musical contralto voice, not ill-trained.
For a time it was fair to hope that she might prove an acceptable,
if not an astonishing artist, could once her stage inexperience be corrected. But the time of correction never came. Hers was not
(after all) so much inexperience as an utter lifelessness—one more
hopelessly cold than anything I have witnessed in a singer so fairly
endowed as she was; a resigned and cool indifference, which had
something of the automaton in its quality, and which, after beginning by wearying, ended by irritating her audiences. The German
tale of the actress contrived by science and worked by springs, who
tumbled into a dead heap of a rouged and leather doll from time to
time, could hardly have had a closer illustration than from this
pretty woman—with a good voice, good training, but with the absence of living charm. To the end of her career—for, at a later
period, Madame Albertazzi sang in English opera—she remained
the same—inanimate beyond the power of intelligence to warm,
or practical experience to quicken into the mere semblance of motion.

Of the next Englishwoman who, in the strange year 1844, made
some impression at our Italian Opera, it would be pleasanter for
me not to speak; but the career seemingly determined for her, the
manner in which it was carried out, and its results, can be overlooked by no historian. The comedy began with a series of exciting and mysterious paragraphs, put forth in the morning papers.
A real treasure, said these, had been discovered at Naples—a young
lady with an exceptional and splendid voice, boundless execution,
and remarkable personal beauty, who was setting on fire the capital
of the Two Sicilies by her appearance in *La Cenerentola*. When
one attestation of this kind after another had prepared the way,
next came hints that there were hopes of securing this Phœnix for
England. A few weeks later we were invited to rejoice that such
hopes were certainties, because then, the print-shops began to tell

of the coming enchantress, in a lithograph which bore out report. A more charming head has not often been shown by the skilful hand that drew it. Further precise and minute warrants "followed suit." It was announced that Madame Pasta had expressed the highest admiration of the coming young lady's talent. She was heralded, in short, not by a mere note, but rather by an opera of preparation, with overture, chorus, orchestra, solo singers, dresses and decorations—all complete, and on the most superb and extensive scale.

Some inquiry, however, ventured in honest curiosity by those, like myself, who could have no dream of the reality, made persons having memories ponder and wonder. Many, like myself, had heard the new Cenerentola at home some years before. Many, like myself, could credit the splendid compass of her voice (of three octaves almost), and its promise of fine quality. But it was less encouraging to recollect certain peculiarities—among these, a measureless courage in ornament, considering the utter deficiency of its execution, a memory more than ordinarily uncertain, an absence of perception when memory failed, and an ignorance of music which six months' training ought to have rectified. Miracles are rare in this age. Then, the plea of nervousness avails little; since those who know music the best are the most ready to admit it. A wrong note on the piano, a false phrase in the voice, may befall any performer overcome with fear, be he old or young; but a deliberately gratuitous change into bad grammar of a musical passage, for the sake of exhibition, or the singing through an entire ballad without any variation in the accompaniment of the notes of the first chord, these things argue qualities out of which it is very hard to fabricate a real artist. These things I had heard, and by their very extremity and strangeness could hardly be forgotten by me.

The curtain drew up for *La Cenerentola,* and Mademoiselle Favanti was discovered in that exquisite introductory scene, than which even Signor Rossini never wrote anything more exquisite. As was the due of so striking-looking a person, as was only natural after the preludes into the value of which few had cared to inquire, the new Cenerentola was welcomed with that sort of universal applause which terrifies, but which yet inspirits its object. And thus, too, when she opened her mouth to sing "Una volta," the natural richness of her lower notes awakened the rapture anew and louder.   But in this very self-same simple fireside ballad she gratuitously introduced a turn flagrantly out of the key—exactly as she had done in old times.   I wondered; but the ballad was called for as vehemently as if Madame Alboni had sung it; and with the repetition came the ignorant turn over again.   It was obviously a cherished grace with the new Cenerentola!

> "Where ignorance is bliss,
> 'Tis folly to be wise."

The opera proceeded in no better fashion and with the loudest plaudits (considering the pretending badness of the performance) ever heard.   Never before—not when Mdlle. Taglioni was young, and Mdlle. Fanny Elssler in the noontide of her witcheries—had "the enthusiasm carried in baskets" to the upper regions rained itself down on the goddess of the night in such number, such enormous size, such costliness of bouquets.   The scene, with all its mock triumph, was humiliating beyond any spectacle of the kind at which I have ever been present, at home or abroad.   Of its sequel no sincere person could entertain one instant's doubt.   Yet the morning after, those at a distance who read, might be excused for believing that a new Malibran—nay, more than a Malibran —had come.

Time, however, may be trusted.   No predetermined support (supposing such ever so lavishly organized), no blowing of the trumpets (supposing the brass ever so Corinthian), can save their victim.   Mdlle. Favanti attempted other characters, in every new one more and more distinctly displaying her unfitness for the greatness thrust upon her; unable to sing, unable to act, unable to recollect her music; still, maintaining an air of self-assertion, not wonderful, considering what the fooling of false praise had been.   Of all the opera feats which I recollect, the most extraordinary was made when she was thrust into *Don Giovanni*, as one capable of taking part in Mozart's master-opera.   In the concerted piece, "L'empio," when she has to support, to answer, to aid her comrades, she was totally lost; and (thanks to Signor Costa) the orchestra and her comrades leaped after her, so as to cover her incapacity for the moment.

But incapacity is not to be covered.   It is sure to display itself, ten times more rudely and crudely, because of the rapacity and credulity of those who protect it. In *La Gazza Ladra,* when she had to sing with Madame Grisi as heroine, as Pippo, she found it expedient to pass off her want of tune, time, and execution, by aid of a laced handkerchief,—in the sweetest stage propriety, belonging to a peasant boy of Palaiseau! No singer on the stage with her could provide for her errors, her omissions, her courageous incompetence. But ere the end of the season she was hissed off the stage (a painful, yet not an unnatural,[1] last act to the farce), to reappear there only once again after the lapse of many years; and again to show that she was the old Cenerentola—no better than she had been.

This an over-true tale—sad, bad, and sorrowful. For who will not follow the so-called artist home into her triumphs, prospects, destroyed hopes? I should not here have tried to tell it again, had it not been for the injury which the false success of so utterly worthless a singer (no matter how gifted by nature) was permitted to be inflicted on those who were set round her during the gingerbread fair of her first triumphs, and for the bitterness with which persecution attended those who ventured to hint in print that Mademoiselle Favanti was *not,* for the present, a second and a better Malibran.

There is one more appearance of a countrywoman on our foreign opera-stage to be recorded—that of the Irish lady, Miss Catherine Hayes. This was made under different circumstances, and many years later. She was a singer who had a right to a hearing at home, in consequence of the real impression made by her in Italy, where her graceful voice and presence and her sensibility had won for her a genuine popularity. She was there accepted as a stranger deserving every courtesy. Her style, too, pleased in Italy, because it approached the long-drawn, false, over-emphatic

---

[1] Not unnatural, perhaps, but surely a relic of barbarism. No woman, were men courteous, should be thus cruelly insulted, unless the woman should have forgot the decencies of woman's modesty. Let those who have placed her in so false a position be brought to account. This has been done in Italy where, after the very bad singing of the wife of a public favourite, *he* was called for, and was hissed violently for allowing his wife to appear. But it is not always that the men of Italy are so temperately courteous. I was present, some years ago, in La Scala, Milan, at the representation of an opera—*Saul*—by Maestro Cannetti. The unfortunate prima donna (who has since gained some reputation) did not please the Lombard dilettanti. When the quick movement of her great air began, some twenty coarse male creatures stood up in their stalls and sang it with her; when she retired, in still more brutal fashion crying, in their harsh Milanese voices—*"Brutta! brutta!"*

style which Italy has liked since Signor Verdi's reign began, but which we have not as yet accepted.   I have noted (by the way), as a characteristic frequent in artists Irish by birth, a tendency towards what is sentimental and deliberate in singing—which is singular in a people so mercurial in temperament as they.   On our English ears it never fails to produce an impression of weariness after a while.   And in our modern days, the old-fashioned spinners-out of our glees, who delighted in a "dying fall" pianissimo—the ballad-singers, who had no mercy on the patience of their listeners—are no longer thought gracious, willowy and expressive.   We have learned that measurement of time is of some value in music: we even drawl a little less on the stage than we did formerly.   Let it be added that this effect to drawl and to slacken time is sure, after a while, to tempt those who attempt it into exaggerations of which they are unaware; that the very style which calls for the nicest possible regulation has within itself an element of disease almost impossible to cure.   Let me again remind my world that an Italian success in nowise ensures an English one, as has been proved by the coldness with which artists, in Italy so popular as Mdes. Frezzolini, Tadolini, and Barbieri-Nini, have been met in London.   We English stand under blame and contempt abroad as a people devoid of delicacy in connoisseurship, whenever we fail to equal the raptures which have been stirred on the other side of the Alps—how far justly or otherwise it would not be my place here to determine.

There is no doubt, however, that Miss Hayes approached nearer the standard of Italian than of English perfection; and ere long her success in her national music, especially at home, was found so much more substantial and available than any to be gained as the representative of Lucia or Linda or Amina, or the sentimental parts which had earned her showers of roses, garlands, bouquets, and sonnets, in Italy, that she did wisely in changing her career, and in principally, thenceforth, confining herself to the concert room.

Now that she is gone, why should it not be said that she was no musician?—and thus was fit, on our stage, for no change or adaptability beyond her two or three sentimental parts (every cantilena in which had to be much elongated), in our concert room for nothing beyond an opera song or two, given with some appearance of vocal style (totally without verbal declamation), and some national ballads, which never seemed to arrive at their end.   Her

"Last Rose of Summer" always seemed to me long-drawn enough to hold out till it should come to be transformed into "The Rose-bud of Spring." She was most gentle, most gracious, yet (because inarticulate) rather wearisome.

Two words, by way of postscript to this chapter on a delicate subject, may be devoted to another of the English ladies who maintained for many years considerable favour on the Italian stage—Madame Albertini—One appearance!

THE YEAR 1845

OPERAS. *La Somnambula, Norma, Il Pirata,* Bellini; *Lucia, L'Elisir, Linda, Roberto Devereux,* Donizetti; *Il Giuramento,* Mercadante; *Cosi fan tutte,* Mozart; *Semiramide, Otello,* Rossini; *Ernani,** Verdi. PRINCIPAL SINGERS. Mdes. Grisi, Castellan,* Rita Borio,* Rossi-Caccia,* Brambilla,* Rosetti; MM. Mario, Moriani, Botelli,* Fornasari, Lablache, Baroilhet,* Corelli. BALLETS. *La Dryade,** *Rosida,** *Le Pas de Quatre.** PRINCIPAL DANCERS. Mdes. Cerito, Grahn,* Carlotta Grisi, Taglioni, The Viennese Children; MM. St. Léon, Perrot. M. Félicien David's *Desert Symphony.*

THE strength of this season lay in the ballet, or rather in a single dance, executed by Mdes. Taglioni, Carlotta Grisi, Cerito, and Grahn. Perhaps the fascination of the "twinkling feet" of these four ladies, grouped as Chalon has put on record, was devised to withdraw attention from the inattention to the interests of opera, and from the gradual substitution of inferior for superior singers, which was obviously the system of management.

The only novelty in opera attempted during the year 1845 was the *Ernani* of Signor Verdi—by this time become an Italian celebrity who was no longer to be overlooked. The first work of his introduced here shared the fate of Bellini's and Donizetti's first works in England. It was received with curiosity rather than sympathy. To myself it gave hopes which have not been justified by its writer's subsequent operas, more popular though they have been. His style, for a moment, struck the ear by a certain rude force and grandeur. How vulgar these have seemed to us, owing to reiteration, will be presently dwelt on.

Ernani was spiritedly performed. The heroine, Madame Rita Borio, was, in every sense of the word, a stout singer, with a robust voice—a lady not in the least afraid of the violent use to which the latest Italian maestro forces his heroines, but able to scream in time, and to shout with breath enough to carry through the most animated and vehement movement of those devised by him. Owing to want of personal attraction, this lady, who proved herself estimable in other music, did not enjoy a success in London such as singers far inferior to herself have since commanded.

To replace Madame Persiani, was brought Madame Castellan; who thenceforward enjoyed, during some years, a settled occupation of trust and variety on our two Italian opera stages. So far as industry and general utility, a pleasing person and a competent voice, entitled their owner to public favour, the new French prima donna was eminently qualified. But she fell short of complete excellence in every point save that of adaptability.   Her voice, an extensive soprano, having both upper and lower notes sufficient in power, was never thoroughly in tune.   The tone, too, of the voice, though not disagreeable, was somehow squeezed in its production. There was no stint of execution on her part; but neither scale, nor shake, nor arpeggio, nor interval was thoroughly wrought out.   In concerted music Madame Castellan's voice (as may be often re-marked with French voices) refused to blend with other voices. Her appearance was genteel and piquant, and her acting in gentle parts was unembarrassed, if not very expressive.   This may ap-pear to be—indeed is—a character made up of negatives; and herein may have lain the cause why Madame Castellan, though she was always courteously received, never excited the slightest en-thusiasm.   One might say of her, once for all, that she spoiled nothing, that she created nothing.   She could be only rated as a prima donna in a second-class opera house.   Her amenity of man-ner, however, and the sedulous care she always showed to keep faith with the public, maintained her long in London; and since she has passed from the stage she has never been replaced by any one equivalent to her.

The third novelty of 1845—also a French lady—stands, I think, in a category altogether different.   Madame Rossi-Caccia was one of those clever persons whose destiny it is, never (so runs their complaint) to have been rightly comprehended.   The solution of their enigma may be that there is little to comprehend, save that affectation which spoils everything, be it ever so cleverly managed or prepared.   The lady was prima donna at the Opéra Comique of Paris for a while.   M. Auber wrote his *Part du Diable* for her there.   She was the heroine, too, of one of the merriest musical farces ever seen—M. Montfort's *Polichinelle* (a little opera which has unaccountably perished).   There, however, she failed to keep her ground.   She was too good for her work.   Her arena (she conceived) was to be a larger stage; and accordingly she passed over into Italy, there to get the stamp of authentication for which so many have tried, and which, with so many, has proved the merest of old delusions.   After this she sang at the Grand Opera of Paris—for which, again, she was too good, or not good enough (I forget which).   On the strength of some of the above pretexts she was brought here, with what result needs not be told.

She was a clever woman of an uncertain age, who had two or three
soprano notes far above an ordinary voice—and her voice was very
ordinary—and who held out on those cruel notes with a fatiguing
persistence, helped out by the play of eyes and of shoulders. I
never saw a woman act with so many shrugs of the latter—
when the emotion became overmastering—as did Madame Rossi-
Caccia.

It will be seen that the French element was already beginning
to take a large share in our Italian Opera House, owing to the decadence of the great Italian art of singing, and to English unwill-
ingness to accept vocalists who could only bawl and gesticulate, in
place of the real women and men who, by their singing and acting,
had for a century past charmed London into a knowledge and a
naturalization of Italian opera. The third new singer, far higher
in class than either of the two ladies, was also French. M. Baroilhet had possessed a winning and rare baritone voice. This, however, had been torn to pieces on the other side of the Alps, where
he had been singing for some years in the operas of the new school,
so-called; and when he came home to Paris not much was left beyond a certain breadth of method and warmth of style, to which his
peculiar appearance added some emphasis and effect. No small
share of the French success of Donizetti's *La Favorita,* commissioned for Madame Stoltz, who then ruled the French Opera, it
was said, and could control its reigning powers "to have or to
leave," was due to M. Baroilhet's singing of the King's song,
"Pour tant d'amour," on which every amateur baritone rushed, till
the tune became as stale as Signor Verdi's "Il balen" is now: neither
tune having vigour to support itself after the first moment of fashion has passed. He was picturesque on the stage, to see—though
his picturesqueness was pushed to the verge of grotesque, and owing much to the stage tailor. The singing went with the face and
figure—at least, when M. Baroilhet was here; his singing having
just those effects and defects which leave an English public doubtful whether the public is to laugh or to cry. It is curious that the
self-same audiences who are insensible to the conventionalisms of
our own stage diction—who will bear any amount of mouthing, or
drawling, or chopping-up of the text in the poetry of Shakespeare
without wincing, under pretext of tradition—remain so undecided
or break out so sarcastically when any manifestation of earnestness,

beyond the pale of their own rubric of attitude or pronunciation, is set before them.

This year, however, other breaches were made in the wall of our anti-Gallican prejudices than by the engagement of the three French singers just mentioned. M. Duprez was here for a second time—the finest dramatic tenor singer I have ever heard and seen on the stage, giving our careless countrymen not merely lessons how to sing, how to act so as to make natural disqualifications forgotten, but absolutely, too, how to speak their own language audibly and accurately. I have not heard since Braham's time—till Mr. Sims Reeves came—the great tenor solo, in the second part of the *Messiah*, "Thy Rebuke," so perfectly sung and said as by M. Duprez. He had had to fight for every word of his English; whereas our English singers seem, on a sort of set principle, to fight against their own language—or, otherwise, never to have learned to read. And the singing of M. Duprez, in this *Messiah* music—in English—was a much harder feat for a born Frenchman, except for a man born with such an indomitable will as himself, than it would be for any Italian singer to transform himself into a few French songs. Oratorio music is utterly beyond the comprehension of our neighbours. They have a notion of Méhul's *Joseph*. They have no reserve in putting the most sacred personages on the stage. They do not understand, or do not care to know, Handel. And yet this great French tenor, in the strength of his feeling for dramatic truth, propriety, and (most of all) his determination never to present himself without doing the best of his best, could master an unfamiliar style of music and a barbarous language (so our neighbours repute it to this day), and could sing when his voice was half gone; and could say when his new speech had hardly come to him—both his singing and his saying having such perfection of intellect (not of organ) as makes the *singing* and still more the *saying* by a foreigner remembered.

During this same year a Belgian company, at another theatre, was giving unmutilated and meritorious versions of the various works in the repertory of French opera, and was habituating our connoisseurs and critics to admit the existence of a third school of music, which is one as remarkable after its kind as the schools of Italy and Germany.

The history of French opera, as part and parcel of the singu-

larly coherent world of French art, has to be written for England.
Even so lately as thirty years ago, when Signor Rossini and M.
Meyerbeer were carrying on the work begun and continued by Lulli,
Rameau, Gluck, Sacchini, Lesueur, Spontini—when *La Muette* had
dazzled all Europe, an opera pronounced by Paganini, as it has
been said, to be the finest opera ever composed—the serious musical drama of France, and its singers, were spoken of by English
dilettanti with mockery. The same people who would take anything German on trust, or swoon in ecstacies over the sickliest and
most trite Italian music, did not so much despise as ignore the existence of a treasury rich in dramatic truth and beauty and musical
skill; and, fixing on certain national peculiarities of voice and manner, heaped ridicule on a race of singers who proved themselves
compatriots of Clairon, Le Kain, Duchesnois, Mars, and Talma.
Such toleration as the comic opera of Paris enjoyed—written by
men no less individual than Grétry, Dalayrac, Monsigny, Philidor,
Berton, Isouard, Boieldieu, and M. Auber—was owing to the
sprightliness of the acting rather than to the sparkle and *esprit* of
the music. I have told with what persistence every French opera
was travestied here to serve the uses of ballet during half of the
period to which these pages refer. It was long and late—perhaps
(in some small degree) owing to the perpetual representations of
a few persons who preferred enjoying *three* to enjoying *two* things
—ere the Englishman, who had enjoyed, in his reading and in his
sympathies, Molière and de Sevigné, and later Châteaubriand and
Hugo, consented to relax his irrational contempt against listening
and approval.

The experiment of 1845, however, met with only partial encouragement. Truth to say, as a body the Belgians, however meritorious and correct, are curiously heavy as musicians. Perhaps they
pay the penalty, belonging to mixed races, of deficiency in nationality; but that there is a German touch in their execution of French
music, and a French humour in their German interpretations, and
something of French and German mixed when they deal with Italian compositions, I have fancied so often as I have thought over
any performances largely enacted by natives of that rich and respectable land.

To return to the Italian Opera House: the performances of M.
Félicien David's *Desert Symphony* were a natural consequence of

the rage which that slight and pleasing work had excited in Paris on its production there. The excellence of our English execution of this symphony must not be forgotten to the credit of Signor Costa, as head of an admirable orchestra. That we fell short of the French raptures over M. David's picturesque work is no wonder, seeing that already the Symphony hardly now exists in Paris. The oriental grace and wildness of certain portions (such as the Danse d'Almées, which is a gem after its kind), could not give permanent life to a composition of such length, in which the constructive and sustaining power was so very small.

Great attempts were made to warm our public into the enjoyment of a troop of dancing children from Vienna—the odds and ends of the once famous children's ballets there. The institution had been broken up owing to the scandals it had originated—scandals too strong for even Austrian supineness in morals to wink at. Certainly if the two dozen girls who came to England were, in the least, fair specimens of what the establishment had produced, there was no compensation (if the word may be degraded so far) in their grace, skill, or promise, for the peril and corruption to which they and their predecessors had been exposed in a licentious metropolis. The show was pitiful and awkward; and (all credit be to English good taste and good feeling—not always to be relied on, however, even should the prodigy be clever, and the monster shocking enough), it was withdrawn, after a few exhibitions had satisfied "the Town" that the said exhibition was worthless and unattractive.

THE YEAR 1846

OPERAS. *I Puritani, La Somnambula,* Bellini; *Il Matrimonio,* Cimarosa; *Linda, Belisario, Anna Bolena, Lucrezia, L'Ajo nell' Imbarazzo,** Donizetti; *Don Giovanni,* Mozart; *Nino,* I Lombardi,* Ernani,* Verdi. PRINCIPAL SINGERS. Mdes. Sanchioli,* Corbari,* Castellan, G. Brambilla,* Grisi, Pasini;* MM. Corelli, Fornasari, Botelli, Mario, Lablache, F. Lablache. BALLETS. *Catarina,* Lalla Rookh.** PRINCIPAL DANCERS. Mdes. Grahn,* Cerito, Taglioni; MM. Perrot, St. Léon.

THE YEAR 1846

HIS was a year of confusion, the principal event of which was a forcible attempt to give Signor Verdi that place on the London stage which he already held in the opera houses of Italy. Two works, as yet unheard, were brought to hearing. The first was *Nino*—a grand opera offered in conjunction with the excitement of the re-opening of the theatre, elaborately, if not tastefully decorated, and with the appearance of a new set of artists and a new conductor.

Nino in England is *Nabucco* in Italy—an Old Testament opera, permitted in Catholic countries, but an opera which must here be rebaptized—even as Signor Rossini's *Mosé* had been for England. We English are not so hard, or so soft, as to be willing to see the personages of Holy Writ acted and sung in theatres. Hagar in the wilderness, Ruth gleaning among the "alien corn," Herodias with the head of John the Baptist in the charger, are subjects of personal exhibition which all thoughtful lovers of art in music must reject, on every principle of reverence and of taste, and from which the thoughtless would recoil,—because, perhaps, they are not so amusing as *La Traviata*. The castigation of *Nabucco* is a measure never to be carried out without loss of strength, character, and reality. Who could bear one of Shakespeare's plays acted from the text of Bowdler?

The other opera by Signor Verdi new to England fared, in one important respect, better than *Nabucco,* in which the frantic and ungracious part of the heroine had been given to Signora Sanchioli— a singer without the slightest charm, who figured strangely on the stage in her amazonian attire, and who screamed in a manner to which British ears were as yet unaccustomed. We have, since that time, been called on to habituate ourselves with *every—all—no* manner of screams in Italian singing. Signora Sanchioli accomplished no popularity, for herself or for the maestro. His *Lombardi*—a work subsequently arranged for the Grand Opera of

Paris as *Jerusalem*—had the aid of Madame Grisi and Signor Mario in the principal parts. The music, even then, betrayed the wear of the lady's peerless voice; and she sang it shyly rather than kindly. Her appearance, in her mediæval dress of crimson and blue veil, was superb. I recollect her figure as I do some picture from a Gothic missal. The sickly cavatina for the tenor, which the barrel-organs made us hate ere "Il balen" was thought of, was given delightfully by Signor Mario; and the rude vigour of certain concerted pieces made itself felt; but the opera did not stand. Even in Italy, I conceive, *I Lombardi* is laid by, as one of the less fortunate works of its writer. *Ernani,* never cordially received in this country, was at its second performance doomed by the miserable company of singers—grandly heralded in the papers—to whom it was entrusted.

The trial of Donizetti's *L'Ajo* was useless. That comic opera is not among his happy comic operas. This was all the musical novelty of the season, with the exception of another attempt to transform M. Auber's operas into ballets, in *Catarina*—a danced version of his extravagant, yet charming, *Diamans de la Couronne*.

This year Signor Costa quitted the Opera; and the orchestra, which he had brought to a point of perfection previously unknown in England, passed into other hands. It was a sign of change that the departure of a conductor could shake an opera house—a sign that discipline, and integrity, and thorough knowledge of the duty in hand by the man who undertakes such duty, be it in the Opera, be it in any other world, make their worth known, soon or late, in this honest country of ours. That the Italian Opera at Her Majesty's Theatre, then our only one, never recovered the loss of Signor Costa, is matter of operatic history. Show followed show, sham succeeded to sham, great singers came and went, but our world had been educated up to a point at which the entire performance was felt to be the real object of interest; and though (for a year or two) this and the other great singer made that meteoric impression which dazzles the public for a while, the year 1846 must be quoted as the first of some years of exhaustion and failure at the old House in the Haymarket.

This was the year when the air began to be stirred from afar by rumours of a new singing marvel, too shy to come to England. A more thoroughly distasteful subject than the machinery set in motion to recommend Mdlle. Jenny Lind cannot pass under any truthful writer's pen. It is not, however, to be escaped from. Never, in our time, have the vacillations and the private virtues of an artist been so ruthlessly advertised, so perpetually kept in sight of the public. The lady herself was, of course, unconscious of the uses to which her charities and her talents were put. If she broke engagements, if she declared, again and again, that nothing would induce her to dare the venture of England, such story of private caprice (or calculation) might have died away, in this busy London world of ours, as a nine days' wonder, had it not been hammered at, and wrought up, had it not been repeated, and speculated on in print, day by day, week by week, month by month. But out of this sagacious use of a history as old as woman's fickleness, and woman's beneficent heart, a lever of curiosity was forged, the force of which seems ridiculously exaggerated at this distance of time. The uses to which it was put were manifold and ingenious. It was worked, with incessant violence, to enable the Opera management to tide over a season of most inferior performances. If one dared to whisper in the pit a suspicion that the orchestra was not what it had been, that some of the new singers, announced so fiercely by trumpets ere they came and after they had come, had not proved so many new Pastas, Malibrans, Sontags, "Yes," (ran the answer), "but what can we do? Jenny Lind is *not* coming!"

So during the season of 1846 everyone was invited to be content, to regret no celebrities departed, to acquiesce in every deteriorated performance—in fact, to put up with the opera on some vague fancy that the future was to be great indeed, though "Jenny Lind was *not* coming." Everyone, however, was *not* content, all glorious and all but unanimous as were the printed plaudits of the increasing success of Her Majesty's Theatre. This is a disagreeable subject, but one from which I cannot shrink, as matter of history. The general tone of the journals during the year 1846 and following years was little creditable to the judgment (assuming it sincere) of those who, day by day, dealt with public opinion, under pretence of directing it. There was no record of failure; none of a growing dissatisfaction among the unbiassed audience; nothing to point out to distant, innocent persons that a system of commanded applause had been organized with great care; that the plaudits, and recalls, and bouquets were unreal, and represented not what lovers of music felt and thought, but what would serve the profits of the manager.   The so-called power of journalism had never a greater rebuke than in the downfall of Her Majesty's Theatre, day by day described as unparagoned in the splendour of its performances, and as enjoying a well-deserved prosperity!   Truth and time may be trusted, in England at least; but the defiance of both, in regard to appreciation of art at its real value, and of attempting to hold fast the ear of "the Town" for the moment, has, in no case which I recollect, during many years of duty on the press, been so complete and so general as in this particular one.

The thing is past and gone, even as a nightmare or a feverish dream pass and go.   Despite of checks and drawbacks, and strange spirts of temporary enthusiasm on the one hand, and on the other of an exclusiveness which is most hurtful to art, the taste for and the culture of music in England have so far advanced that I conceive it would be now impossible to force success as success was forced in the day to which I refer.

SIGNOR MARIO

THERE have been better singers, there have been better musicians, there may have been better voices, than Signor Mario. There has been no more favourite artist on the stage, in the memory of man or of woman, than he. It was not, however, till the season of 1846 that he took the place of which no wear and tear of time has been able to deprive him. The admiration is easy to explain, referable, as it has been, to nature and circumstance rather than to artistic perfection.

The last word (as the French have it) has yet to be said on the subject of amateur art. There may be difficulty in crediting it with certain good qualities without introducing confusion of ideas among those who would listen justly, and without discouraging labour in those who would study. This, however, may be pointed out. Let the vocation be ever so real, let the ambition be ever so honourable, there may be in all professional education one tendency to be watched—a too direct and anxious reference to results, to immediate praise and popularity, and this in no world more than in music; because there personal exhibition enters more largely as an element than in any other exercise of the imagination. The vanity and self-assertion of amateurs, as a class, need not be commented nor laughed at here; but the best of their class have hardly been allowed their dues, as showing glimpses of an elegant and refined fancy, belonging in part to circumstance, in part to social position. So long as the general education of the artist is little attended to, so long as it is held that nimble fingers, a flexible throat, and an instant power of reading a score, that invention of melodies and combination of chords, absolve their owner from the possession of any other knowledge or accomplishment, there will be occasionally apparent some advantage on the side of those whom the pleasure of attempting some expression of what is beautiful, and not the business of life, urges forward. In the midst of much that is doleful and ridiculously affected and pretending, there will be found, however sparingly, from time to time, something to remind the world that gentle nurture and liberal cultivation have a distinct value and influence, that a Lulli brought from his cooking-furnaces, and a Mendelssohn breathing the best air of intelligence, affection, and culture from his cradle days, do not enter into the lists on the same terms. That "antecedents" are terribly abused is of no consequence to the argument; because when a name and an escutcheon are brought to market, as a make-weight for the song ill sung, or the picture badly drawn, the trader, by such transaction, becomes more vulgar than the veriest child of the kennel, who struggles his way to success through poverty and hardship with an imperfect sense of that which is wanting to him. To assert that they are without value is false and unphilosophical, a dream of the levellers: one which, borne out, would make an end of every hope, every thought, every gracious prompting or guidance, by which the human creature is armed for life.

It will not satisfy many of Signor Mario's enthusiastic admirers to be told that, throughout his career, he has never wholly got beyond amateurship—has never been a thorough artist, armed at all points for his duties before the public. Such, however, is the case. The charm of personal appearance and graceful demeanour, borne out by a voice the persuasive sweetness of which can never have been exceeded, has fascinated everyone, the stern as well as the sentimental, into forgetting incompleteness and deficiency, which diligent and thoughtful study might have remedied ere Rubini's successor had been on the stage a couple of years. There has been no desire, no possibility, of reckoning with one so genially endowed by nature, with so much of the poet and the painter in his composition, and of the nobleman in his bearing. Lines, rules, precedents, comparisons, must sometimes be forgotten; and it is well. Those do not know the least, or judge the worst, who fairly surrender themselves to their sympathies—when they cannot help it.

In one point the career of Signor Mario has been peculiar—it might be said, unique. He will live in the world's memory as the best opera lover ever seen; as one who in a range of parts, always difficult, oftentimes insipid, never failed to give a charm and a probability to the scene, to the like of which the world has been unaccustomed. It is one thing to warble a song as did Rubini, and to sigh out a part in a duet; but to be Count Almaviva, or Gennaro, in *Lucrezia,* or Raoul, in *Les Huguenots,* demands not only beauty of voice and person and easy youth of bearing, but certain qualities, also, akin to those which rule the stage in Orlando and Romeo. There must be that feeling of youth which, in some happily gifted persons, never grows old, there must be that abandonment to the sensation of the moment which no study can entirely prepare. The passion duet, in the fourth act of M. Meyerbeer's greatest opera, as acted by Signor Mario, is a thing to be forgotten by no one that has ever seen it. The tenderness, the passion, the struggle, the fury, the inevitable necessity at last to abandon even the partner of the lover's passion, when the terrible bell of St. Bartholemew rings out, and when the massacre night begins, under the eyes of the man faithless to his faith, and entrapped (so to say) into a love alien from it,—these things, helped by no ordinary youth and beauty of person, of voice, of pictorial and picturesque fancy, and of natural refinement in breeding, were represented by Signor Mario as we shall possibly never see them represented again. In the former duel scene of the same opera (here most cruelly cut short) he lacked weight, having to reserve his voice for the tremendous coda of it; but there has been no tenor singing and acting like those of the love duet in the fourth act of that opera.

On the other hand, there have been certain of Signor Mario's characters as inefficient, and little satisfactory, as the others have been bright, buoyant, and impassioned. Without reference to the musical violence done to Mozart, one might have pointed him out as the man of men born to play Don Juan in the opera; yet his attempt was a cold, feeble, ineffective failure as a piece of acting— one which no practice could have brought in the least nearer our ideal of the libertine hero.

Again, there has been small invention in Signor Mario's career. I can call to mind nothing "created" by him (as the French phrase it), except it be the walking lover in *Don Pasquale,* which creation resolves itself into the Serenade. In one respect he arrived at an unlucky time, coming after Rubini, whose peculiar voice tempted composers to write what no one save Rubini could sing thoroughly. Thus in Signor Mario's singing of *I Puritani,* in *La Somnambula,* and *Lucia* there has always been much to desire. Comparison betwixt him and his predecessor was inevitable. His last act in *La Favorita* may be cited as containing his most highly finished singing, in some portions of which the mixture of intense passion and exquisite vocal delicacy exhibited by his predecessor was almost equalled.   In florid music there has been always something wanting; but the art of execution bids fair to be lost among men.   The singer who can give, in all their fulness and brilliancy, the airs of *Otello,* does not exist.   The splendid songs of parade and passion in *Zelmira* are virtually lost, it is too much to be feared, for ever.

It must not be forgotten that, in one delightful branch of his art, Signor Mario has never been surpassed, if equalled—as a singer of Romances.   Here, again, gentle training "will out."   Who does not know the wonderful Frenchman of chamber concerts, laced to a waist, dyed, if not rouged, to a nicety, with a voice as hard as his face, with intensely subduing gloves, such as only grow on French hands, the man who sings his inevitable "Prière du Soir," or the still more inevitable "Ma Mère," or the still most inevitable small ditty about a "little child"?   But who is there that, having passed beyond the veriest childishness in music, does not suffer resentfully under the vulgarities of such virtuous simplicity?   Who does not know the Italian of musical private life, more wonderful still, since his very private musical knowledge lies in some half-a-dozen stale songs, which he cannot accompany, which nobody had better have written, yet who comes and goes in England, and who gives concerts and gets pupils, lives more easily, and dies richer, than many an accomplished gentleman and real poet has done? What is done and suffered in this matter of Romances in "the marble halls" of our country is terrible to think of, impossible to represent.   All the dearer, then, for its rarity, is the pleasure given by such choice chamber music as the best songs of Schubert, Mendelssohn, Gordigiani, and Meyerbeer, when they are sung with poetry and intelligence.

By none have they been rendered more perfectly than by Signor Mario, the character of amateurship which pervaded his talent adding an elegance, and something of particularity, to the speaking of the words and the delivery of the music.   As a singer of Romances he has never been exceeded, rarely equalled.

One more good gift may be added to the list just offered, in which, again, the value of tastes and pursuits collateral with those of the profession adopted may be traced.   The painter's eye, as well as the lover's honeyed tongue, have had no small part in the success of the charming tenor. Few who have trod the stage have trod it dressed to such perfection as Signor Mario. His characters recur to us as do the happiest portraits of Veronese, or Tintoretto, or Bronzino, which grow into the mind as so many faces and figures recollected by their beauty, well set off by waving scarf or floating feather. There is more in this than the stage-tailor's craft,—a touch of poetry, never to be undervalued, whatever be the form taken by it. Those who sneer at taste in dress, harmony of colour, proportion of form, might as well disparage perfume or speak ill of a pleasant chord in music. The abuse of fashion made by the fop has nothing to do with the use of such honest means of embellishment as are within the reach of every one who has an eye, and who is calm enough to recollect that youth and middle age— the morning, the noon, and the afternoon—are not one and the same; and who will set himself forth without false promises or pretexts, as well as his years allow him. No mistake appears to me greater than to confound this sense and feeling with personal vanity or silly coxcombry. They are not given to everyone. Nothing can well be more revolting than the writhings of the ugly to get out of their ugliness by the aid of fine clothes. Well have these been lashed by Mr. Carlyle and by Mr. Thackeray. But the love of beauty is distinct from, and above, all that is temporary and trumpery; and, above all men, the man who presents himself on the stage must be encouraged to understand and to consider this as a part of his art, and of his intercourse with the public. I have seen this by no men so well comprehended as by Signor Lablache and Signor Mario.

SIGNOR VERDI'S OPERAS

CHARACTERISTICS

SIGNOR VERDI is the last Italian opera composer of whom there is need to speak in detail here—the only writer of his country representing, during the last fifteen years, that Maestro of better days, whose music was heard from one end of Europe to the other. He is the only modern man among them having a style, —for better for worse.

Yet many salient features of this style are not Signor Verdi's own. The crescendo, and the use—not abuse—of unison, had been suggested by Donizetti; the form of cabaletta, in which the phrase leaps and starts, rather than flows, by Frederico Ricci; the employment of syncopation, by Signor Pacini; the excess of appoggiatura, by Bellini. No matter; by new combination known materials make a new whole. How much of Gluck is there in Mozart's operas, how much of Paër in Signor Rossini's! Almost all great men have appropriated largely—Bach, Haydn, and Beethoven being, in music, the three most remarkable exceptions. Generally, however, the noble thieves (our own Handel the noblest) have originated as many good things as they have appropriated, thereby making their works sources, treasuries, authorities to be consulted in turn, if not models to be imitated. This is not Signor Verdi's case, neither can it be the case of any popular artist who belongs to a time of decadence. Every attempt to copy him has resulted in producing something extravagantly ridiculous. The young sculptor who could take Bernini as a type would give out works qualifying him for no more distinguished gallery than one in Bedlam. Bernini was the greatest man of a bad time.

There is a mixture of grandeur in portions of Signor Verdi's operas, alternated with puerilities, which is impossible to be outdone in its triteness and folly. In *Ernani,* the first opera by him (as I have said) brought to England, the septet in the first act, the great finale, "O sommo Carlo," and the final terzet, surprised the ear by their dignity and passion, by a certain novelty in the cast of phrase, and by a certain power—rude and feverish, it may be, but still real.   The Settimino (as it is called) in *Ernani* is excellent, especially in reference to the close.   And a composer will no more neglect his closes than will a speaker his periods.   The three next of Signor Verdi's operas produced here—*Nabucco, I Lombardi,* and *I due Foscari*—weakened the first favourable impression; for in each and all of them the strain and violence were repeated.   It became obvious that the new composer relied on effect, not sound knowledge; that he preferred ferocious and gloomy stories; that rant, in short, was the expression most congenial to his genius.   In his earlier operas this vigour was borne out by a naked ferocity of instrumentation, which had a certain attraction when it was heard for the first time.   And thus there have been gigantic men, who have overawed the crowd till the moment when the crowd has perceived that huge stature with them did not imply strength, nor a bullying aspect bravery—till the fragmentary weakness of the tall figure, and the stolidity of the great face, have been appreciated at a second look.

It would seem as if, in proportion to the composer's advancement in his career, the exhausting monotony of this manner of forcing effect had suggested itself to him.   Signor Verdi has obviously shown earnest solicitude to vary, to enrich, and to temper his orchestral effects in his later operas.   He has, also, in them— as in the quartet of *Rigoletto,* and one or two scenes from *Il Trovatore*—been more happily and simply inspired than in his earlier works; but the style to which he has chosen to cling and abide, the style of a bad musical time, ill wrought out in Italy, has remained essentially the same in all—spasmodic, tawdry, untruthful, depending on musical effects of a lower order and coarser quality than those of any Italian predecessor.

Signor Verdi is, generally, the most *untender* of Italians, past, present (let it be hoped), to come.   The broad cantabile in triple rhythms (9-8 or 12-8) which he allots to his lovers, and which is found so advantageous by singers who have never learned to sing but who have a long breath—singers whose voices are heavy, because they have never been trained—has only a make-believe sentimentality.   But this humour of Signor Verdi's may be one of situation and chance rather than of any aridity of nature.   The "Miserere" scene in *Il Trovatore,* commencing with the slow air for the heroine, and the half-asleep song for the gipsy-mother in the last act of the same opera, which is delicious, picturesque, and charming, testify this doubt.   There is in all of these a sweet, affectionate mournfulness, which raises them high among examples of their class, and which indicates, not that the composer is incapable to conceive other emotions than those of fierce, over-wrought passion, but that the composer has fallen on evil days, when the stimulus given to certain features and details of his art—if that were to be popular—may have corroded out of him much desire to express hopes, fears, sorrows, less over-strained than those of melodrama.   Often, however, when the gentle affections appear in the outrageous subjects which he has preferred, he sinks down, as if unequal to his task.   The part of his buffoon's daughter, in the opera of *Rigoletto* (M. Victor Hugo's *Le Roi s'amuse* transformed), is cold, childish, puerile.   The air sung by her when she retires to sleep on the evening of the outrage is but a lackadaisical yawn.   Even in the quartet of the last act, happily combined, her share amounts to little more than a chain of disconnected sobs,[1]—tragedy as physical in its way as the cough of the Camellia lady.   These devices belong to low art.   We have lived to see operas with a sneezing chorus (in time), with a chorus of dogs that bark, and other such prosaic compliments.   Why not as well present the effects of cold in the head?—to go no further in the category of maladies and sorrows accompanied by symptomatic noises.   Let me recall, as a fit subject for comparison, Desdemona's agitated air, in the second act of Signor Rossini's grand *Otello.*   There, too, the vocal phrase is broken, but only for a short time; and the broken phrase is so sustained by the orchestra as to avert anything like a dislocated effect.   How this broken phrase is set off by the wondrous burst of bravura, in which pas-

---

[1] That the same sort of devices may be turned in music to different use can hardly be better proved than by comparing the heroine's part of Gilda in the *Rigoletto* quartet, in the terzet from *I due Foscari,* and of ecstasy in the finale to the second act of *Il Trovatore,* with the false pathos of Fiordiligi and Dorabella in the parting quintet in *Cosi fan tutte.*   In this piece it has always seemed to me that Mozart wished his audience to laugh at the overdone grief of the fickle fair ones (thus preparing for their punishment), and had written in caricature style.   Signor Verdi employs the self-same receipt, in serious earnest, to picture bitter despair or breathless rapture.

sionate despair and resolution run riot without breaking the bounds of beauty in music,—how, on its resumption, it is interrupted by the entrance of the chorus,—are so many strokes of that genius which cannot be extolled too highly in praise. But the effects in that splendid song are exceptional—repeated nowhere else by Signor Rossini, though, in general, he has not been scrupulous in repeating his popular effects. In Signor Verdi's operas, the hysterical element is as sure to have a large place as are incitements for the singer to use the utmost force of his voice.

The absence of anything like gaiety in Signor Verdi's music is curious, the supper scene in *La Traviata* making the exception which proves the rule; and the gaiety there is of orgy rather than of sprightly revel. Light-heartedness, indeed, seems to have vanished from Italian opera, without any compensating serious science having taken its place. The attempts made by Signor Verdi at dance music in the opening scene of *Rigoletto* are paltry to the extreme: so is the masquerade music in the second act of *La Traviata*. Think of Weber's dances in *Silvana, Preciosa, Der Freischütz, Oberon;* think of Signor Rossini's ballets in *Guillaume Tell;* think of those belonging to M. Auber—of his *Muette* (on a subject lurid enough) ; think of the entire first act of his exquisite *Domino Noir;* think of M. Meyerbeer's admirable and piquant dance music combined in *Le Prophète;* and the absence of elegance with mirth in this last of the Italians, such as makes an union of dance and song so charming, by way of relief (the scene admitting it) becomes very dreary. We dance, when we are in Signor Verdi's company, on a volcano: and then we do not dance well, his tunes being bad.

With all these faults—grave ones, calculated to destroy and degrade taste beyond those of any Italian composer in the long list—Signor Verdi has one merit, and this is a great one—earnestness in attempting dramatic expression. He is not tame or timid in his movements on his stilts. Some of his concerted pieces combine a group of contrasted emotions, within the conditions of regular musical form, which shows an advance on his predecessors. The finale (I think to the second act) from *Nabucco,* and the last scene from *Il Trovatore,* can be instanced. His recitative is oftentimes careful in its declamation, though of late—seduced, it may be fancied, by the example of M. Meyerbeer—he has leaned too constantly to the form of recitative accompanied, closely approaching melody, which can only be used by a master-hand without giving to the musical drama a cloying heaviness.

Signor Verdi is not, however, to be disdained, as a shallow, or perversely insincere, man should be. It is evident,—howsoever incomplete may have been his training, howsoever mistaken his aspirations must be proved, and thought to have been and to be—that he *has* aspired: and in this aspiration he is separated far from the *dolce far niente* folk, who, once having got art and its resources in their hands, have made of the same, toys, or means of money-getting. What there is good in his music betokens a certain elevation of instinct and ambition, with most paltry musical culture, working with poor executants, and during an epoch of artistic decay, only rescued from utter corruption by heavings of revolution. A like appearance is to be seen in the time present of German music. The waters are out: for the moment there seems small chance of calling them back; but, while fixing attention steadily and without fear on the rush of the tide in a false direction—while attempting to discriminate what is fact from what is frenzy, in any movement, helped on by enthusiasm and accredited by fashion—lies the best chance of turning the stream on its reflux into a healthier channel, and of strengthening all who really love art in views of reform, and in steadfastness to those great principles which are unchanging, howsoever the alphabet of their expression is modified, as years, and scores of years, pass and are gathered to their forefathers.

THE YEAR 1847

HER MAJESTY'S THEATRE

OPERAS. *La Somnambula, I Puritani, Norma,* Bellini; *La Favorita,* Lucia, La Figlia del Reggimento,** Donizetti; *Robert le Diable,* Meyerbeer; *Le Nozze di Figaro,* Mozart; *Nino, Ernani, I due Foscari,* I Lombardi, I Masnadieri,** Verdi. PRINCIPAL SINGERS. Mdes. Sanchioli, Castellan, De Montenegro,* Jenny Lind;* MM. Gardoni,* Superchi,* Bouche,* Coletti, Fraschini,* Staudigl, Lablache, F. Lablache. BALLET. *Coralia.* PRINCIPAL DANCERS. Mdes. Rosati,* Marie Taglioni,* Grahn, Carlotta Grisi.

THE YEAR 1847

ROM this time forth, during some years, there were two opera houses. The secession of many artists and of a large part of the orchestra and chorus, and that in the wake of their conductor, left Her Majesty's Theatre very bare. Possibly it was an inevitable device that, as provision for expected performances, there should be a provision of promises,—singular to recollect, now that their utterly unsubstantial basis is known. It was announced that M. Meyerbeer was to bring his *Camp de Silèsie* to London—that opera which he has never allowed to travel beyond the barriers of Berlin, aware, it may be fancied, of its weakness. It was undertaken that Mendelssohn should, in the same season, produce his opera of *The Tempest*. There was, thirdly, to be a new opera by Signor Verdi.

Of these three promises, the last alone was performed. It may be doubted whether anything beyond the merest preliminary negotiations had been entered into with the two great German masters. The subject of Shakespeare's delicious faëry dream had always attracted Mendelssohn. So long ere this time as the date of his residence in Düsseldorf he had been in consultation with Herr Immermann on the best form of arranging Shakespeare's *Tempest* for music. I believe that even there may have been one or two pieces sketched, if not composed by him, for the drama which never could come to pass. But in the autumn of this year in question, 1847, during the two memorable days I spent with him at Interlaken, a few weeks before his decease, he spoke with earnest displeasure at the unwarrantable manner in which his name had been traded on by the management of a particular theatre. He had, he told me, positively rejected the book as written by M. Scribe, and had declined to compose it until it was wholly remodelled. Yet after this the venture was made of advertising it in the theatre as in his hands; of specifying the artists included in the cast—nay, and of circulating printed illustrations of the principal scenes.   In no case has the tampering with expectation gone further.   The result will be seen a year or two later.

Such a parade of promises was possibly a desperate necessity, because, under the existing state of affairs, a large amount of novelty was a matter of life and death.   This year, it will be seen, not a single work by Signor Rossini was produced.   Beyond the introduction of *I due Foscari,* by Signor Verdi—an opera which England has declined to accept on any terms—the Maestro himself arrived with a work expressly written for the theatre—perhaps his most paltry work—*I Masnadieri,* which merely can survive recollection by the stage appearance of Mdlle. Lind, who looked Schiller's Amalia to the life, and by a violoncello solo in the Introduction, which first showed London what a consummate master of his instrument we had acquired in Signor Piatti.   These Verdi operas were failures; but two of Donizetti's operas new to England were also introduced—two of his best serious and comic operas, and both of them successful.   *La Favorita* and *La Figlia* have proved real additions to the narrowing repertory of the Italian theatre, both—the fact is worth marking—ascribable to French influence.

Thus much of the music.   There was small chance of any new female singer, save *the* one, being allowed to please; and Madame Montenegro did not deserve to do so.   The men fared somewhat better; and one—Signor Gardoni—by his charm of person and of voice (somewhat slight though the latter has proved) did more to reconcile the public to the loss of Signor Mario than could have been expected as possible.   A word is his due as the due of a real artist who, from first to last, has finished every phrase that he has sung, and who has pointed every word that he has said. There has always been the real Italian elegance—and that more universal elegance which belongs to no country—in Signor Gardoni.   Signor Fraschini, though originally gifted with greater vocal power, was less fortunate.   Fourteen years ago we were little used to the coarse and stentorian bawling which the Italian tenors have of late affected.   The newcomer, naturally anxious to recommend himself by the arts which had delighted his own people, seemed to become more and more violent in proportion as the "sensation" failed to be excited.   But he piled up the agony, forte on forte, in vain.   That so much noise should be received so coolly was somewhat whimsical, bitter disappointment though it must have been to one misled by home raptures. Alas! I already look back to Signor Fraschini as a moderate, if not a temperate, Italian tenor, when compared with many who have since made the ears of right-minded persons suffer.

Herr Staudigl's appearance in Italian opera was an utter failure. With one exception, I have not heard even a German basso so awkward at the southern language as he was. Signor Coletti's return was an acquisition, as an available, expressive, sound singer (of the modern school) should be; and such small success as *I due Foscari* gained at Her Majesty's Theatre was referable to his appearance as the Doge in the last act of that dreary setting of what Moore happily called, in a letter to Byron, "one of those violent Venetian stories." In this, however, as I shall have to state in a future page, truly skilful and impressive as Signor Coletti proved himself to be, he was outdone by the only other representative of the character who has attempted it in England—Signor Ronconi.

MADEMOISELLE JENNY LIND

T is impossible, when treating the marvellous sensation produced at our Italian Opera by Mdlle. Jenny
Lind, to confine the story to the gamut or the book
of exercises, to the scene acted with emotion, to the
audience delirious with enthusiasm. The circumstances must be recalled which had paved the way for the new
singer's success with as much certainty as singularity. We have
read with contempt of Gabrielli's caprices, of Catalani's magnificent extravagances (I have seen that glorious-looking woman
waited on in a concert ante-room, by a page bearing a salver piled
with clean gloves) ; but nothing, in any time, has equalled the
amount of influence brought from the outside to bear on the reception of a singer, who, lacking such outward influences, would
have been received as only one among many (one *after* a few)
great singers; whereas, owing to such accessory excitements, she
was held in this country, for a while, to be *the* one, and the one
alone.

In a position of great difficulty it was the policy of the manager
of Her Majesty's Theatre, menaced by a formidable opposition,
to seek hither and thither for some attraction to replace those
which had, in a body, seceded from him. Europe was not rich
just then—being poorer now. For some years past we had been
hearing of a young Swedish lady with a marvellous voice, from
whom much was to be expected. First she had been read of in
one of Miss Bremer's novels, *The Home*—how she was the darling of the Opera House in Stockholm; next, from Berlin, where
her apparition was indeed a godsend among the clumsy and exaggerated women who strode the stage, screaming as they strode.
The two great German composers had pronounced in her favour
panegyrics which, as usual, grew in importation. With these
came details of private life, and authentications of private virtue,
just as eagerly minute as if they were not, of necessity, assumed—
since private life and private virtue do not bare their modesty and

their secrets to the paragraph-maker. Last of all, the herald-trumpets spoke of charities done, in a tone as if charity was the exception, not the rule, among musical artists. Now this is a theory than which one more foolhardy, more false, could hardly be propounded. Great singers have, from time immemorial, given out of both hands, have too little regarded themselves, too largely turned their singing gifts to account. Howsoever vain, voluptuous, and thoughtless some among them have been, the amount of alms-giving and unselfish assistance ministered by them, without thought of notoriety or repayment, in the midst of hurried and distracting lives, in spite of uncertain gains, in the face of ingratitude, has never been stated, much of it having been concealed. Enough, however, is known to everyone conversant with music and with musicians to make the recommendation of any single singer, as charity incarnate, cruelly unjust to a hundred others, inasmuch as it implied that singers' charity was a new thing in this world of ours before the year of grace 1847.

Nor was this all. After curiosity had been stirred to the utmost came the further provocatives of doubt and disappointment. It was asserted on evidence which was past question that Mdlle. Lind would not come to England, that no argument could prevail on her to change a resolution announced as irrevocable by word and by pen. The game of suspense was never more artfully played. It is curious to recall, as matter of history, how for months the mind of that opera world which craves something to wonder about, was irritated and kept alive by tales of mysterious vacillations, persuasions, negotiations—plenipotentiaries sent to mediate, and bringing back hints and hopes, but not downright assurances; and all this after the treaty had been signed and sealed! By whom all this machinery was originated it is of no consequence here to examine. It had racked our opera world into a state of fever, and elevated it into a firm faith, moreover, that that which had cost so much trouble to secure must be, indeed, something unspeakably precious.

No theatre can have displayed a scene of greater excitement than on the evening when it was to be proved how far the wonder, so far-fetched and dearly bought, merited all that had been promised for her. She appeared as Alice, in *Robert*—an appearance not to be risked by any singer in the least nervous. The girl, dragged hastily down the stage in the midst of a crowd, has at once, and when out of breath, to begin on an accented note, without time to think or to look around her.   I have never seen anyone so composed as Mdlle. Lind was on that night. Though the thunder of welcome was loud and long enough to stop the orchestra, and to bewilder a veteran, and though it was acknowledged with due modesty, her hands did not tremble—one even arranged a ring on the finger of the other—and her voice spoke out as firmly as if neither fear nor failure was possible.   To me, the absence and the semblance of emotion, at once, in the midst of such overcoming excitement, were strange.   Nine hundred among the thousand interpreted what they saw in a reading entirely opposite.   They were magnetized once for all, in those few first moments.   I see (as I write) the smile with which Mendelssohn, whose enjoyment of Mdlle. Lind's talent was unlimited, turned round and looked at me, as if a load of anxiety had been taken off his mind.   His attachment to Mdlle. Lind's genius as a singer was unbounded, and with it his desire for her success.

Her companions on the stage might have been celestial singers and actors, or the reverse, that night: no one cared for them, no one followed the opera.   Partisanship had been fermented to such a fever heat, interest had been bespoken by such a long-drawn series of hints, mysteries, accidents—or planned measures—that excellence so real as that of the new singer was sure to be accepted as that super-excellence in the dazzling blaze of which things good or bad alike disappear.

The scenes of Alice, thoroughly well given, and perfectly suited to the powers of their giver, were waited for, listened to in breathless silence, and received with applause which was neither encouragement nor appreciation nor enthusiasm so much as idolatry. Woe to those during that season who ventured to say or to write that any other great singer had ever sung in the Haymarket Opera House!   To my cost I know that they were consigned to such ignominy as belongs to the idiotic slanderer.   Old and seemingly solid friendships were broken, and for ever, in that year.   It was a curious experience to sit and to wait for what should come next, and to wonder whether it really *was* the case that music had never been heard till the year 1847.

From that first moment till the end of that opera season nothing else was thought about, nothing else talked about, but the new Alice, the new Somnambula, the new Maria in Donizetti's charming comic opera—his best.   Pages could be filled by describing the excesses of the public.   Since the days when the world fought for hours at the pit door to see the seventh farewell of Siddons, nothing had been seen in the least approaching the scenes at the entrance of the theatre when Mdlle. Lind sang.   Prices rose to a fabulous height.   In short, the town, sacred and profane, went mad about "the Swedish nightingale."

How far the triumph was well-deserved in its extravagance was a question scouted for the moment as the rankest and most presumptuous heresy.   No one would for a moment suffer the chorus of idolatry which attended this extraordinary woman to be for a moment interrupted by any discussion of her genius and talent, as compared with those of any former singer.

It can now, however, without treason be recorded that Mdlle. Lind's voice was a soprano, two octaves in compass—from D to D—having a possible higher note or two, available on rare occasions; and that the lower half of the register and the upper one were of two distinct qualities.   The former was not strong,—veiled, if not husky, and apt to be out of tune.   The latter was rich, brilliant, and powerful—finest in its highest portions.   It can be told that the power of respiration was possessed by Mdlle. Lind in the highest perfection; that she could turn her "very long breath" to account in every gradation of tone; and thus, by subduing her upper notes, and giving out her lower ones with great care, could conceal the disproportions of her organ.   I imagine that her voice must have been fatigued by incessant early use on the stage.   It has been said that she only brought it into its admirable state of command after years of use, and, probably, imperfect methods of delivering it; and that the acute and intelligent professor to whom she repaired in Paris for counsel and instruction entirely refused the latter, until she had given the girl's wearied voice chance of refreshment, by rest for a considerable period.

Her execution was great; and, as is always the case with voices originally reluctant, seemed greater than it really was.   Her shake (a grace ridiculously despised of late) was true and brilliant; her taste in ornament was altogether original.   In a song from *Bea-*

trice di Tenda which she adopted there was a chromatic cadence, ascending to E in altissimo, and descending to the note whence it had risen, which could not be paragoned, of late days, as an evidence of mastery and accomplishment.   She used her pianissimo tones so as to make them resemble an effect of ventriloquism.   On every note that she sang, in every bar that she delivered, a skilled and careful musician was to be detected.

No precise appreciation of her expression is possible.   "It is the soul that sees," says Crabbe.   Not a little of the effect produced by the artist on his audience is brought thither by the latter, who cannot stay to enquire how and wherefore his sympathies are engaged.   Whatsoever were the predisposing causes, and let them be allowed for ever so largely, Mdlle. Lind did without doubt satisfy the larger number of her auditors, by giving them the impression that she was the possessor of deep and true feeling.   This satisfaction I only shared at intervals.   I will endeavour to offer such reasons for this qualified admiration as can be given in a matter so delicate, and to support them by an illustration or two.

It was disadvantageous to Mdlle. Lind that she had, throughout her career, to sing in strange languages,—German, Italian, last of all English.   Though she mastered all the three with her wonted industry, she delivered none of them with finished clearness.   This gave more heaviness to her style than is consistent with real expression.   There was always in her singing an element of conflict, beside that which might be discerned in the management of her voice.

Of all the singers whom I have ever heard Mdlle. Lind was perhaps the most assiduous.   Her resolution to offer the very best of her best to her public seemed part and parcel of her nature and of her conscience.   Not a note was neglected by her, not a phrase slurred over.   Unlike many of the Italians, who spare themselves in uninteresting passages of any given opera to shine out in some favourite piece of display, she went through her entire part with a zeal which it was impossible not to admire, and which could not be too generally adopted as a principle by everyone, great or small, who presents himself to an audience.   But perhaps owing to this remarkable strenuousness, many of her effects on the stage appeared over-calculated.   Everything was brought out into an equally high relief. And thus her best part was that of Julia,[1] in Spontini's *La Vestale*—a part in which there must be effort from beginning to end, and this not only because of the story, but from the nature of Spontini's music. The faithless Vestal has not an instant of repose. In the beginning of the tale she has to hide her secret, and then to master her passion in the face of thousands, when her warrior lover returns home, and when to her is confided the agony of crowning him. Then she has to consent to break her vows by admitting him into the temple at night; and, during the passionate interchange of feelings long pent up in a shroud, with the "warm, living love" of one used to conquest, and not disposed to yield, the sacred fire which the Priestess has to ward expires. There remains for her only to sacrifice herself, in furtherance of her lover's escape; to be publicly disgraced, to be doomed, to be rescued from the sepulchre prepared for her by a miracle. There is not a moment of calm, I repeat, in the part of Spontini's Julia. Yet it does not demand first-class tragic genius to fill it. On both grounds it suited Mdlle. Lind's powers admirably; and it is a pity that, owing to our English antipathy to the opera, which seems unconquerable, our public never saw so striking and finished a personification, and one in which nature and art wrought in such perfect concord.

That Mdlle. Lind made strange mistakes, in consulting her own personality rather than the play, was to be seen in her Norma. I had heard those wondrous discoverers, the German critical public, delight in her reading as "maidenly"—praise original, to say the least of it, when the well-known story is remembered. Elaborately wrought as it was, it was pale, weak, as compared with the rendering of the real Norma. Even her most thorough-going admirers in this country could find nothing better to say than that the part was too full of revengeful and stormy passion and of remorse for it to be in anywise rightly presented by one in nature so devoutly different.

Her Alice, in M. Meyerbeer's *Robert*, was excellent throughout. The F and G sharp in her upper voice, called out in the final trio, and delivered with admirable breadth, were sufficient to stamp her as a peculiar singer and a great musician. She threw

[1] *Modern German Music*, vol. ii., p. 351.

much devotional feeling into her acting. It was found so delightful that, in progress of time, could be seen the opera of *Robert,* presented at Her Majesty's Theatre, offered with two acts cut out, —those, I mean, in which the Princess, a rival woman to Alice, appears. Her Amina, in *La Somnambula,* was the character in which she made the most effect on her public. The largo in the last scene, given in a penetrating whisper, while she let the flowers, one by one, of the treasured token-nosegay strew the stage, fascinated the audience, and most justly. It was new, it was true, it served to exhibit all the singer's best qualities. She did not sing the final rondo half so well as Madame Persiani. Her Lucia, in Donizetti's sickly opera, was better as a whole—though, as the opera is closed, not by the Bride of Lammermoor, but by Ravenswood, the part was less congenial to a singer who seemed resolved to dominate beyond any artist whom I have seen, than one in which she could wind up any story which she had begun. She was the only Lucia (as was pointed out to me by M. Berlioz) who prepared for the last dismal heart-break, by her agony in the moment when she is impressed with the falsehood of her lover by her haughty and tyrannical brother. Her madness was fearfully touching in proportion as it had been foreseen. In *La Figlia del Reggimento* (another of her most admired characters), she was surpassed—strange to say!—by her elder successor, Sontag, as to life, as to vulgarity, as to vocal brilliancy. It was the fashion and the passion to extol her as an incomparable singer of Mozart's music, but her Suzanna was stiff, heavy, conscientious: the *disinvoltura* (we have no precise English equivalent) required, co-existent with a sincere musical rendering of every note and phrase, was not there. I liked much her Adina in *L'Elisir,*—more than the generality of her idolators. There was a perverse caprice in her reading of the character, a quick and sharp and strange brilliancy in some of her ornaments, which made it by much the best presentation of the village coquette that I recollect. Perhaps by drawing out the essential ungraciousness of the character she may have spoilt her own chances of pleasing her subjects in it. In England we are singularly averse to anything like mixture or complexity of emotions—even though it *was* an Englishman who called up "the serpent of old Nile," Cleopatra.

Such are some of those characteristics of Mdlle. Lind as a

dramatic singer, the perpetual recurrence of which in her performances make me recollect them with more calmness than was endurable to the frenzied folk of the hour, who crowded into the theatre to come out vehement in rapture.

One more remark, in conclusion, may be thought to bear upon the subject. During her stage career, Mdlle. Lind created very little. Her Vielka, in M. Meyerbeer's *Camp of Silesia* (written for Berlin, and subsequently altered into *L'Etoile du Nord* for Paris), is the only character of her own which was successful. Her Amalia, in Signor Verdi's *I Masnadieri,* could not have pleased had it been given by Saint Cecilia and Melpomene in one, so utterly worthless was the music. In short, Mdlle. Lind's opera repertory was limited,—one which must have exposed her on every side to comparisons should she have remained on the stage till enthusiasm cooled, as it must inevitably have done. If she became aware of this, and if such conviction had its part in her determination to give up the theatre for the concert room, the conviction was a wise one. In a rambling book such as this I may be allowed to digress, and as a pleasure to put on record the admirable qualities of the Swedish lady as a concert singer. The wild, queer, northern tunes brought here by her, her careful expression of some of Mozart's great airs, her mastery over such a piece of execution as "the Bird Song" in Haydn's *Creation,* and lastly, the grandeur of inspiration with which the "Sanctus" of angels in Mendelssohn's *Elijah* was led by her (the culminating point in that oratorio), are so many things to leave on the mind of all who have heard them, as many indelible prints. These are the triumphs, in my poor judgment, which will stamp Madame Lind-Goldschmidt's name in the Golden Book of singers.

THE YEAR 1847

ROYAL ITALIAN OPERA

OPERAS. *La Somnambula, I Puritani, Norma,* Bellini; *Lucia, Maria di Rohan,* L'Elisir, Lucrezia Borgia,* Donizetti; *Don Giovanni, Le Nozze di Figaro,* Mozart; *Semiramide, L'Italiana, Il Barbiere, La Gazza Ladra, La Donna del Lago,* Rossini; *I due Foscari, Ernani,* Verdi. PRINCIPAL SINGERS. Mdes. Grisi, Persiani, Alboni,* Steffanone,* Corbari, Ronconi; MM. Tamburini, Tagliafico,* Polonini, Ronconi, Salvi,* Mario, Marini,* Rovere,* Bellini.* BALLETS. *Manon Lescaut, La Rosiera.* PRINCIPAL DANCERS. Mdes. Dumilatre, Fanny Elssler, Fuoco.*

THE YEAR 1847

I has already been told that, earlier than 1846, dissatisfaction in the opera performances at Her Majesty's Theatre—so loudly recommended in print, so systematically weakened and impaired—was beginning to be general. Ears are stubborn facts. The increasing inferiority of the company as a whole was not to be concealed by the unanimous praises of which it was the object. It has been told that the theatre was always crowded, that the audience was always rapturous. The time had been a golden time for those who made bouquets, since the rain of them was abundant and increasing. But spectators who cared the least for tales behind the curtain, of managerial disloyalty or artistic exaction, and who were the most willing to repose an average faith in all the papers put forth, remembered the good days that had been; and felt that however loud might be the trumpeting, however brilliantly put forth the procession of actors and singers, all vaunted as better than the best who had gone before them—the Opera was virtually in a state of downfall and deterioration. The departure of one long before known as among the best musical conductors in Europe, and with it the dilution of orchestra and chorus, passed over seemingly without any change in public favour. Nothing, apparently, could be more prosperous, more popular, or beyond the power of revolt or opposition to interfere with.

During the season of 1846, however, it was announced that the few great singers left in Her Majesty's Theatre (Lablache excepted), and with them the orchestra and chorus, in a body, had followed Signor Costa; and that a new theatre for foreign musical performances would be opened with the new season. The tale was denied and derided, as something too wild to have any reality; till it was known that the architect was already in possession of Covent Garden Theatre, with a plan for its entire reconstruction, that the works were in steady and rapid progress, and that engagements on a most ample scale of grandeur and individual excellence were signed and sealed. The fact, in short, was no longer to be questioned. The new undertaking was to be faced, destroyed, and ruined; or else the old one must needs give way.

It would serve no good turn further to enter into the private history of this musical event, with all its loops and turns—to recall the green room tales and their contradictions, which agitated those who are concerned in such matters. It is enough to have lived for a while in the cauldron of scandal, without stirring its waters afresh. The new theatre did not tumble down like a house of cards. The officers of Justice did not enter with writs, at the eleventh hour, to lay the strong hand of prohibition on any acting or singing being attempted in an establishment already known, said its solvent well-wishers, to be insolvent. The Lord Chamberlain did not refuse his license, as it was promised for him that he should do. The singers were forthcoming on the day of rehearsal, which took place in the midst of scaffoldings, artificers, and every other apparent interruption and sign of incompleteness. At last, on the 6th of April, the Royal Italian Opera opened its doors with a fine performance of *Semiramide,* in which, besides the excitement of the first night of a new undertaking, there was an attraction of late increasingly rare—the appearance of a new singer of the highest class, Mademoiselle Alboni.

Most of the other events of the first season of the Royal Italian Opera were virtually so many experiments or pioneers. Madame Steffanone was new—a steady, painstaking lady, with a sufficient voice, but no attraction which would entitle her to first honours. She appeared in *Ernani* without herself or the opera exciting the slightest attention. Madame Ronconi was in every respect inferior. Some years ere this, as Mademoiselle Giannoni, she had excited a certain attention at the Lyceum Theatre in Signor Coppola's poor *Nina.* But she did not justify any promise.

This year the new establishment came no nearer grand opera, as it was afterwards displayed there, than by giving *Lucrezia Borgia* with great force, in which Madame Grisi and Signor Mario brought their performances to that perfection which held out so long—and Madame Alboni's Brindisi had to be sung again and again, so jovial was it—and by closing the season with a splendid revival of Signor Rossini's *Donna del Lago.* The one blot on this was the coarse singing of the Roderick Dhu, Signor Bettini—

a very bad tenor, of whom there is no need to speak further, save to put on record that all the brilliancy of the airs of parade—written (if I am not mistaken) for a great singer, Nozzari—was coolly expunged, because the singer had never learned his art. But then, how fresh sounded the music of the first act of that delicious opera!—winding up with the animated "Chorus of Bards," given with a numerical strength never assembled before in England; how welcome after the fierce or feeble music of the later Italians, who had seemed for a while to push this master of genius from his stool! If the music cannot hope to keep the stage (as is too likely), it may not be solely because the art of singing it adequately has all but perished, but in part from the utter nullity of the second act, which, however strengthened by the lovely quartet and duet from *Bianca and Faliero,* is virtually a concert in costume, without an incident, or a spark of dramatic interest. In the final varied air, which, with some alteration, the composer—at once as thrifty, as facile, and as unscrupulous as Handel had been before him—reproduced in *Zelmira,* Madame Grisi that year displayed a grandeur of style, a finish, a "triumphancy," in which there was something of conscious power, conscious beauty, and intentional challenge. She was resolute—it is now fifteen years ago—in proving that she *had not* finished her career, neither that she would be driven from her throne, as Roxana, by any Statira who might or could or should or would arrive.

MADEMOISELLE ALBONI

ALWAYS connect one of Talfourd's happy critical phrases (how happy they were!)—in respect to an actress (I think Miss Chester) who played Mrs. Sullen some forty years ago, and who, he said, had "corn and wine and oil" in her looks—with Madame Alboni. There was never such a personation of teeming and genial prosperity seen in woman's form. Her face, with its broad, sunny, Italian beauty, incapable of frown, and her figure, were given out by nature in some happy mood of mortal defiance to tragedy and all its works; the features so regularly beautiful, the face so obstinately cheery, without variety yet without vulgarity.

Nor was ever voice in more entire harmony with face and figure than was Mademoiselle Alboni's. Hers was a rich, deep, real contralto, of two octaves from G to G, as sweet as honey, but not intensely expressive; and with that tremulous quality which reminds fanciful speculators of the quiver in the air of the calm, blazing summer's noon. I recollect no low Italian voice so luscious.

Since that day the genial contralto has herself changed singularly little—save in consequence of attempts made to extend her voice; and these (after its register is settled) *must* impair its tone. Her stage position with the public has been the same,—with no advance, if little retreat. That she has held no theatre for a long period is easily to be accounted for, without the slightest depreciation of a talent so rich, so equable, so borne out by technical accompaniments. Nature did not limit her means by the excess of personal comeliness bestowed on her. The bulk of Lablache was small impediment to his versatile assumption of the most different and difficult characters. Those who are familiar with the Parisian theatres a quarter of a century since must remember Mademoiselle Mante as one of the most highly-finished actresses belonging to the great period of the Théâtre Français, when Mademoiselle Mars reigned there. That lady absolutely appeared to derive stateliness and grandeur from peculiarities which would have weighed down and choked nine out of ten women. It has been the absence of vivacity, of variety of dramatic instinct, which has made Madame Alboni's many delicious qualities pall after a time. Her singing has been always too monochromatic. To one or two of her favourite pieces—such as the Swiss rondo in *Betly,* and the supper song in *Lucrezia Borgia*—she gave a certain character and animation; but these were exceptions to her general manner. Nor was this redeemed by any variety in vocal resource. Once having heard any song by Madame Alboni, it was to be heard, for ever afterwards, unchanged and the same. This has been the case with other great singers, especially with Madame Pasta, who never altered a phrase or an ornament when they were once selected and settled. But the difference is this—Madame Pasta, by the resistless geniality of her genius, always contrived (as I have said) to deceive her hearers into thinking that she was delighting them for the first time. Even when one laid in wait for a cadenza, or a passage, or a phrase remembered as precious, when the same arrived it always produced the surprise of sounding better than had been expected. It was not so with Madame Alboni. There is a part of every audience that will listen only tranquilly, after a time, to the most mellow of voices, to the most exact musical execution, unless with the same qualities other elements to charm are joined.

Some consciousness of this kind seems to have suggested itself to the great contralto singer and to have excited her to a restlessness of career singularly at variance with a physical placidity so remarkable as hers. By way of enlarging the circle of her attractions, she resolved, as has been said, upon the experiment of extending her voice upwards. This is an experiment never to be tried with success, except, perhaps, in early youth. The required high notes were forthcoming. But the entire texture of the voice was injured: its luscious quality, and some of its power, were inevitably lost, without its gaining the qualities of effect longed for. Madame Alboni has, during her career, sung the music for Ninetta, Zerlina, Amina (even!), and Rosina: and always went through the task correctly, and, for a while, in tune; but the voice remained always a spoiled contralto; though enfeebled, heavy, and, by its displacement, rendered incapable of predominating in music, as the leading voice of the quartet must do. It was only, therefore, by frequently changing the arena of her exhibitions that Madame Alboni, in her altered state, could keep the reputation which had originally by right belonged to her; and which now could only in part be maintained by curiosity, and past pleasant remembrances. The pecuniary profit of the result (a soprano being notoriously more "worthy"—to borrow a grammar phrase—in the treasurer's book than a contralto) has nothing to do with a question of art argued before the curtain.

Enough, by way of general character, prefacing what may be hereafter said in regard to a great and successful artist; if not of the first class as a genius, almost, if not altogether, the last of the great Italian singers. The last truth may be accounted for by the fact that Madame Alboni's real training never began till she had left her own land behind her. Nor was it wonderful that, when this gorgeous voice and capital method and charming execution of hers were first heard, at the Royal Italian Opera, in the display music of Arsace, our public was entranced to such a spellbound delight as may be enjoyed in the island of lotus-eaters. There might be less grandeur in her than with Pisaroni, less fire than with Malibran; but that delicious satisfaction to the ear, that perfect musical finish, that composure (the verging of which towards indolence could not at first be detected) amounted to a new sensation. To Mademoiselle Alboni, then unmarried, assuredly fell the honours of the first night of the new theatre. During the season, too, she sang through the entire range of music belonging to her voice, with the same calmness, vocal perfection, and undisturbed, undisputed triumph. If I recollect right, as Pippo in *La Gazza* she had to sing the entire first solo, in the duet "Ebben per mia memoria," three times over—not greatly to the satisfacttion of the Ninetta, such duet having been omitted in the season 1834, which, in the Ninetta, had brought to light the gracious promise and the extraordinary power of the identical Ninetta of 1847—Madame Grisi.

SIGNOR RONCONI

I HAVE now to speak of a great artist, in every respect the reverse of the delicious singer just parted with. Greater could not be the contrast in every attribute and qualification than between the excellent contralto, with her incomparable voice, her undramatic style, her brilliant execution, and her grand Coreggio face, and the baritone, with his wondrously limited means so shaped and turned to account by genius as to make every limit, every defect, forgotten and forgiven. It was not till the Royal Italian Opera House was opened that the English had the remotest idea of the wonderful endowments of Signor Ronconi as an actor, and their power to make forgotten vocal defects which, with any one else, must have been fatal and decisive. There are few instances of a voice so limited in compass (hardly exceeding an octave), so inferior in quality, so weak, so habitually out of tune as his. Nor has its owner ever displayed any compensating executive power. Volubility there has been none, nor variety in ornament—one close, of the simplest possible form, doing duty perpetually, in this, marking the entire contrast between him and his predecessor, Signor Tamburini. Skill of phrasing there has been, especially in the languid slow movements affected to satiety by Bellini and Donizetti. I dwell on these facts all the more emphatically because it will be next to impossible for the persons of the next generation to conceive the slender physical means on which his popularity has been built; and (what makes the wonder more strange) in many of the characters which that magnificently gifted artist and singer, Lablache, had delighted to present. And more, there has not been anything like personal beauty or presence to make amends for deficiencies of tone. The low stature, the features, unmarked and commonplace when silent, promising nothing to an audience, yet which could express a dignity of bearing, a tragic passion which cannot be exceeded, or an exuberance of the wildest, quaintest, most whimsical, most spontaneous comedy, flung out by animal spirits in mirth's most tameless humour,—these things we have seen, and have forgotten personal insignificance, vocal power below mediocrity, every falling short, every disqualification, in the spell of strong, real sensibility. I owe some of my best opera evenings to Signor Ronconi; and looking back, cannot resist trying to specify a few, difficult though the task be of putting on record effects so sudden, so transient, and in his case, I fancy, so little studied beforehand.

The first of these—in conjunction (to be fair) with the delicious singing of the new contralto, who was encored in every note of her part of Gondi—"broke the fall" of Donizetti's *Maria di Rohan*—not a strong opera, in which the heroine's part, of itself null, was lost by its being entrusted to Madame Ronconi, a lady who insisted on singing, little to the pleasure of our public, and for whose sake (as it has been elsewhere commemorated) her husband, though himself a first favourite, was visited with condign displeasure in a certain Italian opera house, for not employing his marital authority to keep his partner quiet. Here she was received with indifference; just tolerated as an appendage to a great artist, but not encouraged to appear a second time.

There have been few such examples of terrible courtly tragedy in Italian opera as Signor Ronconi's Chevreuse, the polished demeanour of his earlier scenes giving a fearful force of contrast to the later ones when the torrent of pent-up passion nears the precipice. In spite of the discrepancy between all our ideas of serious and sentimental music and the old French dresses which we are accustomed to associate with the Dorantes and Alcestes of Molière's dramas, the terror of the last scene, when (betwixt his teeth, almost) the great artist uttered the line,

"Sull' uscio tremendo lo sguardo figgiamo,"

clutching, the while, the weak and guilty woman by her wrist, as he dragged her to the door behind which her falsity was screened, was something fearful, a sound to chill the blood, a sight to stop the breath.

Then, again, it was Signor Ronconi's dignity and force, as the Doge, which saved *I due Foscari* from utter condemnation at the new theatre—a feat all the more remarkable from his being grouped in that opera with Madame Grisi and Signor Mario, neither of whom found power in it to move the audience. The subtlety of his by-play in the last act was rare, original, and real.

In this last act of *I due Foscari*, the old, iron, noble Doge, tortured betwixt the heart of a father and the duties of a monarch (half a slave to the jealous and corrupt and haughty folk who had invested him with supremacy), had to sit mute while the lady, distracted at the impending death of her lover (his son, doomed by the Doge), vents prayers, tears, and, these last being fruitless, maledictions against the sovereign who will not pardon—against the father, who is as deaf to the voice of nature as the "nether millstone"; and the Doge is old, with a foretaste in him of death, bred of the resolution which has decreed his son's death, in obedience to his inexorable duty to Venice. How the Doge of whom I am speaking sat in his chair of state, with a hand on each elbow of it as moveless and impassive as the thing of wood by Giovanni Bellini pictured in our National Gallery (a picture to haunt one); while the woman—not singing to him, but to the stalls—flung out her agony in a Verdi cavatina, I shall never forget.

But the modern ordinances of Italian opera, including Verdi's cavatina, will have everything done twice—will have the agony all over again—and, that the prima donna may take rest (because her agony must be more agonized the second than the first time), the stupid form is that of making a loud noise during several bars, —a poor imitation of Signor Rossini's poor fillings-up.

During this pause, the hands of the Doge were unclenched from the elbows of his chair. He looked sad, weary, weak—leaned back, as if himself ready to give up the ghost; but when the woman, after the allotted bars of noise, began again her second-time agony, it was wondrous to see how the old sovereign turned in his chair, with the regal endurance of one who says, "I must endure to the end," and again gathered his own misery into his old father's heart, and shut it up close till the woman had ended. Unable to grant her petition, unable to free his son, after such a scene, the aged man, when left alone, could only rave till his heart broke. Signor Ronconi's Doge is not to be forgotten by those who do not treat art as a toy, or the singer's art as something entirely distinct from dramatic truth.

Then, how is it to be forgotten that this Doge was presented by the same man whose quack doctor in *Elisir* showed that wondrous, professionally-haggard charlatan, Dulcamara—more of a machine than a human being, glib, miserable, worn-out, yet unable to be quiet for a single second? The lean quack, and the horrible horse, and the shabby chaise, and the utterly disrespectable puffery of the man and his drugs by the very creature who obviously had the least belief in their efficacy, as might be heard in the monotone of his voice (and the horse and chaise were, obviously, inventions of Signor Ronconi's), make up a whole almost unique in farce opera.

Almost—yet not altogether so; because I cannot help commemorating the starved, miserable poet in *Matilda di Shabran*—a wretched droll, belonging to low Italian farce, but somehow patched up by this great southern man into a character; without recalling his Papageno, in *Die Zauberflöte*—not

"The poor bird-boy with his roasted sloes,"

be-sung by Bloomfield, but the bird-creature, half-man, half parokeet, "who could charm the bird from the tree," (as Mrs. Hardcastle said of Tony Lumpkin). Anything more utterly ridiculous can never have been conceived or executed than this presentation so carried out.

I recall these examples because they will perhaps be among the less familiar of those by which the versatility of this remarkable artist is proved. One could write a page on his Barber, in Signor Rossini's master-work; a paragraph on his Duke in *Lucrezia Borgia,* an exhibition of dangerous, suspicious, sinister malice, such as the stage has rarely shown; another on his Podestà in *La Gazza Ladra* (in these two characters bringing him into close rivalry with Lablache—a rivalry from which he issued unharmed); and last, and almost best, of his creations, his Masetto (as signal a success as his Don Juan had been a signal mistake—one of his two mistakes, the other being Guillaume Tell)—if the matter in hand was a complete history. But fortunately this is not a thing possible to be produced here, Signor Ronconi being, happily for tragedy and comedy, still on the stage.

THE YEAR 1848

HER MAJESTY'S THEATRE

OPERAS. *La Somnambula, I Puritani,* Bellini; *Lucrezia Borgia, La Figlia, Linda, L'Elisir, Don Pasquale,* Donizetti; *Robert le Diable,* Meyerbeer; *Le Nozze,* Mozart; *Il Barbiere,* Rossini; *Ernani, Attila, I due Foscari, Nino,* Verdi. PRINCIPAL SINGERS. Mdes. Cruvelli,* Vera,* Abbadia,* Schwartz,* Lind, Tadolini;* MM. Cuzzani,* Gardoni, Beletti,* Lablache, F. Lablache, Bouche, Coletti, Labocetta,* Sims Reeves.* BALLETS. *Fiorita,* *The Four Seasons.* PRINCIPAL DANCERS. Mdes. M. Taglioni, Cerito, Rosati, Carlotta Grisi, M. St. Léon.

THE YEAR 1848

HE season of 1848 made it obvious that Mademoiselle Lind was an artist who exhausted as much as she assisted any theatre at which she sang. Her own prestige was still great; but it became evident that she was not easily to be worked as a member of a company—that her repertory was very limited, and one in which, seemingly, she sought for undivided predominance. The additions to her list of characters this year were in *L'Elisir, Lucia,* and *I Puritani.* Seeing that in the second opera a strong tenor, as having the last word, must efface the effect of the soprano, there was only a graceful tenor to Mademoiselle Lind's Lucia, and the opera pleased, as though it had been a pleasure taken by Lady Grace, "soberly"—in spite of a great and new excellence introduced into it by the heroine—already mentioned—her preparation for the catastrophe of The Bride's madness.

The misfortune to a theatre of a success so preternaturally forced as hers, is to destroy the chances of any who aspire to make a position beside the idol. The two new ladies brought here to sing when she could not were heard by the public with the most royal indifference; which, on grounds totally opposite, neither merited. The first was a young singer, then of high promise; this was Mademoiselle Cruvelli; the second was a lady who (if no longer in the bloom of her talent) had gained, deservedly, a universal Italian reputation; this was Madame Tadolini.

Though Mademoiselle Cruvelli proved, a year or two later, in London and in Paris, the most disappointing person whom I have ever heard, when she arrived in London for Mademoiselle Lind's second season she had more of the qualities which excite expectation than belong to ninety-nine out of a hundred stage singers— youth, a presence commanding, if somewhat peculiar (with a difference, recalling that of Mademoiselle Fanny Elssler), a superb voice, almost three octaves in compass, and a fervour and ambition which it could not be then foreseen would take their after-forms of reckless and perverse eccentricity.   She gained, as time went on, some of the appearance, some of the reality, of a vocalist; but with every such gain in skill and in position there seemed to come a loss —an added inconsistency, wildness, disregard of such usages as belong to progress, justified by no temporary popularity, whether here or over the water.   Towards the close of her theatrical career there were hazardous musical freaks ventured, at the Grand Opera of Paris, by Mademoiselle Cruvelli, hardly to be precedented. She thought it becoming to alter a rhythm, in a duet from *Les Huguenots,* from triple to common tempo.   The curiosities of her reading of the striking temple scene in the second act of Spontini's *Vestale,* where she turned her back on her duty to the artists about to enter, and gesticulated to the stalls, are before my eyes.   But in the year of which I now speak, Mademoiselle Cruvelli was rich in promise as few have been.   Prophecy itself would have been puzzled to discern how this might be falsified.   But when she sang carefully (a little like a scholar), and acted discreetly (yet obviously with intelligence), she passed unregarded—always theatrically applauded, but without any person concerned in her place of trial paying apparent attention to one, in most respects, then so extraordinary.

Madame Tadolini fared yet worse.   Her years were unfairly counted against her.   She fell on a soil wholly uncongenial to a southern woman who has been famous at home, and whose rights to fame were far from having died out.   There was small care or pains taken to conceal from her that she was merely a stop-gap. The opera, *Linda,* in which she appeared, has never been a popular one in England.   She was ill dressed, and some of her vocal freshness and accomplishment had, no doubt, departed from her: and accordingly she went as she came, without exciting the slightest interest in the public.

One artist new to England—Signor Beletti—took his ground here at once as the basso cantante next to Signor Tamburini who had been heard for twenty years.   That he has since improved his position in this country, as a serious concert singer of the highest order, need hardly be added.   The two new Italian tenors were worthless.   Our redoubtable countryman, Mr. Sims Reeves (probably the best English tenor who has ever existed), sang once only

—owing, it was said before the curtain, to misunderstandings behind it.

We were still not habituated to Signor Verdi's violent music; and thus his *Attila* was rejected in London. An attempt was made by Mademoiselle Cruvelli, by extra animation in the amazonian part of its heroine, to "improve" (as divines have it) the political events of the insurrectionary year 1848. But the fire was not sacred: flame did not kindle our cold hearts; the patriotic shout fell on deaf ears.

The year, in brief, in spite of every outward sign of honour and glory, was felt to be virtually one announcing decomposition and embarrassment.

THE YEAR 1848

ROYAL ITALIAN OPERA

OPERAS. *La Somnambula, Gli Montecchi,* Bellini; *Lucia, La Favorita, Lucrezia,* Donizetti; *La Prova d'un Opera Seria,* Gnecco; *Les Huguenots,** Meyerbeer; *Don Giovanni,* Mozart; *Il Tancredi, La Donna del Lago, La Cenerentola, Guillaume Tell, Il Barbiere, Semiramide,* Rossini. PRINCIPAL SINGERS. Mdes. Persiani, Alboni, Castellan, Grisi, Viardot; MM. Salvi, Polonini, Corradi-Setti,* Roger,* Mario, Tamburini, Flavio,* Ronconi, Marini. PRINCIPAL DANCER. Mdlle. Fabbri.

THE YEAR 1848

HIS year placed the artistic success of the new opera theatre beyond possible question. Rumours were circulated before the curtain of the Haymarket Opera House [1] with eager alacrity, speaking of wreck and ruin as imminent; and these were proved not to be baseless by subsequent disclosures in the law courts of heavy losses endured by the original capitalists. But to close a theatre in which a public finds enjoyment, and from which good things are to be expected, is a catastrophe harder to bring about than the outer world, unaware of the fascination of such speculations, could be readily made to believe. Musically the performances at the Royal Italian Opera were of a magnificence which entirely bore down the attraction of the rival theatre, great and intoxicating as it was, in the presence of a singer who had driven the world, sacred and profane, well-nigh frantic. The productions of *La Favorita* and *Les Huguenots,* on a scale of splendour totally unattempted before, settled the question of character, with a decision beyond all power of cavil or cabal to shake.

The former opera—Donizetti's best serious work—had never till then been relished in England. In truth, to counterbalance the painful nature of the story it required, for this country, such impassioned singing and acting as those of Madame Grisi and Signor Mario, and such a lavish splendour of pictorial decoration and choral solemnity as was thrown into the impressive monastery act. Even with all these advantages and accessories, *La Favorita* has never been so popular with us as *Lucrezia Borgia,* though it is by much the finer opera of the two.

Then, too, public attention was absorbed by the revelation of M. Meyerbeer's brilliant dramatic genius, which had till then been denied, or grudgingly admitted here. *Les Huguenots* had been produced in Paris twelve years earlier, and a performance of it, on a reduced scale, had been offered in London by a Belgian and

[1] Her Majesty's Theatre.—*E. N.*

by a German company; but our critics and connoisseurs had ignored it, with small exception; and those who spoke of it enthusiastically from having heard it in Paris (I may allude among them to myself), were treated with ridicule or silence. Like all dramatic music, it is little fit for the concert room,—as little fit as Donna Anna's great recitative, or the murder duet in *Otello*. Neither can it be effectively performed by a handful of artists in a corner. Had it not been for Madame Viardot's engagement we might never have made its acquaintance, for the Italian artists derided it then. "Chinese music," I think they called it; and but for the animating presence of the Valentine, most of its great situations would have passed off coldly. It may be said to have been produced "against the grain," though no pains and splendour in preparation had been denied it, and the cast was a strong one. It was produced on a Court night, "when our Royalties came in state"; and, so far as I can recollect, the opera was "commanded." But from the evening of its production at Covent Garden Theatre, our public was grasped by that grand musical tragedy with a hold which, it will be seen, has not yet been loosened.

The revival of *Tancredi,* though the singing of Madame Persiani and Madame Alboni was delicious, produced no effect. Neither did that of Bellini's weak *Gli Montecchi,* in spite of Madame Viardot's picturesqueness and power as Romeo (especially displayed in the second act). Neither could all the beauty of *Guillaume Tell* establish that opera—a feat which has not been accomplished till the present year, 1861. That cleverest but most mannered of French tenors, M. Roger, found no favour here. Though the day of French grand opera was, clearly, at last come, as the inevitable resource against Italian penury, the time for French singers had not yet arrived,—the reception on the English stage of M. Duprez (though he came to England when in his wane) making the exception to the general indifference.

M. MEYERBEER'S OPERAS

CHARACTERISTICS

IT may be too early to offer a complete character of an artist whose remarkable talent so nearly approaches genius as to make the distinction a matter of the most extreme nicety. But the pre-eminent position held by M. Meyerbeer as a composer in our foreign opera houses since the year 1848 makes the attempt a matter of necessity.

He cannot be numbered amongst the musicians whose individuality asserted itself at once. But men must be valued in art by what they do, not by when they do it,—and again, not by quantity alone but by quality. Such promise as there is in M. Meyerbeer's earlier operas confines itself to a display of the old known Italian forms. Even in *Il Crociato,* which reveals a perceptibly advancing ambition, that which is faded and borrowed predominates. There is an inherent leanness in the ideas, in spite of the semblance of great pomp and brilliancy. Though he was born and trained in Germany, there is little or nothing of the home-spirit in the music of Weber's fellow-pupil. When he wrote for Italy he was unable, like Hasse and other of his countrymen who have adopted the southern stage, thoroughly to Italianize himself, to assume the ease and the *disinvoltura* which characterize all the theatrical music of the south. In fact, till the Grand Opera of Paris, with all its resources,—in those days more vast than were to be found elsewhere,—was open to him, M. Meyerbeer did not find his style or his vocation, which was to produce elaborate dramas in music of the eclectic school.

The operas since produced by him are more difficult to analyze than even the generality of specimens of eclectic art, so intricate is the mixture of many elements—the mosaic of what is precious with what is trite—which they display; so far beyond the beaten track of rule and precedent do they travel in their course.

M. Meyerbeer's timidity in construction,[1] the absence of sustaining breadth in his inspirations, may in part be ascribed to his having studied under Vogler (Weber's master, too), a man of genius, but in some degree eccentric, many of whose principles and practices have been pronounced unsound by the thoroughly instructed. The original vein of melody, however, can hardly have been rich. No tune of M. Meyerbeer's has become a household word.   On the other hand, no one has shown so much patience in research for effect, such an indomitable ambition as he.   Stage combination cannot go further than in the quarrel scene in the Pré aux Clercs, in the third act of *Les Huguenots*—than in the cathedral scene in *Le Prophète*—than in the first finale to *L'Etoile*.   This last, however—as many an old Mass for four choirs and more could testify—is an affair of calculation, not inspiration, a feat the difficulty of which seems to be greater than it is, and to the accomplishment of which some nature and grace in idea must inevitably be sacrificed, since the pieces to be enwrought into such a mosaic must necessarily be made of a particular and geometrical shape, the themes only becoming tractable in proportion as they are small in limit and insipid.   There is far more of real, individual excellence, far more of material added to the musician's stores, in M. Meyerbeer's treatment of the orchestra.   For this, no less than for colour in painting, there must, I have always held, be natural instinct, a happiness of touch and arrangement not to be communicated by precept.   It is true that some of M. Meyerbeer's discoveries and effects belong to the curiosities of music, and as such will not bear repetition; that he too often affects those instrumental mixtures which startle rather than satisfy; that sometimes he neglects

---

[1] That this amounts to want of resource can hardly be questioned. Experienced as M. Meyerbeer is, and restlessly in quest of effect, his devices of modulation and progression are strangely few; and his favourite one, a close chromatic sequence, gives a feeling of narrowness as distinct from breadth, and of uneasiness, at variance with that impression of frankness and nature so desirable in all composition, especially for voices. It is observable, again, that in his elaborate pieces M. Meyerbeer appears frequently embarrassed how to return to his key, and that their close by no means corresponds with their commencement. Writers of the new school, it is true, too largely show a disposition to fling off this necessity, in their search for what is vague and their avoidance of commonplace; but the emancipation, when defended as a principle, can merely be regarded as a movement of decomposition, which, if taken into conjunction with the annihilation of rhythm and "the concealment of melody" (a phrase we have lived to hear gravely used), would go far to throw music back into the chaos from which the art struggled slowly into life-breath and beauty.

that portion of the orchestra, the quartet of stringed instruments, in which its life blood may be said to reside. But besides all this there is something real, precious, altogether the artist's own, in the instrumental settings of his operas, which must be contemplated with pleasure,—though they cannot be appealed to as a model without danger of exaggeration and conceit on the part of the imitator. There is nothing less satisfactory than the music of those who have taken M. Meyerbeer's combinations and triumphs as their point of departure.

M. Meyerbeer's most striking individuality will be found in rhythm. In this branch of his art he is so strong as to be able to conceal inequalities which, in the hands of any artist less strong, would be fatal to the ear's pleasure. Of the hundreds who have marched to the grand Coronation tune in *Le Prophète* there are probably not ten people who recollect that the first phrase of that gorgeous march is one of five bars. No one, again, has given such stateliness and variety to the somewhat formal measure of the minuet as he has done. The minuet which opens the last act of *Les Huguenots* (now too frequently omitted, owing to the length of the opera) has a combination of stateliness and variety which, till he came, had not been found. But M. Meyerbeer's dance music is so bold, brilliant, seductive and characteristic as to form a feature of as much importance as beauty. It was to the charm of the ballet and the pantomime that *Robert* owed much of its first success. It is the vivacity and seizing grace of the ballets which carry off the heaviness of the third act of *Le Prophète*, unrelieved as the act is (which is always dangerous) by the contrast of a woman's voice.

In this portion of his music we seem to touch the most spontaneous side of M. Meyerbeer's talent. Though not unfrequently commonplace in his vocal melodies, though seldom, if ever, able to furnish a good second part to a tune, let its opening phrase have been ever so attractive, the elegance of his dance music is as striking as is its originality. There is nothing fragmentary in it, no want of breath; but everywhere an affluent, luxurious fancy, a piquancy, a pomp, a sentiment, as may be demanded, raising that which is only accessory and ornamental to a consequence which it has acquired in few other hands. M. Meyerbeer's extreme *fidgettiness* in notation (no other word than this colloquial one so precisely expresses my meaning) is calculated to increase the impression of patchwork which the eye receives when studying one of his scores. Many of the half-bars perpetually poked in by him, to the utter damage of orderly symmetry, are merely so many expressions of a rallentando movement which the master has been resolute to regulate, so as to reduce the singer into a condition of an obsequious automaton. This is needless, wrong, and wearying to those on whom every composer must depend, as depriving them of their individuality. To me a Geneva box is as expressive as the interpreter who is so nipped and trimmed and padded that he can only raise his eyebrows, or prolong his breath for one second's or for three seconds' time, just as the master shall please. There can be no true musical execution without freedom; and freedom means playing—playing with singing among other plays.

But in the annals of musical works produced by a man of great success it may be said, without malice, that nothing has been produced at once so elaborate and so altered as M. Meyerbeer's operas. There are tales of mischief and intrigue current in the world, before the curtain, which are too droll in their exaggeration to pass without the strongest protest. Living folk still record tales how, when *Robert le Diable* was coming, people were hired,—"*dormeurs*,"—to sleep in the pit, possibly to snore, every evening when *Guillaume Tell* was performed. What avail professional sleepers, whether seven or seventy and seven? "The little finger" of *Guillaume Tell* is more precious than the whole body of *Robert*.

I allude openly to these children's tales because they inevitably enter into such a book as mine. The certainty is that M. Meyerbeer has always shown himself undecided. The first dramatic idea, with him, would seem to go little beyond his yielding to the temptation of a period, a trait of local colour, a subject, and its developments and transformations, till the last moment when it appears to be at the mercy of chance—then to be ruled by some accessory consideration referable to other things than musical purpose or continuous thought.

Robert, it has been said by Dr. Véron in his *Memoirs* (and Dr. Véron was the manager of the Grand Opera when *Robert* was adventured), was made and re-made ere it took its present form. The scene of resuscitation in the ruined convent owed its ghastly colour to a stage manager, who fancied something newer and more awful than the ballet of simpering women with wreaths and garlands, laid out for it. The two grand operas which followed *Robert* at the same theatre have been more largely modified and reconsidered. The fourth act of *Les Huguenots,* that masterpiece of dramatic effect, stands in its present form owing to Nourrit, the singer. It was originally intended that the St. Bartholomew massacre should be organized by Queen Marguerite, and not by the father of the heroine; but it was pointed out that the interest attaching to the presence of Valentine, as an involuntary and horror-stricken witness, would be impaired by the predominance on the stage of another female character,—and the change for the better was accordingly made. Yet more, the grand duet with which the act now closes—*that* duet of passion and agony, which every subsequent tragical composer has tried to emulate—that duet, which has been commented on as an unparagoned proof of force on the part of the master who could produce such effects with two voices, after such an overcoming and astounding a chorus as "the Blessing of the Swords," was an afterthought, wrought out in complaisance to Nourrit, who felt that the situation of the two lovers in the drama not only admitted but demanded such an encounter, such an outburst, such a confession, wrung out by the terror of such a parting, in such a place, at such a time. Certainly, never was suggestion adopted and acted upon with more power and felicity. This duet is perhaps the most brilliant illustration contributed by music to the chapter of accidents.

Still greater are understood to have been the changes made in *Le Prophète,* because more long-drawn was the period of its gestation. It was contrived and "cast on" for Nourrit, possibly at the instance of that poetical artist,—the most intellectually gifted of tenors on record. Yet the opera did not see the light till Nourrit's successor (M. Duprez) had vanished from the French stage, and, in him, the only artist whose peculiar qualities and excellencies would have enabled him to do entire musical and dramatic justice to the arduous part of John of Leyden,—the lover, the son, the self-abused fanatic, struck down in his hour of pride and triumph by shame, remorse, and retribution. Till now, only one half of so mixed and difficult a character has been conceived and wrought out. *This* representative has given us the love and the personal charm, the filial affection, the suppliant weakness, dissembling to avoid the horror of detection, the Sardanapalus touch of voluptuousness with which wreck and ruin and death are invested with all the wreaths and robes of revelry, half reckless, half melancholy. *The other singer* may have been more sufficient to the drama in the scenes where the false fanatics tempt the true dreamer, and where he, in his turn, overrules the rising rebellion by the command of his presence, in the moment of hazard; but I have never seen anything like a complete conception of the character, so wide in its range of emotions, and might have doubted its possibility had I not remembered the admirable, subtle, and riveting dramatic treatment of Eleazar in *La Juive* (the Shylock of opera) by M. Duprez.

The difficulty of finding any adequate representative of the principal false-hero-character, and the circumstance of one of the greatest creative artists whom the world has ever seen being within reach at the moment when the drama was to be given, may have caused the extensive alterations, almost amounting to reconstruction, which *Le Prophète* underwent, with M. Roger and Madame Viardot as its leading personages. The mother (a character, by strange chance, new to serious opera) was, from a secondary figure, transformed into a principal one; and the betrothed bride of the fanatic leader (the outrage on which bride, by feudal exaction, was one main motive of his rebellion, and of his yielding to the false counsels of the Anabaptist fanatics) was deprived of her original importance to the story. The gain was great and peculiar, inasmuch as it placed a new type—that of the devoted and devout burgher woman, without youth or beauty—on the opera stage; but the drama and the music, if considered as a whole, lost by it. Something of the contrast which is so essential to a long and serious work was taken away, something of proportion destroyed.

In another point of view, M. Meyerbeer's over-solicitude must result in dangerous change to every work so calculated as are his works, when they are produced under new circumstances. It has cost *Les Huguenots* some of its most charming music,—and, in England, more than this. The original commencement of the opera is now annihilated everywhere; and yet the original commencement of the opera has a courtly elegance and finish, a delicacy of phrase, a distinction of form, such as cannot be packed away or suppressed without loss to the great picture and damage to the Master, who has shown himself as capable of seizing in music the chameleon colours of artificial society as of grasping the rude customs of rough, natural character. Then the amount of complication, the resolution to demand from every executing voice its extremest services, which are peculiar to M. Meyerbeer's operas, render a perfect execution of them so difficult as to be the exception, not the rule. There has been no perfect execution of any among them save at the time and place of their first production. That which can be obtained after months of preparation in Paris, from artists excited to prodigious feats by the perpetual presence of one merciless in exaction, can only at very rare intervals be produced elsewhere. I shall speak of the subsequent works of M. Meyerbeer in some detail, as is due to their importance to modern opera.

MADAME PAULINE VIARDOT

ONE of the greatest first-class singers of any time is now to be set in her place so far as I can do it,— a woman of genius peculiar, inasmuch as it is universal. The gibe of "inspired idiocy" has been too often thrown by their contemners against musicians —most of all, executant musicians. It is well, once in a life's experience, to have known, seen, and proved that the culture of art to its highest point, in a world mistrusted unfairly as one of exclusive sensual seduction, neither narrows nor precludes nor preoccupies the artist so as to limit the play of fancy, or the exercise of wholesome affection, or the intelligence which will keep abreast of its time. Let the excuse be taken away once for all from the torpid and mercenary who would shelter themselves behind it, let the reproach be once for all silenced in the mouths of superficial bystanders. There was no more consummate, devoted, thoroughly-musical musician than the composer of *Elijah;* yet he was the man of wit, the man of reading, the man of society, the man of many languages, the man of other arts and other worlds than his own. His, however, is not a solitary instance, without parallel.

Madame Viardot—born Pauline Garcia—from her outset in life stood before the public in a position difficult to occupy, under the disadvantageous shelter of a family name. There have been mediocre tribes of stage and concert people, it is true, who have been helped and placed by the incident of birth,—such folk as the four singing sisters Heinefetter, and as many singing sisters Vespermann. In a singing family there is, mostly, a duet, a better and a worse voice, a train and a train-bearer; and the worse voice gets dragged up by supporting the better one. Such, however, was not the case with Pauline Garcia. Malibran had gone years before her time of coming came; and the melancholy circumstances of so painful a death, after so meteoric a career as Malibran's, enhanced a reputation which had been already in itself formidable enough. Her younger sister had to face the world of art uncompanioned, and without having natural attractions equal to those of her father's daughter, who had already a second time made the name glorious.

The Italian stage, at the time when Pauline Garcia ventured on it, was filled by a woman in her prime of beauty, with a voice almost faultless; possessing a rare shrewdness of appropriation, if not powers of invention, a nature rich in dramatic impulse, untiring health, unfailing equality, and who, by this wonderful combination of qualities, kept her throne at the Italian Opera against all comers and goers for a quarter of a century, and (past denial) satisfied her audiences more completely than Malibran herself—Madame Pasta's successor—had done, to the point of making some among them speak of her as of one on whom Madame Pasta's mantle had fallen.

Well, this new Garcia, with a figure hardly formed, with a face which every experience and every year must soften and harmonize, with a voice in no respect excellent or equal, though of extensive compass, with an amount of sensitiveness which robbed her of half her power, came out in the grand singers' days of Italian opera in London, and in a part most arduous, on every ground of memory, comparison, and intrinsic difficulty—Desdemona in *Otello*. Nothing stranger, more incomplete in its completeness, more unspeakably indicating a new and masterful artist, can be recorded than that first appearance. She looked older than her years; her frame (then a mere reed) quivered this way and that; her character-dress seemed to puzzle her, and the motion of her hands as much. Her voice was hardly settled, even within its own after-conditions; and yet, paradoxical as it may seem, she was at ease on the stage, because she brought thither instinct for acting, experience of music, knowledge how to sing, and consummate intelligence. There could be no doubt with anyone who saw that Desdemona on that night, that another great career was begun.

Her first song in that opera, an air introduced to replace the original air by its composer—which is weak, besides being identical with one in *La Donna del Lago*—placed her extraordinary vocal preparation past dispute, the scena being one of as much difficulty as ingenuity, written by Signor Costa. In the second act, her treatment of the agitated movement in the finale, which precedes the startling and terrible entrance of Desdemona's father, was astounding in its passion and the brilliancy of its musical display, if considered as forming part of a first performance of one so young. All the Malibran fire, courage, and accomplishment without limit were in it,—but something else besides, and (some of us fancied) beyond these.

This first performance, however, seized the musicians more powerfully than it fascinated the public. To be real, to be serious, to be thoroughly armed and prepared, to be at once young and old, new and experienced, is not enough. Particular qualities are not to be dispensed with in England when the public mind is in a certain state. The absence of regular beauty can sometimes, but not always, be forgiven. Then this young girl had another drawback in the very completeness of her talent. It was hard to believe that she *could be* so young, if capable to sing with such perfect execution and such enthusiasm: nor had the voice from the first ever a *young* sound. Here and there were tones of an engaging tenderness, but, here and there, tones of a less winning quality. In spite of an art which has never (at so early an age) been exceeded in amount, it was to be felt that nature had given her a rebel to subdue, not a vassal to command, in her voice. From the first she chose to possess certain upper notes which must needs be fabricated, and which never could be produced without the appearance of effort. By this despotic exercise of will it is possible that her real voice—a limited mezzo-soprano—may have been weakened. Unless the frame be more than usually robust, the process (as I have said elsewhere) is always more or less perilous. But in these days everyone will sing altissimo—basses where tenors used to disport themselves, tenors in regions as high as those devoted by Handel to his contralti, while contralti must now possess themselves of soprano notes, by hook or by crook, and soprani are compelled to *speak,* where formerly they were content to warble. There is no good in lamenting over this tendency; there is small possibility of controlling it; but its influence on the art of singing is hardly to be questioned.

The impression made on our London world by the new singer was, at first, greater in the concert room than on the stage; and yet, there she had to measure herself against a no less accomplished mistress of the subtlest art of vocal finish than Madame Persiani. Among the most perfect things of their kind ever heard were the duet-cadences in the duets from *Tancredi* which they used to present; and these were mostly combined and composed by the girl—higher in taste than the similar ornaments which Malibran and Sontag had executed, though sometimes, like those, a little far-fetched. I have never become wholly reconciled to the cunningly modulated instrumental cadences which Madame Pasta first introduced, and which the Garcia sisters elaborated, in the less modulated music of the Italian school. The garniture may overlay, as much as it sets off, the material which it is meant to decorate.

After one or two seasons of questionable success—not questionable appreciation—Madame Viardot disappeared from France and England for a considerable period. She was to be heard of in Russia, in Germany, in Austria, as making her way upwards, always at first and afterwards most largely among the musicians and the poets and the persons of highest culture and intelligence. It was rumoured that she had ripened and chastened her powers as an actress. It was as perpetually rumoured that she had lost her voice, the truth of the matter having always been that every fresh audience had to become accustomed to the original defects of the voice. At last, as has been noted, she came to our Royal Italian Opera with the prelude of this mixed reputation, and with the disadvantage, again, of the wonderful early promise, or rather performance, being remembered.

Every circumstance connected with Madame Viardot's reappearance was badly devised, and attended by still worse fortune. She was to appear in *La Somnambula,* in this provoking comparison on every side—with her recollected sister, with Madame Persiani, with Mdlle. Lind, whose best part was Amina. As if these things were not enough, the tenor, experienced in Elvino's music, and the delight of our public, with whom she was to have appeared, was "indisposed" when the evening came (the word has many stage meanings), and there was found a Spanish gentleman, Senhor Puíg, who sang as Signor Flavio—used, it was said, to the opera—and in company with whom (I believe, without rehearsal) she had to go through her own ordeal.

That she passed through it so well I have always regarded as a wonder. That the impression on a thoughtless general public was in part disappointment, in part confirmation of rumour, was no wonder. She was nervous; the rebel voice more than once refused to obey her command; she had to avoid acting in order not to be put wrong by a stranger. Still, the great artist was to be recognized by all who had eyes to see and ears to hear. I have never seen a somnambulist heroine whose sleep was so dead as Madame Viardot's. The warmth and flexibility of her execution, throughout marked by new touches, told in her first and her last air (though the rondo, to be just, has been sung by no one so well as by Madame Persiani). What she was next to do, and where she was to be, in a theatre where every throne seemed to be occupied by those who sat firm, it was hard to divine.

The doubt was prolonged, and the fight made hard, by every possible circumstance and accident. But the resolute artist gained ground and won her way, in spite of rivalry, in spite of opportunity denied. When beyond the walls of the theatre, her resources were seen to be boundless—to embrace every language to which music is sung, every style in which music can be written, whether ancient or modern, severe or florid, sacred or profane, strictly composed or nationally wild. Without tediously drawing out a list, it may be asserted that nothing comparable to its length and variety is on record in the annals of singers—save, as may be seen, in the achievements of Sontag.

It was not till *Les Huguenots* was given "on command" (an opera, as has been said, then avoided with aversion by all the Italian artists), that Madame Viardot, placed in her right position, and in music till then neglected because ill-rendered here, established a reputation different from, and superior to, that of any other prima donna within the compass of these recollections. The effect which was to be produced in it seemed to strike conviction that the opera was not so much "foolishness" into Madame Grisi, who subsequently, in consequence of Madame Viardot's deferred arrival, appropriated the part, and, with it, took as tradition some of her predecessor's inventions—especially those of listening terror, in the striking conspiracy scene. Something of the kind Madame Alboni had done, by copying one of Madame Viardot's changes in one of her favourite show-pieces, the *Cenerentola* rondo. The above is history—not dispraise to the imitators, but, however, due to the inventor, the latter a figure, in art as in science—alas!—how often unfairly overlooked.

I have elsewhere adverted to Madame Viardot's admirable performance of a character unbecoming to her voice—that of Rachel, in M. Halévy's *La Juive*. The music of that opera has been unfairly depreciated in England, and her acting in it was passed over, save by the few. Her other great success, then, in England, was in M. Meyerbeer's *Prophète*,—an opera so thoroughly identified with herself, and so animated by her probable performance of a character (however improbable) high-toned and new in an opera, that it has lived a languishing life here since she has been withdrawn from it, as compared with the former work. The intrinsic merits of this opera will be discussed elsewhere; but here it must be repeated that our artist could set on the scene a homely burgher woman, with only maternal love and devotion to give her interest, and could so harmonize the improbabilities of a violent and gloomy story, and of music too much forced, as to make the world, for a while, accept it for its composer's masterpiece. When the story of M. Meyerbeer's operas is finally written it may prove that he was as much indebted to Madame Viardot for suggestion in *Le Prophète* as he was to Nourrit in *Les Huguenots*.

This originating faculty,—in spite of many drawbacks, which are never to be lost sight of by those who admit while they admire,— accompanied by great versatility, gives Madame Viardot a place of her own, not to be disputed. It has been proved, once, twice, thrice—to name a second example, in the calm oratorio music given by Signor Costa to the Child of the Temple, Samuel, in his *Eli*, the tone of which, not easy to take without becoming insipid, has been copied by every other singer. It was proved by her bringing out, in the same oratorio world, the recitative of Jezebel, in *Elijah*, which, till Madame Viardot declaimed it, had passed unnoticed. It has been proved, once more, and perhaps most significantly of all, in her latest and most arduous undertaking—the revival of Gluck's *Orphée,* and the triumph of it in modern Paris, as beyond any triumph which the most sanguine and enthusiastic lover of the ancients could have anticipated. It is something to have lived to see such an event, in musical days during which Signor Verdi is King.

My strong conviction it has long been, matured by study and experience, that Gluck is as truly Lord and King of serious musical drama as Handel is of oratorio. As an illustration in music of the power of music, *Orphée* may stand face to face with *Alexander's Feast*. Of the two works it is the one less marked by time.

Patched, altered, transformed, at first—written (it may be) in haste and carelessness—there is no other opera in the world's long list which, with merely three female voices and a chorus, can return to the stage like this, in days like ours, to make the heart throb and the eyes fill. The scene of Orpheus with the demons, his lament over Eurydice, when she is a second time reft from him, have never passed out of memory as concert-music; but who, till the other day, bethought him of the sadness of the funeral introduction, or the more resistless fancy and pathos of the scene in the Elysian Fields? What, in tenderness and delicious melody, can exceed the chorus of the beatified Shades, who first console Orpheus unseen, and then place the hand of the wife, given back to life and love, in *his* hand? There is nothing in the range of drama or poetry—not even the burial of Ophelia, neither the dirge over Fidele, in *Cymbeline*—more affecting than this simple chorus: there is nothing of the same tone in opera to equal it. The awful and menacing wrath of the infernal warders of the Land of Shadows, and their resistance to Love, stronger than death, gradually yielding to the charm of his persuasions, might, I verily believe, be more readily produced than those quiet bars of melody and harmony combined. Even in recollection—as the holiest aspects of nature do, as does some real emotion of past times, all the more touching because of its quietness and unexpectedness—it moves me beyond the power of description by epithet.

To dwell on the selectness and delicacy of Gluck's orchestral writing (a merit too largely overlooked in him) to point out how his devices as well as his melodies have been reproduced—what they have suggested—would lead into tedious specifications and comparisons. It is more to the purpose to insist on the extreme difficulty of his music; difficult, because the finest union of poetical conception and musical skill and dramatic truth without a shade of exaggeration are rare; difficult, as are Miranda, and Perdita, and Volumina, for the actress. It may be doubted whether such a perfect representative of Orpheus ever trod the stage, as Madame Viardot. The part, originally written for an artificial Italian contralto, was subsequently transposed so as to suit a high tenor French voice. That either Guadagni or Legros can have satisfied the eye may be also doubted. The Frenchman, we know, was affected and grimacing in his action. As personated by Madame

Viardot it left nothing to desire. Her want of regularity of feature and of prettiness helped, instead of impairing, the sadness and solemnity of the mourner's countenance; the supple and statuesque grace of her figure gave interest and meaning to every step and every attitude. Yet, after the first scene (which recalled Poussin's well-known picture of "I too in Arcadia"), there was not a single effect that might be called a *pose* or a prepared gesture. The slight, yet not childish, youth, with the yearning that maketh the heart sick, questioning the white groups of shadows that moved slowly through the Elysian Fields, without finding his beloved one; the wondrous thrill of ecstacy which spoke in every fibre of the frame, in the lip quivering with a smile of rapture too great to bear, in the eye humid with delight, as it had been wet with grief, at the moment of recognition and of granted prayer; these things may have been dreamed of, but assuredly were never expressed before. Such perfect embodiment of feeling and fable can hardly be looked for twice. There could be no second group of Niobe!

Further, the peculiar quality of Madame Viardot's voice—its unevenness, its occasional harshness and feebleness, consistent with tones of the gentlest sweetness—was turned by her to account with rare felicity, as giving the variety of light and shade to every word of soliloquy, to every appeal of dialogue. A more perfect and honeyed voice might have recalled the woman too often to fit with the idea of the youth. Her musical handling of so peculiar an instrument will take place in the highest annals of art. After the mournful woefulness of the opening scenes, the kindling of hope and courage when Love points the way to the rescue were expressed by her as by one whom reverence had tied fast, but who felt that its law gave freedom to the believer—her bravura at the end of the first act (the interpolation of which was sanctioned by Gluck, though the music is Bertoni's or Guadagni's—at all events, not his own) showed the artist to be supreme in another light—in that grandeur of execution belonging to the old school, rapidly becoming a lost art. The torrents of roulades, the chains of notes, unmeaning in themselves, were flung out with such exactness, limitless volubility, and majesty as to convert what is essentially a commonplace piece of parade into one of those displays of passionate enthusiasm to which nothing less florid could give scope. As affording relief and contrast, they are not merely pardonable, they are defensible; and thus only to be despised by the indolence of the day, which, in obedience to false taste and narrow pedantry, has allowed one essential branch of art to fall into disuse.

How completely Madame Viardot effected this marvel was shown in a scene of which I was eye-witness. When *Orphée* was given at the Royal Italian Opera in 1860 (not well given, though with some effect, thanks to Gluck's music), the Orphée of the Théâtre Lyrique in Paris, then in London, sang to a circle of amateurs and opera frequenters this stupendous bravura. "Why was this cut out at Covent Garden?" was the question which went round when the plaudits had ceased. The air had *not been* suppressed, but had been toiled at by one without comprehension of its quality, or means to work it out. Here it had passed without recognition. The singer had imitated a few of Madame Viardot's attitudes, had followed some of her readings; but this exhibition of the sorcery which knows where to find gold, by the aid of divination, purpose, and science, was above her reach.

It would have been impossible to have spoken of Madame Viardot's peculiar career—begun, carried through, and continued under difficulties—and to have omitted mention of her Orpheus, though it has not been presented to the public in London, and though, to dwell on it, I have been led beyond the precise limits of my subject.

THE YEAR 1849

HER MAJESTY'S THEATRE

OPERAS. *Norma, La Somnambula,* Bellini; *Il Matrimonio,* Cimarosa; *La Favorita, Linda,* Donizetti; *Robert,* Meyerbeer; *Don Giovanni, Le Nozze,* Mozart; *La Cenerentola, Il Barbiere, Semiramide, La Gazza Ladra, Otello,* Rossini; *I due Foscari,** Verdi. PRINCIPAL SINGERS. Mdes. Alboni, Van Gelder (Giuliani),* Parodi,* Lind, Rossi-Sontag; MM. Gardoni, Beletti, Lablache, F. Lablache, Bordas,* Coletti, Calzolari,* Bartolini.* BALLETS. *Le Diable à Quatre, Electra.* PRINCIPAL DANCERS. Mdes. Carlotta Grisi, Rosati, M. Taglioni.

THE YEAR 1849

SIGNOR ROSSINI'S music, which had been all but banished from Her Majesty's Theatre for a couple of seasons (Mademoiselle Lind not being, apparently, a* ease in his operas), returned there this year, in consequence of changes in the company which rendered performances of the newer refectory not attractive. Signor Verdi's star (as may be seen) had waned—not to brighten in England until his real popularity arrived in *Il Trovatore,* and (more's the discredit!) *La Traviata.* There was no attempt to promise or to produce any new work. The thing to be done, clearly, was to "keep the theatre going," in some manner or other. It was no longer a case of art, but of artists.

The return of Madame Sontag to the stage, as one of the most remarkable events in the biography of singers, claims a separate notice. Another curious appearance was made in the person of Mademoiselle Parodi. Of this young lady persons conversant with the theatres across the Alps had been hearing for some years. It had been told them that she was the tragic singer on whom Madame Pasta had let fall her mantle, that she had been watched, cherished, counselled, approved, by that admirable artist. The supremacy of the departed Queen of musical tragedy has, by the way, been in nothing more remarkably displayed than by the manner in which her approval has been fictitiously worked to recommend inferior singers about to cross the Alps, before they have arrived. It seemed and sounded like disloyalty and scepticism to all that is most real to venture a word, thought, or line of dispraise in regard to the woman of whom Madame Pasta was said to have said "that she was destined to succeed her." I have known in my time, at least, half a score of such heroines.

Mademoiselle Parodi, however, was something better than the ordinary pretenders. She had sung a few times at Milan, or near it, with uncertain effect; but such fact tells nothing from a distance. The assurances, again and again repeated (and this time from no sources open to suspicion) excited in many—myself among the number—the keenest curiosity and expectation.

To those who had never heard or seen Madame Pasta, Mademoiselle Parodi appeared, on the stage, strange-looking, yet rather handsome, having a voice steadily out of tune, and a certain largeness of style which was offered to conceal the want of thorough training.   To those who *did* recollect that great artist, the appearance of Mademoiselle Parodi was painfully tantalizing.   One who wrote at the moment compared it to the China plate sent home from China by the manufacturers there, who, having found a crack in the pattern plate, reproduced, with painful consciousness, the crack throughout the service commissioned from them.   I find the simile recurs to me irresistibly when I am recollecting Mademoiselle Parodi, in reference to my distinct recollections as compared with those of the mighty and impassioned original artist whose career she aspired to reproduce.   There was something of the grand conception, something of the excellent declamation of her predecessor, in this young lady's performances—something of preparation, which separated her from the thoughtless and shapeless girls who are now to be seen flying at the highest stage occupation; but there was something, too—in itself and finally fatal—of the double. The voice was absolutely like Madame Pasta's broken and incomplete voice.   Like hers it was husky; like hers, it was out of tune; only, this time, from first to last.   The original Norma and Medea could so excite herself during the course of a performance that towards the close of it—even when all means seemed to be gone— her magnificent power to move and to satisfy were revealed without a drawback.   For those minutes it was well worth any one's while to wait.   Mademoiselle Parodi had all the organic defects of the elder woman—some of the instincts which encouraged us to fancy that the cloud that wrapped her in the outset might clear off.   But the cloud never cleared.   She presented a singular imitation of Madame Pasta's voice out of tune, and taste in ornament and step and smile—till the last; all the more singular because she was obviously no mocking-bird, bent to mimic the song of somebody else, but a sincere and careful artist.   I have been told that once or twice in private, on the nights when her voice answered to her call, she sang admirably.   Once, too, she produced a real effect on her audience, and in music for which no one could have imagined her fitted—I mean the sea song in *La Tempesta* of M. Halévy.

We had now come to a time at which the supply of Italian opera with Italian singers could no longer be counted on, and when the names of French and German and Belgian artists began to figure largely in the programmes of the year. Madame Van Gelder, who sang as Madame Giuliani, was a well-trained artist with by no means a disagreeable voice—a fairly good second lady. M. Bordas was a thoroughly untutored vocalist, with no presence, no dramatic power,—a man only to be remembered by his name on a list. The only other singer worth a word was Signor Calzolari, with a light tenor voice, somewhat worn, but capable of some execution, —the last singer (till the other day, when M. Belart arrived) who has not been obliged deliberately to omit a large portion of the brilliant passages in Signor Rossini's lighter music. When I have, of late, heard this and the other bawler (to whom Nature had given means to work withal) extolled as a singer in the "grand style" because of his incompetence and inflexibility, I have been, as often, whimsically reminded of the "City Madam" (no fictitious Mrs. Harris, but a real mother with an actual daughter), who said, with a delicious pride in her hope of the family, "She's a dear, true English child—*she* won't learn French."

THE COUNTESS ROSSI

T HE career of Henrietta Sontag, born at Coblenz, on the Rhine, in 1805, the child of actors, was one so singular in its chances and changes that had she not been beautiful and fascinating as a woman, and the greatest German female singer of the century, there is enough in its vicissitudes to furnish matter for a romance. To her consummate charm and merit as an artist justice has not yet been done.

She cannot have enjoyed that perfect vocal education by which singers more favourably circumstanced have profited. Nature, however, had given her a soprano voice of rare and delicate quality, with a sweetness which, in my memory, was only shared by [1] two voices so delicate as hers, and which I have never heard in the voice of any other German woman, be it strong or small. Though not precisely rich it was mellow in tone. The compass of it was two perfect octaves, with a note or two more. This voice was trained principally at the Conservatory in Prague; but the child who began stage life when she was six years old, in the *Donauweibchen* of Kauer, had that sort of indomitable persistence in herself (gentle as she looked, with her blue eyes and her pale brown hair) which goes far to make amends for insufficient training. She must have early made herself, or been made, a musician; for among the feats of her early time was the singing the part of The Princess in Boieldieu's *Jean de Paris* (a favourite opera in Germany) at a moment's notice. But hers, at first, was not the talent which seems the most to seize her countrymen. They do not dislike exaggeration in singing, but call the same "hearty." The appreciation of beauty of sound in the human voice is sparingly given them. Sontag was essentially a singer, not a declamatory artist. Everything that she did must be presented by the agency of grace. As years drew on, emotion and warmth increasingly animated her perform-

---

[1] Those of Madame Stockhausen and Madame Cinti-Damoreau.

ances; but when she began she could do little more than look lovely, display her beautiful voice and careful finish, and be steady as a rock in her execution. Obviously both nature and grace had marked her out for a certain occupation; and thus it was by good chance that the girl arrived at Vienna during the time of Signor Rossini's triumph there and the predominance of Italian opera, and while a singer so accomplished as Madame Mainvielle Fodor was still to be heard. But though Henrietta Sontag's tendencies were towards all that is elegant and florid in southern music, it must not be forgotten that for her the last great German opera—Weber's *Euryanthe*—was written. That he consulted her style more than it was his wont to flatter his singers may be heard in the finale of its first act, and also in the duet with tenor of act the second—so curiously resembling in its melody one of Signor Rossini's *Tancredi* duets. Further, so consummate a musician was she found, so competent to grapple with the most harassing difficulties of unvocal vocal music, that she was chosen by Beethoven as the leading solo voice in his *Missa Solennis,* the extreme difficulty of which has never been exceeded. It may be questioned whether ever artist appeared before the public who, during her career, sang through such a wide range of music; but her natural taste obviously directed her to Italian opera. In this her greatest successes were won, both at Vienna and Berlin. The people became fanatic in admiration of her. The tale is not forgotten of a party of German youths drinking her health, at a joyous supper, in champagne, out of one of her satin shoes which had been stolen for the purpose. The Continent presently rang with the name of one who was as much of a Faëry Princess as of a wonder, if half the tales that went around could be true.

And she *was,* indeed, lovely when she first dared the ordeal of measuring herself, in France and England, against the great southern artists who sang in Italian opera. In her springtime, the musical drama was not the polyglot world which necessity has latterly made it. The taste of French and English amateurs was fastidious. Many shared the Great Frederick of Prussia's indisposition to hear Mara, "because she was a German singer"; many more were prepared to criticize the beautiful young Rhinelander severely, as one who had been over-praised by national partiality. She had, on her arrival in Paris, some imperfections to polish down; she was accused of being sometimes too violent in giving out certain notes; of mistaken method in her execution. She was found reserved, timid, and cold in her acting. But she made good her place among such great Italians as Pisaroni and Madame Pasta, and in rivalry of an artist no less astounding and redoubtable than Maria Malibran; and with the excellent, modest sense of a true artist she added such polish as was wanting to her singing, and some warmth to her personifications of such characters as Desdemona and Donna Anna. She is understood to have made Madame Pasta a subject of close and attentive study; and month after month, at all events, developed on the stage an amount of power the existence of which, at her outset, was doubted. She never could transform herself into an impassioned tragedian; but by the spell of sensibility, taste, and propriety, and of her personal attractions, she established and advanced herself in public favour under circumstances of no common difficulty. In London, though enthusiasm did not get to the length of a shoe for a champagne glass, it took forms no less characteristic of English idolatry. The Sunday papers told of Dukes dying for her, of Marquises only waiting to offer her their coronets at her feet. Royalty itself was said to have mingled in the dance. Her dress, always exquisite, though too laboured, set fashions. Colours and race horses were called by her name; and (not the least significant tribute to her fascinations) a fashionable publisher tickled "the Town's" curiosity by announcing as forthcoming "Travelling Sketches, by Mademoiselle Sontag!"

She had a secret, however; and, like other singers' secrets, it did not get into the Sunday papers. Everyone knows the mysterious Romeo to whom Juliet's faith is plighted, and for whose sake she has promised to leave the stage, so soon as the apron shall be full enough of gold to build the cottage in which Private Life is to dwell,—or else he is the infatuated nobleman, waiting the death of some ancestor with many quarterings on the family 'scutcheon, ere he dare best it with the bright "or azur" of genius, brought in to enliven dull nobility. A merry and a motley list could be drawn out of the expectant lovers of singers, who have only, in fact, existed in the heads of scandal or of paragraph-mongers. Henrietta Sontag *had* a real history of this class to interweave into the story of her artist-career,—and a history long-time secret and unsuspected. There *was* a young Italian nobleman to whom she was betrothed, waiting till their united fortunes should justify their marriage; and she smiled, and sang, and said "No" to everybody and to everything, and, it may be averred, had never written a word of the advertised Sketches, and in the very freshest hour of her youth, beauty, and triumph as a singer, suddenly disappeared from the stage into court-life, as the wife of a diplomat—ere long, an ambassador. That all this might be done in all due order, the King of Prussia paid his tribute to her renown, and made his wedding-present by bestowing on her a patent of nobility. The daughter of the people was extinct. She had her escutcheon and quarterings and a "von" to her maiden name— as was only befitting one who was thenceforth to figure in court circles.

Twenty years passed—in Brussels, in St. Petersburg, in Berlin— but she was never forgotten. Her story, gossips said, was intended to be shadowed forth, "with a difference," in *L'Ambassadrice* of Scribe and M. Auber, written for the only equal she ever possessed—Madame Cinti-Damoreau. Travellers (I may recall, among others, the lady of "the Baltic Letters,") able to penetrate the mysteries of august life, brought home tales from time to time of her popularity, of the preservation of her good looks, and here and there somebody told of her singing. Everyone, however, conceived her to be dead and gone for the public, past recall.

The troubles of 1848 broke out, however; and Mademoiselle Lind having irrevocably left the stage, and having set sail for America, something must be done for the Haymarket Opera, which the Covent Garden Opera was pressing hard. And one May-day, with as many flourishes as pen can make and epithet colour, out came the news that, "owing to family circumstances," the Countess Rossi had consented to resume her profession. What was more, forth came a small book in green and gold, devoted to her former and more recent history, and which, in so many plain words, pointed to the necessities which had prompted her return to Her Majesty's Theatre as a special instance of Divine interposition!! in favour of a deserving home of aristocratic entertainment!!!

These circumstances of her return to the stage must be dwelt on; for a more curious and noticeable event is not on opera record.

No revival has ever been made under circumstances of greater peril. Every possible means of exhausting a theatre by success had been resorted to in the popularity and departure of Mademoiselle Jenny Lind. During the period of its duration, the voice of the public (as I have said) became rancorous and persecuting to those who considered her as a great singer where other great singers had been, but who did not consider her as the greatest of great singers who had ever been. It was dangerous, in society, to offer a word of comparison on the subject. It was as dangerous to be silent, when silence was construed as dissent, and dissent was assumed to be so much utter and interested malignity. The old opera days, so charmingly chronicled by Walpole, when Lady Brown (whose Sunday music scandalized so many) flew into rages at and forbid her house to such of her guests as did not rage with her in deification of her own peculiar prima donna, seemed to be revived—so true it is that there is no past earthly folly or frenzy which may not be reproduced in any present generation.

Thus, however great was the stroke of good fortune which could replace the Swedish lady by an ambassadress whom adverse fates compelled to reappear on the scene of her old triumphs after twenty years of court-life, for herself it was an adventure little short of desperate. However the circumstances of her story might be worked out to its uttermost, however all honest people must have felt real sympathy for the mature woman, remembered as so charming in her girlish days, about to measure her present against her past self, it was all the more felt a more fearful hazard for her to measure her musical and dramatic accomplishments against those of a predecessor whose tantalizing disappearance from the stage had rendered her, on many grounds, more than ever an object of fanatical worship.

But Madame Sontag (such was to be now her name) had not slept during the score of years when Grisis and Persianis and Linds were coming and going. She had never laid aside the care and culture of her delicious voice during her episode of ante-chamber work and monotonous court splendour. She sang in public, as an amateur, once or twice for charitable purposes. In private noble circles she was frequently to be heard. The Berlin gossips fifteen years ago, who seemed to resent the exaltation of a girl from among the people to a place of "state and ancientry," had many sharp stories of the willingness of the new-made Countess to sing at court parties if any other amateur appeared there who ran a risk of being found attractive. There was a laughable tale of her thus breaking silence, on the occasion of a French lady (not noble) appearing at Court whose romances had won her some social success,—and singing down her poor little rival, past chance of retrieval. But who that knew Berlin fifteen years ago does not know the enjoyed spite and bitterness of every disparaging story that could be there spread, so as to make artists hate and oppose each other, and circle sit in judgment on circle?[1] Is it not proved at this very hour by the turning out of the rag-bag of evil scandal hoarded up by a rag-picker, in his lifetime admitted to decent society as a man of letters—Varnhagen von Ense? Is it not proved, in a no less significant form, by the avoidance of that real artist and nobleman by nature, Felix Mendelssohn, to settle among his own beloved family in that city of wicked talk? There could be no doubt that the Countess Rossi's whole heart and soul were in the opera; but I never found proved—and, during some acquaintance, I never traced in her—that sort of spiteful rivalry which I have heard imputed to her. She knew her own value; she was honourably anxious to have it owned; but I believe her to have been heart-sound and sweet-tempered—a little vain, as her early career may explain, a little grand, as a singing ambassadress of twenty years' standing may be permitted to be, but, in every fibre of her frame, an honest, real artist; as such, willing to "let live," albeit very desirous to "live" herself. Though part of the advertisement of her return was the coronetted Album handed to her, from which "the Countess" (as she was pointedly called) was intended to strike terror into plebeian audiences when she appeared as a public concert singer—though in private society (where she sang very sparingly, and then only as an amateur) she was generally to be remarked as the most carefully dressed, and most wearily elegant, among the crowd of aristocratic ladies, —the change was immediate, the pleasure was keen and vivid, when she could enter into some question of music with any one more willing to discuss it than eager to compliment her. Her eye brightened, her conversation (never peculiarly intellectual) became animated. She was in her own world again, in her own sphere of

[1] *Modern German Music,* vol. i., p. 158.

legitimate charm and influence. The smile passed, and the face resumed its company-look of insipid suavity, if some Star or Garter lounged up, to talk the regulation nothings which a high-bred man of rank is allowed, in good society, to talk to one still a beauty and an ex-ambassadress. I cannot but think that she rejoiced in her return to the stage, anxious though the moment must have been for her and hers.

There was no need of misgiving on the occasion, at all events. The first notes of Linda's Polacca were sufficient to assure every one who filled the theatre—some out of financial anxiety, some out of envious rivalry, some out of affectionate recollection, some out of mere curiosity, now that the artist was in her old place again, whether the woman had not lost too much of what the girl had been to make the step chargeable with vanity or unjustifiable cupidity. But all went wondrously well. No magic could restore to her voice an upper note or two which time had taken; but the skill, grace, and precision with which she turned to account every atom of power she still possessed, the incomparable steadiness with which she wrought out her composer's intentions—she carried through the part, from first to last, without the slightest failure or sign of weariness—seemed a triumph. She was greeted—as she deserved to be—as a beloved old friend come home again in the late sunnier days.

But it was not at the moment of Madame Sontag's reappearance that we could advert to all the difficulty which added to the honour of its success. She came back under musical conditions entirely changed since she had left the stage—to an orchestra far stronger than that which had supported her voice when it was younger, and to a new world of operas. Into this she ventured with an intrepid industry not to be overpraised, with every new part enhancing the respect of every real lover of music. During the short period of these new performances at Her Majesty's Theatre, which was not equivalent to two complete opera seasons, not merely did Madame Sontag go through the range of her old characters—Susanna, Rosina, Desdemona, Donna Anna, and the like—but she presented herself in seven or eight operas which had not existed when she left the stage—Bellini's *Somnambula*, Donizetti's *Linda, La Figlia del Reggimento, Don Pasquale; Le Tre Nozze*, of Signor Alary, *La Tempesta*, by M. Halévy—the last two works involving what the French call "creation," otherwise the production of a part never before represented. In one of the favourite characters of her predecessor, the elder artist beat the younger one hollow. This was as Maria, in Donizetti's *La Figlia,* which Mdlle. Lind may be said to have brought to England, and considered as her special property. Not merely as displaying vocal art, but in point of dramatic intention, was Madame Sontag by much the higher of the two; and this in spite of her greater age. She was the more archly military in the camp; and in the lesson scene of the second act,—where the reclaimed daughter of the Regiment has to endure the weariness of being trained as a fine lady—the outbreak of old habits and propensities, shown in her vulgarly tasteless finery, in her petulant behaviour, told in the very tones of her voice, made as gay and real a piece of comedy as could be enjoyed.

With myself, the real value of Madame Sontag grew night after night, as her variety, her conscientious steadiness, and her adroit use of diminished powers were thus mercilessly tested. In one respect, compared with everyone who had been in my time, she was alone, in right, perhaps, of the studies of her early days, as a singer of Mozart's music. In this she displayed a taste, a suavity, a solid knowledge, and yet a temperate liberty; the true style was wrought out—a style which possibly no mere southern can ever acquire. She had the Vienna traditions. Traces of this have been shown in England by Madame Van Hasselt-Barth, by Mdlle. Jenny Lutzer (now Madame Dingelstedt), and later by Mdlle. Anna Zerr—one of those excruciating high soprani whose ungraceful screams, however correct or flexible as to notes, make the most patient people desire anodynes; but the easy, equable flow demanded by Mozart's compositions—so melodious, so wondrously sustained, so sentimental (dare I say, so rarely impassioned)— that assertion of individuality which distinguishes a singer from a machine, when dealing with singers' music—that charm which belongs to a keen appreciation of elegance, but which can only be perfected when nature has been genial—have never been so perfectly combined (in my experience) as in her. Her Susanna was, from first to last, a study—not altogether the Susanna of Beaumarchais, but wholly the Susanna of Mozart.

It is impossible, then, to rate the claims of this beautiful and accomplished woman too highly. She had not genius, but she had grace in no common degree of bounty; and with grace, that honourable and untiring desire to give her best, and nothing less than her best, which is more frequently found among northern than southern singers. The latter are apt to have "tempers"; to sulk, or to lounge; to decline all duties that do not bring the reward of immediate applause; to rule, in short, by caprice. She ruled by constancy. Her respect for her public amounted to true nobility, which implies due consideration of others as well as of one's self.

But if her life (as I must think) had, on the whole, been a weary one—and this with no desire to make it such on the part of those who surrounded her—its close, after her return to the stage, was as painful a story as has been often told. What I have tried to present, in the above characteristics and recollections, as something without precedent, failed to strike the public as such; and this is no wonder. Audiences cannot, should not, be expected to weigh and wait, and take a series of performances in the aggregate, and consider beauties with reference to difficulties. In spite of her incomparable exertions to uphold and revive a tottering and exhausted theatre, the engagement of Madame Sontag was understood not to have fulfilled the expectations of those who had contracted it. She had, however, to work out her contract, and in so doing to make acquaintance with artist life under conditions which had no existence when she had quitted the stage. Then the rapid railway transport of our times, which enables the manager to transfer his apprenticed subjects to a fresh place each day, and to call on them for exhibition every night, had not been thought of. This, however, including a Scottish tour during a most harsh winter, Madame Sontag now battled through bravely and without adverting to its hardship—so especially severe for one with a voice so delicate as hers, and past maturity, moreover. Her best was to be done: for her art, for her family, for her manager. I remember hearing her tell, with pretty fatigue (and, for once, some slight regret for the ease and luxury of her court life), how, on the occasion of a railway accident, she had been compelled to struggle through the snow on foot for some miles, to arrive in time for her concert, with the coronetted book. This, however, was got through. When she was free from her English obligations, then came the wear and tear of a career in America, where she had to present herself as successor to one in whose honour hotel rooms had been garnished (by Mr. Barnum) with silver locks, engraved with scriptural mottoes. Through America this remarkable artist steadily and gracefully sang her way, bespeaking no particular indulgence, but winning her audiences wherever she went. In an unfortunate moment it fell to her lot to go down to Mexico. There the pestilence seized her at the moment when her task, in one respect, was nearly accomplished—that of reinstating her family fortunes—when, possibly, the hour was fast coming at which even *her* quiet resolution would have made it impossible for her to fight with time much longer.

Her name should be royally remembered in the noble family restored by her exertions. Her name is here respectfully commemorated—not as Countess Rossi, but as Henrietta Sontag.

THE YEAR 1849

ROYAL ITALIAN OPERA

OPERAS. *Masaniello,** Auber; *La Somnambula,* Bellini; *Il Matrimonio,* Cimarosa; *Linda, Lucrezia Borgia,* Donizetti; *Robert le Diable, Les Huguenots, Le Prophète,** Meyerbeer; *Le Nozze, Don Giovanni,* Mozart; *Semiramide, Il Barbiere, La Donna del Lago,* Rossini. PRINCIPAL SINGERS. Mdes. Dorus-Gras,* Catharine Hayes,* De Meric,* Angri,* Grisi, Persiani, Corbari, Viardot; MM. Mario, Massol,* Tamburini, Salvi, Marini, Sims Reeves, Tagliafico, Polonini, Ronconi. PRINCIPAL DANCER. Madame Pauline Leroux.

MASANIELLO was at last creditably performed in London, with Signor Mario for its hero (singing and looking the Neapolitan fisherman delightfully), for its Fenella, Mdlle. Leroux, and for its other two principal characters, Madame Dorus-Gras and M. Massol,—another proof how, year by year, our foreign musical theatres have had more and more to draw on other lands than Italy for their singers. Madame Dorus-Gras, though never able to lay by her nationality so as to group well with her playfellows, and though deficient in that last elegance which distinguished Madame Cinti and Madame Sontag, was nevertheless an excellent artist, with a combined firmness and volubility of execution which have not been exceeded, and were especially welcome in French music, heard in a concert room. On the stage she pleased less. Her appearance was *not* significant. She was lifeless as an actress. She never mastered Italian, having never mastered French, owing to her Low Country extraction. For all this, her Alice in *Robert* was excellent. She sang the opening song, "Va dit elle," and the semi-Scottish romance, "Quand j'ai quitté la Normandie," more thoroughly in the metallic, exact style which M. Meyerbeer's music demands, than any other singer whom I have heard attempt the part.

We had a Greek lady, too, Mdlle. Angri, in the place of Mdlle. Alboni,—one to whose talent the epithet of eccentric must be applied. Her voice, a contralto, was unique in its quality,—even, easy, hollow, without lusciousness, a little hoarse, without much expression, but it was a voice that *told*. Its volubility was remarkable; there was no difficulty that she did not play with, frivolously and rapidly, as a person half-tamed might do, endowed with amazing natural powers, to whom composure is impossible. Her face and figure lent themselves well to disguise. She wore doublet and hose without the slightest diffidence of sex—without, however, the slightest immodesty. She had instincts for acting. But there seemed to be something uncouth and wild which interposed betwixt her and her English audiences. She never got their sympathy; on the contrary she tired, as those who fail to fulfil the expectations they have excited must always end in doing; and she left the Italian Opera, after a season or two, without leaving behind her an impression or a regret.

The appearance of Mr. Sims Reeves in Italian opera did not as yet bear out the promise made by him in English, on his immediate return from Italy, nor foreshow the career since run by this admirable and real singer. He failed to "fall on his feet" on the foreign opera stage in England—why, it would not be altogether easy to explain: in part, no doubt, from the disinclination which certain audiences have "to their own people," from the same causes as barred our Italian Opera stage to the last of the Kembles, who had been the delight of Naples. A study of our English fastidiousness, relieved with corresponding laxity in allowance, would be worth the care of any historian of manners.

It was less singular that Miss Catharine Hayes, who for a while had been a leading favourite at La Scala in Milan, and aspired to the same position here, should be disappointed in her attempt. We had not as yet descended to the level at which one so irregularly cultivated as she proved herself to be could appear a finished artist. But of her separate mention has been already made.

In 1849 two other foreign artists appeared for the first time elsewhere in London, who have since figured largely in Italian opera. The one was a Belgian lady, Mdlle. Charton, whose agreeable voice and talent made her acceptable in light French operas to all listeners whose Parisian experience was not great, and who did not mark in her that provincial air which must be cast aside ere its wearer can take first rank in a metropolis. The other was Herr Formes, who, as one of a bad German company, created a real sensation by his singing in *Die Zauberflöte*. Never was man endowed with a more majestic voice and presence to work with in his art than he. I can call to mind no other deep bass voice, so deep, so sonorous, so equal as his in 1849, nor did I ever see anyone move with more dignity than did he, then, as High Priest. From the first he possessed himself of the sympathies of the English, who have always been as ready to welcome German as they have been to mistrust French singers. From one so young, so striking in appearance, so obviously endowed with that original talent for the stage which no study can altogether replace, there was much indeed in those days to be expected, especially at a period when the supply of Italian singers was beginning to fall so short.

M. MEYERBEER'S OPERAS

THE production of *Le Prophète* in Paris and in London was the musical event of the troubled year 1849. The reader may be spared retrospect of the extent to which curiosity had been tormented during thirteen years, in regard to this third grand French opera by M. Meyerbeer. Enough to say that "the golden time" in which so serious and singular a work might have set forth to its fullest effect was lost by its composer's hesitation in confiding it to the French theatre during the reign there of M. Duprez. The part of John of Leyden—lover, son, fanatic, penitent—has never been played and sung as it might and would have been by that splendid musical and dramatic artist.

The opera is itself worth a study as an experiment, till then untried, to transport musical drama across its ordinary frontier. A tale which religious and political fanaticism pervades as an element would have tempted few composers save the writer of *Les Huguenots*. But having touched the Puritan in Marcel (a figure not till then indicated in music [1]), it was natural that he should be tempted further still in the same little-trodden path. It was natural that he should forget that what seduces the artist in his study does not always equally delight a mixed audience. The three Anabaptists grouped in place of a single bass voice were, because of their sombre nature, a perilous novelty. Neither is fanaticism, whether it be sincere or hypocritical, a subject readily to be treated in music, because that demands simpler and less unmixed emotions, be they strong or gentle, for its themes. There is no distinct intimation of irony possible in the art. It is difficult

---

[1] It is among the anecdotes which many believe (and in some degree confirmed by the letters just published), that Mendelssohn forbore finishing and giving to the world his *Reformation Symphony,* (a work destined for an anniversary), in consequence of finding the well-known Lutheran psalm-tune destined to figure there, appropriated by M. Meyerbeer.

to intimate that a coronation which is taking place is one of a self-deluded impostor, not of a real king; it is hard to convey the impression of semi-insanity in the canticle with which a religious chief rouses his superstitious soldiers from mutiny and moves them to impossible feats. The actors and the framework of the story must here help the musician. M. Meyerbeer has possibly gone as far as man can go, by characterization in music, to surmount the difficulty; but that, in so doing, he has introduced an element of strain and exaggeration into his opera, the effect of which is felt by many among his audience who do not trouble themselves to search out the cause, is true.

Le Prophète, again, is peculiar as being the first serious opera relying for its principal female interest on the character of the mother. The wife reigns as queen in *Alceste* and *Fidelio;* the outraged revengeful woman in *Medea* and *Norma;* but the pathos of maternal tenderness and devotion, pure of all passion, had been hitherto unattempted till it was tried in this opera. This selection even in this case largely arose from chance. In the first draft of the drama, it has been said, the Prophet's love, wrested from him by the despot, was destined to be the heroine; and, as the drama stands, she still awkwardly crosses the impassioned scenes of its fourth and fifth acts with the purpose of retribution. But the character was virtually effaced from the moment that Madame Viardot was associated with the production of the tragedy, since it was felt by author and musician how admirably she was fitted by nature to add to the gallery of portraits a figure which as yet did not exist there. Her remarkable power of identification with the character set before her was in this case aided by person and voice. The mature burgher woman, in her quaint costume, the pale, tear-worn devotee, searching from city to city for traces of the lost one, and struck with a pious horror at finding him a tool in the hands of hypocritical blasphemy, was till then a being entirely beyond the pale of the ordinary prima donna's comprehension; one to the presentation of which there must go as much simplicity as subtle art, as much of tenderness as of force, as much renunciation of woman's ordinary coquetries as of skill to impress all hearts by the picture of homely love, and desolate grief, and religious enthusiasm.

It is not too much to say that this combination to its utmost force and fineness was wrought out by Madame Viardot, but (the character being an exceptional one) to the disadvantage of every successor. There *can* be no reading of Fides save hers; and thus the opera, compared with *Les Huguenots,* has languished when others have attempted her part—either by copying, as did Mdlle. Wagner and Madame Stoltz, or by attempting, as did Madame Alboni, to carry it through musically, leaving all the dramatic passion and power wisely untouched.

The above peculiarities, then, have had an influence on the present popularity of *Le Prophète,* an influence neither inconsiderable nor unjust. Whether any state of the stage will arrive at which they will be thought merits, not drawbacks, remains for others to see. Meanwhile it is true that they have somewhat chilled admiration for the remarkable musical beauties which the opera contains, some among these separate beauties more attractive than any in *Les Huguenots.* I will not dwell on the droning chant of the preaching Anabaptists, but recall the charming duettino of the two women in the first act (as fresh and real as its writer's chamber-duet, "Mère Grande"); in the second act, on the song of John of Leyden, the arioso for Fides, "Ah, mon fils," and the commencement of the quartet of men which closes the act. The entire movement may have been an attempt to outdo the terzetto of men in *Guillaume Tell,* even as the "Blessing of the Swords," in *Les Huguenots,* may have been suggested by the Swiss conspiracy scene of Signor Rossini's opera; but the opening is excellent, clear, decided, and altogether M. Meyerbeer's own.

Then in the third act of *Le Prophète,* the relief given to its heaviness (as I have said) by the dance music, amounts to a master-stroke of genius. There is nothing more varied, more piquant, more original, more picturesque, than the music of this ballet, prefaced by the chorus with the arrival of the skaters, followed out by the waltz, by the exquisite Redowa (in which a touch of the rhythm of the minuet in *Les Huguenots* occurs), and after the Ice Quadrille—which bears incomparable company to the evolutions on the stage—by the galop, when the rout of peasants and suttlers light their lanterns and start homewards. It is easy to stigmatize these things in opera as empirical; but who can stop or stay, if the intrinsic fascination of them makes its print in the mind? I was brought back to recall this excellent beauty of epi-

sode in M. Meyerbeer's work while listening to the no less delicious Greek chorus with dance, "Parez vos fronts," in Gluck's
Alceste. In a sombre story, such as is *Le Prophète*, the musical
light and cheerfulness let in (supposing opera conventions admitted—and what is opera but conventional, even as regards
drama?) are as precious as brilliant.

Afterwards, before the false Prophet appears on the scene,
comes the Revolt chorus—turbulent, odd, broken (yet full of
musical ideas), which passes scarcely perceived in the drama, but
which is the best revolt, perhaps, on the musical stage, the best
preparation for the entrance of the false Prophet, resolute to
quell the revolt, that could have been contrived. Yet in Paris, till
the very last moment of producing the opera, everything was left
under conditions of modification till the great scene for the
Prophet arrived. In Paris, the prayer in this was suppressed, by
way of meeting the means and the powers of M. Roger. In London, where this was restored, a portion of the after-canticle (containing most beautiful phrases) was retrenched, in consideration
of Signor Mario's strength. As represented both by the French
and the Italian tenor, the scene retains only half its power: as
written, it lays an overburden on any possible Prophet.

In the fourth act, before the cathedral scene comes, there is
still the petition of the worn-out pilgrim, which is one of M.
Meyerbeer's best romances. But in Paris, more than, as yet, in
England, the best of such petitions and romances cannot stop the
action of a great drama in music without protest; and the song,
therefore, can only be received as a preparation for the entry of
the heroine into the cathedral scene. The duet which intervenes,
betwixt the mother and the wandering bride of the false Prophet,
is a forced piece of ingenuity. Not so the grand scene which follows, and which virtually *is Le Prophète*. No more superb example of musical effect exists in drama. The march is gorgeous
in its opening beyond precedent of stage marches, choicely rich in
the melody of the trio. Then comes the organ behind the scenes,
with the church anthem (the latter as sanctimonious as the former
was gorgeous), broken by the imprecations of the distracted
woman, who hears the praises of the false Prophet; her heart the
while moved by the sacrilegious wickedness of him who has
spirited away her son. Next follows the chant of the children

with their censers (curiously lame in the second strophe), all wrought up, with consummate art of climax, to the instant at which the false Prophet, having quelled a revolt, intoxicated, self-deluded, crowned, conceives himself—*is* to himself—divinely inspired. The thunderbolt falls, in the moment of terrible recognition. The wild appeal of the mother, bewildered by surprise and horror, and the weary, wearing yearning of months of pilgrimage; the more fearful struggle still in the heart of the impostor, with the knives of the fanatic fiends who have goaded him into the blasphemous crime close at hand; all this is treated by M. Meyerbeer with the grasp of a giant, able to control the surge of the most tremendous and unlooked-for emotions.

This grand concerted piece, leading, by a chain of its writer's favourite modulations, to the climax of explosion in the scene of the false miracle, is well worth comparing, by those who study effect, with similar movements by Signor Verdi, as containing an example of the broken (or sobbing) phrase used, as expressive of suspense, to its uttermost.

It was perhaps inevitable that the pretended miracle, in which the impostor pretends to restore reason to an insane stranger, and persuades his mother to deny his identity, should rely on the actors more than the music. Such a situation is beyond the power of sound to express, let the transcendentalists say what they will. And indeed it may here be told that this scene might not have retained its present form had any other actress than Madame Viardot "created" (as the French say) its principal part, remembering as I do how, at the last rehearsals, not only every trait and turn of the situation were studied with anxiety, almost hesitation, by Scribe; how there were consultations about shortenings, total omissions; and how Ary Scheffer—that most poetical of modern religious artists, and passionately fond of music—watched its composition as though he had been painting a picture.

Le Prophète of London had a vast advantage over that of Paris in the remarkable personal beauty of Signor Mario, whose appearance in his coronation robes reminded one of some Bishop-Saint in a picture by Van Eyck or Dürer, and who could bring to bear a play of feature, without grimace, into scene of false fascination, entirely beyond the reach of the clever French artist, M. Roger, who originally sustained the character. There can be nothing grander in combination than the sweep of the procession from the cathedral, after the false miracle has been accomplished, with the "Dominum salvum fac" pealing behind the scenes from the organ, and the people shouting almost in adoration. It is a moment of pomp and splendour, never outdone in stage-music. M. Meyerbeer is a composer by moments.

Here, however, *Le Prophète* might and should have ended, but for that inconvenient thing, poetical justice. The fifth act, though nothing is left unattempted which could serve the purpose of effect, is inferior throughout. The grand air of parade with which it opens, howsoever mystified by Madame Viardot's amazing fervour, is queer and tormented as a song. The duet betwixt the mother who asserts herself and the son who repents comes too late in the story, and is curiously cut short at last, as if its composer had felt it misplaced. The elaborate terzet, in which the lost love of the false Prophet reappears, is fierce, difficult, wholly ineffective, though obviously laboured, with the intention of making it one of the important pieces of the opera. The last song at the banquet after the manner of Sardanapalus, where the false Prophet indulges in a voluptuous vengeance and expiation for all the past evil done, and quits the scene—no penitent, but one who conquers his conquerors —with the festal wreath on his head and the festal wine-cup in his hand, does little essentially to redeem the feebleness of this act. The catastrophe belongs to the scene painter and the stage manager. It is not because the bacchanal is vulgarised by its being so closely identical with an Irish street song—"Paddy Carey." Such things have happened before, and will happen again. Handel used a Welsh air in his *Acis,* a Calabrian bag-pipe tune in his *Messiah.* It is because, in the working-up of the familiar phrases, the composer shows himself unequal to the situation,—as if the indecisions and changes of thirteen years' preparation (and half as many months of rehearsal), had left him without clear-sightedness or distinct vigour fit to close the long legend, probable or improbable.

The production of *Le Prophète* may be said to have saved the new Italian Opera House, then notoriously floundering in embarrassments, with a company which was a republic, and, for the time, in a state of discontent amounting to anarchy. Though the first performances were all that was incorrect and incomplete, though the three Anabaptists (without meaning any hypocrisy) sang as falsely as false Anabaptists can sing, though Miss Hayes was insecure, as, indeed, she was always in all new operas, and though Signor Mario had not mastered the difficult intervals of the miracle scene, *Le Prophète* produced an effect not to be forgotten.   It had seemed from the first, to some, that this might not last so long as the effect produced by *Les Huguenots,* but the subsequent course of the opera has, till now, hardly justified the prophecy.   The charm of Madame Viardot's splendid personification wore itself out, because, I must repeat, of the stilted and untruthful nature of the situations.   A year or two later Madame Grisi, always active and intelligent in adopting what she had seen more original artists do, attempted the character, without success.   Yet I fancy that, allowing for the want of one or the other actress, or even of one or other Prophet (the real one being yet to come), and admitting the gloom of the story, and its limited fitness for music, this opera may keep its proportion and its place by the side of the more universal musical drama which it followed—at a very long interval.

M. AUBER'S OPERAS

CHARACTERISTICS

THE musical dramas of M. Auber form, in every respect, a group too remarkable to be passed over. They have sparingly penetrated into Italy; but they have kept the German stage awake, and preserved it from death of the weary dullness and inanity which have fallen on it since Weber was laid to rest, and they have been found pungently necessary in this country; because here, though we have accepted Signor Verdi (with a protest), we have *not* accepted the swarm of second-hand composers in the manner of Signor Verdi, who seem able to cheer easy Italian audiences from carnival to carnival, and whose works die, as the saying is, "like flies." On the other hand, M. Auber, as the type of modern French composers—not able to rise into serious music, and yet able to suspend attention, to charm the ear, and to satisfy the musician's mind by graces and delicacies entirely peculiar to himself—has become, I repeat, in some sort a necessity in England: because here we have not yet arrived at the point of accrediting bad music for fashion's sake, though we have permitted the entry of very paltry musical executants, who have arrived and traded under false colours.

The life of this noticeable composer has been a singular one. He has never, apparently, been disturbed with an idea or a curiosity beyond the barriers of Paris, never seems to have troubled himself with aspirations for foreign fame, never with the idea that there were other theatres than those lying on the rival sides of the Boulevards. He began to write late, as these precocious times of ours go, when young gentlemen aged fourteen are to be received as so many new Mozarts (because Mozart wrote when he was fourteen). But when M. Auber began to write, he began to write as few of these new quasi-Mozarts begin—with a style of his own. It was neither Grétry, nor Boieldieu, nor Dalayrac, nor Monsigny, nor Berton, that M. Auber tried to write over again. It was no emulation of German composers, it was no copying of Italian writers: it was true "French of Paris," and not French after the school of "Stratford atte Bowe"; and it was a "French of Paris" from which confused Germany,—and England, athirst for new operas, no matter whence they come,—have been very glad to derive aliment and variety.

If M. Auber has been always superficial as to feeling, he has been always wondrously elegant as to *costume*. There is no deep science in his *Masaniello,* but there is the fervid south of Naples in it. The unaccompanied prayer in the revolt scene—said to have been devised as a movement for a Mass—the tarantella, the whole tissue of the work, is something fiery, volcanic, alien to French nature and to French habits, something, withal, having a charm for the moment, and a lasting charm also. Then the form of the opera is wholly new—an opera with its principal part a mimic one. Long as it is, it is slight. It contains no grand finale, little, if any, elaborate concerted music, only one duet of high pretension (that duet urged and speeded, as if with flashes of fire, by the orchestra). In short, the work is "trivial" (as we are now invited to accept of the epithet) for a grand opera,—full of ballads and dances and of everything else which (it may be assumed) is impure, and improper, and idle; nevertheless, under its own conditions, a real, permanent work, animated with the life of genius, which will keep it alive.

To no other work, on so large a scale, contributed by M. Auber to the Grand Opera of Paris, can the same praise apply. *Gustave* is carefully wrought, the opening and the close of its overture (under French conditions) delicious, the Galoppe unparagoned among Galoppes. Here, however, it may be seen that the master has spread himself over too wide a canvas. The passion is cold—howsoever, not torn to tatters, as it has been since torn by Signor Verdi, the other day (1861), when aspiring to *re*-set the story (no modest proceeding). In his *Lac des Fées,* the capital student-march which opens the overture, the faëry-chorus, which hangs in the ear with a fascination, even though the fairies be French fairies, the frank, bold, natural hunters' chorus, are all that can be recollected; in *L'Enfant Prodigue,* positively nothing.

But then in comic opera who has been comparable to M. Auber?

—save Signor Rossini, and he only once, in *Il Barbiere*. It has been the fashion to forget that Donizetti's *L'Elisir* was a *re*-setting of the book of M. Auber's *Le Philtre*. The French setting of the story (as I have said) is the better, brighter one of the two. Then *L'Ambassadrice* (most illogically reputed to have been written at Madame Sontag's retirement from the stage and diplomatic marriage) has some comic numbers and graceful melodies of the first quality. The lesson scene, where the real singer endeavours to sing false so as to conceal her singers' origin, and subsequently becomes unable to resist breaking out into every imaginable brilliant passage (as a sort of compensation to herself for the slavery into which she had thrust her genius), is one of the most legitimately delicious and whimsical things extant in the library of opera of any time.

After *L'Ambassadrice—before* any other comic opera save *Il Barbiere*—comes *Le Domino Noir,* to Scribe's happiest, gayest book, written just at that juncture of a man's life when his power of contrivance is complete, and does not wander away into complication. To myself, twenty years ere I had thought of setting English words to it, the charm of that work was rivetting, as one containing something bright, gamesome, delicate, courtly, which exists nowhere else. The music of the first, or ball act, with its quadrille, and bolero, and waltz behind the scenes, with the delicious romance of the "Dama Duende" (Faëry Lady) who drops the nosegay close to the youth feigning sleep, in order that he may enjoy the enchantment, is incomparable, save in *Il Barbiere*. And incomparable is the supper song of Gil Perez, the convent porter, in the second act, with its burden "Deo gratias."

The third, or what may be called the nuns', act of the opera, has that fresh character (first in the talk of a barn-yard, which men are told excites a society of secluded women, next in its religious, feminine feeling) which are almost—altogether—without paragon. It seems like yesterday that I heard Madame Cinti-Damoreau sing the solo with the harp accompaniment to the canticle, which opens with the organ. I can only record the effect by an epithet which may appear overstrained; it was *celestial*.

What, again, of its kind, can be more elegant, and in places more melodious, than *Fra Diavolo?* which, again, is another of the world's *stock* pieces,—music to revel in, without any fatal seduction. If he has been rarely deep, M. Auber is never dull. He falls short of his mark in situations of profound pathos (save, perhaps, in the sleep-song of *Masaniello*). He is greatly behind his Italian brethren in those mad scenes which they so largely affect. He is always light and piquant for voices, delicious in his treatment of the orchestra, and, at this moment of writing (1861) —though, I believe, the patriarch of opera writers (born, it is said, in 1784), having begun to compose at an age when other men have died exhausted by precocious labour—is for that very reason, perhaps, the lightest-hearted, lightest-handed man, still pouring out fragments of pearls and spangles of pure gold on the stage.

To return: I cannot but recollect the bright bits (no false jewels) in *Le Diamant de la Couronne,* the song for the heroine (with a burden), the Spanish duet in the bolero style for the two women; I cannot but allude to the delicious prelude to the overture to *La Sirène,* to much of the music to *Lestocq,* to the laughing song in *Manon Lescaut,* to the piquant overture to *Le Cheval de Bronze,* —a disappointing opera, however, the disappointment of which has always seemed to me strange, so quaintly comical is the story.

With all this, it is as remarkable as it is unfair that, among musicians, when talk is going round, and this person praises that portentous piece of counterpoint, and the other analyses some new chord the ugliness of which has led to its being neglected by most former composers, the name of this brilliant man is hardly, if ever, to be heard. His is the next name among composers belonging to the last thirty years which should be heard after that of Signor Rossini, the number and extent of the works produced by him taken into account, and, with these, the beauties which they contain.

THE YEAR 1850

HER MAJESTY'S THEATRE

OPERAS. *I Puritani, Gli Montecchi, Norma,* Bellini; *Il Matrimonio,* Cimarosa; *Lucia, Don Pasquale, L'Elisir, Lucrezia, La Figlia,* Donizetti; *La Tempesta,** Halévy; *Medea,* Mayer; *Don Giovanni,* Mozart; *Ernani, I Lombardi, Nino,* Verdi. PRINCIPAL SINGERS. Mdes. Parodi, Giuliani, Hayes, Rossi-Sontag, Frezzolini, Bertrand,* Fiorentini;* MM. Michelli,* Beletti, Sims Reeves, Lorenzo,* Calzolari, Lablache, Baucardé,* Coletti, Gardoni. PRINCIPAL DANCERS. Mdes. Ferraris, Carlotta Grisi.

THE YEAR 1850

HE downward course of Her Majesty's Theatre became more and more evident. Such hope as had been placed in the financial result of Madame Sontag's reappearance died out. She was heard with pleasure but without enthusiasm. To myself, the amount of resource which she displayed, considering her age, seemed then, as now, marvellous, a feat almost by itself in the history of opera. But the public did not appreciate this as it deserved. The theatre was falling out of repute, and nothing could save it. None of the new singers excited the slightest sensation. There was, in fact, only one event during the season—the production of *La Tempesta,* by MM. Scribe and Halévy.

I have always thought it an unhappy, though not an unnatural idea, that of arranging Shakespeare's *Tempest* in the form of an opera, to be set by Mendelssohn. The success in faëry-land which he had gained in his *Midsummer Night's Dream* Overture, and which ought to have deterred every one from tempting him to a second enterprise of the kind, was the ground of the mistaken calculation,—a mistake, however, which will be fallen into again and again, so long as the world prefers repetition to novelty. To start merely one difficulty—who *can* present the invisible Ariel on the stage, save as the outburst of a fountain, or as a flash of volcano-fire, or as lightning, or as the shooting of a star? A mime *must* do it; and, however well it be done (and we have seen it as well done as it *can* be done), the dream is gone. The mime flying on stiff wires, be she, he, or it ever so tiny, ever so musical in voice, ever so tricksy in action (a combination not the easiest in the world to realise), lingers long behind imagination; or else makes a gross piece of elf-work before an unpoetical—not therefore necessarily a coarse—public. Then, admirable as was Scribe's stage-manipulation—able, in less aerial visions, to make impossibility forgotten, to reconcile the sharpest discords, to keep up curiosity at the expense of common sense—he was, after all, a Frenchman. Now the French are not to be trusted with Shakespeare, save under protest against the alliance. They *will* clip, and curl, and oil the mane of the lion; they *will* plane down and polish the crevices in the marble rock. Whether it be a Dumas who fits up *Hamlet* with a new catastrophe of corpses round about the Ghost; or a Dudevant, who, out of the fulness of her æsthetic respect, mends *As you like it;* or a Scribe, commissioned to do his best for dancers, singers, machinists, and composer; the result is always the same. The story of *The Tempest,* being at once too simple and dreamy as it stood, was to be rendered piquant by bringing out into coarse light what Shakespeare had only hinted in passing, and by troubling with intrigues the poetical love of Ferdinand and Miranda. A "situation" was to be made out of the odious pursuit of Prospero's daughter by Caliban. Sycorax was endowed with a machinery of witchwork. A final suspense was contrived, in which the heroine was beguiled to the verge of taking her lover's life by the malicious persuasions of her demon enemies.

Though the drama itself had fascinated Mendelssohn, such conventional monstrosities as these thrust into it, by the most skilled of handicraftsmen, were rejected by him at once. He declared that he would not treat the opera book as it stood—this, after his progress in the work, and its date of positive production, and pictures of the performers in character, had been advertised in the London papers!—and, in fact, he never composed a note to it; and threw the matter aside, in displeasure at the engagements entered into without his concurrence.

To supply his place was not easy, especially for a management which had, by promise, confidently undertaken other duties for M. Meyerbeer. The number of possible successors was not large. Among skilled living musicians, there was no one to be found more available than M. Halévy. If he was rarely fanciful, he was never vulgar in his music; if seldom spontaneous, he was always ingenious, and wrote like one to whom all the resources of his art are known. A strange compound of facility with meagre imagination, he put forth to the world few works, few acts, few scenes, which arrest attention or excite rapture. Here and there, as in *La Juive,* are touches of grandeur and emotion. *Les Mousquetaires* breathes the air of the old French Court; *Le Val d'Andorre* has a rustic mountain-quaintness which is no less national; but this makes a brief list of notable pieces, the number and extent of their maker's productions considered. In writing for England, M. Halévy was trammelled by conditions not calculated to nourish fresh and genial inspiration. He had for the second time to set an Italian text (having in his early days written a *Clari* for Malibran); to give life and colour to one principal character, in the form of dance and pantomimic music, in which his strength has never lain; and, lastly, for his heroine to accept a singer who, however incomparable as an artist (and who so incomparable as Sontag?) must needs be spared and cherished within restricted limits as to compass and power when her voice was to be provided for anew.

Produced under all these conditions, I have always felt that *La Tempesta* has more real merit than the world agreed to award it. If not at his best, the composer did himself no discredit in it with those who can think and make allowance. A prayer on board ship, in the impossible "Storm" prologue, a delicate chorus of elves, who time the flights of the dancing Ariel, the great finale to the second act, where Caliban is made to dance, brutified with wine (including a frank, spirited sea-song and burden), in which, as I have said, Mademoiselle Parodi achieved her solitary English success, are all good, effective, and simpler than is the wont of their composer. Yet seldom, by comparison, did the freshness of a real and artless melody seem so deliciously welcome as in Arne's "Where the bee sucks" (since called by certain French historians "Dr. Arne,"— *an English melody*), introduced among the pantomimic music, with as much tact as delicacy, by the Parisian composer.

All was done to produce *La Tempesta* worthily and well that Her Majesty's Theatre could do. The author and the composer were summoned to England; and it is pleasant to remember with what a simple and sensible cordiality Scribe seemed to enjoy his visit and took his place in society. Frenchman to the core, as every line of his hundreds of dramas proves, I remember no Frenchman whose nationality sat so easily on him in our country, as his. By neither look, word, nor sign, could it be inferred that any sight was strange to him, any usage difficult to reconcile with the Median and Persian statutes of French propriety. Yet he was neither flattering, nor insipid, so much as quietly gay—as self-assured as a well-bred man should be, and therefore considerate of the claims of everyone else. More cheerful and agreeable in intercourse no distinguished stranger and comic author could be. (Your comic author is sometimes woefully dreary company in private.)

Most pleasant, too, was Halévy, just gone (March, 1862), respecting whom, therefore, some personal and memorial words may be now permitted, and none the less because the same would especially commemorate the agreeable impression made on all who knew him in this country. He was singularly pleasing and intelligent in intercourse. He was able to get rid of himself and his operas, to take a courteous and clear-sighted pleasure in all the novelties that London offers to Parisian eyes. In fact, after having read the academical discourses which, as the Secretary of the Institut, it was his business to prepare, it may be now fairly said—what during his time of life and artistic production could not have been said without gratuitous incivility—that he had more general intelligence than special genius. The musical talent which he possessed was exclusively Parisian. Anywhere else, save in the capital of France, I have never heard his stage works without a feeling of shortcoming and weariness. The very peculiarities of his style—an extreme illustration of that musical suspense in which the French delight, calling the same, "distinction"—demand French text, French actors, French audiences. I recollect the man, in both capitals, as tenfold more frank and attractive than his music.

The best singers in the company were assembled to give every possible strength and spirit to the drama. The Caliban of Lablache was alike remarkable as a piece of personation and of good taste. Had it not been so, the very hazardous scenes of the monster's persecution of Miranda could not have been allowed on the stage. In these, too, Madame Sontag's delicacy and reserve stood the drama in good stead. The rest of the company had worked with no less good will; the music had been studied to a nicety rarely attained since Signor Costa had left the theatre. There was rich and tasteful scenery. But *La Tempesta* could not live. It was even received with less favour when it was subsequently given at the Italian Opera House in Paris, though there (by way of improvement), the last act was entirely omitted. In England, as yet, Halévy has no public.

The disheartening lethargy which, in spite of every attempt to force applause, and to counterfeit the appearance of success, was creeping over the old opera house, got hold of the ballet too. It seemed totally impossible to excite any interest or curiosity. But we still read, morning after morning, of triumph after triumph, of enormous gains and successes; and the farce, melancholy as it was, was kept up for still a year or two longer, as bravely as if the end had not been from the first to be clearly foreseen.

THE YEAR 1850

ROYAL ITALIAN OPERA

OPERAS. *Masaniello,* Auber; *Lucrezia Borgia, L'Elisir,* Donizetti; *La Juive,** Halévy; *Les Huguenots, Robert le Diable, Le Prophète,* Meyerbeer; *Don Giovanni,* Mozart; *Moise, La Donna del Lago, La Gazza Ladra, Otello,* Rossini; *Nabucco,* Verdi; *Il Franco Arciero,* Weber. PRINCIPAL SINGERS. Mdes. Castellan, Vera, De Méric, Grisi, Viardot; MM. Maralti,** Formes, Tamberlik,** Zelger,** Massol, Polonini, Mario, Tamburini, Ronconi.

THE YEAR 1850

THIS was a season of splendid performances, memorable for many things. Year by year the taste for grand opera spread and increased in England. Year by year the execution became finer and finer.

Der Freischütz in its Italian dress, and with recitatives excellently adjusted by Signor Costa, was relished by others more than by myself. German music and southern words do not agree; nor has the experiment of translation ever succeeded, whether the work be one of Spohr's, or *Fidelio,* or this most German of German operas, a goblin tale. The terrors of the Wolf's Glen lose half their terror when "done into Italian." Neither is recitative introduced in place of spoken dialogue often happy. A certain lightness and proportion are sacrificed, without any compensation in the form of solidity or grandeur being added. I have found this in M. Auber's *Fra Diavolo,* in M. Meyerbeer's *L'Etoile,* in every other work thus *stiffened*—but in no case so heavily as in the case of the ultra-German popular legend. A like essay was made at Paris, with the incomprehensible recitatives of M. Berlioz; but there the result was virtually the same as here. At Covent Garden, however, *Il Franco Arciero* enjoyed one advantage, in *not* being sung by Italian artists, Mddle. Vera excepted. The tenor, Signor Maralti, was Belgian. The Caspar of Herr Formes has been always one of his favourite characters—the type of all he could do best in opera, and with less left undone than in other parts. Madame Castellan, on the other hand, was inefficient as the heroine, her style having a certain restlessness which was especially ill-fitted for German music. She was always, moreover, slightly uncertain in tune. On the whole, I have heard the opera produce far greater effect in many a fifth-rate German town than it produced when given with the splendid band and chorus of Covent Garden Theatre. There it did not retain its place in the repertory.

On recalling this careful performance, in conjunction with the Italian version of *Oberon,* presented during a later season at Her

Majesty's Theatre, it seems clear to me that the quality which makes a composer adaptable to a southern language, whatever his country—be he a Bohemian Gluck, who could write an *Orfeo* for Italy, or a Saxon Hasse, who was as voluminous and popular in his day as Donizetti—was more entirely wanting to Weber than to anyone so excellent as a melodist that could be named; and this from no perverse antipathy, so much as from an original diversity of nature. Far from his entertaining the former, Weber has left concert scenas (as many, I think, as six) to Italian text, in which the Italian form has been studied. But these are faded, flat imitations, without a trace among them of the spirit which inspired the dances in *Preciosa*—the romance of Adolar and the May song in *Euryanthe,* and the delicious mermaid tune, "O 'tis pleasant to float on the sea," in *Oberon.* Now Beethoven was rugged and uncompromising enough; but in what *he* wrote to Italian words, as the terzet "Tremate," and the scena "Ah, perfido!" none of his freshness was lost, whereas it may be said that a suavity was imposed on him by the conditions of his language. Since Weber's death the Germans have not had an operatic melodist. Schubert's Lieder, in like manner, sound utterly unprofitable (even when a Mario adopts one of them) when divorced from their original text.

But if *Der Freischütz* gained here a limited success, disappointing to connoisseurs, how much more vexatious was the fate of an Italian opera, produced during the same Italian season; one of which I cannot think without the quickest possible sensations of pleasure. This is the *Moïse* of Signor Rossini—yet another cruelly mortifying proof that some of the finest music which its writer poured forth is buried, beyond power of man and woman to raise it, beneath the weight of a wrong story. Nor is this heaviness referable to the subject being Biblical, and as such rejected by English decorum. Even if we could consent to such an offence as seeing the persons of Holy Writ presented on the stage, the legend, as a legend, is badly arranged. The plagues and the portents which interpose for the rescue and defence of an injured people, and for the destruction of tyrannical crime, poorly compensate for the absence of anything like interest in the characters. There is some colour in the grand recitatives given to the prophet, but this is all. The lover and the tyrant have small difference between them. The women are thoroughly insipid. There remain, then, as engines of stage excitement, the supernatural night, the storm with the destruction of the idol, and the final flight of the captives, with the familiar chorus (half-an-hour's work, as the tale goes), which turned the scale in the fortunes of the opera when it was produced in Italy. Yet the composer seems to have been aware that it contained some of his most glorious music, by the unusual care which he bestowed on enriching and re-casting it when it was presented on the Parisian stage. The new introduction and the new finale to the third ace—*Moise*, in brief, as a French whole,—was unknown to our public till 1850.

Of the magnificence of the new matter added to the old work, what can be said that is too high in praise? There is no contrast in music—no, not even in Handel's stupendous *Israel*—stronger than that between the slow, restless, moaning Darkness chorus (a long andante maestoso, unlike any other movement existing in Signor Rossini's operas), and the stretto following the delicious round, "Mi manca la voce," in which a form of crescendo, dear to the master, and more than once abused by him, is worked out, with vivacity and climax, in their happiest forms of expression. It is idle to object that the receipt is one well known—that the means are not such as would be employed by a countryman of Bach or Beethoven. The effect produced is resistless, owing to the exceeding felicity of the phrases (in particular the coda) and the amazing animation of the orchestra. The singers sang it in London as if fire, not blood, was coursing through their veins. A storm of delight burst from every corner of the full theatre. I remember no moment of greater musical excitement.

This, too, was in no small part aided by the force and fervour of the then new tenor, Signor Tamberlik, who, from his first half-hour on the London stage, possessed himself of "the town" as the only alternative to Signor Mario which our audiences were willing to accredit. The secret of our sympathy for this artist—happily, as I write, able and vigorous—may be analysed by readers of the hour. One may tell those of the future that the voice, howsoever effective, and in its upper notes capable of great power, can hardly be called a charming one—though warm with the south—neither regulated by an unimpeachable method. I conceive that its owner may have begun to sing ere it was thoroughly settled—may have never thoroughly followed up those exercises of vocalization on which alone there is a real dependence to be placed, relying rather on natural fervour and readiness than on studies such as made Rubini and M. Duprez respectively so complete. There have been many moments when Signor Tamberlik has reminded me of both these great artists; but throughout every entire part committed to him there has been no escaping from a sense of irregularity—or rather call it want of that last finish which gives an artist his place among first-class artists. Before he came to England the voice of Signor Tamberlik had contracted the habit of vibration which always, more or less, gives an impression of fatigue and premature decay, though in reality it is merely an ill fashion—a relic of Paganini's treatment of his strings, a peculiarity wondrously turned to account by Rubini when his sustaining power began to desert him, and absolutely, in many of his best performances, producing an effect of emotion not attainable by other means. Then however quick, available, and firm as a musician—endowed, it is said, with a capital memory (in all this differing from his brother tenor)—the last, nicest sense of measurement of time is not among Signor Tamberlik's secrets. Without this there is no perfect satisfaction. Nevertheless, surprisingly rare is the gift even among real, sound musicians. I think of Hummel's ritardando passages on the pianoforte, at the distance of long, long years, and of the tempo rubato of Madame Pasta, of the accent of Madame Persiani, of the support given to every movement in which he was engaged by Lablache, and of Rubini's sensibility, which he could exchange for any amount of animation (in singing) both in musical rhythm and reason, and of the incomparable declamation of M. Duprez, and thus cannot help ranging my admirations accordingly.

Still, there was no hearing Signor Tamberlik during a single act of an opera without being aware that he was a man who could sway his public. Then it was charming, and not common, to listen to Italian words delivered with so pure and true an accent. The English have become so polyglot of late that the beauty of language bids fair to become effaced, and the value of vowels and consonants to vocal music runs some danger of being forgotten. The saying of Signor Tamberlik's recitative has often reconciled me to some disappointment in his manner of singing it.

Lastly, a leading phrase—the culminating passage in that amazing stretto—enabled Signor Tamberlik to display all his energy and sympathetic warmth within a short compass. The two told with the might of a whirlwind. The house, as Kean said, "rose at him." As a further contribution to this *Moïse*, Signor Tamberlik could bring a profile as remarkable as one on a Roman coin, which gave no ordinary dignity to the "feeble lover" of the antique story. And seeing that personal appearance has something to do with the reception of every drama, it is to be recollected that in this very revival of "Il nuovo Mose" the aspect of Signor Tamburini, one of the handsomest men ever seen on the stage (but, lucklessly, dressed for the occasion no doubt from some authentic monument), with bare arms and bracelets, a spangled petticoat and bodice, and false hair plaited at the sides of his face, had something to do with the cool reception of the work. Those even who loved the music as I do could not forbear a laugh. The figure, supposing it Egyptian of the period, was too absurd to be tolerated.

M. Meyerbeer's *Robert* was once more attempted this year, with the new tenor for the hero, with Signor Mario for the Raimbaud, and Madame Grisi (the most resolute of opera queens to retain her throne by trying at everything which every singer had done) was the Alice. A more complete mistake was never made. The opera has never been liked here, in spite of the fashion of foreign currency. But the greatest mistake was the Bertram of Herr Formes, who this year (as has been told) was for the first time transferred to the Italian stage,—a Bertram who floundered about like an ill-advised bat, so as to hamper every creature concerned with him by his acting, without in the slightest degree redeeming the over-weening predominance by any musical correctness or beauty. It was a hard and real disappointment—the first of a long list.

Another costly and striking production was that of *La Juive*, M. Halévy's best serious opera, selected in mutual deference to such interest as its composer's visit to England excited. The fate of *La Juive* throughout Europe is worth a word or two. It can be nowhere said to have succeeded. There is not one single air from it which has become popular. Yet the music is not altogether unworthy of the story—the most powerful opera book in the modern list; one, though, it has been said, which, with his characteristic disdain, Signor Rossini rejected in favour of M. Jouy's insipid *Guillaume Tell*. The drama, too, lends itself to that show of spectacle which is almost essential to works on so large a scale. Then there is novelty in the disposition of the characters—introduced, it has been said, at the instance of Nourrit (a real inventor), who was weary of love parts. Eleazar offers as fine scope for the tenor who is disposed to act as, in its different style, does Otello. There must be life in any creation that can keep the stage for a quarter of a century; yet it would be difficult to name a tragedy which has lived so frigidly as *La Juive*. In London it had the advantage of Madame Viardot's acting as the heroine, of which I have spoken elsewhere. The music is beyond her legitimate compass, but she sang it sublimely. Signor Mario's inefficiency and want of effect as Eleazar were made curious by the fact circulated before the curtain that he had anxiously desired to play the part—having, in fact, been the only singer who has gained entrance for a bar of M. Halévy's music in England, by his delicious execution of an air from *Guido and Ginevra*. But the cast in its weakness or strength mattered little, I suspect. I fancy that the composer has certain qualities which will always render our audiences impenetrable to his merits. There is a certain hard cleverness which is particularly distasteful to us,—a measure in full of that spirit which, presented in a smaller quantity, makes us indifferent to Spontini and virtually underrate Cherubini. For precisely this reason it may be that M. Halévy's music loses more when executed out of Paris than any other music so really sterling. It is the best French ware of the second class.

I have often speculated on the interval that may yet elapse before we really possess the catholic spirit in art of which we conceive ourselves possessed; how long it may be ere we recognize that curiously self-consistent nationality of style which runs through every expression of the imagination in France, and which animates works of every school with a distinction as marked as that of Italian beauty or German idealism. When that good time of possession shall come we shall have three pleasures, instead of two, in foreign opera music; and among the most abiding of these may be our pleasure in the opera of France.

THE YEAR 1851

HER MAJESTY'S THEATRE

OPERAS. *Le Tre Nozze,** Alary; *Gustave, Masaniello, L'Enfant Prodigue,** La Corbeille d'Oranges,** Auber; *Les Quatre Fils Aymon,* Balfe; *La Somnambula, Norma,* Bellini; *Fidelio,* Beethoven; *Lucia, Lucrezia, Linda,* Donizetti; *Le Nozze,* Mozart; *La Cenerentola,* Rossini; *Florinda,** Thalberg. PRINCIPAL SINGERS. Mdes. Duprez,* Fiorentini, Ugalde,* Feller,* Alaimo,* Sontag-Rossi, Alboni, Nau,* Barbieri-Nini,* Bertrand, Giuliani, Cruvelli; MM. Lorenzo, Bilanchè,* Romagnoli,* Poultier,* Calzolari, Lablache, F. Lablache, Coletti, Pardini,* Massol, Ferranti,* Sims Reeves, Scapini,* Gardoni. BALLET. *L'Isle des Amours.* PRINCIPAL DANCERS. Mdes. Ferraris, Carlotta Grisi, Monti (*Pantomimist*).

THE YEAR 1851

OW little of Italy there was in Her Majesty's Theatre during the Great Exhibition year 1851, the
foregoing list curiously shows. There was no stint
of enterprise, however much miscalculation. Generally speaking, the music was more accurately prepared than it had been for some seasons past.

The attempt to enrich the Italian repertory by M. Auber's grand
operas has only succeeded in the case of *La Muette*. Strictly
speaking, that bright Neapolitan story hardly comes within the
designation, so few of the great musical pieces are developed.
There is a much closer attempt at the style in *Gustave* and *L'Enfant Prodigue,* and therefore they are less successful, the composer
always suffering when serious music on a grand scale is to be attempted. A great building of alabaster would have a poor appearance, in nowise suggesting the preciousness of the material.
Yet *Gustave* is full of delicious music finely wrought, beginning
with the first notes of the overture, which has a fascination approaching those which open Signor Rossini's opera preludes. I
was never fully aware of the value of this music till I was, in the
year 1861, hearing the assault made by Signor Verdi on the same
story. It seems strange to those who know a certain affectation
to be one characteristic of French opera composers, that the Italian
should be the less natural of the two; but such is the case.

The version of *L'Enfant Prodigue* pleased less, and deservedly
so, in spite of the admirable singing of Madame Sontag, who did
wonders with the weak music of her part. Not only did the Biblical origin of the story weigh against it in England, but M.
Scribe's mistake in reproducing the great situation of parent and
child—already set forth far more forcibly in *Le Prophète*—could
not fail to be felt. *La Corbeille d'Oranges* was inferior to both.
This is a thoroughly paltry opera, written expressly for one who
was no actress, on a story which may be said to have reminded the
spectators not of the ripe but of the squeezed orange. To this

tale music was fitted, under the idea of producing a part calculated to exhibit the remarkable vocal powers of Madame Alboni, which should not make any demand on her acting. A poorer work was never thrown off by the pen of a clever man.

Florinda had greater peculiarity as an entire novelty, and moreover as an essay at opera composition made by a splendid and popular instrumentalist. That the habit of thinking and writing for the pianoforte is not favourable to such enterprises has been proved often and again. Steibelt, whose sonatas and concertos contain tunes enough to stock the brains of fifty of the men of these our degenerate days, could not manage to throw life into his *Romeo and Juliet*. Hummel's *Matilda von Guise* is still less known. As a melodist M. Thalberg is not to be compared with either of his predecessors, though a grandeur and breadth in some of his combinations might be thought to foreshow vigour in dramatic effect, and of this there were passing traces in this drama. I recollect one agitated concerted piece, where the device, so common in comic opera, of expressing confusion by setting a profusion of words each to its note, was used to good effect in a scene of tragic combination; but all the rest has left on me an impression of extreme dryness and laudably careful writing—nothing more. The story—one of the pieces by M. Scribe which had long hung on hand—was one of small interest. Everyone, however, concerned in the matter fought their best for its success—in particular Lablache, who was doing his utmost for his son-in-law.

That marvellous and versatile actor—then, too, not very far from the close of his career—did still more in behalf of another opera. He absolutely danced to Madame Sontag's polka song in *Le Tre Nozze* of Signor Alary. This opera, again (though never was light comedy more wanted by way of repose and variety) failed to please. The music was slight and faded, containing few happy phrases. The polka song, however, lingers in our concert rooms, the fashion of singing dance music, when a show-piece is wanted, having of late years superseded the yet more foolish habit of singing instrumental airs with variations, introduced by Catalani.

A better fate ought to have attended *Les Quatre Fils Aymon,*— to my thinking Mr. Balfe's best opera, on a quaint and lively story, and with a nice combination (I think till then untried) of a

group of four ladies, manœuvred with and against a group of four
gentlemen.   The lot of this work has been as capricious as that
of Donizetti's *Fille du Regiment* (one of *his* best operas).   Both
were written for the Opéra Comique of Paris, where neither was
successful; both have obtained a wide popularity elsewhere.   During some years there was hardly a German opera house where
The Sons of Aymon was not awkwardly performed and heartily
received,—an opera of delicious freshness and deep merit if it be
compared with the silly *Stradella* of M. von Flotow, which may
be said to have superseded it, and which still keeps the German
stage.   Here an attempt to set it in English, during the operatic
management of Mr. Maddox, at the Princess's Theatre, can be
hardly said to have made it known.   It was a disadvantage that,
when this opera was given in its Italian dress, the heroine was
not represented, as originally intended, by Madame Sontag, who
had come to coldness and correspondence with her manager, but
by Mademoiselle Cruvelli, whose eccentricities were more apparent
in comic than in serious opera.   In the latter, they were lauded
up to the skies by her admirers as so many new readings of the
passions.   But for all that, the part song of the four young
knights, graceful and *gaillard* in no common degree, and the garden finale to the second act on the darkened stage, built on a
melody graceful and mysterious—as a thread of moonshine creeping through some wood-opening—are not to be forgotten.   The
opera, it is true, is slight, and the instrumentation more slighted
than that of later operas by Mr. Balfe; but it occurs to me now
as one which would well repay the labour of re-touching, because
built on a happy dramatic thought, and thus containing some elegant and arresting musical ideas.

Only two of the ladies,—a sixth part of those who appeared in
1851,—were Italians.   The training, however, of Mademoiselle
Duprez under her accomplished father entirely justified her appearing in Italian opera.   It was a pleasure to hear one so young
as herself so honestly prepared for her profession.   There was
no common promise in her appearance, since it was then to be
hoped that time would bring power to her extensive soprano voice,
at that time, doubtless, too slender for a large theatre and a grand
opera.   There was already little to be added in musical taste and
acquirement.   She sang as one having a style.   That time hardly

fulfilled the hope is as well known as that she is one of the very few thoroughly finished singers competent to execute anything that can be written for the voice, now on the stage. Never was prima donna called on for a larger amount of resources than the lady who had to "create" the part of Catherine, in M. Meyerbeer's *L'Etoile*. The part is one of extreme difficulty and fatigue, which sets in early—the heroine leaving the stage for scarce a moment during the first act, and yet at the close of the opera having to cope alone with two flutes in that arduous piece of display expressly calculated to show off Mademoiselle Jenny Lind's then lustrous upper notes. The valiant manner in which this was sustained from beginning to end by one so slenderly endowed with power, and during a long and uninterrupted run of months, cannot be forgotten—though its price (as might have been seen) was injury and enfeeblement of the voice, possibly never to be repaired.

The second French lady named, who at that time had a high repute in Paris—Madame Ugalde—was not fortunate in her attempt to transform herself into an Italian artist. With all her vocal cleverness and audacity, her musical accent, and a dash of true dramatic instinct here and there, she was always an unattractive singer. A want of refinement as distinct from accuracy or finish ran through all her performances. She was too conscious, too emphatic, and too audacious. Then her voice, though skilled in every possible exercise, and not incapable of breadth in the cantabile style, when it was needed, had been trained in the French school, and was, in its best days, not agreeable, because of a certain harpsichord tone—something of the quill and something of the wire—which ran through its compass. She came here with great ambitions, it was said, having desired to make her first appearance on our Italian stage as Semiramide, with not one solitary requisite for the part, save command over any given number of notes in a roulade. Her disappointment must have been great; for in *L'Enfant Prodigue*—where, besides playing the Dalilah who seduces the son from his duty, she sang a little ballad as a camel-boy, more pungently than artlessly—she was entirely eclipsed by Madame Sontag, to whom was allotted the less marked character and music, and from whom, moreover, all disposition to support and to favour her behind the curtain had passed away.

The third, a French-American singer, Mademoiselle Nau, had

held for many years a useful and respectable position at the Grand Opera of Paris, M. Auber having written the part of the Fairy in his *Lac des Fées* for her. A more coldly correct singer, with a very small voice, is seldom to be heard. I have found this lifelessness so frequent among American singers—who, during late years, have been numerous, and some of them accomplished—as to be involuntarily tempted to speculate on this chill as a characteristic. If there be reason in this, the phenomenon is odd, as occurring among a people of many peoples, so full of life, curiosity, and caprice—one to be matched against the languors in music of the mercurial Irish, who, as a race of singers, have a provoking habit of dragging their time. There is no accounting for these physical peculiarities; but no one that has ever looked closely at imaginative art can fail to recognize their existence and repetition.

On the whole, the most successful performance of the Great Exhibition year was that of *Fidelio,* in which Mademoiselle Cruvelli was ably supported by Mr. Sims Reeves. In this music our admirable English tenor was as ripe as the lady was crude. He drew out from the vocal music and finished all in it that is tuneable and lovely, without any sacrifice of declamation or dramatic force, without being overborne by the orchestra, without constraining the latter to any complaisance for the singers. But even then Mr. Sims Reeves was far beneath the point which he has since reached by care and thought and real artistic feeling. As to *Fidelio,* howsoever symphonically superb it be, the opera is one in which there is no judging of a vocalist's qualities; and accordingly Mademoiselle Cruvelli's powerful and extensive voice suited the music; and its composer had chained his executants too fast for her to attempt those vagaries which, with success, and by the encouragement of injudicious admirers, became at a later period so prominent in her performances. Up to this time there had been some improvement in the arrangement and command of the admirable materials given to the lady by nature; but henceforward the misuse of them increased so steadily, and with it her exactions and caprices as an artist, that it was a case of relief, not for regret, when she left the stage.

THE YEAR 1851

ROYAL ITALIAN OPERA

OPERAS. *Masaniello,* Auber; *Fidelio,* Beethoven; *Lucrezia Borgia, La Favorita, L'Elisir,* Donizetti; *Saffo,** Gounod; *Robert, Le Prophète, Les Huguenots,* Meyerbeer; *Don Giovanni, Il Flauto Magico,* Mozart; *Semiramide, La Donna del Lago,* Rossini; *Il Franco Arciero,* Weber. PRINCIPAL SINGERS. Mdes. Grisi, Angri, Castellan, Bertrandi,* Viardot, Zerr,* L. Pyne;* MM. Salvatori,* Tamberlik, Formes, Stigelli,* Bianchi, Tagliafico, Ronconi, Mario, Ciaffei,* Tamburini.

THE YEAR 1851

THE foregoing list of operas will show an increase of the tendency towards works of the German school. In its second season, however, the Italianized version of *Der Freischütz* proved unattractive, in spite of the appearance of Signor Tamberlik in the tenor part. Nor could the same artist's excellent singing as Florestan overcome the apathy of the public to the version of *Fidelio* performed in Covent Garden for the first time. The audience encored one of the magnificent four *Leonora* overtures prefixed to the second act; but the performance as a whole was somehow not right, not German; careful, but languid. Madame Castellan did her utmost to be womanly; but she was neither sufficiently intense nor touching as Leonora, and the music tore her voice—an organ which had never been altogether regulated. The opera, I have become more and more convinced on every return to it, is one only to be enjoyed under certain conditions and certain limitations, in spite of the affecting nature of its story, in spite of the beauties of idea and enrichment which it contains—the affecting Prisoners' Chorus, the thrilling grave-digging scene in the vault, and the luxury of instrumental beauty lavished over the work, so as only Beethoven could lavish it. The strain on all the singers, ascribable to the master's indifference to vocal convenience or beauty, the heaviness of certain portions—as, for instance, the close of the first finale (one of Beethoven's least happy inspirations)—bear with an oppressive effect on both artists and audiences, except they be relieved and brightened by nationality of humour in those who execute.

A most careful effort was made to perform *Il Flauto Magico* in the most perfect manner. The wholesale admirers of particular schools and masters refuse to admit the extreme wearisomeness of this elaborate puzzle, decked as it is with admirable music, when the opera is presented on the stage, and regard all admission of the same as frivolous blasphemy. It would be wearisome to recapitulate the reasons why neither that which is serious, nor that which is comic, nor that which is sentimental, nor that which is fantastic, tell as they ought when setting forth a story which no one can assert to be either mystical, or allegorical, or a simple imitation of Carlo Gozzi's faëry extravaganzas, awkwardly executed. In proportion as the nature of drama in music is understood, will the regret deepen that one so consummate in science, so shrewd in discernment, and so boundless in musical idea as Mozart, should so carelessly, to please the worthless manager of a popular theatre (for such was Schikaneder), have thrown away the richest veils and garlands and jewels of his art, in decorating a thing not so much disproportioned as having no ascertainable form. In themselves, what can be fresher than the melodies, more stately than the solemn choruses, more sprightly than the music given to the lighter characters? We have known them so long, and have loved them so well, as concert and home music, that by many it will be till the end of time thought a flat heresy to say that their place, heard in a detached form, is in the concert room——but not as parts of a drama which has no clear meaning on the stage.

The music was most carefully rendered by Madame Grisi, Signor Mario, and excellently by Herr Formes, who was heard and seen to his best advantage in Sarastro. Every conceivable quaintness and unpremeditated freak were thrown into the part of Papageno by Signor Ronconi; and the smaller part of Papagena was taken with zeal and relish by Madame Viardot. Then, for Queen of Night, an agile and clever singer, possessor of the acute notes requisite for the part,—and, it was to be presumed, the true Vienna tradition,—had been imported from Austria in Mademoiselle Anna Zerr.

This was a very curious artist, belonging to a class larger than people take pains to recollect,—the highest soprani of the old school of vocal writing, from whom any amount of volubility and execution *above the stave* was to be demanded. It may be doubted whether there have ever existed so many singers of the kind as during the past quarter of a century. How its existence is to be reconciled with the cry of complaint against the raised diapason of modern times, as rendering the old music impossible to be sung, baffles comprehension. The feat, when it is done, is worth little, and it may be counterfeited by adroit trickery. By this, is believed, La Bastardella (Lucrezia Agujari, who sang in London at Burney's concerts in the Pantheon for £100 a night), who was the wonder-singer of Mozart's time, produced those topmost notes— up to CC *alt.*—which so amazed the composer, and may have inspired him with his fancy of writing for such marvellous folk,—as is obvious in his *Die Entführung* and the opera now spoken of. If the feat, however, be not elegantly mastered, the effect is more than worthless—one to recall the pain of a surgical operation, howsoever it may strike the vulgar with surprise.   Mademoiselle Zerr, like many of her German sisters, was more strenuous than easy. Her voice was shrill and harsh.   She gave the slow movements of her grand airs in the true, broad, sensitive style which Mozart's cantabiles demand; but in her bravuras the hearer was irresistibly reminded of a pea-hen masquerading as a lark.   When all had been done, and done correctly, and the *Astrafiammante* looked triumphantly round for the great applause, which came plentifully from the lovers of amazement, one took breath, thankful that the operation was over!   On one evening she was replaced, at an hour's warning, and with as much gain as loss to the performance, by Miss Louisa Pyne, who had never till then attempted Italian opera—another illustration of the mastery with which our best English artists can assume various occupations in foreign music; in none, possibly, complete, but as a body more steady, meritorious, and prepared, than the singers of Italy, Germany, or France, so called on, could prove themselves.   This may be because we have, till now, no great stage style nor stage music of our own, and because our vocalists must have, therefore, a reference to, and a dependence on, the music of foreign countries; and because, as a company, they are more skilled musicians than those of other lands.

The revival of *Il Flauto*, however interesting by reason of its completeness, and precious as affording the student an opportunity of considering a work of art so famous in its true light, could not often be repeated.

The latest attempt of any mark at bringing forward a new composer at either of the opera houses was the production of M. Gounod's *Sapho*.   This took place too late in the season of 1851 for the opera to have had any chance of establishing itself, supposing that other adverse circumstances had not opposed themselves to the immediate reception of the new writer in this country.

On one alone of these is it worth while to return for a moment
—the pertinacious resistance of a portion of the English public
(and this by no means its least refined and cultivated section) to
everything that is new. Through this had Beethoven to fight, and
Signor Rossini, and, later, M. Meyerbeer. Even after Mendelssohn had fascinated England by his amazing first appearances
in *The Midsummer Night's Dream* overture and his pianoforte
Concert-Stück, there was a lull in curiosity and interest of some
half a dozen years' duration respecting him. It would be vastly
inconvenient, after all, to a multitude of easy-going connoisseurs
if the new man were to turn out a new genius! It is hard to regard bigotry like this without impatience; and the worst consequence of it is that adventurous spirits who have more enthusiasm
than judgment, and who are irked by hearing certain names told
over and over and over again in a sort of cuckoo-hymn, which it
costs small trouble to sing, are driven into licence for liberty, and
in their irritation lose all power of discriminating that which is
bad from that whch seems good. The singular and noticeable
outbreak in Germany which, for a while, bade fair to destroy there
all love of what is real and beautiful in art—the greatness thrust
on Herr Wagner—could never have happened were there not
abroad and talking in the world—not in the opera world alone—
too many persons such as those who, in answer to any curiosity expressed about *Sapho,* would reply, "But why don't they give us
Don Juan?"

To a few hearers—since then grown into a European public—
neither the warmest welcome nor the most bleak indifference could
alter the conviction that among the composers who have appeared
during the past twenty-five years, M. Gounod was the most promising one, as showing the greatest combination of sterling science,
beauty of idea, freshness of fancy, and individuality of style. Before a note of *Sapho* was written, certain sacred Roman Catholic
compositions and some exquisite settings of French verse had made
it clear to some of the acutest judges and most profound musicians
living that in him, at last, something new and true had come,—
may I not say, the most poetical of French musicians that has till
now written? By some of these the composer's name was mentioned to me; and the same curiosity and hope which urged me to

undertake a day-and-night journey to Weimar, in the expectation of great things from Herr Wagner (also on the instigation of those whom I trusted), took me to Paris, to hear for myself.

I conceive *Sapho* to be the best *first* opera ever written by a composer—Beethoven's *Fidelio* (his first and last) excepted. The story was not well fancied, and its writer—M. Emile Augier, whose delicious little drama, *La Cigüe,* had already shown how irony could be introduced into antique art—inwrought into this old tale a thread not so much of comedy as of political sarcasm, a humour unpresentable in music. Possibly, too, the old wells are dried up. Though the present generation may be tormented by weak reproductions of Greek sculpture, by new Venuses painted, or unpainted, and similar affectations, till the end of its term, it may prove that Greek opera was exhausted by Gluck. Sacchini's *Œdipe* has vanished. The transcendent *Medea* of Cherubini is inaccessible. There is a time for everything. A new Parthenon is almost as improbable to be built as a new Bamberg Cathedral.

Yet after every qualification has been made, there will be found in the *Sapho* of M. Gounod enough of what is new and true to stamp its composer—a certain placid grandeur of line, a richness of colour, not, perhaps, sufficiently various, an elegance and tenderness of melody, which belong to no preceding model. The harmonies, it is true, are in the taste of the time, which inclines to what is vague; but to this charge those of Mendelssohn are liable, and still more those of Chopin. In his predilection for writing on a ground bass, M. Gounod does not follow the modern fashion. I question if the device has been often in the theatre more happily employed than in Sappho's song and chorus in the second act, and than in the Shepherd's lay on the rock in the final scene, which contrasts, in its exquisite wildness, with the grand and desolate lyric of the heroine ere she buries her despair in the waves. The entire close of the opera may be compared, in its simplicity, its power to move, with Signor Rossini's masterpiece of expression, the third act of *Otello*. Exquisitely graceful, too, are some of the lighter portions of the work,[1] such as the chorus of girls who greet the heroine when she arrives to compete for the prize of

[1] The grace of these has been since more gaily and variously exemplified in certain portions of M. Gounod's *Medicin malgré lui;* more signally still in his ballet music. All that belongs to *La Nonne Sanglante* is capital,—only exceeded by that

song, and the duet in which Sappho's rival, Glycera, cajoles the old voluptuary.   Many, many more happy passages and pertinent thoughts could be specified, to which the world has begun to do justice.   A return to this opera, in spite of the drawbacks of subject and story, is as possible as was the return of the German public to *Fidelio,* the entire failure of which on its production so blanked the expectations of Beethoven's friends and self.

Though *Sapho* was well received by the audience, in spite of our habitual timidity in approval of the work of one hitherto unknown, the wrath and ridicule outpoured by most of the censors of the press were too vehement and curious not to be put on record. The event has not justified the sagacity of those who jeered at and assailed the music, and who declared that any expectation invested in its writer was only so much sheer hallucination.   There is dispraise of a quality which defeats its own object.   The fact has to be swallowed and digested, that already the composer of *Sapho,* the choruses to *Ulysse, Le Médecin malgré lui, Faust, Philémon et Baucis,* a superb Cecilian Mass, two. excellent symphonies, and half a hundred songs and romances which may be ranged not far from Schubert's, and above any others existing in France, is now one of the very few individual men left to whom musical Europe is looking for its pleasure.

And here, since digression is a part of recollection, it may be allowed me to dwell on this aforesaid *Faust* by M. Gounod, as I did a score of years since on the operas of M. Meyerbeer—now so indispensable, then visited with such bitter contempt by our critics, who would neither give ear to the music nor endure the praise of it by any writer.   Labour, however, is somehow thriftlessly bestowed by the persons who would instruct some of us that black is yellow.   There are many with whom first and last impressions are one.   It is possible to force one's self into an admission of cleverness; but to try to enjoy that which is not attractive is a stupid exercise, to say the least of it—one hopelessly undertaken by those who have real opinions, principles, and fancies of their own.

of M. Meyerbeer. There is one Hungarian dance, in particular (with a ground bass), which is of the very highest quality for character, spirit, and elegance. There are few, if any, stage waltzes with a chorus so fresh, so simple, and so resistless, as that in M. Gounod's *Faust.*

It may be doubted (let it be said at the outset) whether *Faust* is a better subject for music than *Hamlet*—whether Marlowe's and Goethe's hero is not a character of a quality so subtle and complex, so fine in its lights, so flickering in its shadows, as to defy the power of sound to express it, if not of stage presentation to exhibit it. Yet it has tempted "all and sundry." Prince Radziwill took Goethe's drama in hand. Spohr, who had a strange desire for being—that which he could not be—fantastic and supernatural (and who showed a choice in his opera books as curiously courageous as his music was timidly orderly)—

"took up the wondrous tale,"

not the tale, however, as told by Goethe, but a version of the story at once dull and fierce, including coarse witch-work, and adventure meant to be lively, but motionless as regards interest. More lately, Schumann, Dr. Liszt, M. Berlioz, have treated the story, and the last-named composer with added spices and condiments which, indeed, are curious—here a Hungarian march, there a diabolical outcry of gibberish made for the occasion—as one might make an Unknown Tongue.

This latest setting of *Faust,* by M. Gounod, if only as being the clearest musical one, is well worth a respectful study. Certain of the German purists, forgetting how even their noble Schiller, when translating Shakespeare for the stage, could interpolate scenes not in our poet's text, have professed themselves as being cruelly outraged because the French composer has stuck so closely to Goethe's text, has used so many of Goethe's words. To us English, who take the last act of *Otello,* including the "Willow Song," so tranquilly—nay, rather say, with such enthusiastic pleasure—this seems only so much churlish pedantry.

In the Introduction, the vague, restless gloom of the old philosopher, weary of the life whose *arcanum* he has been unable to find, the sounds of rural and young people passing without, the resolution to end one mystery of existence by attempting another yet untried, the mystery beyond the grave, are excellently coloured, and characterized in a manner which is free, graphic, original. Less so—and this may be noted throughout the work—is the tone of Mephistopheles; perhaps because that worthy is as little susceptible of being wrought out in music as Shakespeare's Iago, fine sarcasm finding in our art no colour.   Be this as it may, the demon is here weak.

Nothing can be imagined more jovial or more original than the Kermesse music which opens the second act, where the tune passes from group to group.   In particular the verse allotted to the old citizens is admirably quaint and melodious.   The combination of all the separate elements at the close of the movement is of itself enough to substantiate M. Gounod's skill as a composer; though a certain vagueness and disposition to push harmonic licence to its utmost must be allowed for, under protest.   As I have said, I cannot fancy the waltz and chorus which close the act (during which dance Margaret crosses the stage to a strain that Mozart might not have disdained to own) exceeded in brightness, novelty, and thorough nature.   No French waltz that I know approaches it in beauty, and in the utter absence of that torment with which our neighbours delight to add piquancy to their dance music.   Till this time Margaret has only been glanced at.   The third and fourth acts bring her out in all the innocence, passion, and woe of her character.   After Faust's delicious monologue in the garden come her old ballad of the King of Thule and her delight at discovering the casket of jewels—so combined as to make an important song of entrance for the heroine.   The allegretto, I observe, has excited lively displeasure among certain German critics, who quarrel with her pretty surprise as being too coquettish—the air having, to make its sins more heinous, the enormity of a long trill to bring back the subject.   How the transcendentalists would set to music the wonderment, the artless, harmless vanity of the child who fancies herself alone, I cannot presume to conceive, though I have every confidence in the power of meagreness of idea to take the form of a pedantic weariness, and to impose on the shallow as so much profundity.   For my poor part, the liveliness of this cabaletta is to me attractive and true to the situation; the closing phrase of it is exquisite in its grace.   It may be pointed out, however, as the most *French* number in the opera.   Then comes a quartet, full of happy touches and charming phrases of melody.   M. Gounod, however, has too great a tendency in his concerted music to interrupt the flow of the melody for the sake of a bit-by-bit accuracy of setting his words, hardly trusting enough to the lights and shades which singers of intelligence can throw into their interpretation, and hardly remembering enough that a movement must not be judged bar by bar, chord by chord, but by its character and colour as a whole. Emotion does not mean too much expression. A reader who would emphasize every word (save, perchance, when reading a "Latter-Day pamphlet") would become terribly fatiguing. The love duet which follows is more complete in this respect—a real love duet, if there was ever such a thing written; one of those inspirations which might have been born among the dews of a summer twilight, and the scent of flowers, and the musical falling of distant waters. The brief adagio which contains the full confession of the pair has a luxury of tenderness and beauty which are unsurpassable. After the parting, the recall of Faust to the fatal interview, it must be owned, is somewhat of an anti-climax, weakening the impression as the act closes.

We are now in the act of shame and remorse, throughout which the composer is almost always at the height of his subject. I wish, though, that he had not felt himself bound to set the spinning song again. As easy would it have been to treat the *Erl King* anew, after Schubert, or the "Willow Song" in *Otello*. A Lenau may have the temerity to handle *Faust* after a Goethe, but it is the temerity (as his melancholy fate proved) of incipient madness. In this case, however, the wonder is that the French composer did not fail more utterly.

From this point to the death of Valentine in duel with the seducer there is not a weak bar. The return of the regiment is one of those seizing pieces of music which are instinct with fire. I shall never forget the riotous enthusiasm which burst out when this magnificent chorus, to which an army of myriads might sweep on its way to victory, electrified the ear at the Théâtre Lyrique on the night of the first performance of the opera. I feel it thrill in my pen as I write. Very wicked is the sarcastic serenade sung under Margaret's window by Mephistopheles—his most wicked music in the opera. The duel trio is in the highest tone of challenge, as chivalresque, after its kind, as the admirable Septuor in *Les Huguenots*. The death of Valentine, and his curse, are painted with a grave and lacerating passion that are of the highest order of expression. It was hard, after this, to deal with the scene in the church, with the tempter at the unwedded mother's ear, taunting her with her shame, and bidding her to leave all hope behind, while the pealing organ and the awful monkish hymn menace her like words of irrevocable doom.   Here M. Gounod's church studies have stood him in great stead.   The solemnity of the organ strain, the naked grimness of the chants, are both venturesome in their awful depth of gloom:—the cry of Margaret's agonised prayer, when the terror becomes intolerable, could hardly be better poured forth.   There are few if any living men who could produce music more worthy of the situation.   Even when Weber and Spohr were writing operas, Goethe himself said that no one could treat it, save, perhaps, M. Meyerbeer.   How nearly that ingenious master of combination, who loves to pile Ossa on Pelion, conscious of his power to accumulate and build up, has approached to the sublimities of the church scene in *Faust,* may be seen in his melodramatic *Robert.*   M. Berlioz, though notoriously afraid of nothing, has wisely not touched it.   He has the Easter hymn, and the student orgy, and the sylphs, and the ghastly ride, and the devils (for whom he has invented a pandemoniacal Unknown Tongue) ; but he has wisely stopped at the portal of the church, and there left the heartbroken penitent alone.

The fifth act, as at present performed, as replacing the Walpurgis music originally written (which was the weakest part of the entire opera), now opens with a hideous and dismal goblin symphony, transferred judiciously from *La Nonne Sanglante* (a work crushed under the monstrous dullness of the story).   After Weber and Meyerbeer had done their worst—the one in the Wolf's Glen, the other in the cloisters of Saint Rosalie—it was no easy matter to find new supernatural colours and combinations. Devilry, like fairyism, in music has only a limited gamut; but in this wild, weird symphony, with its wail of wordless voices, fitful as the bitter blast of midnight sweeping cloud-borne across a blasted heath, M. Gounod has added some notes to the scale of effect.   There is something new in its terrors—a vague, yet not utterly formless horror, such as raises expectation.   Though for contrast's sake, I suppose, was next introduced the transformation which brings us into the midst of the bacchanal orgies of the old pagan deities, and though there is a suave and stately voluptuousness in the chorus, and an animation in the goblet song for Faust, this is one of the portions of the opera which moves me the least.

Not so the final scene in the prison, with the despair of the crazed victim, the maddening recognition of her lover, the temptation to fly, and at last the outburst of supplication, and faith, and delicious hope, and the willing farewell to life of one who sees pardon leaning from heaven for the crime which has wrought such bitter misery. These are here touched with a master's hand. The passion sweeps like a whirlwind to the catastrophe. There is no indecision, no faltering, nothing to hold back a climax the effect of which, when it arrives, is overwhelming, if it be only moderately well rendered.

In one respect *Faust* was admirably presented in Paris; and indeed the opera stage has rarely seen a poet's imagining more completely wrought out than in the Margaret of Madame Miolan-Carvalho. I had for some few years watched the progress of this exquisitely finished artist with great interest before she had begun to excite any attention in her own country, finding in her performances a sensibility rarely combined with such measureless execution as hers—and it has been fancied hardly possible to a voice in quality like hers, a high and thin soprano, with little volume of tone; but I was not prepared for the delicacy of colouring, the innocence, the tenderness of the earlier scenes, and the warmth of passion and remorse and repentance which one then so slight in frame (to see the very painter's Margaret) could throw into the drama as it went on. Rarely has there been a personation more complete, rarely one more delightful. Those know only one small part of this consummate artist's skill (if even they know her as an incomparable Cherubino, and as most brilliant among the brilliant in such a fantastic extravaganza as La Reine Topaze) that have not seen her in this remarkable *Faust* by M. Gounod. Wherefore an opera successful throughout the continent has been till now withheld from our opera stage, during a period when, to stave off utter famine, we are compelled to have recourse to translations from the French,—let the sybils declare. (1862).

THE YEAR 1852

HER MAJESTY'S THEATRE

OPERAS. *Norma, I Puritani, La Somnambula,* Bellini; *Maria di Rohan, Lucia, Don Pasquale,* Donizetti; *Casilda,** H.R.H. the Duke of Saxe-Coburg; *La Prova d'un Opera Seria,* Gnecco; *Don Giovanni,* Mozart; *L'Italiana, Il Barbiere, Semiramide, La Cenerentola,* Rossini; *Ernani,* Verdi. PRINCIPAL SINGERS. Mdes. Fiorentini, Bertrandi, Cruvelli, Feller, De la Grange,* Favanti, Charton;* MM. Ferlotti, Calzolari, Gardoni, Lablache, *Beletti, De Bassini.** BALLET. *Zélie.* PRINCIPAL DANCERS. Mdes. Guy Stephan, Rosati.

THE YEAR 1852

HIS year, at last, an Italian opera season was gone through without a single female Italian singer. But it was evident that the impending ruin of the theatre could not be averted much longer, and that shifts and expedients, as reckless as they were fruitless, must needs be resorted to.

The change for the worse in Mademoiselle Cruvelli began to show itself strongly this season. More at ease with her public than formerly, and by panegyric encouraged to rate herself as equal, if not superior, to the greatest of her predecessors, she began, in fancy, to originate—in reality, to neglect. Every now and then some wild burst of energy in her singing displayed the glorious compass of her voice, but also that its freshness was even then departing; while her acting, though it was animated enough, perpetually missed its mark owing to her extreme self-occupation. She was triumphantly heedless of all her companions on the stage. In her great scenes she was always too soon or too late. She preferred to fly into a fury before the word was spoken that should set fire to the train. She would fall into an attitude just after the moment for the attitude had gone by. Then she performed strange evolutions with her drapery by way of being statuesque, and exhibited things more strange with her costume when it was not antique, by way of being pictorial. So well were these propensities of hers known that later, when, as Queen of the Grand Opera of Paris, she deliberately altered the rhythm of the leading phrase of a grand duet in *Les Huguenots,* the world said, "Only Mademoiselle Cruvelli's way"; and when, a few months later, the choice of some coming opera was in debate, loungers reported, rather admiringly than otherwise, that "this time there was to be a part with bare arms in it, for Mademoiselle Cruvelli!"

Such amateurs as were not yet disabused in regard to the reality of Italian reputations, or who for themselves admired the new manner of bald and violent singing, had for some years been speaking of Signor de Bassini in terms so high as to excite curiosity in regard to his real value. In 1852 he was a handsome man with a fine voice: with something of the style which is, happily, not yet here accepted for real style, and in the management of his voice with some dramatic energy. But our public was not worthy of him, as I have, again and again, heard said of singers many degrees less interesting than himself, in the theatres of Italy—by dilettanti raised nearer the seventh heaven of rapture in proportion to the noise which could be made by tragedy queen, lover pursued by jealousy, or uncle cruel and bold. He could do little to save our sinking theatre.

Everything, in short, conspired to hasten the decay and downfall of the old opera house, which, for many a year past, had possessed such great artists, and had exhibited one new Italian composer in his prime after another. But there are people whom no adversity will instruct; and the world was once more invited to wait and believe on the strength of a rumour, and an incident too curious to be forgotten, as a matter of dramatic recollection.

So remarkable had been the attention and ferment stirred by Mdlle. Jenny Lind's indecision and breach of contract, by the paragraphs in the papers, and the proceedings in the courts of law, of which she was the object, that hers was thought a fashion good to be followed by other singers, in no respect so well worth quarrelling for. At the time spoken of, a tall, handsome young lady, with a finer mezzo-soprano voice than is general in her country, with a real talent for the stage, was creating a great sensation in Berlin by singing in *Le Prophète* in close imitation of the original Fides. It is always wise to mistrust such close imitations who appear so immediately after their models have shown themselves, though for a while they thrive. It is particularly unwise when the enthusiasm is Berlin enthusiasm. Any one who had witnessed the fits of rapture into which one half of the Prussian capital was thrown by Mdlle. Löwe's imperfect singing might be excused from entertaining extraordinary expectations of Mdlle. Johanna Wagner.[1] Before she was heard in London—in the year 1853—I had an opportunity of studying her talent in the Prussian capital, and of finding it in no respect equal to the reputation so loudly trum-

---

[1] The daughter of Richard Wagner's elder brother Albert.—E. N.

peted. She was one of the many who sing without having learned
to sing. Her voice—an originally limited one, robust rather than
rich in tone—was already strained and uncertain, delivered after
a bad method, and incapable of moderate flexibility, as was to be
felt when she toiled through Mozart's air, "Parto," from *La
Clemenza,* with its clarinet obbligato. She wore man's attire well
and decorously, but she had too much of the elaborate and atti-
tudinizing style of her country to be acceptable as an actress, especially in the Italian drama, where the passion, if it cannot be
made to seem spontaneous, becomes intolerable. Such opinions
were shared by the English public when she *did* appear.

In 1851, however, Mademoiselle Wagner arrived in England,
as Mademoiselle Lind had done, under engagement to sing at both
opera houses, having broken a first contract because of the superior
advantage and security of the second one. Here, then, was a
second of those quarrels in which managers delight, as in drums
which summon the world to the show; here were more of conflict-
ing rumour, more of paragraph-making, more of costly appeal to
courts of law, more of running to and fro, more of examining
witnesses. Mademoiselle Wagner had only presented herself at
a solitary rehearsal of *Le Prophète* at Covent Garden Theatre
when she was laid under prohibition by the judicial authority, and
was prevented from appearing in either opera house till the quarrel should be settled. It was during the litigation on this case that
a letter from her father was produced, containing the contemptuous phrase, "that one only *could* go to England to get money," the
publication of which excited such lively indignation. The ignorance of, or contempt for, what passes in this country, which
has prevailed in Germany, during the last quarter of a century,
among second-rate musicians, must have been already known to
any who had passed about among them, and heard them speak
freely. Handel, Haydn, Beethoven, Weber, Spohr, Mendelssohn,
knew better! But in my goings to and fro I have heard things
regarding this country of a contemptuous strangeness, as ridiculous
as they were overcharged and inconsistent. Twelve years ago, in
the town which tolerated the introduction of "Mein Herz ist am
Rhein," in the lesson scene of *Il Barbiere*—and this not by the
Rosina, but by the Barber—I was informed that we had no singers
in England. Six years later I was gravely instructed by a Fräulein

who had a repertory of some four songs, that she was coming to London to fill the blank existing in our oratorios: herself cognizant of some two and a half by Handel! How this can arise in a day like ours it seems hard to understand; but the idea of our ignorance is still as fixed, among certain of the Germans, as was that among the French of our "God-dam," so ingeniously recorded by Beaumarchais, or the wonderful Gallic superstition under which a French playwright enabled our Lord Mayor of London (a perfect Gog of greatness on the other side of the channel) to transport the Heir Apparent of the British Crown to the United States!

Let these things be as they may, whatever Mademoiselle Johanna Wagner might have effected had she appeared as agreed on in her original compact, the excitement of her non-appearance and the confident promises of a legal verdict in favour of Her Majesty's Theatre could not ward off the ruin which its manager had for some years been preparing with such blind assiduity. The public had lost all faith in the theatre, as was not wonderful—all trust in the daily reports of the superiority and success of every new singer. It had been said, for some time, that private assistance had been strained to the very uttermost; and the truth of the tale was proved in the fact that the old Haymarket opera house closed A. D. 1851—not to re-open for three years—for the first time since it had been rebuilt by its Polish architect Novosielski.

THE YEAR 1852

ROYAL ITALIAN OPERA

OPERAS. *La Somnambula, Norma, I Puritani,* Bellini; *Maria di Rohan, I Martiri,** *Lucia, Lucrezia, L'Elisir,* Donizetti; *La Juive,* Halévy; *Pietro il Grande,** Jullien; *Les Huguenots, Le Prophète,* Meyerbeer; *Don Giovanni, Il Flauto Magico,* Mozart; *Guillaume Tell, Il Barbiere, Otello,* Rossini; *Faust,** Spohr. PRINCIPAL SINGERS. Mdes. Castellan, Seguin,* Julienne,* Grisi, Zerr Bosio;* MM. Mario, Tamberlik, Ronconi, Ander,* Stigelli, Tagliafico, Bartolini, Gueymard,* Formes, Galvani, Negrini.*

THE YEAR 1852

THREE new operas were produced, each as distinct one from the other as well could be. *I Martiri,* by Donizetti, was arranged for the Grand Opera at Paris, from the *Poliuto* written for Naples, which is said to have cost poor Nourrit his life. On quitting France, unable to face the inevitable succession to his throne of M. Duprez, that poetical but too sensitive artist conceived the desperate idea of transforming himself into an Italian singer. He *would* not see that his day was done! The disfavour with which his attempt was received at the Teatro San Carlo, where he appeared in this *Poliuto,* exasperated his distress of mind, already verging on insanity, and brought about the act of self-destruction—one of the saddest stories of compulsory retreat in the annals of the stage.

I Martiri, though supported in Paris by Duprez, whose singing of the "Credo" was prodigiously admired by our neighbours, in no respect bore out the favour which had attended *La Favorita.* The opera is diffuse, the story is dull, containing a mixture of false paganism and stage Christianity which the English have not yet learned to endure in opera. Then the music is generally weak in effect till the final duet of enthusiasm, which, of its kind,—including the inevitable modern use of unison,—offers good room for display to strong singers, though less exciting, perhaps, than the final duet in *La Favorita.* Here it was taken by Signor Tamberlik and Madame Julienne—the latter a French or Belgian lady who had already sung in London, and who now aspired to serious Italian opera. She was entitled to do this by the quality of her voice,—a real soprano, full and vehement rather than rich,—and by her good stage intentions. But the favourable impression made by the duet died away in subsequent performances of this and the following year. Her appearance was not prepossessing; and even in 1852 (nor till the last, it may be said), had any newcomer the very slightest possible chance of disputing the occupation so triumphantly and despotically held by Madame Grisi.

Her resolution not merely to have and to hold her own but to take from others all that could interfere with her supremacy, during this very season, led the last-named remarkable prima donna into one of her few mistakes—her attack on Madame Viardot's great and self-created part in *Le Prophète*. Her failure was as complete on this occasion as it had been many years before, when she had been tempted to appear for once only as Romeo—it may be, in the hope of establishing beyond question her succession to Madame Pasta.

The second opera new to our Italian stage was the *Faust* of Spohr, which the veteran composer came to England to conduct in person. I have elsewhere [1] attempted to characterize the opera music of this peculiar composer, who in his choice of subjects and intention was so romantic, in his execution so mannered and insipid, and to point out why, even in his own country, the popularity of all his works, excepting those especially written for the violin, had waned during his lifetime, and how admiration had passed off into placid, weary respect. Even with that best will to relish and to cherish German opera in England, which prevailed for some quarter of a century among our amateurs, Spohr's musical dramas have been from the first found soporific. "How many more lamentations are there to be?" said one of the most accomplished German musicians living to me, while waiting for the third act of *Jessonda*. Even the excellent performance at Covent Garden Theatre (allowing for the disadvantages which attend translated German Opera), even the incomparable orchestra, the chorus not to be matched in Europe, even the veritable presence of the composer, could do nothing to change our apathetic respect into real enjoyment. All was done that could be done in honour of an honourable guest, whose farewell visit to England this was understood to be; but it was done with no result.

It would be hard to name any distinguished musician—as a man meriting the highest respect, and almost beloved in his own circle elect—who, to the outer world, seemed so cold and ungracious as Spohr. Others have been as thoroughly self-engrossed—Spontini, for instance—but more courteous. I shall not soon forget how I have heard Kalkbrenner, when elderly, mow down every other

[1] *Modern German Music*, vol. ii., p. 88.

pianist and writer for the piano more modern than Haydn (Bee-thoven among the number) with "a golden axe"—here admitting prettiness, there excusing an odd chord or two, anon remarking on peculiarities of execution as very courageous. But all this was elegantly administered. In the same humour, also, were the sar-casms of John Cramer directed against players who played what he could not play. But these were cases of self-assertion in court dress. Spohr's was a case of callous, bovine indifference to every one except Spohr. He did not care—rather he did not know—whom he trampled down under the flat hoof of his intense pre-occupation. Yet the composer of *Faust* had not led a secluded life, to excuse his want of geniality in manner. In his early days he had travelled much, had mixed with men of many classes; and though in his later years he found himself under a hard and un-complying taskmaster in the Elector of Cassel, who seemed to take a pleasure in thwarting him, Spohr had seen courts, and had been honoured at them. There is no want of elegance in his music. A large portion of it is surcharged with a sort of faded grace, which cloys. In person he was singularly dignified; but in behaviour his phlegmatic self-importance, and indifference to the claims of oth-ers, amounted to incivility. During this last visit of his to London he was to be met in every musical circle of any significance; but he strode about through them careless whom he inconvenienced, less gratified by cordial attempts contrived to do him honour than made impatient by the hot weather; or else would sit dry, solemn, and inattentive, without one solitary kind word to say to younger musicians whom he had not till then known, or offering the slight-est token of interest in any German music unless it was Spohr's. I suppose he could laugh, but I never even saw him smile. He seemed,—in the world, at least,—to have no courtesy for women, no notice for children; to take everything set before him as a mat-ter of course, to give nothing in return.

This phlegm of self-occupation (I know not how better to char-acterize it), this orderly calmness, maintained without effort, be-cause without consideration for others, is to be felt in his music, and may be fancied as a reason why it loses hold on those the readiest to admit its many excellent qualities. Studied, as it were, from a distance, it is striking by its individuality: considered more intimately it wearies by its monotony, till the hearer is apt to be-

come unjust. We were grateful to have an opportunity of studying *Faust* so carefully performed; and Spohr had changed, and
amplified, and introduced other music (a grand air from his
Zweikampf among the number) to fit the old work for the new
house in London: but few, if any, of our opera-goers desired to
sit through the opera a second time. Nor could it be said that
on this occasion the German music was betrayed by the Italian
artists. Signor Ronconi, though insufficient in voice, played and
looked the character of Faust admirably, and sang with unusual
care. Signor Tamberlik's Ugo excited the only enthusiasm of the
evening. Such failure as there was in the completeness of the
execution of Spohr's opera belonged to the Germans—Mademoiselle Zerr and Herr Formes.

The third novelty of this season was as different in character
from the one just mentioned as is a rope-dancer (who cannot
dance) covered with tags and spangles and tawdry ribbons, from a
well-executed but rather oppressive German statue, cast in bronze.
That unlucky day on which it was decreed that money should be
wasted in setting forth a grand opera by Jullien is a date which
belongs to the realm behind the curtain. When will there be another such character before it as the composer of that opera?
Absurd as he was, a charlatan who had succeeded in deceiving
himself, wasteful, vain, disorderly, the man was made for better
things. There was good in him; a sort of pompous, comical, per-
verted enthusiasm—but real the while—for what was good.
Parisian critics, who recollect well their own Tivoli Gardens,
where he had his dance orchestra, and know England as Parisian
critics do (not at all), have told the French world that here he
was reputed as great a man as Beethoven. Between such wondrous deification and utter disgust there is still some truth to be
told, now that the eccentric, tawdry creature who so delighted in
himself and in his embroidered coats and in his shirt-fronts—
those wonderful works of stitchery—is no more. If Jullien was
ignorant, as one so tossed about in land and sea in his boyhood
could hardly help being, he had much mother wit and kind-
heartedness. He could be and was humane and considerate to
the people under his control; and this, too, when no credit was to
be won by it. He was further liberal to them until his money
matters fell into that chaos in which struggling folk have neither

time nor breath to be nice, and in which only the really strong have self-denial enough to be honest.

He had deluded himself (bystanders aiding in the folly) into conceiving that he had a real genius for composition. When the news of Mendelssohn's sudden death reached him at a rehearsal he stopped his band, smote his forehead with a tragical blow, in which there was a touch of genuine dismay and regret, and exclaimed to the bearer of the tidings, "This is what happens to all people of genius!—*I* will never compose any more!" He had a humorous instinct for odd orchestral mixtures of sound, largely wrought out by the first-rate players whom, in the first days of his prosperity, he gathered about him. Year by year his "Quadrilles" grew more and more elaborate, aspiring, and tremendous. Avalanches—Fires at sea—Earthquakes—Storms—Sacks of towns—Explosions in citadels—all melting off into some thunder of hilarity, loyalty, or thanksgiving at the close, were there. Whether he really wrote the amazing productions in question, or merely designed them, leaving others to work them out and to correct any very glaring faults of harmony, is a mystery hardly worth solving. They have vanished for ever, now that his lovely and inspired behaviour is no more.

But that such a man should have been accredited in producing an opera at such an establishment as Covent Garden Theatre is among the wonders of the time; and more, that such a man should wake the morning after *Pietro il Grande* was performed, and find himself put into companionship with M. Meyerbeer before a reading public! It was no wonder that one so feather-brained, so scheming, so grandiose in his expectations and self-conceit should become bewildered, and at last lose such small amount of ballast as he had ever carried. Of the opera itself it would be waste of time and patience to speak, superbly put on the stage as it was, with a luxury of characteristic Russian dresses, and soberly sung by no less experienced artists than Mademoiselle Anna Zerr and Signor Tamberlik, for heroine and hero. The attempt at practising on public credulity in bringing it forward was a piteous mistake, which must have worked, and did work, its own punishment. No cost had been spared in presenting it. The scenery was complicated, the dresses were gorgeous. There were dances, processions (for aught I recollect, a battle and fireworks). The entire affair was perilous, as drawing down ridicule on a management professing such high aims as that of Covent Garden Theatre. Fortunately it happened at the very close of the season, and the folly could be swept out of sight and memory before the curtain drew up in 1853.

Among new singers, the only permanent acquisition made to either opera house in 1852 was that of Madame Bosio, the value of which, however, was imperfectly promised by her first appearance in *L'Elisir*. Of her person everyone could judge; but her voice seemed that evening to be wiry, strange, perpetually out of tune, and her execution to be wild and ambitious. I remember no first appearance much more scant in musical promise, of one who was destined during her short career to become so deservedly great a favourite. But Madame Bosio was curiously made up of contradictions. Her features were irregular and ill-formed; yet on the stage she passed for more than pleasing—almost for a beauty. Her manner, which in private was inelegant after the first courtesies were over, had in public a certain condescending gracefulness which made up for coldness. Next to Madame Sontag, Madame Bosio was the most ladylike person whom I have seen on the stage of the Italian Opera. This demeanour of hers, and her happy taste (or fortune, as may be) in dress, had no small influence on the rapid growth of her popularity, which grew to exceed that of Madame Persiani, the lady whom she replaced, and by many was thought to surpass, though in no respect her equal as a singer.

There is no odder subject for speculation than the analysis of what is called "charm," and the power of assuming it commanded by certain persons who have no inherent appreciation of it. The power as certainly exists as does the power to impress by nobility of nature and generosity of heart in many whose manners are rough, and whose speech is ill-selected. Of Madame Bosio I shall have to speak again, in the record of later seasons.

THE YEAR 1853

ROYAL ITALIAN OPERA

PRINCIPAL OPERAS. *Masaniello,* Auber; *Norma, I Puritani,* Bellini; *Benvenuto Cellini,** Berlioz; *L'Elisir, Maria di Rohan, Lucrezia Borgia, La Favorita,* Donizetti; *Robert le Diable, Le Prophète,* Meyerbeer; *Don Giovanni,* Mozart; *Il Barbiere, Guillaume Tell,* Rossini; *Jessonda,** Spohr.

PRINCIPAL SINGERS. Mdes. Castellan, Bosio, Grisi, Albini,* Nantier-Didiée, Julienne-Dejean, Medori,* Tedesco;* MM. Mario, Tamberlik, Ronconi, Formes, Lucchesi,* Stigelli, Beletti.

I find no mention of *Les Huguenots* in my notes of the year, but that opera was certainly given.

THE "old house," then, was fairly beaten out of the field by the new one. And after all that had been whispered, and asserted, and published in print, the Italian Opera in Covent Garden had entirely superseded the house in the Haymarket, with all its traditional fashion. How certain persons had clung to this, with a constancy peculiar to loyal England, can hardly be believed. They had sworn (and, I am convinced, honestly) that to drive five minutes further towards so vulgar a locality was impossible—forgetting how the playhouses there had been mobbed by persons of taste, intelligence, and rank to see John Kemble and Mrs. Siddons. They had overlooked in their own dear domain the extinction of Fop's Alley, and such sights in the pit as misbehaviours which would have made a chapter on manners in Mrs. Trollope's American experiences. They had endured bad music, they had defended inferior performances, on the plea that it would not do for any manager to yield to the dictation of a subordinate (the onus of the new establishment having been conveniently laid on Signor Costa's separation from the theatre). They had appealed to this and to the other printed praise of every performer, male or female, who had appeared in turn; while also they had virtually declared that, when one particular star had vanished, the entertainment was no longer worth frequenting. But there was no questioning the fact that, long before 1853 set in, the tide, fashionable and unfashionable, had turned to Covent Garden to hear great musical performances, and that in 1853 "the dear old house" was closed.

Mine is no miserable story of personal scandals, of undertakings ventured without money, of mortgages and bargains, of quarrels in the face of ruin, of the fathomless and endless proceedings of Chancery. Our law reports have told that there had been enough and to spare of all such hindrances and drawbacks on the Haymarket Opera house from the time when its walls were raised. But it must be stated that one cause of wreck and disaster was the desertion of the theatre, owing to the systematic deterioration of its musical performances, for which the temporary frenzy (the word is not too strong) excited by one wonder offered no equivalent. Real retrenchment of luxuries is economy; but the setting forth of counterfeit and inferior wares as equal to past splendid realities is an experiment on credit, intelligence, and patience which (no matter how it be sustained) can come to only one issue.

Three operas, not hitherto heard in England, were produced during the season. The first was Signor Verdi's *Rigoletto,* in which, for the first time, that composer took some real hold of our public. It is by some spoken of as Signor Verdi's best work. I have always found it dull, dismal, and weak, the ball-room music in the first scene clear of anything like vivacity, the music for the hunchbacked court buffoon,—M. Victor Hugo's Triboulet from his *Le Roi s'amuse,*—colourless, and to depend entirely on the actor's power of shifting from one mood to the other—from the ribald's silly wit to the devouring anxiety of a father who knows that he hides a fair daughter from the eyes of unscrupulous libertinism. Even Rigoletto's outburst of horror and rage, after the outrage has been committed which destroys two lives, is merely the old, familiar, flagrant cabaletta which has done duty again and again one hundred times. It would be hard to name anything in the shape of an air of exhibition more puerile and affected than the song of Gilda when she retires to her chamber—singing as she goes—on the night of her abduction. Then the bad weather which finds the desolate fair rambling close to the house of the hired assassin, which is to prove so fatal to the ill-starred daughter of the court servant, has no bitterness in its wind and rain. One excellent piece, however, *Rigoletto* does contain—that quartet in which, while the libertine Duke and Maddalena, the assassin's sister and decoy, are toying within the wretched hovel, the daughter and the father are shivering in the storm without. This is most ingeniously and effectively combined. Further, the Duke has a popular song the frivolity of which is not misplaced; and on these two numbers, on the coarse but forcible horror of the revolting story, and on the exceeding fitness of the actors to their parts, may be ascribed such favour as *Rigoletto* has gained in England. As the buffoon it would be impossible to exceed Signor Ronconi,—in the hour of his buffoonery so pliant and degraded, so superstitiously terrified beneath the curse of the old nobleman whom he is bidden to mock on the way to the scaffold, when alone with his child, showing the restless love and suspicion of an animal; after her abduction, so rueful in his attempts to be gay, as he creeps to and fro among the courtiers, eye and ear alert to discover any trace of her hiding-place, convulsed with fury and vengeance when too late he finds her, and when she flings herself into his arms, hopelessly outraged! Nothing, again, could be more character-istic, heartless, careless, and withal fascinating, than Signor Mario as the Duke—the very charming royal rake, whom ladies have been heard to excuse as more sinned against than sinning, his beauty set off to perfection by his old Italian costume, a figure for Bronzino to have painted. Yet more, in *Rigoletto* Madame Bosio made the first of those many advances forward which have been noticed; and was graceful, tender, and innocent, the very picture of one unable to cope with wrong, who had nothing left her, having been wronged, save to die. Signor Tagliafico was excellent as Sparafucile, the bravo; and his sister Maddalena was no less ex-cellently personated by Madame Nantier-Didiée. Her gay, hand-some face, her winning mezzo-soprano voice, not without a Cremona tone in it, redeeming the voice from lusciousness, and her neat, lively execution, were all displayed in this part, short as it is. For such occupation as falls to the share of a first-rate singer of the second class, this lady has never been exceeded. Subsequently when, tempted by ambition, and because of the scarcity of competent singers, she has tried to win first honours as a contralto, the natural limits of her powers have made themselves felt, and she has lost rather than gained in public favour. In try-ing too high flights she may have somewhat sprained her wings.

The second new opera, *Benvenuto Cellini,* is to be described as a real curiosity. For a year or two previous to this period, M. Berlioz, having made his great powers as an orchestral conductor known to us, and his almost equally great critical acuteness when it is brought to bear on subjects which interest him, had secured a certain attention for his instrumental compositions. They had made that sort of half tempting, half tantalizing impression which turns out well or ill for the works which are the object of it, in proportion to the amount of real truth, structure, and meaning they may prove to contain. Then, late in the autumn of 1852, Dr.

Liszt, always chivalrous in coming to the rescue of genius neglected or unfairly treated, had brought about a representation, in the little theatre at Weimar, of this *Benvenuto Cellini,* which, on its production at Paris, had been cruelly maltreated. The late Grand Duchess of Saxe-Weimar, a lady of rare musical accomplishment —gracious, and able to be liberal in all matters of art,—had interested herself in the performance, and had contributed largely to its production in the utmost perfection within such narrow limits. I was present at that performance, the excitement of which was remarkable—almost amounting to a contagion not to be resisted. Goethe's little town, in 1853, was taking no small credit to itself as having brought forward the new musician who was to set the world on fire—Herr Wagner. There was something of self-glorification in this, if there was much also of that honest conviction which is indispensable to any temporary victory gained by fanaticism. In those days M. Berlioz was rated by the Germans as among the transcendentalists—as a man who had suffered martyrdom in frivolous France, and had been neglected by ignorant England because he was in advance of the time. Every nerve was strained by sincere faith and good-will to place his *Benvenuto Cellini* in the list of operas before which the world was to bow down, in forgetfulness of the Mozarts, Webers, Rossinis, as a race of well-meaning, worn-out pedants or triflers, who had amused an indolent public, unwilling and unable to think, and whose day was gone. The performance was nothing short of marvellous, for the difficulties to be overcome were enormous. The little orchestra did wonders in following the intricacies of the score; the singers (but, to be sure, they had been inured to Herr Wagner's operas) were steady in their parts, and if they sang too mechanically it was the fault not of themselves but of their composer. He was present, the audience was heartily rapturous, and German rapture (how different from Italian ecstacy) is very seducing for the moment. The real beauties, then, of this perplexed and provoking work were brought as near to the comprehension and sympathy of those who heard it as they will probably be ever brought. I was honestly interested by the experiment, and warmed by the cordiality of its manner, into forgetting the partisanship which belonged to it—though not convinced by the music.

Such having been the impression made by the composer in England, the tale of the triumph of *Benvenuto Cellini* at Weimar, which gathered amplitude by the way, made the trial of the opera here a natural if somewhat a courageous experiment. The performance was prepared with great care, and the composer himself presided in the orchestra. The evening was one of the most melancholy evenings which I ever passed in any theatre.

Benvenuto Cellini failed more decidedly than any foreign opera I recollect to have seen performed in London. At an early period of the evening the humour of the audience began to show itself, and the painful spectacle had to be endured of seeing the composer conducting his own work through every stage of its condemnation. Be such an exercise of justice warranted or not, it is impossible to be present at any scene of the kind without real feelings of concern —concern in this case heightened by thinking how much good labour on good material had been thrown away, out of systematic perversity.

It will surprise those who only recollect *Benvenuto Cellini* by its performance, on going through the published music, to find how considerable is the amount of real idea existing in it. In no other of its writer's works is the melody so abundant or so natural. Too often M. Berlioz bases his compositions on mere groups of notes, which have no claim to be considered as phrases, but are such as might be thrown together at haphazard, or (what is almost equivalent) by a fixed resolution to use what everyone else has rejected. Betwixt incompleteness of early study, a disposition to rebel and to resist belonging to a certain French period, and a too partial delight in the last compositions of Beethoven, the value of clearness as indispensable to a work of art—most of all a work of music, in which rhythm claims so large a part—seems to have been for ever lost by him. Not altogether to be classed with the writers of a late period in Germany, whose annulment of form may be referred to ignorance and incompetence, in his case the unselect accumulation of feature and detail produces almost the same effect of distress and confusion to the ear as theirs. It is his delight, in place of setting out his thoughts, to cover them. If the voice has a happy phrase—and in this *Benvenuto* some very happy ones have to be found (I will instance, among others, the duet of the lovers in the first act)—it is so smothered or hampered by a distracting instrumentation that only the most cultivated experience can recognize it. Often a burthen otherwise, repetition of the theme is so disguised, from a dread of being commonplace (which, by the way, is among the commonest fears of the unintelligent and half-instructed), that it passes unperceived; or there will be some allusion to it thrust in to some distant and heterogeneous part of the work, which throws out the most apt attention. There is a terzetto in the first act of *Benvenuto* in which, by way of too faithfully expressing the mystery of those who conspire "aside" (as the stage phrase is), a bright and animated musical phrase, of more sustained length than is frequent with the writer, is divided into such shreds, and with such ineffective changes of rhythm in the accompaniment, as entirely to be lost by those who have not a more minute acquaintance with the score than should be expected from any earthly audience.

Then the ease of the singers is disregarded with a despotism which is virtually another confession of weakness. As music, the scene in the second act, known in another form as its composer's happiest overture, the *Roman Carnival,* has the true Italian spirit of the joyous time; but the chorus singers are so run out of breath, and are so perpetually called on to catch or snatch at some passage which ought to be struck off with the sharpest decision, that the real spirit instinct in the music is thoroughly driven out of it.

These things are noted, not to depreciate a man of no common ingenuity and acuteness, so much as to suggest wherefore, owing to their misdirection, he has till now missed the reward which belongs to consistent labour and high aspiration. Among the most singular of modern phenomena is the verdict on the compositions of M. Berlioz which must be passed by those who judge him according to his own code of criticism. Again and again as he has done, repudiating what is obscure, and every deification of ugliness (for which the French world has largely to thank the French *convulsionnaire* school of writers), it is wonderful, as illustrating self-delusion, to see how perpetually he has turned out of the broad and clear way of musical composition to court obscurity and uncouthness. And the result has been that in spite of all his real fancy and invention, especially in orchestral sonority, his career as a composer has been virtually a prolonged struggle, unrelieved by a permanent success. It may be doubted whether, when his own personal influences as an admirable conductor of a certain music, as a man notorious for wit of word and pen, as a combatant who, right or wrong, has fought for his own system, have passed away, the works of M. Berlioz, pretentious though they are, and in some sense poetical, will keep their place; and the sympathy which every generous person must feel for one so earnestly striving, so often discouraged, so partially accepted, is strengthened by the vexing conviction that his case is not one of vacant vanity mistaking its occupation, so much as of a self-will that has deluded its possessor into a labyrinth from which there is little reasonable prospect of his extrication.

Of Spohr's *Jessonda* it is sufficient to say that it shared the fate of his *Faust*. It was listened to with respect, and parted from with feelings of relieved *ennui*.

Towards the close of the season two ladies arrived—Madame Medori and Madame Tedesco—from both of whom something was to be expected. The former—a Belgian lady—if I mistake not had been largely about the world, unable to find a home anywhere, ere she came to London. We had heard, from those who ought to have known better, that her voice was superb—almost without a peer among soprani; that she possessed no small amount of dramatic fire; that she was to be, in truth, a real acquisition to any grand opera company. It was a pity that all this should prove a mistake. Madame Medori was strong enough, in every respect, it is true, to satisfy the most exigent admirers of what is vehement; but her voice had acquired the habit of vibration to so terrible an extent that on a long note it seemed sometimes first too sharp, and then too flat, or *vice versa,* ere it settled itself; and Madame Medori had a propensity for long notes. There was an undaunted rudeness in her manner, that bespoke either a nature without refinement, or one which had been vulgarized by practise in inferior theatres before inferior audiences. Such a triumphant person (a wit once said that vulgarity was always triumphant) appears to her worst advantage in the company of well-instructed, well-bred persons—since, from false notions of self-assertion, she is too apt to display every defect she possesses, in the highest relief; want of ease, and the consciousness (not to be put aside) that she is unpopular, adding new points that must displease bystanders to those which are already part and parcel of her nature. The audience stared at her, and were puzzled at her boisterous ways. She came and went in silence; but it became evident that England was no home for Madame Medori. After London she tried Naples, after Naples the Grand Opera of Paris, with the same result everywhere.

Madame Tedesco, a mezzo-soprano, was unable to gain a footing here, for reasons totally opposite to those which rendered us averse to enthroning so riotous a person as the last mentioned one by way of opera queen. She had then a precious voice, and commanded that which Madame Alboni tried for—a rich mezzo-soprano, two octaves and more in compass, of equal quality from its lowest to its highest notes. I am inclined, on recollection, to consider it the most perfect organ of its kind that I have ever heard. But never was voice more completely thrown away. The want is hard to specify, for it was everywhere. Hers was a voice that can never have studied; it was also a voice without inflexion, without light or shade in it (things entirely distinct from piano and forte), without power of execution, though it went duly up scales, and down the same, with a sort of composure more irritating than downright failure. Nothing but that placidity (shall it be called?) of temperament which is not to be animated by praise or blame, could have prevented its owner from taking a first rank among singers, could have supported her through the scene which (as I have said) I had some years before witnessed at Milan, when she had to sing throughout an opera—*Saul,* by Maestro Cannetti— in La Scala, with the brutal accompaniment of a pit full of men— lovers of music, too!—who greeted her with a storm of opprobrious insults so often as she appeared, and, by way of a delightful joke, absolutely sang through the quick movement of her grand air with her. The scene excites disgust and indignation as I write; and as I write I see the quiet, impassive figure on the stage come and go, and continue her part as firmly and quietly as if there had been dead silence round her. When I saw Madame Tedesco here and in Paris, some ten years later, after she had succeeded better in more hospitable places, and had added some little to her vocal experience, it was impossible to avoid fancying that what then I had admired as indomitable pride, as a resolution not to give her unmanly enemies the satisfaction of conceiving they had conquered her, might be ascribable to other qualities.

On the whole, this season strengthened the impression, which was already too strong, that the dearth of such singers as we had heard in former times was becoming, year by year, greater, and tended to fix attention increasingly on what in reality has proved essentially the main musical stay and support of the Royal Italian Opera—its orchestra and chorus. Insomuch as the band of the Grand Opera in Paris—incomparable in 1836—had become slack, and feeble, and slovenly; insomuch as theatrical orchestras so celebrated as those of Berlin, Vienna, Munich, and Frankfort (under Guhr) had disappointed the traveller; the increasing merit and spirit of our own rose by comparison. Foreigners—even those, like Herr Wagner the elder,[1] who had conceived that England was a place only good to make money in—began to speak of its superior brilliancy, its amazing readiness in reading at sight, and its entire subjugation to its conductor; the last not merely won by musical acuteness but by moral promptitude, considerateness, and honour.

[1] See p. 80.—*E. N.*

THE YEAR 1854

ROYAL ITALIAN OPERA

PRINCIPAL OPERAS. *Norma,* Bellini; *Fidelio,* Beethoven; *L'Elisir d'Amore, Don Pasquale,* Donizetti; *La Prova d'un Opera Seria,* Gnecco; *Le Prophète,* Meyerbeer; *Don Giovanni,* Mozart; *Guillaume Tell, Matilda di Shabran, Otello, Il Barbiere, Il Conte Ory,* Rossini; *Ernani, Rigoletto,* Verdi. PRINCIPAL SINGERS. Mdes. Marai,* Nantier-Didiée, Bosio, Grisi, Viardot, Cruvelli;* MM. Ronconi, Tamberlik, Mario, Lucchesi, Susini, Tagliafico, Lablache.

T HERE was nothing this year at Covent Garden Theatre that called for remark, save the accession to the company of Signor Lablache, the first of Madame Grisi's many farewell performances, an inroad made by Mademoiselle Cruvelli, the result of which in no respect bore out her popularity in the Haymarket, the appearance of Mademoiselle Marai, a useful and pleasing second woman, whose voice, after a season or two, somehow dwindled away, and the production of Signor Rossini's delicious *Il Conte Ory*. On the whole the season was a supine one; and such stir as might be found in the opera world was among the Germans at Drury Lane.

The delicious *Il Conte Ory* has, with all the beauty of its music, never been a favourite anywhere. Even in the theatre for which it was written, the Grand Opera of Paris, where it still keeps its place, even when Madame Cinti-Damoreau was the heroine, giving to the music all the playfulness, finish, and sweetness which could possibly be given, the work was heard with but a tranquil pleasure. Like the excellent *Le Philtre* of M. Auber (which, as I have elsewhere said, entirely outdoes *L'Elisir*, the Italian setting of the same fancy) it is too delicate for a large stage. But like other of Signor Rossini's operas—may it not be said, all of them, *Il Barbiere*, *La Gazza*, and *Otello* excepted?—the music suffers for the story; and the composer, by his want of selection or disdain, proved once again his own enemy. The rakish Don Juan of the old French ballad, who, with his band, enters the house of the retired Countess, disguised as nuns, as a character turns out to be more disagreeable than droll; and even the questionable adventure is not happily arranged so as to keep animation in the story alive, though Scribe had a hand in its arrangement. The book, in truth, is little less stupid than that of *Matilda di Shabran*, with which opera it pairs off somehow. It bears the appearance of its origin—a determination to turn to account the music of an occasional opera, *Le Voy-*

age à Rheims, written in commemoration of the coronation of Charles Tenth of France, and in Paris performed by a bevy of singers such as no magic could call together now. The composer was then already entering on the last stage of his career. What entire transformations have passed over every world, most entire, perhaps, over his own, since then. Yet he is still living and still jesting!

It will be seen, on turning to *Il Conte Ory,* that the master was already in train for that alteration in his style which led to such magnificent results in *Guillaume Tell.* Without having lost one iota of the freshness of those days during which the introduction to *La Cenerentola* and the sestet were thrown off, and the capital concerted piece, "Oh guardate," in *Il Turco,* a felicitous curiousness in the modulations is to be observed, a crispness of finish, a resolution to make effect by disappointing the ear, which not only bespeaks the master's known familiarity with the great music of the greatest classical writers, but also his wondrous tact in conforming to the taste of the new public whom he was to fascinate. *Il Conte Ory* is essentially a French opera; and, as every French opera must do, loses by being sung with Italian words.

Yet, be it French or Italian, what is there in vocal music that can exceed the final trio, ridiculous though the situation may be? The life, the unexpectedness, the delicious union of the voices (to repeat an epithet), without undue platitude or perplexing intricacy, the dainty orchestral touches modestly, not timidly, introduced, precisely in those places where the ear is the most surely reached, make this trio, of its kind, a masterpiece, one not requiring the distortion of unnatural study for its comprehension, but which at first hearing speaks home; and which, if examined later, will repay the examiner as every specimen in which beauty, symmetry, fancy, and spirit are combined must do.

By an odd coincidence, this year was given in London another comic opera, and another masterpiece, which has mainly failed to produce its due effect, since the time of its first production, because of the feebleness of the story—*Die Entführung,* or *Il Seraglio,* of Mozart, which was executed rather than sung, by a coarse German company, at Drury Lane Theatre.

This year again there was an attempt at French comic opera at the St. James's Theatre, insufficiently made—as, indeed, could not be avoided. It is obviously impossible to transplant all the elaborate machinery of Parisian theatres to this distance; and on the piquancy of every detail no small portion of effect depends. Heard out of Paris, even in such opulent towns as Bordeaux (with its magnificent theatre), Marseilles, Lyons, French comic opera loses much of its brightness. When it is provincial it is impoverished in no small degree. This may be thought to imply a criticism on the music, as of an inferior class—if proved to be so largely dependent on execution; but I should rather point the moral against the amount of excellence in performance to be procured in the country. For the comic opera of France there must be neat and pungent singing (if with beauty of voice so much the better, but our neighbours are not famous for beautiful voices), cleverness in speaking, so large a share has dialogue in the pleasure, adroitness and propriety in action, so as to contribute to making an entire picture, and, last of all, perfect taste in costume. Then there must be an excellent orchestra for accompaniment which (in these days of orchestral writing, when the score is surcharged with half a score of instruments not dreamed of half a century ago) cannot be a small one. All these things are provided for in Paris by government assistance. In England, with the best will, and the greatest liberality imaginable, they can but be shadowed out, only presented in outline. The first lady in this French opera company was Madame Cabel—one of those peculiar singers so numerous in France, who have execution almost without limit, an infinity of dash and adroitness, but no style and no sensibility. In Paris—though subsequently M. Meyerbeer *did* select Madame Cabel as the heroine of his Breton opera —there was always a touch of what is provincial (to use the word with no contemptuous sense) in Madame Cabel's performances, in spite of her voice, which was superior in quality to the voices of her sister singers. I found her, there as here, second-rate; but her flights and her feats, for a few evenings, astonished and attracted our public, and did their part in familiarizing English amateurs with enjoyment in French opera.

THE YEAR 1855

ROYAL ITALIAN OPERA

PRINCIPAL OPERAS. *I Puritani, Norma,* Bellini; *Fidelio,* Beethoven; *L'Elisir d'Amore, Lucrezia Borgia,* Donizetti; *Don Giovanni,* Mozart; *L'Etoile du Nord, Le Prophète,* Meyerbeer; *Il Conte Ory, Il Barbiere, Otello,* Rossini; *Ernani, Il Trovatore,* Verdi. PRINCIPAL SINGERS. Mdes. Bosio, Marai, Bürdé-Ney,* Nantier-Didée, Viardot, Rüdersdorff,* Grisi, Bäur;* MM. Gardoni, Tagliafico, Zelger, Lucchesi, Formes, Graziani,* Mario, Tamberlik, Lablache.

THE YEAR 1855

HE year 1855, though a prosperous opera year, was not rich in variety. Two new works, however, were given, both of which must be dwelt upon. *Il Conte Ory,* with Signor Gardoni the graceful hero, was repeated. *Fidelio* was tried again, for the introduction of a German lady—on that evening when Napoleon the Third, Emperor of France, visited Covent Garden Theatre in state with our Sovereign Lady. What a strange commentary on chance and change was this, to those who recollected our imperial guest as the quiet and retiring frequenter of a box at the old opera house, before and after the expedition to Boulogne; and who recalled the derision which had attended the very few who then dared to speak of that event as one which might as probably have turned for better, as it did for worse, to him who adventured it! The tale of its accidents has, possibly, yet to be told.

Signor Verdi, this year, at last arrived at his real popularity in England—not equalling that of Bellini, but surpassing that of Donizetti—by the production of his *Il Trovatore,* the work among his works in which his best qualities are combined, and in which indications scattered throughout earlier productions present themselves in the form of their most complete fulfilment.

The story, it need not be told, is of the most paltry quality; one that might have been gathered from some extinct novel of the Minerva Press,—in place of the Spanish romance, little known on this side of the Pyrenees, from which it was derived. What is more, it is next to unintelligible. But the library of drama numbers some curious modern examples of interest and success excited, independent of clearness of narrative or sequence of events. There are stories that get hold of the public, if even every approved artifice of that neat carpentry, which was carried to such a wonderful refinement by Scribe, be violated in their contrivance; and the tale of *Il Trovatore* is among them. To this day many persons have not found out the right and wrong betwixt the false child roasted by the gipsy and mistaken vengeance and the true one, spared, and mistaken, and flung into all manner of miserable dilemmas, and at last beheaded, in order to give the avenging Fury an opportunity of saying to her noble persecutor, *"He was thy brother!"*

No work which is to last can be constructed on such an invention as this, because every half century has its new extravagancies: whereas truth, and love, and self-denial have been the same, in their simpler workings, ever since the world began. The most intricate combinations of Scribe will go out of fashion. For the moment, however, the tangled monstrosity of the story of *Il Trovatore* was overlooked in the admiration of Signor Verdi's music.

On this work, as the favourite Italian opera of to-day, or yesterday, there might seem no need to descant, did it not in some sort contain, as has been said, a quintessence of all that Signor Verdi has derived, combined, and originated, with something of his own, and might it not thus become an object of some curiosity to those who may read and refer, long after it has been swept off the stage, not, impossibly, after a musical stage has ceased to exist. The mixture of platitude with rugged invention, the struggle to express passion, the attempt at effect, in two important points (the "Miserere" one of these) wholly successful,—have been equalled by Signor Verdi in no subsequent opera; nor did he before, nor has he since, been so happy in tenderness, in beauty, in melody. "Il-Balen" has been the ruling London tune for five years, as undeniably as "Di tanti palpiti" was the tune some forty years ago, when barrel organs were (and brass bands) as one to ten!

One of the points in *Il Trovatore* which may be found worthy of remembering, after this or the other tune has passed into the limbo of old tunes, is Signor Verdi's essay at vocal Spanish gipsy colour. The chorus of waifs and strays opening the second act has an uncouthness, a bar or two of Oriental drawl, before the Italian anvils begin, which must remind anyone of such real gipsy music as can be heard and seen in Spain. Thus also is the monotonous, inexpressive narration of the gipsy mother, Azucena, to be animated only by her own passion,—all the more truthful (possibly) from its want of character. No melody really exists among those people; and the wild cries which they give out could not be reduced to notation, were it not for the dance which they accompany. Signor Verdi may have comprehended this, though with insufficient means of expression; at all events, some notion of the kind is to be found in what may be called the characteristic music of *Il Trovatore*.

There is much more in the "Miserere" scene—a picturesque beauty, and an originality not to be doubted or denied by anyone to whom the stage speaks,—though the leading phrase of the concerted piece might never have been found, had not there been an apparition scene in *Semiramide,* in which Signor Rossini had shown how terror might be told in rhythm. The introductory air for the heroine is new in its forms of melody and accent; and the combination of her voice with the voice of her lover—and with the chorus also, unseen—is captivating.

Il Trovatore (or rather, the heroine of this dismal opera) was introduced here, under some difficulties, by a German lady who had not sung in Italian ere she came to this country—Madame Bürde-Ney. It would be hard, even among her richly-gifted countrywomen, to name a soprano voice more rich, more sweet, more even, than hers. It was a voice better taught, too, than the generality of German voices—a voice delivered without force and inequality, with due regard to beauty of tone and grace in ornament. But the new language and new accent hampered Madame Ney; and her powers as an actress here seemed to be only limited. Thus the main requisite for the performance of Signor Verdi's music—a certain violence of emphasis and expression—was denied to it; and such spirit as could be thrown into the opera was contributed by Madame Viardot in the dismal character of the Spanish gipsy mother. Her few bars of cantabile in the last scene, where sleep comes over her while she sings, were among the most exquisitely beautiful and pathetic things heard on any stage.

The song "Il balen" exhibited to its best advantage one of the most perfect baritone voices ever bestowed on mortal in Signor Graziani. Such an organ bestowed by nature as his is a golden inheritance; one, however, which has tempted many another beside himself to rely too exclusively on nature. Be the song ever so lovely, be the voice ever so round, and full, and honeyed, the charm of "Il balen" must wear out in time, when not supported or varied by other attractions. It has, apparently, done so in the present case.

Possibly, too, *Il Trovatore* has already lost that popularity, in all

its fulness, which its music enjoyed for awhile. There is no returning to the work as a whole, for reasons already indicated—the
essentially superficial and showy nature of its effects.

Totally different in character was the other new opera of the
year. *L'Etoile du Nord* has been justly styled by that acute critic,
M. Berlioz, as the most highly-finished example of M. Meyerbeer's peculiar manner which that master of combination has given
to the world. It must be evident, however, to all who consider
the work, that his subtlety of combination has betrayed him, not
merely in the ordinance of the music, but also in the arrangement
of the story. Never did Scribe—who could bring into one play
the Heptameron of Marguerite of Navarre, and into another comedy everything possible and impossible, so as to make a heroine out
of La Maupin, the strange amazonian opera singer—twist and
torture his imagination and control over stage trickery more artfully (and less successfully) than in the case of the *Silesian Camp*
—a stupid work, written for the inauguration of a new theatre at
Berlin, as a sort of occasional court opera, intended to glorify the
Great Frederick and his flute-playing—when the same must needs
be transformed into a Russian story of Paris. But this turning,
and dyeing, and twisting process is opposed to all simplicity of invention; and within its coils and loops and ties there is too much
chance of the most clear-sighted man, the man most solicitous for
effect, losing his way, or being strangled. Till the end of the second act the story of *L'Etoile* moves, it is true—not probably, but
with an improbability which is found moving. Later follows one
piece of musical display after another—a trio for three men full of
cleverness (left out in Paris, but in London admirably executed),
a long mad scene for the heroine, including her trio, with two
flutes (a portion added to the old, original Prussian opera, in order
to exhibit the remarkable power over tone and breath commanded
by Mademoiselle Lind)—but nothing that leads the tale to any conclusion which is natural, or can be admitted for romance's sake.
This may be ascribable to delay, timidity, to an over-solicitude as to
effect, nourished and cherished by every success, by every experience; since the score of *L'Etoile* contains pages full of pure, original
ideas, as clearly designed as they are sharply wrought out. To
instance—a rare enjoyment and humour (not over-refined, it is

true) and a capital combination of two women's voices and tongues, are to be found in the suttler-duet in the tent scene of the second act, such as raise that piece, in a musical point of view, far above the level of manufacture. It is comical and artistic; and in both respects of the best quality.

Elsewhere, with all his ingenuity, M. Meyerbeer has been in some degree paralysed by the requisitions of a story arranged and re-arranged, and by his own desire to outdo himself. In the finale to the first act there are three choruses—the bridal one of peasants, that of the recruits, that of the drinkers, each having a melodic phrase of its own; and the three are so inwrought that, when the frank, brilliant winding-up comes, there is left no impression of patchiness or dislocation. But the eye, on perusal, is aware of this, not the ear; and the phrases themselves, meanwhile, must have suffered in the resolution to pare them into a working—or, as theatrical folk have it,—a practicable shape.

The combination of the old and commonplace Dessauer March, at the close of the second act, with the fife quickstep (which is no tune) and the Cossack military music (which is yet less a tune) with the prayer and chorus of principal voices, laid out so as to accom-modate themselves to the emergency desired, affords another ex-ample of what is not genius and not effect, howsoever it may ex-cite wonderment in the ignorant world.

But in the second act of this *L'Etoile* there is a coarse camp ele-ment not existing—not indicated—in any other musical drama. And in this we may touch the peculiar genius of M. Meyerbeer; and in this I can see, on recollection, how Lablache—who was al-ways contriving, always understanding, always inventing—found his last amusement and occupation in personating the gross, semi-stupid savage, transformed into a military official, and thereupon bewildered into a conspiracy, who ties fast the knot of such story as exists in this strange opera.

I cannot conceive that there was ever a veteran artist who, on the eve of his departure, left so fresh, so distinct a print of his foot on the ground, as Lablache left in the character of Gritzenko. He could not have done this had there not been some incitement to enable him so to do—in the rough, real animation inevitably be-longing to a military opera, which excited him, and brought out every particle of his powers—vocally, but not intellectually, failing.

This last personation by Lablache was among those masterpieces which it is as well to remember as to regret, seeing that what man has done, man may do. I think that he was content with it himself. The only time, during a quarter of a century's public intercourse, that I had the honour of speaking to him was when he sought occasion to express his pleasure in respect to a few honest words of mine, with regard to this opera and his share in it. "You have made," he said to me, "an old man very happy."

Otherwise, in many respects, *L'Etoile* went amiss in London. The hero, Herr Formes, could not satisfy anyone who had seen the original Pierre of M. Bataille. He did not sing the music perfectly. He acted too much in critical junctures. Then, though Madame Bosio as the heroine was charming and delicate, and in her disguise of doublet and hose what a Rosalind should be, and though, as her peasant sister-in-law Prascovia, Mademoiselle Marai did her best, the two picaroon suttler women in the second act (most essential to the story and the music, and how excellent in Paris!) were condescending in London—half ashamed, thoroughly doleful. They drummed as a pair of disguised princesses might do; they sang their capital duet without fire, or fun, or accent. All the intricate and clever and effective music that belongs to them fell dead on London ears. The fault, in fact, might perhaps lie with the master, from his having sought in opera what cannot be produced in it—a union perfectly balanced, of music, song and farce,— and this may always bar the work from chances of its being adequately represented in the most complete of musical theatres out of Paris. There women can act without beauty and can sing without voices, and draw out every point to the uttermost of its pungency, without pedantry or caricature. The loss to this second act of the original language and the original vivandières can hardly be over-estimated. But the entire opera is cruelly lamed by translation, for many reasons. One of these is the amount of staccato music. From first to last there is a perpetual application of word to note, at variance with all Italian fancies as to singing, and as to what the singer should be expected to do; and, save in broad comedy, creating a perpetual impression of fatigue to the listener. There is one quiet tune, which was *the* final tune of the Prussian opera, re-made for Paris, and which passed almost unobserved when *L'Etoile* was given at Berlin. Yet even that quiet tune—

the heroine's prayer at the end of the first act—wants a second part. Then the romance for the basso in the last act, intended to be penitent, expressive, and suave, is in reality mawkish—a song to be avoided rather than courted by any singer, as one without nature, however seemingly simple.

Under Parisian conditions these peculiarities were little felt, the restlessness of character passed unperceived; but on being paraphrased it became dry and tedious, and to this may be ascribed the limitation of the success of the opera, as compared with others by its writer. In none has he been more individual, in few more melodious. The gipsy rondo in the first act, the song with chorus of girls given to the peasant bride, the Cossack dancer's tune in the camp, the jolly infantry song, with its irresistible brethren, in the third act Prascovia's little romance, are all specimens of the master in his happiest mood, "snatches of song" clear and sweet enough to make one regret that there is so much of mere "snatch" in M. Meyerbeer's works, and that any effort on his part to work out a theme or a subject is so often accompanied by loss of power, timidity, mannerism, and the use of recondite expedients to conceal real poverty of resource.

L'Etoile, again, suffers on the Italian stage by the substitution of sung for spoken recitative, and by M. Meyerbeer's substitution of recitative accompanied for the free musical talk, with a chord to sustain it, by aid of which the composers of past times connected their dramatic situations and their display pieces. Rich as is this modern manner of working, it nevertheless surcharges the work with ornament—deprives the hearer of any chance of rest, and stiffens an opera into a symphony four hours long. There is no breathing, no waiting; and the set musical pieces, whether they be songs, choruses, or elaborate combinations, when arrived at, have already lost some of their importance, owing to over-preparation.

Such are a few outlines of M. Meyerbeer's fourth French opera, as presented in Italian here. How far its success might have justified the care and cost lavished on its production cannot be ascertained; for the fire at Covent Garden Theatre swept it away, —I can hardly fancy with much hope of its frequent return. The work is throughout Parisian, and not, like *Les Huguenots*, universal.

There were more farewell performances of Madame Grisi, in some of which her obvious resolution not to be displaced seemed absolutely to restore her to her splendid powers of other days. Her career may be said to have been remarkable in the length of its autumn.

THE YEAR 1856

HER MAJESTY'S THEATRE

OPERAS. *La Somnambula,* Bellini; *La Figlia, Lucrezia, Don Pasquale,* Donizetti; *La Cenerentola, Tancredi,* Rossini; *Il Trovatore, La Traviata,* Verdi. PRINCIPAL SINGERS. Mdes. Alboni, Rizzi, Albertini,* Piccolomini,* Wagner,* Amadei,* Bauer; * MM. Calzolari, Beneventano,* Zuccone,* Baillou,* Salviani,* Bouché, Baucardé, Reichardt, C. Braham.* BALLET. *Le Corsaire.* PRINCIPAL DANCERS. Mdlles. Marie Taglioni, Rosati.

THE YEAR 1856

ER Majesty's Theatre reopened with every outward sign of prosperity. The house was crammed nightly; to all appearance the audience was delighted with the singers, good, bad, and indifferent; and one artist was brought forward to reproduce the golden days of Mademoiselle Lind, and who absolutely did, for a short time, fascinate the foolish part of our opera public into a belief that in her arrived a new revelation.

There had been the usual trumpets blown beforehand, with some variation in the tunes. After tales of Swedish parsonage houses, after the coronetted book handed to "the Countess" to sing from, after the volume published in proof that Madame Sontag's return was an interposition of a special Providence on behalf of a temple of art fit object for such peculiar care, after the facsimile of Madame Pasta promised in the daughter of her adoption and the inheritress of her secrets, invention could hardly have been easy; seeing, too, that it had already been tried in half a score of less prosperous forms. There had been the Viennese children, rescued, it was said, from the clutch of the Jesuits, in whose spiritual welfare virtuous sovereigns had been interested. There had been a negro woman, with some of the inborn musical skill belonging to her race, paraded with the insulting title of The Black Malibran. There had been the mystery of no mystery belonging to Donna Lola Montez—absolutely brought to dance on the stage as the daughter of the celebrated Toreador Montez, at a time when she had no less absolutely, beyond her indomitable impudence, fewer requisites for her dancing appearance before our public than those taken by her to Paris, and which, on her disgraceful failure at the Grand Opera, drew from M. Jules Janin one of the most lacerating and bitter pieces of criticism ever provoked by audacity. After all these devices, which must have cost labour to discover them, and after the ruin which they had helped to bring on the theatre, it seemed strange that a new campaign should be tried again, on no grounds

of art more solid than those of appeals to the old worn-out quack-
eries.   But it was so; and apart from the real attraction to musicians of Madame Alboni, who never sang better than she did on
the reopening night of the "old house," and the next piquant promise of the certain appearance of that engagement-breaker, Mademoiselle Johanna Wagner, whom our Courts of Law—and whom
commissioners sent out to examine her—had exalted into a surpassing value, strange to those who had fathomed her real worth as
a singer, London was prepared for the advent of a dazzling beauty
—the favourite pupil of the most renowned singing-master in Italy,
Signor Romani, a young lady of noble Roman family, driven by her
irresistible propensities for the musical drama into open variance
with her relations (this clause in the legend was not of the newest) ;
and, to clench and crown all—A CARDINAL'S NIECE!

The little lady herself, I believe, may have never set the wondrous tale a-going.   But her career and her popularity in England
were odd, and the story thereof is not to be escaped from.

No greater sign of the decay of the old Italian art of singing
could have been shown than in the temporary success of Mademoiselle Piccolomini.   Her voice was weak and limited—a mezzo-
soprano hardly one octave and a half in compass.   She was not
sure in her intonation; she had no execution.   That which was
wanting she supplied by a behaviour which enchanted several of
the persons who sit in the stalls.   Her best appearance was in *La
Traviata*.   The music of the first act pleased, perhaps, because it
is almost the solitary act of gay music from the composer's pen;
and her effrontery of behaviour passed for being dramatically true
to the character, and not, as it afterwards proved, her habitual
manner of accosting her public.   In the repulsive death act, too,
she had one or two good moments of serious emotion, though this
was driven at times to the verge of caricature, as when every clause
of her last song was interrupted by the cough which belongs to the
character.   But the essential homeliness of her "reading" of a part
which could only be redeemed by a certain born refinement indicated
in the frail heroine, was to be seen when Madame Bosio undertook
it at the rival opera house; and when, by the superior delicacy of
her treatment of it as an actress, she effaced the forwardness of her
predecessor.   To compare the two as singers would be simply
ridiculous.   *La Traviata* showed all Mademoiselle Piccolomini's

paltry resources.   She never improved in her singing, but she exaggerated the gaieties and gravities of attitude and gesture in every subsequent attempt.

Never did any young lady, whose private claims to modest respect were so great as hers are known to be, with such self-denial fling off their protection in her resolution to lay hold of her public at all risks.   Her performances at times approached offence against maidenly reticence and delicacy.   They were the *slang* of the musical theatre—no other word will characterize them; and *slang* has no place in opera, be it even the broadest opera buffa.   When she played Zerlina, in *Don Giovanni,* such virtue as there was between the two seemed absolutely on the side of the libertine hero, so much invitation was thrown into the peasant girl's rusticity. Musically the little lady was essentially a vaudeville singer,—a Columbine born to make eyes over an apron with pockets, to trick the Pantaloon of the piece, to outrun the Harlequin, and to enjoy her own saucy confidence on the occasion of her success—with those before the footlights, and the orchestra.

But Mademoiselle Piccolomini had one great gift—that of speaking Italian with a beautiful, easy, finished pronunciation and accent, such as few have possessed, and she had an air of impertinent youth; and so, for a while, she prevailed where less appetizing pretenders to favour had failed to prevail before her. Further, she was patriotic; and in Italy she had harangued serenaders—even as Madame Schroeder-Devrient did in Dresden—from a balcony, with her hair let down, even as Mademoiselle Rachel prudentially consented to do, when, grasping the republican flag, she propitiated the Red People in Paris of 1848 by declaiming to music "La Marseillaise" (to be repaid afterwards by her being compelled to re-enact "the sensation" at the order of a New York public).   But neither magic nor management nor her delicious Italian speech could transform Mademoiselle Piccolomini into an artist who had a year's right to keep any musical stage of importance.   The old and the young gentlemen did their best for her; and she repaid their best, so far as the demeanour which they admired, and her own capital Italian accent could do, to make amends for singing utterly worthless.   But the show could not last, even in days like ours, when singers are few.   It was worn out ere she left the stage, and accordingly, for every world concerned, it is surely the best that Mademoiselle Piccolomini vanished, and early, from inferior singing, pretty acting, and equivocal by-play—into private marriage.

By way of adding to the excitement there arose—or, it may be said, there was got up—a controversy concerning the good or bad morals of *La Traviata,* as a piece to be accredited or condemned. That there is an unwholesome interest in the story is evident from the fact of its having been the first of a series of bad dramas which have since taken possession of the Parisian theatre, for the exhibition of simple and compound female frailty in modern guise. The fulminations against it, as excessive in its licence, must have been felt as ridiculous by any one familiar with the musical stage; who is compelled to admit that the opera house can never have been considered as a place in which our art has been devoted to the service and illustration of that only which is high, and pure, and righteous. It was the commonplace nature of the sin and shame and sorrow which revolted such persons as were really revolted, and which absolutely provoked a manager's defence of the tale, as conveying a salutary warning to the young men of our times! The serviceable hypocrisy of such a plea was inevitable, as a reply and a retaliation, a wretched expedient to pique the jaded palates of playgoers; though but in harmony with that state of French society which could delight in the dreary, morbid social anatomies of Balzac's novels.

It may be questioned if anything could furnish a stronger argument to those who attack stage representations than the manner in which the Parisian stream of vicious fashion drew in not only the impure but the pure, than the spectacle of a faithful wife and a devoted mother, such as Madame Rose Chéri was, lending herself to the personation of all that is destroyed and depraved, by illustrating a world in which even such illusions as can cling to such disorders belonging to it, are ended by shame and misery.

But it might have been seen that whatever was the temptation of the spoken drama, *La Dame aux Camélias* was a story untenable for music. Consumption for one who is to sing! A ballet with a lame Sylphide would be as rational. Yet the opera, which failed signally on its first production (as better works have also done) became, for a while, a universal favourite here; and the tale, and the music, and the little lady who brought the two hither, delighted a section of our public; and they were seriously discussed, as though dramatic worth and reality had been in both. They served their turn—till a year later, when Madame Bosio, as I have said, by the elegance of her singing and performances made the want of refinement in Mademoiselle Piccolomini so obvious as to hasten the destruction of a spell which, to the discredit of our musical taste, had lasted far too long.

One of the events of the year 1856 which, though not presented on any opera stage, was not to be forgotten, was Madame Viardot's singing of a scene for Meduse—the music by Lulli. The music was stiff—bald (as modern critics might put it)—but true, as affording scope to the highest and the most free declamation, and having a grandeur of line (to adopt the artist's phrase), which can only come of grand imagination.

I have already adverted to the appearance and disappearance, at the Haymarket opera, of our countrywoman who sang as Madame Albertini;[1] and who, in Italy, enjoyed during some years a success analogous to that gained by Madame Schoberlechner, Madame Gazzaniga, and half a hundred of those mediocrities whom the depreciated taste of the time has fostered into a short life. She arrived in England, so far as could be guessed, under some strange idea that London was to be stormed, even as Italian cities had been by her. When will the foreigner's fixed idea—so strangely ignorant—of musical England be corrected? Mr. Ebers, in his curious book concerning the Italian Opera, told that when Madame Borgondio, a prima donna now nameless and never famous, came to try her fortune in this island, she dragged across the Alps with her her own pianoforte; being afraid of finding none in this desolate home of Broadwood and Erard. I have myself been gravely asked by a German conductor of repute and research, within the last six years—and without any sarcasm meant—whether there were any chorus singers in England. But the English dilettante, or artist who has grown into foreign life, as to a second nature, is a character, so far as I know, yet more hopeless to deal with—whether he be the student enamoured of Bürschen

---

[1] Chorley means Madame Albertazzi, who began life as Emma Howson.

rudeness in Germany, or the opera-goer, inured to bad music, bad orchestras, bad singers, in Italy, who raises his eyes in pity for a less enlightened tourist, that can protest against the noise he has been hearing the night before, and against the man who treats, as something *fossil,* every suggestion that the brawling, bawling fancies of the hour, during a time of transition and discomposure, when orchestral and vocal music are in conflict, need not surpass, because they are *of* the hour, those triumphs of art, won by study, which have enrolled the names of some former—and happily still (some living) singers—in a record imperishable so long as music shall exist.

Nevertheless Madame Albertini, though it was not convenient for her (or the theatre) to sing a second time—was hailed by the convenient audience as every one of her predecessors there had been before her. She did not use a good voice badly, so far as I recollect, nor like one uninstructed—so much as like one having a voice, without a spark of musical or dramatic intelligence.

I have now to speak of a third disappointment and a far more ponderous one, in the failure of Mademoiselle Johanna Wagner.

This, as I have said, was one of the ladies who make themselves interesting by breaking contracts, and who also seems to have cherished the strange fancy that in coming to England she was invading a savage country, where gold grew. It seems stranger that, beforehand, these German folk have not learned that England nourished Handel, that England commissioned Haydn (that from English influence came Haydn's greatest lasting work, *The Creation*), that from England could money be sent to Beethoven, when (fantastically, as is evident) he conceived himself dying of want. But this is not their instruction. They have "bettered it," as Shylock says; and accordingly the lady, reputed to be a great artist, having made a first engagement in London, was deceived or entangled into the facilities or the difficulties of a second engagement, became an object of contest in Courts of Law, and an object not the least in the world acceptable in the Court of Courtesy, howsoever attractive as an object of curiosity. Once, the breach of an engagement can be found charming; but it is a mistake to try the trick a second time, especially on so small a capital of qualifications as was the lady's.

Be these things as they may, Mademoiselle Wagner arrived too late in our solid money-grubbing England to do her purse or her theatre much service.

The voice had not recovered the weariness which was to be heard in it at Berlin, in 1852, when I heard it there; because the voice had not been rightly trained. She was most striking to see, but the mechanical vehemence of second-hand German acting proves less attractive in London than at Berlin. *There,* as part of a picture (got up by machinery), and as addressing a public to whom the style of elaborate violence is congenial, it can be submitted to. Here it seems extravagant, pedantic, and distasteful, in no common degree. The German actor's alphabet (I do not here speak of such admirable artists as Seydelmann or Emil Devrient, who make a law for themselves out of a pedantic formula), has always struck me as singular and limited. I have a book in which dancing is taught by diagrams: *"Here bend—there twirl—when you offer hands across—smile,"* and so forth; and I think that this book must be the textbook for many actors whom I have seen on the German operatic stage. One can count their steps whether in advance or retreat. They kiss in time; they go mad telegraphically. This may be very meritorious; it is clearly most popular in Prussia; but here it is not found welcome, after the first impression of strenuousness has passed over.

Considered as a singer, the claims of Mademoiselle Wagner were very meagre. She must have had originally a fine mezzo-soprano voice. She can never have learned how to produce or how to use it. Whether as Romeo, or Tancredi, or Lucrezia Borgia, the insubordinate toughness of the organ could not be concealed. Though she dashed at every difficulty with an intrepidity only to be found in German singers, none was, in very deed, mastered. Then the surroundings and supports of the new heroine were beneath mediocrity. I will pass over them, for the sake of charity and civility. Not even the loudest efforts of commissioned praise could delude the public into enduring these performances, or accepting them as successful.

Elsewhere I have adverted to the fatal and impracticable mistake made by the Germans in all that concerns appreciation and practice of the singer's craft. The question is, however, worth returning on, if music is to live on the stage in any other form than that of tasteless declamation accompanied by an orchestra—nay, too, and for the interests of instrumental music,—lest the time should come when everything like executive facility, charm of tone, and grace of manner, shall be discouraged, in the violin player or the clarinet player or the pianoforte player, as they have lately been in the throat and chest and lips of the Rosina, or Fiordiligi, or Susanna of the hour. The monstrosity of imagining the progress of art insured by stripping it of any resource is among the abuses of modern times, which really can only impose on the understandings of rational beings by the force of impudence. There is a rudeness against which the highest breeding can make no head, a blank courage of falsehood which almost destroys the possibility of power to investigate, and the musical fallacy referred to is, in its world, as flagrant as these social assumptions. To disdain material is to reduce art into savagery; to paint with three colours instead of six is to go back to the china plate, or the old heraldic pictures of the Blue Lion and the Green Man. Yet now, under pretext of eschewing meretricious devices, the singer who commands the entire range of his voice, real or acquired—be the music quick or slow, brilliant or expressive—is becoming so rare in Germany and Italy that a mass of musical works, which have a life and beauty of their own, are vanishing out of notice, because of the depreciated state of modern execution. Those gracious resources of old fancy, which added the last charm and polish to composition (space being expressly provided for them by the composer), lie under the ban of disapproval—and this in a time which has seen the revival of decorative art so signally brought about as almost to promise new combinations, new luxuries, new pleasures, to deck such idea as in these wasted times, when invention is so outworn, may still present itself.

THE YEAR 1856

ROYAL ITALIAN OPERA

OPERAS. *I Puritani,* Bellini; *L'Elisir, Lucrezia,* Donizetti; *Don Giovanni,* Mozart; *Le Comte Ory,* Rossini; *Il Trovatore, Rigoletto,* Verdi.
PRINCIPAL SINGERS. Mdes. Bosio, Maria, Grisi, Devries,* Bürde-Ney, Nantier-Didiée; MM. Tamberlik, Graziani, Tagliafico, Gardoni, Ronconi, Formes, Neri-Baraldi.*

THE YEAR 1856

T HE destruction by fire of Covent Garden Theatre was the great opera event of this year; one which was thought by many—perhaps hoped by a few to be—conclusive as to the fortunes or misfortunes of Italian opera in this country. Though no terror was added to the catastrophe by the loss of life, the same was sufficiently dismal and startling.

To keep together the band, the chorus, and the principal artists, in the hope of better days, was all that was possible, and the Lyceum Theatre, being fortunately accessible, offered a shelter to the Royal Italian Opera. Some of the performances gained by transfer to the smaller locality—those, especially, of Signor Rossini's music, in which Madame Bosio distinguished herself by the grace and finish of her singing. Hers was a case of nightly improvement. She began, too, to act with sensibility, if not with force; and succeeded to more than the favour with which Madame Persiani had been regarded, though less consummate a mistress of her art, and less various in her ornaments.

Truly delicious was one of the works presented, which, for many a long year, had not been heard in London, Signor Rossini's *Comte Ory*. Like its maker's *Moïse,* it must pay the penalty of his thoughtlessness, or of his arrogance, as may be. The story is not worth the music. The coarse, chivalresque old French ballad, in which the Brigand Count assails the household of a Lady Eglantine, as subject for an opera comes off third best, after *Don Juan,* and after *Zampa*. The story is one to be avoided rather than treated; and this must have been felt by Scribe, who nevertheless was not scrupulous in avoidance of questionable matter. It is a sensual farce when presented on the stage; nothing more.

On this unpromising canvas the musical embroidery of the original bad pattern is lovely enough to rise to the point of being magical. There is not a bad melody, there is not an ugly bar in *Comte Ory*. Its writer—thrifty and predatory, as, before him, Handel

363

had been (there are more analogies between the genius of these two great men than have been till now set forth)—used again, and wrought up in 1828, for *Comte Ory,* materials which had been flung into an operetta of the moment, *Un Viaggio a Rheims,* written in the year 1825 for the coronation of Charles the Tenth of France, and sung by such a company of artists as it would be impossible in these days to assemble.   But for the benefit of the prudes and the pedants, the treatment of the first finale may be pointed out as an example of the uttermost mastery over vocal effect attained in modern times and under modern forms. Throughout this finale the entire treatment of the bass voice, as supporting, animating, answering its comrades, is as new as it is brilliant.

In the second act, the drinking chorus of the roistering Count and his troop, who have arrived to flutter the dove-cote, is not to be overlooked, though to some it may seem only so much stage music.   The wonderful and willing adaptation of an Italian to the French style was never more clearly shown than here.   After the Count's charge of the convent, the original story must needs be suppressed; but music could not help breaking out in the final trio. As regards the combination of voices, I know nothing more exquisite than this movement; and more exquisitely it could not have been rendered than by Madame Bosio, Madame Nantier-Didiée, and Signor Gardoni.

To turn the artists to account, certain opera concerts in the nave of the Crystal Palace at Sydenham were organised—novel, attractive, fantastic entertainments, in preparation of which the exhibition of any musical research was impossible, and which owed much charm to the peculiarities of scene.

THE YEAR 1857

ROYAL ITALIAN OPERA

PRINCIPAL OPERAS. *Fra Diavolo,* Auber; *I Puritani, La Somnambula,* Bellini; *Maria di Rohan, Lucia, La Favorita,* Donizetti; *Il Trovatore, La Traviata,* Verdi. PRINCIPAL SINGERS. Mdes. Grisi, Bosio, Balfe,* Parepa,* Marai, Nantier-Didiée, Devries;* MM. Mario, Gardoni, Neri-Baraldi, Ronconi, Polonini, Zelger. PRINCIPAL DANCER. Madame Cerito.

THE YEAR 1857

THE performances of the Royal Italian Company were this year resumed at the Lyceum Theatre, under the accustomed cloud of rumours. There would be no new theatre, said those who were afraid of one. The resources of "the old house" had been refreshed by yet another miraculous interposition; and the old favourites who had been affronted thence, seven years before, on the plea of their being worn out, were about to be brought back thither in triumph—as if the value of an artist was to be changed by a removal from the Strand to Charing Cross! It is a real gratification to think of the ruin which attends all such malicious attempts to injure; most of all, when "the shop over the way" has any connexion with the arts, whose mission, say the preachers, is to humanise mankind.

This second Lyceum Season, like the former one, being merely provisional, it followed that no great amount of novelty could be attempted. Yet there was one, too remarkable in the finished perfection with which it was presented, not to be remembered with the liveliest pleasure—the Italian version of M. Auber's *Fra Diavolo*.

In London, where this opera was dressed for the Italian stage, with sung, for spoken, recitative, something of its artless vivacity might be lost, even though the composer had made additions and allowed interpolations from other operas so as to enhance the importance of its scale. But never can the music have been so deliciously sung and played as by Madame Bosio, Mademoiselle Marai, Signor Gardoni, Signor Ronconi (whose travelling Englishman in a nankeen suit was incomparable as a piece of whimsical farce), Signor Neri-Baraldi, and the two brigands, Signor Tagliafico and M. Zelger. One and all seemed to enjoy the gay coquettish music and the frolic of the story, which even the tragical ending of the bewitching robber hero fails somehow to sadden. I remember no instance of execution throughout more even, more smooth, more fine, and more lively. When, a year later, the same opera was transferred to the more vast stage of the new theatre, some parts of its vivacity and grace were gone, since every effect must needs be in some degree exaggerated.

Then the distasteful and feeble opera of *La Traviata* was represented at the Lyceum Theatre to such a perfection as to give the death-blow to the success of the lady who brought it to this country, being there sung and played to perfection by Madame Bosio, with that half-elegance, half-distraction of manner which alone could make such a heroine supportable for the purposes of musical art. Whereas Mademoiselle Piccolomini (on the stage) was the willing grisette, Madame Bosio was the woman whom bad chances had driven into fitful recklessness. She sang the music of the first act admirably. In the two others there is little or nothing worth the trouble of singing.

THE YEAR 1857

HER MAJESTY'S THEATRE

PRINCIPAL OPERAS. *I Puritani*, Bellini; *La Favorita, La Figlia del Reggimento, L'Elisir d'Amore*, Donizetti; *Don Giovanni, Le Nozze*, Mozart; *Il Barbiere*, Rossini; *Il Trovatore*, Verdi. PRINCIPAL SINGERS. Mdes. Spezzia,* Ortolani,* Piccolomini, Alboni; MM. Reichardt,* Stecchi-Botardi.* Beneventano,* Giuglini,* Bélart,* Rossi,* Corsi,* C. Braham, Beletti, Vialetti. BALLET. *Esmeralda.* PRINCIPAL DANCERS. Mdes. Roati, Marie Taglioni, Pocchini; * M. Charles.

THE YEAR 1857

THE events of this year clearly foreshowed the decay and second closing of Her Majesty's Theatre, which shortly afterwards came to pass. No new operas were promised, nor performed. The fury of admiration for Mademoiselle Piccolomini declined as rapidly as it had risen. The attempt to raise it in Paris had been tried; but Paris, besides its settled habit of pouting at everything which London has discovered, has an audience for its Italian opera different from ours. The latter has become shifting, variable, in every respect liable to be abused by false reports. During the year of a certain mania I saw the sum of fourteen guineas for a box,—no matter for what, no matter to hear whom,—to hold four people, paid away, and the box accepted as a favour by its fortunate holder. The maker-out of the voucher of the box aforesaid observed, drily, to his comrade at the desk, while he was blotting his ticket, *"Railway People!"*

This sort of random speculation and extravagance of ours, this blind or deaf wish to be amused by the newest thing in fashion,—which has changed the character of our foreign opera audiences —while it has in no respect checked the love for an understanding of the best music, which has also marvellously advanced in England, has—*had* at least five years ago—touched far more remotely the frequenters of the Italian opera in Paris. Though fashion had abandoned it some years earlier (when I first knew Paris, no English dilettante would confess to entering any other musical theatre), there was still an audience, leavened to some degree by a few connoisseurs, who had no scenic splendour to seduce them, no orchestra such as ours to entice ears enjoying orchestral effect, to be made happy by compensation for make-believe singing. They found Mademoiselle Piccolomini a consummate example of this— a nonpareil among counterfeits. They sent her away, accordingly, in high disdain, and with a little of the dear old comfortable contempt against English musical stupidity. That which is true in a reproach will stick to its victim. The "figure" of London folly began to decline in regard to her fascinations, though in the country it was maintained for a while longer; but here, her shrugs and nods and winks and utter vocal inefficiency were all too powerless (and it was well) to save a waning theatre.

As to the new Italian lady, Mademoiselle Spezzia,—the original *Traviata,*—a few words will suffice. She was a lady of good presence, with a voice of sufficient compass and power, and some passion in her acting. But her voice was an ungracious one; or else it had been ineradicably ruined by the mistaken modern habits and practices which have superseded those of the by-past school of training. Every note was disfigured by a sort of tough vibration, which entirely neutralized every other such good quality as its owner may have originally possessed. Her fate, though, was a hard one; because, after having been heralded with the inevitable flourish of trumpets, she was in an unusually short time treated with that unmistakable neglect which amounts to positive discourtesy. I best remember her in connection with the one fragment of Mendelssohn's opera which has been performed on any stage: the finale to *Loreley,* given at Her Majesty's Theatre only once, as part of a concert in costume. To this she was wholly unequal, without sufficient power of voice, without an idea of the required style.

If Mademoiselle Spezzia may be commemorated as a fair specimen of the forcible prima donna of modern Italy—a degree lower in acquirement than such vehement ladies as Mdes. Schoberlechner and Gazzaniga, whom it never was thought prudent to invite to England, great as had been their renown at degenerated Milan and Naples—Mademoiselle Ortolani was in some degree a comparative specimen of what now passes in the south for light or florid singing; since she attempted all the feats that the Persianis of better days had accomplished, and which were, in 1857, partly reproduced by the rapidly improving Madame Bosio. This was done not without a certain incomplete power over florid execution, which might have beguiled her audience for a while had her natural powers been more genial; but her voice was shrill and wiry, qualities which are more easily pardoned (who can explain why?) in French than in Italian voices. She chose, too, for her appearance, *I Puritani,* an ill-advised selection, since for her it was hopeless to think of doing that which a Persiani, a Lind, and a Bosio had failed in doing. In this part, her variations were odd rather than effective. The part of Elvira is one of sentiment as well as of vocal brilliancy. In the former the lady could hardly be called competent. As regards the latter, we were not yet so tolerant of counterfeit work as are our neighbours over the Alps. The filigree work must be of pure, not mosaic, gold. The lace must be real, and of the finest flaxen thread; the patterns of both must be of good style; and if new, not therefore fantastically disproportionate or we will have none of them in first-class theatres.

There were several new gentlemen. It had been said, before Signor Corsi arrived, that in him we were to have a tragic actor whose Nabucco and Rigoletto were to efface those of Signor Ronconi. What effacement there was, was in the tones of his voice, which was utterly destroyed ere he sang here; more so even, I think, than those of Signor Salvatori, in whom disappointment had kept such an ill pace with his foreign reputation. I can hardly imagine Signor Corsi to have been ever anything more than a meritorious singer. But under such circumstances as his, of crippled and decaying powers, the benefit of the doubt may fairly be given. The artist who appears, when past his prime, before a public of foreigners, with no old gratitude to endear him to them, does so at a perilous disadvantage. Signor Vialetti (a native of France, if I mistake not) proved himself, as he has been since found, a useful accessory member of a company.

Nor were these the only strangers. There was Signor Beneventano the bold (warranted, also, as beautiful), who had been promised to us as the coming Don Juan of Don Juans, even as Signor Fornasari had been in former, more credulous, times; but who came, and was seen, and did not conquer; and passed away, in spite of apparent triumphs, with a more deserved rapidity than Signor Fornasari had done.

Let me pass to something more genuine, and name two artists of real merit who also appeared during this strange season—a pair of tenors as widely dissimilar one from the other as two tenors can be, Signor Giuglini and M. Bélart. I have no need to dwell on the gratification produced by the suavity of voice of the former gentleman, a welcome variety after the stentorian exhibitions to which we have of late been unluckily habituated in the new singers from Italy; and by that certain elegance of style which some, nevertheless, have complained of as cold, languid, and over-elongated. I have no need to mention him as the most satisfactory importation which has arrived since that of Signor Tamberlik, since these are things to be heard and tested by all who please at this moment of writing. It is permissible, however, to dwell on the charm, apparently fast vanishing into empty air, which belongs to a real Italian singer. The "fatal gift of beauty," by nature belonging to Italy, made itself nowhere more felt than in the singer's art, and even, till a recent period, might be found among voices untutored and of no remarkable quality. The common street folk who used to sing "La sorte mia tiranna," or "Benedetta sia la madre," to guitar and gironda, before Donay's or Pedrocchi's coffee houses, or in such wondrous open-air theatres as St. Mark's Place, Venice, or beneath the plane-tree walk at Cadenabbia, which leads up to the Villa Sommariva, on the lake of Como, used to be, somehow, more in the form and belonging to the order of singers than any other set of people among whom I have travelled. Latterly the decline has been sadly perceptible. We are now rapidly approaching a period when the Italian opera houses, on this side of the Alps at least, must be maintained by French, German, English, and absolutely American singers; and it need not surprise anyone should the chronicler who, thirty years hence, shall attempt a task such as mine now rapidly approaching its close, have to point to Signor Giuglini as the last of Italian tenors, in whom some of the graces of "the good old days" still lingered.

M. Bélart—deceased while these pages were passing through the press—was a real singer, a Basque, or Spaniard, if I mistake not, endowed with no great power or fascination of voice, lifeless, not to say insignificant, on the stage—and this not merely in person but also in dramatic conception. But he had vocal fire, nerve, brilliancy, in no common degree, and is a tenor not to be forgotten, as having been able to sing the bravuras of Signor Rossini as they were written—further as a man having much of the earnest and modest self-respect which mark the true artist. In other days, when the singer was not required to act according to our unhappy (or happy?) modern fashion, M. Bélart would have been rated as an acquisition compared with such helpless people as Curioni, who were "first lovers" when I began to know Italian opera in London. He was a real artist,—as a man quiet, not vain, but a little tedious.

Neither the sentimental nor the showy tenor could restore the falling fortunes of Her Majesty's Theatre.   Galvanized into the semblance of some life by false spells—opportunity helping the operation, in the catastrophe which had befallen the rival establishment—no unprejudiced looker-on could doubt what the result was to be at an early period; nor could feel amazed when the virtually dead body sank back again into its tomb.

This year, I may say by way of postscript, I had an opportunity abroad, as well as at home, of verifying the desolation which had swept over the world of Italian opera singing and composition. To be just, however, during this year, too, I heard the only good orchestral performance execution I have ever encountered in that country—I mean that in the Carlo Felice Theatre at Genoa, so ably presided over by Il Cavaliere Mariani.   The exquisite sentiment of this gentleman, as conductor of southern music (I will venture to say unparalleled in Italy), left nothing to be desired.   The band, a very fair one, though not equal to our London and Paris orchestras, then numbered some accomplished artists, Signor Venzano, whose vocal waltz has given his name a certain vogue, being among the number.   But I shall remember, as one of the highest musical treats of its kind which I have ever enjoyed—the *reading* of the pantomimic music which accompanies the final scene of *Linda di Chamouni*.   In itself, as a picture of the struggle betwixt insanity and reason, the music is thin, common, and conventional. But as I have heard a great singer, by the force of feeling and conception, intensify some poor song, so as to give it the semblance of emotion (and who has not heard this that is familiar with modern Italian opera?) so the admirable feeling of the conductor in question for the situation enabled him to carry the sympathies of his orchestra with him, and, it may be said without absurdity, to make it *sing*—with an impassioned and melancholy fitfulness, with a tear in every string, a sigh of yearning in every note breathed, so as to produce an effect inconceivable to those who have not heard it.   I recollect nothing so perfect by way of concerted instrumental expression save one in the antipodes of the world of music—a certain performance of the Funeral March in Beethoven's Eroica Symphony, under Herr Hiller's direction, heard a year or two later at the Whitsuntide Musical Festival at Cologne.

An opera by Signor Pedrotti (who is considered one of the most promising masters of young Italy) *Tutti in Maschera*—given in a new little theatre which just then had been opened in the thickly-peopled suburb of San Pier d'Arena, beyond the lighthouse—had been prepared by the same careful and competent hand,[1] and thus stood a better chance of success than it could have got anywhere else. More, of course, nothing was to be expected from the singers; the music struck me at the time as containing something more like honest composition than we have been used of late to find in Italy, especially a finale in which a couple of different subjects are ingeniously wrought together.

That same year I heard a posthumous opera by one Signor Ferrari, *L'Ultimo Giorno di Suli,* a violent piece of rant, violently ranted through in the handsome Canobbiana Theatre at Milan, by singers whom, to avoid giving pain, I will not name; and *Crispino e Comare,* a feeble work by one of the Riccis, at a minor theatre in the Lombard capital. It was given a few weeks later in London by a fourth-rate company, brought hither with the mistaken notion of establishing the novelties and the singers of modern Italian opera buffa. The insipidity of the music was only equalled by the badness of the performers; one alone of whom stood out as not merely endurable, but showing a certain promise in the guise of ready humorous exaggeration, which he has since, in some measure, followed out. This was Signor Ciampi, who has still, happily, time in abundance before him to ripen into a clever and original buffo singer; and who, happily for his good chances, has exchanged Italy for England.

My last Italian experience of 1857 was gathered in the splendid Carignano Theatre at Turin, then gorgeous, and looking as if lined from vaulted roof to pit with cloth of gold. There I heard Sig-

---

[1] I cannot resist reminding the reader of what, though not utterly unknown in London, is still, as yet, too little known here—the choice and expressive beauty of Signor Mariani's songs. Though something of the bright and artless fancy of the elder Italian melodists be wanting to them, though in the more ambitious among them there may be too obvious a strain after the vocal effects of Signor Verdi and the instrumental accompaniments in which M. Meyerbeer delights, the best of them have a beauty and a charm which place them by the side of, and in point of solidity and science above, the Tuscan songs of Gordigiani,—the Schubert of Italy.

nor Verdi's *Aroldo,* an altered, and, it was said, an improved, version of his *Stifellio,* on a story not clear to understand, save that it was truculent and mysterious in no common degree; that there are in it tyrants, assassins, I think—I am sure a raving prima donna—and abundance of church music behind the scenes.   I find in my notes, too, mention of an agreeably consistent overture to this violent story, in the form of a Galoppe, and of the utterly disproportionate predominance of the brazen instruments.   *Aroldo* then, I think must take its place among its writer's weaker works (ridiculous though the epithet seems, after the foregoing description). The fury of the heroine, Madame Gariboldi-Bassi, and of the lover, Signor Negrini, was not less whimsically at variance with the indifference of the Piedmontese public.   The work, however, for aught I know, may since have righted itself; for I have never heard an opera more furiously hissed than was *Viscardello* (the Papal version of *Rigoletto*) at Rome, in the year 1851; although that unequal work is now everywhere.   So, also, *La Traviata* failed on the night of its birth.

In truth, the impression which must be more and more forced on everyone the deeper that examination goes, amounts to this— that Italian connoisseurship is defunct; that the necessity for excitement, which in music has been growing up for the past thirty years with the rapidity of the faëry bean-stalk, has brought the public into that state in which good and bad have no longer a meaning or a distinction.   But enough of a long and not a very cheerful postscript.

THE YEAR 1858

HER MAJESTY'S THEATRE

PRINCIPAL OPERAS. *La Zingara,** Balfe; *Don Pasquale,* Donizetti; *Les Huguenots,* Meyerbeer; *Le Nozze, Don Giovanni,* Mozart; *La Serva Padrona,* Paisiello; *Il Trovatore, Nabucco, Luisa Miller,** Verdi. PRINCIPAL SINGERS. Mdes. Alboni, Piccolomini, Sannier,* Tietjens,* Ortolani; MM. Giuglini, Belletti, Vialetti, Rossi, Bélart, Aldighieri, Benevontano, Castelli.*

ROYAL ITALIAN OPERA

PRINCIPAL OPERAS. *Fra Diavolo,* Auber; *Norma,* Bellini; *Lucrezia,* Donizetti; *Martha,** Flotow; *Zampa,* Hérold; *Les Huguenots,* Meyerbeer; *Don Giovanni,* Mozart; *La Traviata, Il Trovatore,* Verdi. PRINCIPAL SINGERS. Mdes. Grisi, Bosio, Parepa, Nantier-Didiée, Marai; MM. Mario, Tamberlik, Gardoni, Neri-Baraldi, Graziani, Ronconi, Tagliafico, Polonini, Zelger.

DRURY LANE

PRINCIPAL OPERAS. *La Somnambula,* Bellini; *Lucrezia,* Donizetti; *Don Juan,* Mozart; *Il Barbiere* Rossini; *Il Trovatore, Rigoletto,* Verdi. PRINCIPAL SINGERS. Mdes. Fumagalli,* Gassier, Salvini-Donatelli,* Viardot, Laura Baxter,* Vaneri,* Persiani, Rudersdorff; MM. C. Braham, Naudin,* Badiali.*

THE YEAR 1858

I N proportion as our own times are neared, any record of recollections becomes more and more difficult. It is obviously impossible freely to characterise newcomers whose talents may not yet have
matured themselves, whose shortcomings may still
be open to correction; almost as impossible (if ever the rights of
privacy are to be solicitously respected) as it would be to put into
print the merits and defects of the man or woman who had been
our neighbour at table yesterday. Of the artists who have taken
an assured position in England, for better for worse, I have had no
hesitation in speaking; but to offer impressions of those whose better or worse days may be still to come would be an ungracious proceeding, to which (were it found ever so piquant by friend or by
foe) no considerate person could resign himself. It is best, therefore, to deal with the performances of this year and the following
one in some points less minutely than formerly.

They were varied and miscellaneous and sufficiently distracting,
seeing that during the season 1857–8 *four* Italian opera houses
were open in London; and this at a period when the supply of Ital-
ion singers had notoriously slackened, when the art of Italian singing had obviously deteriorated, and when the repertory of opera in
Italian had manifestly to be fed from foreign sources.

To the opera buffa at the St. James Theatre I have already adverted. There appeared, among other southern strangers, a real
Neapolitan Pulcinello, who, with a mask on his face, and a costume
not unlike that of a cook, leaped and gesticulated, and conceived
himself unaccountably funny. Well-a-day for such home favourites as can content the easy-going people of Naples, when they have
to exhibit behind London gas-light! But this particular Pulcinello
(in whose case, I am sure, that no pain can be given by the plainest
speaking of one's mind in English) was,—supposing him viewed
from any Neapolitan point of view, whether from Santa Lucia or
the Chiatamone, or from a stall in the Theatre San Carlino, or a

corner shop in the Strada del Toledo, where water barrels go round like the wheels of a mystical water-mill—a remarkably dreary companion, a mime who could have enlivened nobody in the capital of the Two Sicilies.   It is a pity when such as he are fooled over to this country of ours with brave expectations.

The wavering policy pursued by the management of Her Majesty's Theatre made itself felt this year.   The season commenced in February—ended, and recommenced later.   It was first to be cheap, and afterwards dear.   Lastly came a *codicil* sort of season to a last dying speech and testament—cheap again.   The only new artist who appeared worthy consideration was Mademoiselle Tietjens.

Of the new operas produced it is easier to speak than to characterise the German lady's superb soprano voice.   The first opera was Mr. Balfe's *Bohemian Girl,* which, in Italian, was given with sung, for spoken, recitative, and was received in its new dress with applause from the many, loud enough to rend the heavens.   But an English grand opera in which, for the sake of encores, ballads must be poked in, no matter how, no matter where, when presented with a southern text, simply becomes a "Deformed Transformed." During the lovely ballad there can be no movement on the scene, and there is no passion in the rhymed platitudes, though these may have drawn tears from the gallery, and may have suggested tunes to the barrel organ.   In a work of this quality there is no opera, as the word is understood among the other countries of Europe.   Further, a musical drama made from the book of a ballet (and who that ever saw it can forget Mademoiselle Fanny Elssler in *Le Gipsy?*) always labours under the disadvantage of requiring pantomimic motion in place of suggested music.   *La Somnambula* is the great exception, because the story of that opera is nearly as simple as the *Simple Story* of Mrs. Inchbald.   There is a fury of rapture, however, with which even a column of decimals would be received if a Rachel or a Ristori were to recite it on the stage.   Though this is not precisely the case in the present instance, the poor *La Zingara* was received, in the year 1858, with a triumph which had never been exceeded, even in the days of the Catalani. As regards Italian repertory—where is it already?

It was pleasant to hear the elegant, if somewhat feeble, operetta by Paisiello, *La Serva Padrona,* which had been long before set by the more charming, more solid, more intense Pergolesi. How pretty, how graceful, the music was! if somewhat weak; music fairly to be measured against that of Mozart's *Schauspiel-Direktor,* which turned up nearly at the same time, and which proved how intimately Mozart had felt the spell of Italy, as Italy was in his youth. That the German had more solidity than the Italian composer might have been divined from the first note of either man's music; but that the German would have never been what he was, without having seen Italy, is no less evident.

Also there was presented a third work, new to our Italian stage —Signor Verdi's *Luisa Miller,* in which Schiller's torturing German burgher drama, *Kabal und Liebe,* was to be pressed into southern opera service.

It has seemed to me that, as one among Signor Verdi's operas, *Luisa Miller,* taken on its own terms of fire, faggot, and rack, is the weakest of the weak. There are staccato screams in it enough to content any lover of shocking excitement; but the entire texture of the music implies (I can but fancy) either a feeble mistake or else a want of power on the part of an artificer, who, obviously (as Signor Verdi does) demanding situation and passion and agony to kindle the fire under his cauldron, has also only one alphabet, one grammar, one dictionary, whatsoever the scene, whatsoever the country—one cantabile, one spasmodic bravura, one feverish crescendo, as the average tools by pressure of which the stress on the public is to be strained out. I cannot conceive any English audience returning to *Luisa Miller,* and fancy that already the opera may be dead in Italy.

———

The year 1858 gave to London a new theatre for Italian opera —so far as the stage and the portion of the house allotted to the audience are concerned, more ample and pompous than any theatre hitherto existing here. It would seem, however, as if, of later days, nothing complete, in all its parts, can be arranged for British uses; that if the public room be grand and spacious, the means of ingress and outlet must needs be pinched; as if, in fact, we were living in a period of architectural compromise and extravagant economy.

The really commodious theatres of Europe, as distinguished

from the magnificent ones, are, I suspect, few in number. The new opera house in Moscow, built by M. Cavos, is generally considered to be the most thoroughly magnificent theatre existing. I confess to a great heresy regarding the glory of the Teatro San Carlo, at Naples, as also that of the Teatro la Scala, at Milan—the latter, however, being the grander of the two, in right of its proportions; both having a certain vast and naked look which no costly decorations can altogether mystify or conceal. The Teatro Carlo Fenice, at Genoa, is, for a theatre of the first class, better proportioned than either of the former, without appearing to be uninhabitable. Throughout the continent (especially in Italy) there are theatres of a second class, the like of which have no existence in this inconsistent and costly London of ours: where it would seem as if no modern architectural purpose can be thoroughly or efficiently wrought out unless it be in a world far more important than the world dramatic—engineering architecture.

Perhaps the theatre which is the most complete in its form and proportions is Professor Semper's new one at Dresden—a building which has further the rare merit of distinctly announcing its purpose in its outward construction. The Comic Opera, at Paris, is terrible for any one to sing in, however pleasant to the eye and comfortable to the spectator. The Théâtre Lyrique of Paris, about to be destroyed—a flat oval, in which everyone was brought near to the stage, and that stage a large one, capable of any amount of scenic effect—seems to have presented one of the best forms of theatres. In regard to acoustic effect, the same is so capricious that I can fancy no lecture, no theory, no experience of such effects able to account for certain successes to be found in theatres constructed by accident.

A thousand things more could be noted in regard to theatres and their peculiarities. One could write a page on Palladio's antique theatre at Vicenza, another on the marble theatre at Pavia. One could call up the thousand recollections which cling to that dingy barn, the Kärnther Thor Theatre in Vienna, which still has been the scene of so many brilliant musical exploits. Then a chapter could be written on open air theatres, not forgetting that one at Herrenhausen, whence our reigning family came over, and in which the Kilmansegges and Schulembergs, and other fat Hanoverian sultanas, may have sat and shivered, sustained through the

damp and the chill of the climate, and under the gloom of the um-
brage, by the delicious and heroic idea that their entertainment was
something charming and French—quite as good as anything at
Versailles.

Again it might not be wholly unprofitable to discuss how far, for
the uses of dramatic representation, the Italians are right or wrong
in darkening the portion of the theatre allotted to the audience,
so as wholly to concentrate the entire interest of the evening on the
play and its actors; even though, strange to say, this is accompanied
by those habits of love-making, coffee-drinking, ice-eating, card-
playing in ante-rooms, which make of the Italian opera houses virtually so many social music-halls, in which nobody pretends to listen to an entire performance, but merely to one song or to one
singer.   Another matter worth propounding and pondering would
be the superiority of the arrangements of scenery in France over
those of England, where we, nevertheless, have such surpassing
scene-painters.   It might be reasonably inquired why in London
the eye should be hurt by scraps and snips and those utterly impossible expositions called "sky-borders"; and wherefore, in Paris,
a street should seem a street, and a wood a wood, and the spectator not there be vexed by any make-believe discrepancy, save that
which belongs to the false reds or crude greens—otherwise to the
badness of colouring from which our neighbours are only now beginning to emancipate themselves.   But the romance and reality
of theatrical architecture must be left to other hands than mine for
the present.

The performers and performances in the new theatre are to be
spoken of, and the novelties which they included.   The improvement of Madame Bosio, from season to season, was never more
evident than in 1858—an improvement which carried off the
trashy music of *La Traviata,* and carried away the part from
Mdlle. Piccolomini.

This, too, was the year of a strange experiment; the one made
by Signor Mario to do what Garcia and Donizelli had done before
him—to lay hands on the character of Don Juan.   Of all these
usurpations, howsoever they be justified by success, there can be
only one opinion.   All such experiments are false in point of taste;
false in point of art; false in point of ambition.   The part naturally attracted Signor Mario, because he is the best operatic tenor

actor who has been seen in our time; because he could present the man to be presented, better in face and costume than any one who has till now played it; and because there was "gentle breeding" in his presentment of the libertine. Yet a more complete mistake I do not recollect. The music became weak and strange and singular in his hands, without the presentation of the drama serving the cause of the usurper.

Of the chances of *Zampa* on the Italian stage in London I have already spoken. The third unfamiliar opera produced during this first year of the new theatre was M. von Flotow's *Martha*. Here we have another ballet set as an opera, another tribute to the animated invention of our allies, and one in which the story, being less gymnastic than other ballet stories put into music, might rationally excite the fancy of a composer. M. von Flotow's *Martha*, without question, enjoys a universal currency, which no subsequent opera by him has, till now, acquired.

Yet it may be fairly asked,—supposing the "Last Rose of Summer" taken away (Moore's amateur refinement on "The Groves of Blarney"),—what would remain to *Martha?* The spinning quartet; the "Good Night"; *not* the "Porter" song (*Porter* here meaning Barclay and Perkins, by way of giving to the part an ancient English colour) a song vapid as is the residue out of a stale vat; and the romance, which, with its Italian words, "M'appari," was made captivating by Signor Mario's voice and passion. The tale, no doubt, is amusing, though as extravagant as any dream that ever disturbed the sleep of an opium eater; but the music is poor, small, hybrid; and except for Thomas Moore, and his amateur liberties which converted an old rollicking Irish song into a sweet sentimental melody, *Martha* could hardly have lived a week.

In the year 1858 there was a fourth Italian opera house—at Drury Lane. In this the noticeable performers were Madame Viardot, Madame Persiani, M. Naudin (a tenor who may have a future to come)', and Signor Badiali, a veteran singer whose "Indian Summer," as Americans have it, was better than the spring of most successors to his occupation. Had this great artist arrived some years earlier he would have made good that lasting place which real artists always keep in England, no matter how counterfeit ones can take it for awhile.

POSTSCRIPT.—The year 1858 gave me yet one more opportunity

of realizing the ruin of Italian music in its own country—and this at one of its most splendid palaces, the Teatro San Carlo of Naples. There I heard Signor Verdi's *Lionello,*—at Rome, *Viscardello,* originally *Rigoletto,*—which may have borne as many other names in as many other towns as Italian censorship pleased. That opera was given at Naples less well than I have heard it given anywhere else. There Signora Fioretti sang in it steadily, without the slightest charm; and there Signor Fraschini seemed less boisterous than he had shown himself in London. But the orchestra was shabby and the chorus was paltry; and the opera, under its castigated form, produced no effect whatsoever. Yet English tourists, with enthusiasm to let, will speak in raptures of any Italian operatic performance, no matter how bad it may be; because the price of entrance is, compared with ours, cheap; and because of the novelty in the audience and in the surroundings, which naturally has so much charm for a people at once so reserved or so imaginative as the English, and who too often appear, when as tourists on the continent, to know small medium between the extremes of love and hate, of blind rapture, or sullen contempt.

THE YEAR 1859

ROYAL ITALIAN OPERA

PRINCIPAL OPERAS. *Dinorah,** Les Huguenots,* Meyerbeer; *Don Giovanni,* Mozart; *La Gazza, Otello,* Rossini; *Il Trovatore, Rigoletto, La Traviata,* Verdi. PRINCIPAL SINGERS. Mdes. Lotti della Santa,* Calderon,* Grisi, Nantier-Didiée, Penco,* Miolan-Carvalho,* Marai; MM. Mario, Gardoni, Tamberlik, Neri-Baraldi, Ronconi, DeBassini, Zelger, Tagliafico.

DRURY LANE

PRINCIPAL SINGERS. Mdes. Balfe, Piccolomini, Guarducci,* Tietjens, Sarolta,* Weisser;* MM. Giuglini, Badiali, Graziani * (a tenor), Bélart, Fagotti,* Vialetti.

The new operas promised were none of them performed.

THE YEAR 1859

THE first event of 1859 was sad enough. The death of Madame Bosio made a vacancy in the opera-world which will not be very soon filled. An artist whose progress was so steady and so complete as hers is so rare (of late times) among the choir of singing-birds that when such a one as she may disappear, the trouble becomes doubly painful. She perished from the Russian climate, and owing to her too incessant labour.

The other event of this year was the production of M. Meyerbeer's latest opera; the opera meant by him to be simple, pleasant —and peasant. It is worth a study.

I have elsewhere pointed out the extent to which M. Meyerbeer has wronged himself owing to his superfluous anxiety. Here is a pathetic, characteristic, and simple village anecdote, dragged out of shape and lengthened, without its being made, in any respect, a great work; an opera rendered difficult to produce and tiresome to hear merely because the charm which lived in the original thought has been exhausted and elongated.

The notion of a divining rod which should bring out the precious metal from the entrails of the earth is possibly, in any event, too far-fetched a fancy to be clad in music. But in this case there was contrived an earlier story (I conceive, invented as a supplement), in which occurs the fire at a farm-house, on a Breton Saint's Day, as a consequence of which fire the girl of the farm grows mad. So that, during the first, the second, and part of the third act of this opera we have a mad heroine.

It is needless to point out how tremendously such a condition loads the actress—especially when, after having been requested to be solidly mad for two acts and three quarters, at the last she must needs waken up in her wet clothing, recover her sanity, and go straightway to be married. It seems too much forgotten by the makers of opera-books, that insanity moves within as narrow limits as faëry work—that the half-visionary remembrances of old thoughts in old tunes has become an engine to excite curiosity and suspense, as hackneyed as the old duet of "He" and "She," in which first the man sang his admiration and secondly the woman responded to the same.   It may be noted as a fact that the employment of this element in music is a comparatively modern one.   The masters of drama resorted to it sparingly.   Setting aside such a tragedy of horror as the *Duchess of Malfi*, Shakespeare may be said to have exhausted it in his straw-crowned Lear and his tender Ophelia; and in the one of these pitiful stories there is a majesty, in the other an exquisite and maidenly beauty, which give to both of the diseased ones as much individuality as belongs to any healthful being of the mind.   But of late there has been a serviceable use of brain-distemperature resorted to by playwrights, especially in opera; the end of which is that no one is frightened, no one hurt, because the audience is perfectly aware that the miracle of cure and redemption will arrive, during the symphony to the cabaletta of the last song of the prima donna.

Besides the *Nina Pazza,* thrice set, the one mad opera which holds some place in the library of musical drama is Paër's *Agnese* —an opera which has vanished, perhaps not to return, though containing some of the best music written by Signor Rossini's predecessor, to whom Signor Rossini is so much beholden for many of its forms and effects.   Opera-goers of a time before mine are still living who go back with fond admiration to Ambrogetti's personification of the shame-crazed father.   Such character, however, as laid in this must have been brought to it by the artist; since the music is even and regular to respectability without freak or distemperature indicated.

We English, long ere this, had already produced something of the class infinitely more characteristic.   In our store of national music, nothing could be named to exceed the mad-songs of Purcell; in particular his "Delirious Lady"—though this (to make the matter more remarkable) is a song of counterfeit insanity, assumed by Altisidora to fool Don Quixote to the top of his bent.   It would be hard to name any recitative in any language more instinct with the wild wayward frenzy of despair, than the one which opens this noble scena—as a specimen of powerful expression, unparagoned, its date considered.   Later compositions could be counted by hundreds—the mad scene in Signor Rossini's *Semira-*

mide, for the most part generously omitted in mercy to the powers of the average Assur, especially to be remembered; but none to exceed glorious John Dryden's "From rosy bowers."

But for better for worse, such productions will always be painful on the stage; almost as painful as the exhibition of physical suffering, or the slow agonies of disease. In *Le Pardon* [1] the sting is drawn by the comfortable assurance which the least experienced opera-goer must feel from the very first that a cure will be wrought ere the curtain falls.   So that while allowing the employment in music of what is wild and stern, of the fierce and the terrible, as shades not to be avoided—supposing the picture to be severe and historical—the long, weary madness of the Breton girl, Dinorah, who, as was to be foreseen, is re-animated into sense and marriage at the Ploermel Saint's day, offered a difficulty rather than a temptation to any composer who desired to mate the madness with musical method.

Our neighbours, as dramatic authors, think otherwise; and thus M. Meyerbeer has been seduced by the local tone of his work into conniving at an extension of a painful, foolish incident.   And what is more, there can be small question as to the fact that, owing to the nature of its subject, *Le Pardon,* simple as it may seem in point of incident and number of characters, has been made curiously difficult to represent.

The music of it, however, is well worth a study, if only because the opera in its form is virtually identical with the form of predilection in England as regards operas, where there must be ballads in any quantity, and of every quality; where the lady is to die, and the lover is to go mad, and the villain is to rejoice, not to "Love, still Love" (as Moore sang it), but to "Ballad, still Ballad."   Viewed in this respect, *Dinorah,* or *Le Pardon,* is a model, in right of the tunes showered over it from the first to the last bar.   The overture, which tells the story of the poor crazed girl, is a puzzle, since it is hard from it to unthread the idea of the Breton farm-house, burnt down on the day of a church festival; the hymn "Sancta Maria" behind the curtain—sung by voices— be it ever so lovely, when thus looked on wants explanation even for such hearers as prefer vagueness in a prelude.   From the first to the last of the two first acts there is an affluence of fresh, wild,

[1] I. e. *Dinorah,* the French title of which is *Le Pardon de Ploermel.*—E. N.

quaint melody (the second part always weaker than the first, but this is M. Meyerbeer's weakness)—remarkable as occurring in the last work of so mature and elaborate a composer. Better snatches of song could be found nowhere in the first act than the cradle song of the poor mad heroine, than the fancy in the duet where she imagines herself reaping—with its delirious coda. Then again there are few if any things better in music than what may be called the formula of the gold diggers,—so rough, so sharply cut, yet so clear. The terzet closing the first act is to be specified as having a freshness, subtlety and beauty beyond the reach of any other living, or of many a dead, writer. The delicious elegance and luxury of instrumentation employed when the subject is returned to, the skill with which interest is heightened and suspended to the very close, the clearness of the ideas, and (what is not habitual with the master) their amplitude, make this terzet something unparagoned, at least in the library of modern music.

In the second act the most popular feature, save for those who care about stage carpentry—"sensation" they call it now—is the shadow dance. But infinitely better, to those who study *Le Pardon* as a wild opera, will be found the snatch of melody which precedes it—a tune which might have been put into the mouth of Ophelia; and infinitely better is the sinister legend of menace, with which the crazed creature denounces the gold-seeker as one marked for death. In these the freshness of the original thought is not marred by any deficiency in working out the same. As "snatches of song," there is nothing better in the whole domain of music. The catastrophe when the sluices burst and the bridge breaks—a combination to be avoided, not courted, by any great musician—is virtually weakly treated by M. Meyerbeer. He has relied on the rotten tree and the bursting-out water, and on a considerable noise in the orchestra. But these things do not make an opera.

The third act of *Le Pardon* is an afterthought, a platitude. The sportsman, the reaper, the goatherds, who successively sing, and afterwards simultaneously chant a morning prayer, are one and all superfluous. The conclusion of the story, depending on the restoration to sanity and matrimony by daylight, of the wet woman fished out of the broken sluices at midnight, can hardly be exceeded in absurdity.

And yet throughout this unnatural opera the peculiar genius of the master will be everywhere traced by those who look beneath the surface; not merely his shortness of breath as regards melodic inspiration, but also his daintiness in instrumental combination. Elaborate, overwrought as the latter may be found, it is still so full of rich beauty, masked by so many touches of quaint, characteristic delicacy, as with all who think largely to redeem it from the charge of being merely a piece of head-work. Most observable, as marking character and predilection, is the excess to which the overture is elaborated; not less observable than the real want of resource with which so long-drawn a composition, containing so many lovely half-melodies and choice episodes, is conducted.

It is almost idle, at so recent a period, to descant on the admirable performance of this work at the Royal Italian Opera, on the grace and finish of Madame Miolan-Carvalho, on the peasant poltroonery of Signor Gardoni, and, last year (1861), the morose rudeness of that accomplished French artist, M. Faure. Nothing of the kind is now attainable in any other European theatre.

I shall be absolved from dwelling on the strangers who appeared for the first time in 1859, some of whom were only birds of passage, who came for once and no more. One fact, however, must be repeated—the cessation of supplies to our Italian Opera Houses from Italy. So far as concerns singers, the schools of Paris have replaced those of Milan, Naples, and Venice.

Of the Italian Opera at Drury Lane there is small need to speak at length. There was rarely ever put forth a more appetizing list of promises, not even in the days when Mendelssohn's *Tempest* was cast and illustrated before a note of its music had been written. Signor Verdi's *Macbeth* (in which opera the part of the Lady had been played with prodigious fire by Madame Viardot in the provinces), Gluck's *Armida* (Gluck's operas being regularly promised by every theatrical manager who would, like Mrs. Jarley, be "calm and classical," but somehow coming scantily to English performance, except as concert music in Manchester), Signor Petrella's *Ione,* or the blind girl of Pompeii (a working out of the graceful and fascinating creation of Sir E. Lytton's Neapolitan Romance), were all promised. Not one of these promises was fulfilled.

THE LAST CHAPTER

HIS is always a weary one to write—having in its very nature something of parting, something testamentary, something, whatever the task may have been, that includes pain, beyond such relief as belongs to a labour completed.

I close this book of sketches with mingled feelings. If it has been welcome to recall various emotions due to a favourite art and pursuit during the course of many years, to pay tribute to what has seemed to me universally beautiful, and thoughtful, and true, it has been impossible the while not to be saddened while noting my recollections. How few are left of the great composers and their interpreters who carried away lovers of music into the faëry-land for which they sought! How many are gone of the playmates whose pleasure in their enchantments added the encouragement of sympathy to my own pleasures!

I cannot conceal from myself that, whatsoever may have been the gain, in technical performance, won by England during the last thirty years, the losses to the great world of art (which is of no country), have been greater. There are no signs on the horizon of great singers, very few of real composers, in the domain to which I have restricted the remembrances here thrown together.

But in truth whether the field be oratorio, symphony, or chamber music, the same tale has to be told. There appears to be little youth of heart, and as little truth of fancy, among those who aspire for first honours. There is skill, no doubt—and I as little doubt, honesty, since the advance in conscientious training among average musicians is indeed remarkable and comforting; but the divine spirit, the soul, the life-breath, that which gives to one man's genius the voice of a clarion, and to another's the persuasion of a breeze that sweeps over the grass, which it scarcely touches—where are they? Is invention dead, or is it buried, like Ogier the Dane, to break its tomb when the spell is taken off, and some true champion penetrates into the heart of the sepulchre?

There is little, at all events for the moment, to afford anything like an oracular answer. Let us see how far speculation can push its torch, so as to pierce the fog impending over an art so lovely, which has so largely entered into our daily life, as ours. It may be urged that, in the story of time and change which I have tried to tell, music has only followed the condition of every imaginative art; that inasmuch as there has been a cycle of architects, first Greek, then Gothic, a cycle of painters, northern and southern, a cycle of dramatists, and that since our age, with all its fertility, all its convenience, all its brilliancy, all its honest appreciation of the lovely things of the past, cannot even reproduce, still less originate, in any of the worlds conquered, enjoyed, and exhausted, it may be now the fate of music, as of her divine sisters in art, to fall away into a sleep: not therefore to be forgotten, not ceasing to influence, yet perhaps never either to waken to her old simple youth or to resume her mature adornment. But there is an answer to this doleful suggestion. Music has always been a capricious art, in no respect bound in its life by analogy to the other arts of imagination, with which it is still closely, inextricably united. The poet can write tranquilly, and lay his verses aside against a better day than the one which neglects him—and in this respect the poet includes the great dramatist, whether he be tragic or comic. The painter can paint his pictures, sell them at indifferent prices, see the door of some private gallery shut over them, and take his leave, during his life-time, of some dream on which he has exercised his finest fancies, his powers most dearly bought by experience. But the musician's work, until it is exhibited before a public, can be only a work incomplete, inasmuch as music has only a theoretical existence till it has been tried by the composer's own conscience, and approved or forgotten by those to whom it is submitted. Nor is there any manner of dragging a public to hear a second time that which, on the first introduction, has left the public indisposed to return. And besides all this, music must somehow or other reflect the manners and fancies of its birth-time and birth-place,—and also the conditions of executive art.

In every respect Europe has seen a wondrous amount of

change during the last century and a half. Whereas the national schools of composition have entirely formed themselves, and split asunder during that period, amateurship has become less exclusive, more cosmopolite. Yet fancy has had its curious ebbs and flows, totally irrespective of fashion. In reply to all the jargon about "points of departure," as to the manner in which one reputation is built on and supersedes another, in which old laws are abrogated, old truths voted obsolete, in favour of more enlightened ideas, it may be emphatically pointed out that during the very time at which the crudities and chaotic beauties of Beethoven's posthumous works began to be seized on as pretexts and models by a school of irrational enthusiasts weary of conformity, the admirable science and fertility of Sebastian Bach, the ancient, began first to be appreciated; while Mendelssohn, the modern, with far more restricted poetical endowments, and a certain formality at times approaching to aridity (if judged by romantic standards), built up as his own individuality the only universal German reputation which has been established since that of Beethoven! The period which has seen the return (after a season of eclipse) to the noble but grave sonatas of Clementi and Dussek has also seen the establishment of the wayward, incomplete, fantastic, yet most fascinating Chopin, on a pedestal of his own. The years during which singers' music has been stamped into bits as so much trash by the Wagners of New Germany, and bawled into a premature destruction of its voice by the Verdis of infuriate Italy, have been also those in which the magnificent vocal music of Handel has been more largely circulated and studied, in all its range, than during the time when it was thrown off.

What is to be got from all these contradictions, all these confusions? A conclusion that music is about to perish, an admission that music is to be emancipated by the annihilation of some among its elements? For me, neither the one nor the other—no lamentation that our "virtue" has eaten up "the cakes and ale" of the future, no credulity in the despotic miracle of bricks made without straw. I believe that original genius may always reappear, and will make for itself some fresh channel. I believe that thoughtful science, not shrinking from retrospect, not averse to discovery, will increasingly refer to record, not to tradition,—will increasingly separate that which is of the hour from that which does not pass away. The "players" have had their riot; the orchestra and its combinations have been driven into that prominence and perfection to which extravagance and corruption may be the inevitable sequel. The turn of the singers may be again to come. I believe that a composer of opera, no matter of what country, may yet arise, who may conciliate charm, science, effect, discovery, and expression, so as to produce a more perfect and enduring whole than the world has hitherto possessed; though we, of the generation rapidly passing away, who remember the music of the last thirty years, may not be there to see.

Fortunately, however, though betwixt Italian indolence and German transcendentalism there is no ordinary confusion and loss in the singers' world, there is increasingly good training in France; and, in this country, a desire among our singers for a vocal superiority, which is stronger than when I began to listen to music —because it is more deeply based than formerly on that musical science and general usefulness which the spread of intercourse and the wide field of foreign art to be commanded (till our own shall renew its nationality) have rendered indispensable. English singing has suffered largely from our national love of the ballad, in which a melancholy execution, *ad libitum,* has been accepted as expressive, and in which "The Banks of Allan Water," "The Last Rose of Summer," and "Auld Robin Gray" never came to an end. We are still, as a nation, deficient in that accent which the French possess in almost a superfluous degree; we are still too much enamoured of long and lovely notes—though the old style of English tunes, which was so largely abused by our second-rate composers at the beginning of the century, has been exchanged for one more modish and quasi-foreign. Our artists, as a body, have something to gain in point of that precision without formality which has to do so much with the meaning of music and the charm of melody. Yet that they have derived benefit from that which has harmed the Germans in their singing,—the increased appreciation of instrumental music—it would not be hard to prove. They have improved, too, as linguists, while the singers of other nations have stood still. In short, there is rally and progress in our world of music, strangely capricious as are its motions. A higher standard of execution is desired and tried for than formerly, a more intelligent rivalry with the artists of other countries. In these polyglot days the English singers stand better before the world than they did thirty years ago.

But these speculations bring me from the domain of recollection so far forward into the world of contemporary criticism as to warn me of a limit to my task. It would be immodest and vexatious to attempt to appraise reputations which can be hardly said, as yet, to have settled themselves; to discuss the merits or demerits of singers of the present time whose ways and means may be modified long after the chronicler from before the curtain has passed away. Let some one else, if not more sincerely desirous of distinguishing diamond from paste, true from false, not less willing to add to the enjoyments of the past those of the present, more capable than myself on some future day, go on with the history of foreign opera in England.

I have done my best to tell a plain tale sincerely.

INDEX

INDEX

403